Baedeker

Brazil

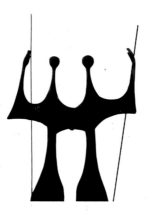

www.baedeker.com

Verlag Karl Baedeker

TOP ATTRACTIONS ★ ★

The Fernando de Noronha archipelago, Rio de Janeiro with its Sugarloaf Mountain, the colonial towns of Ouro Preto or Mariana, the bubbling cauldron that is Salvador – the list of top sights in Brazil is endless. To help make sense of what is on offer, here is our guide to the country's must-sees.

1 ★ ★ Manaus
City of millions in the heart of the lush rainforest ▶ **page 279**

3 ★ ★ Belém
Splendid colonial architecture in the Amazon metropolis ▶ **page 166**

2 ★ ★ Ilha de Marajó
River island in the Amazon, with rich and varied scenery ▶ **page 174**

4 ★ ★ Fernando de Noronha
Atlantic island paradise, under the strict protection of conservation law ▶ **page 230**

BAEDEKER'S BEST TIPS

From all the tips in this book, we have compiled the most interesting for you here! Experience and enjoy the best of what Brazil has to offer.

⚠ Wings Of Madness
Find out about the fascinating life of Brazilian aviation pioneer Alberto Santos-Dumont. ▶ page 74

⚠ A night at the manor house
The owners of the listed fazenda Pé do Morro offer guests board and lodgings – as well as horses to explore the natural surroundings. ▶ page 139

⚠ Two-masted boats off Angra dos Reis
Islands and beaches aplenty, best reached by pleasure boat ▶ page 153

⚠ Calling all divers!
Thanks to the clear waters, there is excellent diving off Arraial do Cabo. ▶ page 166

⚠ Dive into the underworld
Explore the underwater caves of Bonito ▶ page 186

⚠ Festival do Inverno
The »winter festival« of Campos do Jordão is a major cultural event. ▶ page 207

⚠ Day trip to Baturité
From Fortaleza to the colonial mountain town ▶ page 243

⚠ On safari
Jeep and boat tours through Iguaçu national park ▶ page 248

⚠ Tunnel trip into the Mina Modelo
Take the pit train into the coal mine of Tubarão ▶ page 272

Cozy evenings with a few beers or the buzz of the carnival
Tips for sporty types and culture vultures, for families travelling with children, for gourmets and nature lovers – there's something for everyone!

Fisherman with his jangada
boat in Fortaleza
▶ page 241

BACKGROUND

PRACTICALITIES

Price Categories

▶ **Hotels**
Luxury: over 460 reais
Mid-range: 160 – 460 reais
Budget: under 160 reais
For a double room with
breakfast

▶ **Restaurants**
Expensive: from 55 reais
Moderate: 28 – 55 reais
Inexpensive: under 28 reais
For a main course

Carnival in Rio de Janeiro: →
high spirits are a must!

Background

AT A GLANCE: WHAT
VISITORS SHOULD KNOW
ABOUT BRAZIL, THE
COUNTRY AND ITS PEOPLE,
ECONOMY AND POLITICS,
SOCIETY AND EVERYDAY
LIFE

GOD IS BRAZILIAN

This is what the Brazilians say themselves, and everybody who knows this South American country will agree. How else to explain all the natural wonders and the ethnic diversity in a single country? In Brazil, visitors can hear the heartbeat of Africa as much as that of Europe, of Indian tribes as well as the Asian immigrants. People of all skin colours live with and alongside each other.

But Brazil has a lot more to offer beyond the current clichés of carnival, samba, beach beauties and football. Of course, visitors entering the colourful fray of the carnival of Salvador da Bahia or giving in to the magic of the samba school parades in Rio de Janeiro's »Sambódromo« carnival arena, will see even their dreams of Brazil surpassed, as carnival in Brazil is passion, danced and sung, with the rules of society temporarily suspended for the pure joy of living.

Collective euphoria

Every year a collective euphoria takes hold of the nation, as social barriers and the norms of society are broken down. Brazilian carnival revellers leave behind the realities of life and transform themselves, like caterpillars turning into colourful butterflies. So the penniless play the glamorous fairytale prince and many a maid in domestic service becomes a fairy princess. Rich and poor, top and bottom are

Young generation *30 % of the Brazilians are less than 15 years old.*

turned upside-down. In the carnival season, only the here and now really counts – and as long as the Brazilian nation expends itself in the festive whirl the worries of everyday life are pushed aside. »Carnaval do Brasil« is a pressure valve that makes bearable – if only for a short time – the blatant injustices of the country's wealth distribution, the glaring social contrasts and the lack of prospects facing the majority of the population. The rest of the year, many Brazilians get by with a blend of resourcefulness and flexibility, making concessions and practicing »the high art of compromise« called »jeito brasileiro«.

Human interaction

The common greeting in Brazil is »tudo bem« – »everything alright« – with the thumb always pointing up: a simple but effective ritual

Carnival
The drums set the rhythm, there is dancing, singing, laughing; everyday worries are forgotten, and having fun becomes a Brazilian's first duty

The Bahia coast
Endless beaches waiting to be explored – by buggy, for example

Architecture
The architectural style of Oscar Niemeyer – as unconventional as it is unique. Niemeyer's creations not only give the cityscape of Brasília its distinctive look, visitors will find his work everywhere in Brazil.

Rainforest
The rainforest might appear menacing sometimes, but it also has a gentle side: the Serra dos Órgãos in bloom.

Beaches, beaches – and more beaches...
With over 7,000km/4,350 miles of coast, beach lovers are spoilt for choice.

Urban jungle
Hectic, chaotic, oversized: twelve million people live and work here. São Paulo truly never sleeps.

practiced all over the country and which many visitors also find extremely infectious. »Calor humano« – human warmth – is how the Brazilians themselves describe their pleasant way of interacting with one another. Extremely sociable, they feel at home even in the hustle-and-bustle and are always looking for the company of other people. Calor humano is exactly what Brazilians often miss when they are abroad – as do many visitors to Brazil once they are back home.

Inexhaustible diversity

The diversity of the landscapes of this huge South American country is matched by the number of possible trips to Brazil, enough to suit everyone's tastes. Whether visitors want to cruise the streams and rivers of the Amazon, lined with gallery forests, or spot crocodiles, capybara water pigs or rare birds in the Pantanal, or maybe prefer the beach to tan their body and – as many Brazilians do – to exhibit it, everyone will find here their very own slice of paradise. Every year, spectacular scenic highlights such as the Iguaçu Falls and the Sugarloaf Mountain of Rio de Janeiro work their spell on thousands of visitors, as do the opera house of Manaus, the architecture of Brasília or the beautiful beaches of the Northeast. The vibrant life in the metropolises of Rio de Janeiro and São Paulo exerts its own special fascination; everything and anything seems possible here, but the clash of social extremes is particularly abrupt and immediate. Even a fleeting visit, however, to

Yanomami
Brazil's cultural diversity is based on its wealth of ethnic groups.

the historical Old Town of Salvador da Bahia or the baroque towns of Minas Gerais such as Ouro Preto, São João del Rei, Tiradentes and Diamantina, becomes a trip back in time to the colonial era, shaped by the gold rush and the discovery of diamonds. Last but not least there is the land of the gaúchos in the south, which, with its European influences, is in a way as foreign to the Brazilians in the Northeast as faraway Europe.

Facts

How many people live in Brazil? How big is the country? Who was the first European in Brazil? What exactly is Candomblé? Who is the best-known author on the contemporary Brazilian literature scene? All will be revealed on the following pages.

Nature

With large tracts of level terrain, the territory of Brazil may be generally divided into **two types of landscape**: the Amazon Basin in the north and the high plateau of the centre and south. The political-administrative division of Brazil into five regions – North (Norte), Northeast (Nordeste), Southeast (Sudeste), South (Sul) and Midwest (Centro-Oeste) – lends itself to a more detailed subdivision of natural habitats, as the individual regions all have their own geographical character. Despite the regional differences, a warm and humid climate prevails, with varying degrees of strong and regular rainfall. Due to the oceanic air masses, these climatic conditions are less pronounced on the Atlantic coastal strip, whilst the humidity in the interior is extremely high owing to countless watercourses and dense tropical vegetation. With their exceedingly hot and humid climate and impenetrable, rampant forests, large tracts of Brazilian territory are practically uninhabitable.

The Brazilian North

With a surface area of some 3.9 million sq km/1.5 million sq miles, the Brazilian North takes up over 45 % of Brazilian territory. The central part is occupied by the Amazon lowlands. North of the Amazon Basin lies the high plateau of Guyana, covered to a large extent with grassland (campos), from which several higher peaks rise – amongst them the **Pico da Neblina**, at 3,014m/9,888ft the highest mountain in Brazil. The south of the region, on the other hand, is characterized by the extensive rock formations of the Brazilian mountain ranges.

Flowing from west to east through the Amazon lowlands, the Amazon measures some 6,500km/4,000 miles in total (over 3,000km/1,850 miles of which is in Brazil), its basin taking up nearly a third of the South American subcontinent. Its tributaries, the Marañon and the Ucayali, rise in Peru. Carrying by far the most water of any river in the world, the Amazon enters Brazil at an altitude of 82m/269ft, so that it only has to overcome a slight gradient to reach the point where it flows into the Atlantic. Only from Manaus onwards do the Brazilians call the river the Amazon, after it has merged with the Rio Negro; the river's middle reaches are called **Solimões**. Along its banks, there are three levels of terraced terrain: the highest being the terra firme, safe from flooding, with the Equatorial rain forest. Below that lies the várzea, which in times of high water – for the southern tributaries, from October to March, for the northern ones from March to July – is flooded, whilst the lowest level, the swampy

The Amazon and its tributaries

← *Not all waters promise a fun splash around: a cayman in the Pantanal*

Facts and Figures Brazil

© Baedeker

Geographical location
► South America

Surface
► 8.5 million sq km/3.3 million sq miles

Capital
► Brasília

Bordering countries
► Argentina, Paraguay, Bolivia, Peru, Colombia, Venezuela, Guyana, Suriname, French Guiana, Uruguay

Population
► 183 million inhabitants
► 22 inhabitants per sq km (57 per sq mile)

► Ethnic groups: 54% white, 39% mulatto and mestizo, 6% black, 1% other, including approx. 730,000 Indians
► Age distribution: over 30% of the population are under 15 years of age, only around 6% are over 65.

Religion
► 74% Catholics
► 15 % Protestants
► Buddhist, Bahá'i, Muslim and Jewish minorities
► Indian natural religions and Afro-Brazilian religions

Languages
► Portuguese
► Approx. 180 Indian idioms

State and administration
► Presidential federal republic
► Parliament (Congresso Nacional): Chamber of Deputies (Câmara dos Deputados) with 513 members, elected for four years, and a Federal Senate (Senado Federal), with 81 members, elected for 8 years
► Head of state and government: Luis Inácio (Lula) da Silva (since 2003)
► Adminstrative structure: 26 states and one Capital Federal District

Economy
► Gross Domestic Product (GDP): 1.4 trillion US$ (2007)
► GDP per capita: 7,600 US$ (2007)
► Unemployment rate: approx. 12%
► Main sectors of economy: services 73%, industry 21%, agriculture 6%

igapó, has plants such as the mangrove that also thrive in an amphibious environment. Where the Amazon merges with the Rio Negro, it spans on average 5km/3.1 miles, while the closer it gets to its mouth, the wider the riverbed becomes. The most violent clash of river and sea water creates the **pororoca**, a high tidal wave that sweeps away everything in its path and surges upriver for many kilometres.

The Amazon's numerous tributaries run parallel to each other, following the gradient of the lowlands. They may be divided into three groups: rios brancos (white rivers), rios negros (black rivers) and clearwater rivers. **Whitewater rivers** such as the Purus and the Madeira cross alluvial land and carry large amounts of detritus and suspended mineral matter, giving them a whitish colour (branco = white). Coming from the Brazilian mountains, the **clearwater rivers** – Rio Tapajós and Rio Xingú – cross rocky terrain and carry little in the way of deposits. Finally, the **blackwater rivers**, such as the Rio Negro, flow through floodplains, organic compounds (humic acids) lending their water a dark colour.

Tributaries

The Northeast: Litoral – Agreste – Sertão

The Nordeste (Northeast) of Brazil consists of three geographically distinct areas: Litoral, Agreste and Sertão. Only penetrating the interior for 60km/37 miles at most, the **coastal strip** (Litoral) consists primarily of a recent sedimentary plain, structured by the many bays, islands, dunes, lagoons and reefs (recifes). Before developing into one of the most densely populated areas of Brazil, this coastal land was covered in lush jungle vegetation, most of which has had to make way for sugar cane plantations.

Litoral

Towards the interior of the country there follows a high plateau no more than 700m/2,300ft in height, the Agreste, mostly tabular in shape, with steeply sloping sides. In many places, its rivers that run down to the plain – e. g. the Itapicuru and the Parnaíba, rising in the Serra da Tabatinga – form waterfalls. The vegetation is sparse and low-growing, with individual trees here and there that lose their leathery leaves in the summer.

Agreste

The Agreste turns finally into the Sertão, the **semi-arid zone**. The highest peak here is the Serra Baturité, covered in lush plant life. The crystalline rock is overlain with thick layers of old sediments, and is often table-like (Chapadas), similar to the Spanish Meseta. The watercourses are reduced to brooks, as a large amount of water evaporates. The landscape is most characterized however by the **caatinga**, with its small scrubby trees and bushes that shed their leaves in the dry season. The recurring periods of drought here may last for several years.

Sertão

The Southeast: serras and restingas

The Sudeste (Southeast), the wealthiest and most populated region of Brazil, does not form a single geographic entity. Reaching from the dry areas of the Northeast to the mountain ranges of the South, it also comprises the eastern part of the Brazilian mountain ranges with peaks of 800m/2,625ft to 1,000m/3,280ft. Serras are the high

Serras

plateau's elevated edges that were either created in a more recent geological era through uplift, or originate in the formation of the broad valleys, through which several of the tributaries of the Amazon and the Rio São Francisco wind their way, mainly in a south-north direction. From south to north, there is firstly the **Serra do Mar**, bounded in places by the ocean, elsewhere touched by lagoons or restingas (coastal plains), which reach their greatest elevation (2,318m/7,605ft) in the **Serra dos Órgãos**. Towards the north follows the **Serra da Mantiqueira**, culminating in the Pico da Bandeira. Even further north rises the **Serra do Espinhaço** with several mountain crests over 1,700m/5,600ft. Towards the Atlantic extends a stretch of coast with more recent layers of strata, which have led to the formation of rocky reefs, lagoons and bays surrounded by sandbanks – foremost among them the **Baía dos Todos os Santos** (All Saints Bay). The foothills of the mountains often edge right up to the coast, making an impressive sight. The most famous example is the conical **Pão de Açúcar** (Sugarloaf) in Guanabara Bay, dominating the skyline of Rio de Janeiro.

The Amazonian rainforest of Brazil can appear both menacing and captivating.

Restingas is the name given to those lowest-lying stretches of coast, **Restingas**
consisting of marine sediment, between the states of Bahia and Santa
Catarina. Mangrove vegetation often shows in the lagoons and the
low coastal terrain that is flooded at high tide. In the interior, west of
São Francisco, the region features deeply eroded terraces of up to
1,000m/3,280ft that rivers have carved up into numerous serras.

The South: Planalto and pampa

In South Brazil (Sul), a subtropical, moderate climate favoured set-   **Planalto**
tlement by Europeans. Geographically, São Paulo state, usually treated as part of the Sudeste (Southeast), belongs to this part of the
country, which consists of an extensive high plateau with a dense
network of rivers, and vegetation that is becoming noticeably different from that of the tropical areas. The **Serra do Mar** divides the
coast from the interior of the country. Its western slopes drop to a
high plateau, with an average height of 500m/1,640ft and drained by
the Rio Paraná and its tributaries, including the Tietê, with a length
of 1,100km/683 miles.

Southwards, the coastal mountains become lower and change into   **Pampa**
savannah-like lowlands (pampa), used mainly for cattle farming. On
the coast, lagoons have formed over time on the predominantly
sandy, loamy soil, such as the **Lagoa dos Patos** (Lagoon of the
Ducks), 7,000 sq km/2,700 sq miles wide and up to 10m/33ft deep.

The Midwest

Due to its considerable distance from the Atlantic, the Midwest   **High plateaus**
(Centro-Oeste), comprising the states of Mato Grosso, Mato Grosso
do Sul and Goiás, as well as the federal district of Brasília, is one of
the most sparsely populated regions in Brazil. It is composed of various undulating high plateaus, mostly covered by savannah-like **campos cerrados**. The watercourses running through the area flow into
the basin of the Rio Paraná and the Amazon. Along the Mato Grosso
high plateau, the watershed runs between the basins of these two rivers. Both the tributaries of the Amazon, running northwards, and
the tributaries of the Paraná, form a large number of waterfalls and
rapids.

In Goiás state, the plateau rises up to over 1,500m/4,920ft (Chapada   **Alluvial land**
dos Veadeiros), gradually levelling out towards the Rio Paraná on
sandy, basalt-rich rocks, to eventually disappear under a blanket of
alluvial land. As for the vegetation, large parts of Mato Grosso and
Goiás are dominated by savannah (campos cerrados), whilst the
more southerly areas are characterized by steppe-like campinas. In
the lower-lying areas with loamy, sandy soil, the **Pantanal**, the landscape changes between the rainy and dry seasons.

Climate

Predominantly tropical climate

Brazil has a mainly tropical climate, apart from the far south, with its subtropical climate. This means there is very little variation in temperature between the seasons. Even in the coldest month, the average temperature in nearly all parts of the country remains over 18 °C/64 F. Nevertheless, temperatures do vary, most between the lowlands and the higher-altitude areas. More pronounced are the differences between the rainy and dry seasons, with all gradations between very wet and very arid. So there are the permanently humid zones in the inner tropics on the Equator, and on the other hand, the semi-arid zones in the marginal tropics. The further south you get in Brazil, the more distinct the seasons become temperature-wise. However, due to the country's geographical position south of the Equator, they work the other way round: summer here lasts from December to March, winter from June to September.

Climatic regions

Despite predominantly tropical conditions, the Brazilian climate is anything but uniform. The country may be divided into four climatic regions: the humid tropical rainforest climate of Amazonia in the north, the tropical rainforest climate on the southeastern coast, the tropical climate with a distinct dry season in the interior to the south of Amazonia, and the subtropical, permanently humid climate of southern Brazil.

The vegetation of Brazil

Any attempt to describe in a few words the overwhelming diversity of plants and animals in Brazil – the country with the highest biodiversity on earth – is doomed to failure. The committed attempt of the ***Flora Brasiliensis*** to cover the Brazilian flora, completed in 1906, required over 20,000 pages. Considering the fact that botanically and zoologically, the Amazonian rainforest is amongst the least explored on earth, the real wealth of plants and animals can only be guessed at.

Rain forest in Amazonia

The tropical rainforest of the Amazon region, called Hylaea by the influential German explorer and naturalist **Alexander von Humboldt** (1769 – 1859), and in Brazil usually called selva, covers nearly the entire Brazilian lowlands. This is a complex vegetation system with many different types of trees, up to 60m/195ft high, sheltering low-growth trees connected by lianas (long, twining plants), with countless types of epiphytes. Around the mouth of the Amazon and in the areas still reached by the tides of the Atlantic, mangroves dominate, free of undergrowth but coupled with plants able to survive in soil regularly flooded by the high tide. Different again is the vegetation in the **igapó**, an area constantly under water; one of the plant species thriving here is the açaí palm. Enriched with nutrients time and

Brasil • Climate charts

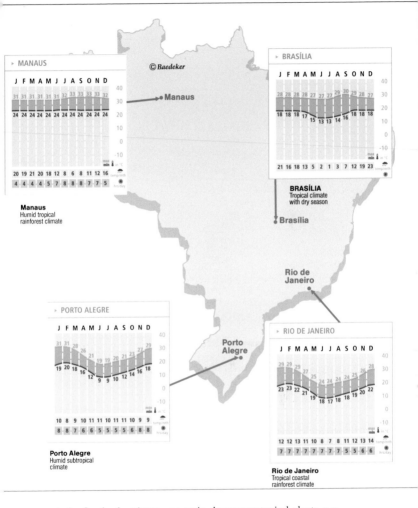

© Baedeker

MANAUS

	J	F	M	A	M	J	J	A	S	O	N	D
	31	31	31	31	31	31	32	33	33	33	33	32
	24	24	24	24	24	24	24	24	24	24	24	24

20	19	21	20	18	12	8	6	8	11	12	16
4	4	4	4	5	7	8	8	8	7	7	5

Manaus
Humid tropical
rainforest climate

BRASÍLIA

	J	F	M	A	M	J	J	A	S	O	N	D
	28	28	28	28	27	27	27	29	30	29	28	27
	18	18	18	17	15	13	13	14	16	18	18	18

21	16	18	13	5	2	1	3	7	12	19	23

BRASÍLIA
Tropical climate
with dry season

PORTO ALEGRE

	J	F	M	A	M	J	J	A	S	O	N	D
	31	31	28	26	21	19	19	20	21	23	27	29
	19	20	18	16	12	9	9	10	12	14	16	18

10	8	9	10	11	11	10	11	11	10	9	9
8	8	7	6	6	5	5	5	6	8	8	8

Porto Alegre
Humid subtropical
climate

RIO DE JANEIRO

	J	F	M	A	M	J	J	A	S	O	N	D
	29	29	29	27	25	24	24	24	25	26	27	28
	23	23	22	21	19	18	17	18	18	19	20	22

12	12	13	11	10	8	7	8	11	12	13	14
7	7	7	7	7	7	7	5	5	6	6

Rio de Janeiro
Tropical coastal
rainforest climate

again by floods, the **várzea** area again shows very typical plants, e. g. the jupati palm and the tall miriti palm. The real rubber tree (not to be confused with the indoor plant of the same name) – called seringueira by the locals – and the cocoa plant prefer the less moist soils of the várzea, at a higher altitude. On **terra firme**, the forests are a little more permeable, as the undergrowth is less dense. Characteristic of this area are the castanheira, the paranut (brazilnut) tree, its capsular fruit (ouriços) harvested at the end of the rainy season, in

Brasil • Vegetation zones

© Baedeker

- Amazonian rainforest
- Pampas Grasslands
- Caatinga shrubland
- Babassú palm forest
- Atlantic rainforest
- Araucaria forests
- Cerrado tropical savannah
- Gran Sabana (savannah)
- Pantanal wetlands

the Tocantins valley in particular, and the caucho, a Brazilian rubber tree growing in the wild. In the middle of the rainforest areas visitors sometimes come across plains covered in high grass, such as the occasionally flooded campos of Marajó island and Amapá federal state. On this alluvial land, grass plants make up the dominant vegetation.

Coastal forest and caatinga in the Northeast
The vegetation in the Northeast displays different characteristics, depending on the distance from or proximity to the Atlantic or the Amazon area. The further you get from the Amazon Basin, the more the rainforest changes, first into caatinga, and then taking on the characteristics of a semi-desert, the **sertão** proper. In the north, the coastal vegetation consists of rampant mangroves and extensive coconut palm plantations. The tropical coastal forest that used to dominate south of Cape São Roque, where the coastal strip is no wider

than 60km/37 miles and shrinks even more beyond Recife, has been partly cut down and replaced by plantations of sugar cane, which thrives on the sandy soil. In the interior sertão, the trees are mainly deciduous, but the type of vegetation characterizing the scenery is the caatinga with its cacti, thorny shrubs and gnarled trees. With the onset of the rainy season, the caatinga turns into an exuberant green thicket of grass plants.

Today, little remains of the once profuse tropical coastal forest (Mata Atlântica) of the Brazilian east; most of it has made way for more lucrative plantations, with the increasing number of people settling in the region not helping. All this points to the fact that the Mata Atlântica between Recife and Porto Alegre is the most threatened rainforest on earth; its salvation now seems practically impossible. The fact that in 1999, the rainforest area of the **»Discovery Coast«** (Costa do Descobrimento) in Bahia and Espírito Santo and the Atlantic forests of Paraná and São Paulo were added to the UNESCO World Heritage list may be a hopeful sign for the preservation – if only in fragments – of the **Mata Atlântica**.

Atlantic rainforest and grassland in the southeast

In the country's interior, the sertão, campos grasslands dominate the scenery, sometimes interspersed with trees (cerrados), as in the upper valley of the Rio São Francisco, sometimes treeless (campos limpos). The semi-desert climate of the mid and lower valley of the São Francisco river has its equivalent in the caatinga.

In the south, characterized by several climate zones and altitudes, the plant cover also shows different characteristics. The northern part is covered in thick, rampant rainforest, at least where it has not been destroyed by human intervention. Moving south, forests with deciduous trees, typical for soils with varying water content and that, on the São Paulo high plateau, cover a major part of the **campos cerrados**, resembling the African savannahs.

Subtropical vegetation in the south

From the south of Minas Gerais state up to the north of Rio Grande do Sul, at an altitude of 400 to 500m/1,300 to 1,600ft, **araucaria forests** (Mata do Pinhal) appear, typical of regions that have a moderate, warm climate and all-year-round precipitation. South of Rio Grande do Sul, grasslands (campinas) dominate.

The vegetation in the Midwest consists mainly of savannah (campos cerrados), occupying large parts of Mato Grosso and Goiás, whilst in the more southerly areas a type of steppe vegetation (campinas) shows. Moister soils also support gallery forests, often with no undergrowth and single-species trees only.

Savannah, steppe and periodical wetlands in the midwest

In the lower-lying regions with loamy, sandy terrain, the **Pantanal**, the scenery changes: periods of heavy precipitation, when the rivers flood the plains, alternate with marked dry spells. Various nutrient-rich types of grass grow here. During the rainy season, the around 200,000 sq km/77,000 sq miles of the Pantanal form a single expanse

At just under 7,400km/4,600 miles, the Brazilian coast offers countless fabulous beaches, such as here in the state of Bahia in the northeast of the country.

of water with large carpets of aquatic plants and many wooded islets, used as a refuge by wild animals such as jaguars, tapirs, capybaras and wild boars, but also domestic cattle. In the dry season, the area reverts to being **one of the most interesting natural reserves on the continent**. The vestigial watercourses and small sea basins left behind after the rains have gone are full of piranhas and alligators and also serve as a haven for countless waterbirds. Savannahs and swampy areas alternate, whilst on the banks of the large rivers lush forests grow rampant, teeming with monkeys.

The Brazilian fauna

The parallel existence of higher mammals, marsupials and indigenous mammals of South America – the toothless placental mammals (Edentata), including those of the order Xenarthra – represents a distinctive feature of the local mammalian life. Amongst the **marsupials**, relatives of the opossum, the dwarf opossum and woolly opossum are the most common. A characteristic of nearly all South American opossums is the prehensile tail, capable of grasping and holding. The last surviving representatives of the order Xenarthra are **sloths, anteaters and armadillos**. Sloths spend the majority of their lives hanging in branches, these herbivores favouring cecropia trees near rivers. Despite their inertia and slowness of movement, which are due to their metabolism, sloths are excellent swimmers.

Anteaters have a long sticky tongue to lick up their food and sharp claws to break up termite mounds. Whilst the giant anteater prefers the savannah habitat, the smaller collared anteater lives both in trees and on the ground; the squirrel-sized silky anteater has completely given up life on the ground.

Anteaters

Bony armour and strong digging claws characterize all armadillos. Sensing vibrations in the soil, some armadillos dig themselves into the ground with lightning speed. Armadillos feed on any organic matter. The South American **lowland tapir** prefers an amphibious environment and is considered to be extremely shy of humans. Nearly completely extinct now, the tapir has a dark-brown pelt, a crested mane at the nape of the neck and a trunk-like snout designed to tear off leaves, twigs and fresh shoots.

Armadillos and tapirs

Brazilian monkeys may be subdivided into **capuchin monkeys and Goeldi's monkeys, as well as marmosets**. All share a preference for forest habitats, and while rarely seen, their audible presence, of the howler monkeys in particular, gives them away. Much more reticence is shown by the pygmy marmosets, weighing only 150g/5.3 ounces, the smallest New World monkeys, who attract attention by bird-like chirping. With a body length of up to 70cm/28 inches and its melancholic air, the gentle woolly monkey is the largest South American monkey, but its numbers are severely threatened.

Monkeys

One of the most-feared predators of South America is the **jaguar**. Villainized in mythology as the bad guy, in a similar way to the European wolf, the jaguar is now almost extinct. Other predators in Brazil are the puma, ocelot and maned wolf, as well as the coati and the raccoon.

Predators

Two types of freshwater dolphin live in the Amazon and its tributaries: one is black and one lighter, with a pink colouring. While the timid sea cows – faced with extinction – are not often seen, the dolphins, about 2m/6.5 ft in size, often follow boats.

Dolphins and sea cows

The birdlife of Brazil, and the Amazon area in particular, is characterized by a richness of species, splendid colours and low population density. The most luxuriant and varied displays of colour are offered by the quintessential tropical bird, the **parrot**. The colourful plumage with which nature blessed them is the reason that they are torn from their natural habitat to lead a wretched existence in cages abroad.

Birds

Alongside the parrot, the **toucan**, with its bright orange, oversized beak and the **colibri** (hummingbird) are the country's best-known tropical birds.

Reptiles   The tropical climate offers the cold-blooded snakes, lizards, turtles, alligators, caymans and crocodiles an ideal terrain. The most prominent lizards are **iguanas and whiptail lizards**; amongst the constrictors, the **anaconda and boa** are feared, while coral snakes and pit vipers paralyse and kill their victims with neurotoxins.

Fish and amphibians   In a country such as Brazil, characterized by an extensive system of rivers, the recorded number of around 3,000 species of freshwater fish comes as no surprise, amongst them (freshwater) sharks, pipe-fish, rays, sawfish and flatfish. At up to three metres'/ten feet long, the largest freshwater fish in the country is the **piracuru**. The most common are the characins, a family of 700 species of freshwater fish related to the carp family. Another is the **piranha**, whose danger is overrated. Tree frogs are in the habit of laying their eggs in the highest treetops, but they are better known for being the much sought-after prey of indigenous hunters, who use their skin secretions as arrow poison, lending these tree-climbing frogs their other name: poison dart frogs.

Natural work of art: the tropical flora and fauna …

An estimated 10 to 30 million species of insect exist worldwide, a considerable proportion of these in the primary forest of Brazil. Unfortunately, the visitor to tropical regions usually becomes acquainted with the rich splendour of this most diverse animal kingdom through its smallest members, the annoying pests that will use a person as a welcome habitat.

Insects

The destruction of the Brazilian rainforest

Blaming the destruction of the Brazilian rainforest on the high demand for tropical timber for the manufacture of upmarket living room furniture is to oversimplify a very complex issue. Extensive agriculture and livestock farming, extraction of mineral resources and slash-and-burn land clearances in particular – caused largely by an inexhaustible supply of landless farmers looking for land to settle, themselves the victims of an extremely unequal distribution of land – form a network of destruction that has already not only eliminated some 20% of the Amazonian jungle, but also over 90% of the tropical coastal forest (Mata Atlântica). The consequences for the Indian population whose living environment is being destroyed, for the flora and fauna as well as the global climate are disastrous. So complex are the causes of the destruction of the Brazilian rainforest that

... is not shy to display its luxuriant colours.

comprehensive strategies are required for safeguarding one of the most important ecosystems on the planet. An integral part of this must be the implementation of Brazil's progressive environmental legislation, with adequate official supervision, **land reforms** as a measure for tackling the extremely unfair structures of land owner-ship, international aid programmes for the protection of the rainforest, **cutting the demand for tropical hardwood** and the eco-logically sustainable stabilization of the economy with, at the same time, reduction of social injustices. As long as Brazil does not move towards a more collective wealth, the unrelenting exploitation of na-ture for economic reasons will continue.

Population · Politics · Economy

In Brazil, the mixing of ethnic groups of diverse origin – the de-scendants of Portuguese colonials, European and Asian immigrants, Africans brought forcibly to Brazil and subjugated Indians – has led to a colourful medley of a population and a cultural diversity that to this day are part of the particular appeal of the country. 53 % of the Brazilian population are white (of which 15 % are of Portuguese de-scent, 11 % Italian, 10 % Spanish and 3 % German), 34 % mixed-race, namely mestizos or caboclos (the descendants of whites and In-dians), mulattoes (the descendants of whites and black) and cafuzos (the descendants of blacks and Indians), 11 % Afro-Brazilians as well as just under 1 % Asians, mainly Japanese. The sad fact that there are now fewer than 200,000 descendants of the estimated 5 million Indi-ans that were living in what is today Brazil when the Portuguese ar-rived in 1500, is the **result of European conquest and colonization**. The Indians are divided into about 200 different ethnic groups speaking 120 different languages or dialects belonging mainly to four linguistic families: Tupí-Guaraní, Gê, Karib and Arawak.

Population make-up

Whilst the Brazilian constitution prohibits all racism, discrimination against ethnic minorities undeniably occurs. There is a clear correla-tion between dark skin colour and lesser economic status and social prestige. The darker the skin, the lower the chance of social mobility. Accordingly, the political, economic and cultural elite of Brazil is predominantly white. The indigenous population traditionally occu-pies an underprivileged position at the fringes of Brazilian society.

Racism

The ethnic heterogeneity of Brazil goes hand in hand with the exis-tence of numerous religions. Whilst Brazil calls itself the world's larg-

Religion

← *An explosive issue: protest against the unequal distribution of land in Brazil*

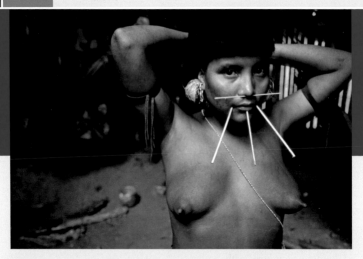

OPPRESSED AND BETRAYED

On paper, protection laws gave Brazilian Indians the right to self-governed reservations as early as 1934. The 1988 democratic constitution even promises them the right to cultural independence and diversity. Noble intentions, not matched by a sorry reality: in fact, in the early 21st century, four fifths of Brazilian Indian reservations continue to be defenceless prey to all kinds of invasion by the white population.

The fault lies with the infamous Decree 1775, thought up by the then minister of justice Jobim in 1996 that stipulates the mandatory hearing of all objections before any demarcation of indigenous land. Just the ticket for gold prospectors, wood exporters and land-squatters, resulting in hundreds of pending lawsuits and the indigenous peoples' living space in many places disputed or acutely threatened.

Low level of interest

In this unequal war of attrition, the successes of the indigenous population have been few and far between, since the interest of the Western world in their fate has significantly tapered off. Who will have registered that the Maxakali tribe in Santa Helena de Minas, led by **Maria Diva Maxakali**, succeeded in seeing off foreign invaders? Even a very different news item from the state of Minas Gerais caused a stir only in Third World circles: in March 2000 – i.e. almost exactly 500 years after the beginning of the conquista – 22 Xacriaba Indians were freed by civil servants of the FUNAI Indian protection agency, after suffering over two months of enslavement on a remote estate. Contempt for Indians as well as threats and attacks are far from being »yesterday's news«, and the dismal life on many reservations is dominated by lethargy and hopelessness. Some have long since degenerated to enclaves of alcoholism, others have extremely high rates of suicide. For gold pros-

Yanomami woman with facial adornments: the constitution allows Indians a right to cultural self-determination and expression, although the reality is somewhat different.

pectors and large estate owners the Indians are at best »**bichos do mato**«, animals from the jungle. They are often seen as having no work ethic or ability to learn, but more like a kind of burden interfering with vested economic interests. The idea of the Indian as a Brazilian with equal rights remains a pious hope in the early 21st century.

Perfidious means

The fate of the **Waimiro-Atriori** serves as an example of the perfidious means mining firms, large farmers, gold prospectors and provincial politicians employ against the Indians. After being almost completely wiped out with boundless brutality by Brazilian regular armed forces during the construction of the BR-174 highway from Manaus to Boa Vista (1968–1977), the few survivors of this tribe were swindled out of a large part of the reservation they had been promised north of Manaus. After satellites had located rich deposits of tin ore in the area, the upper reaches of Rio Uatuma were swiftly renamed »Rio Pitinga«. This clever manoeuvre paved the way for the subsequent dispossession of the Waimiro-Atroari, as according to the law, Rio Uatuma constituted the reservation border, with no mention anywhere of Rio Pitinga.

Enduring violence

Has the country's bloody past been overcome? Yes and no: for the celebrations, on 22 April 2000, of the 500th anniversary of the »discovery« of Brazil by Pedro Alvares Cabral, police used such excessive force against demonstrating Indians that Carlos Mares, president of FUNAI at the time, resigned in protest. In the same year, an Indian who, after a visit to Brasília, slept off his inebriation at a bus stop, was doused with petrol by white youths and set alight. Abroad, neither of these two incidents warranted any meaningful reaction; no ambassador was called in to report, no head of government in Europe or North America was heard to demand, loud and clear, the **protection of the indigenous minorities**. If there really is a vague hope to preserve the diversity of the indigenous ways of life in Brazil, it stands and falls with the watchful interest of politics, media and the public in the »First World«. A prerequisite for the preservation of Indian culture is the sustainable securing of living spaces for indigenous peoples. If Brazil's constitution of 1988 is really meant to guarantee the effective survival of Indian peoples in the 21st century, there must be no withholding, ignoring or looking away. Otherwise, the legislation remains a mere façade for the West.

est Catholic country, along with Protestant, Muslim, Jewish and Indian-animist influences, it is most of all **syncretic combinations** of African religions with Catholic traditions that add to the religious diversity. Despite the statistical dominance of pure Catholicism, the official church, with its conservative bent, is increasingly losing its followers, many of whom look to satisfy their religious needs with various cults (in the wider sense of the word): the Evangelical Pentecostal movement (Igreja Universal do Reino de Deus) in particular, as well as the syncretic Afro-Brazilian religions.

State and administration

State system According to the constitution of 5 October 1988 and the referendum on the final state system of 21 April 1993, the **Federal Republic of Brazil** (República Federativa do Brasil) is a presidential federal republic, with Brasília as capital.

Parliament The legislative National Congress (Congresso Nacional) consists of two chambers, the Federal Senate (Senado Federal) with 81 seats – three for each federal state or district – and the Chamber of Deputies (Câmara dos Deputados) with 513 delegates. Whilst the members of the Chamber of Deputies are elected every four years by propor-

The weather-beaten face of a farm worker in Mato Grosso

tional representation, Senators stay in office for eight years. Every four years, partial elections are held where alternately one or two thirds of Senators are elected using majority voting. All citizens are eligible to vote from the age of 16.

Government

At the head of government stands the president, elected every four years directly by the people. The president nominates the cabinet. The 1997 constitutional amendment allowed the re-election, once only, of the president, whose term of office had previously been limited to one legislative period.

Parties

Brazilian parties have traditionally been very much geared towards personalities rather than political agendas. The majority of the parties are small narrow interest groups and populist parties with marginal importance. Few parties have considerably shaped the most recent history of Brazil: the **Partido do Movimento Democrático Brasileiro (PMDB)** is the successor to the MDP – the official opposition party during the military dictatorship from 1964 onwards – and is considered a centre-ground party. In 1988, the **Partido da Social-Democracia Brasileira (PSDB)**, the Brazilian Social Democratic Party, split from the PMDB. The **Partido dos Trabalhadores (PT)** was founded in 1979 by unionists, intellectuals and left-wing groups and is considered a modern programme-oriented party of the left. The **Partido da Frente Liberal (PFL)** occupies ground right of the centre.

Legal system

Brazil's formal constitutional structure is based on the constitution of 1988. Despite modern legislation and a large number of judicial institutions, there are some parts of the country where the authority of the state is scarcely present, which is why in Brazil formal law only applies in part, and private law enforcement is not unusual. Escalating political corruption, the power of the drug cartels, the murder of street children and rural workers and the unspeakable treatment of prisoners illustrate that the country is far from enforcing current law – only 10% of all homicides are solved.

Administration

Brazil is divided into **27 federal states**, including the Federal District of Brasília. Every federal state has its own constitution as well as its own parliament, with a governor at the head of affairs. One level below the federal states there are over 9,000 districts and just under 5,000 cities and municipalities.

Economic development

The economic development of Brazil, from an agrarian national economy to an emerging market country with a broad industrial base, is characterized by alternating heady **economic booms** with the invariably recurring freefalls into the depths of economic **recession**. Up to the middle of the 20th century, Brazil was an agrarian society,

Federal Districts Map

RORAIMA
AMAPÁ
AMAZONAS
PARÁ
© Baedeker
MARANHÃO
CEARÁ
RIO GRANDE
DO NORTE
PARAÍBA
PIAUÍ
PERNAMBUCO
ACRE
RONDÔNIA
TOCANTINS
ALAGOAS
SERGIPE
BAHIA
MATO GROSSO
Bundesdistrikt
Brasília
GOIÁS
MINAS GERAIS
MATO GROSSO
DO SUL
ESPÍRITO
SANTO
SÃO PAULO
RIO DE
JANEIRO
PARANÁ
SANTA
CATARINA
RIO GRANDE
DO SUL

- North = (Norte)
- Northeast = (Nordeste)
- Midwest = (Centro-Oeste)
- Southeast = (Sudeste)
- South = (Sul)

geared towards the export of wood, sugar, gold and coffee. The low level of crop diversification led to a heavy dependency on the world market and regular slumps in export sales.

Promoting industry

From 1956 onwards, under **President Juscelino Kubitschek**, an intense industrialization policy, largely financed by the state, was set under way. A high rate of inflation and political instability spelt the abrupt end, in 1961, of this phase of revival based on industrial development. From 1970 onwards, under the military junta, the economy started to prosper strongly again, leading to an economic boom which was to change not only the structure of the Brazilian economy, but of society as a whole: the rapid development of urban industrial centres led to a rural exodus and a structural change from a mainly rural to a more urban society, with levels of urbanization currently around 80 %. The military government's lack of moderation led it – dazzled by the scale of the economic boom and in the belief it would last forever – to draw up monumental development projects for the economy and implement them on credit.

Boom and bust

With the oil crisis of 1979 and the resultant explosion of interest rates, the Brazilian population had to pick up the bill, in the form of unemployment and social decline. Only the far-reaching economic reforms of the early 1990s – a strict fiscal policy, financial reforms, the liberalization of trade and the deregulation and privatization of state companies – led to the gradual consolidation of the economy. However, it took the establishment of the real as the new currency in 1994 (Plano Real), initiated by the finance minister at the time, and later President **Fernando Henrique Cardoso**, to halt the runaway inflation. Economic growth, price stability and the increase in real earnings for the lower income brackets were the result of Cardoso's economic policy, until in 1998 the Asian crisis took hold of Brazil too, shaking the world's trust in Brazil's financial strength.

Recovery of the economy

Following the relaxation of the stringent exchange rate controls and the floating of the real in 1999, the Brazilian currency lost 44% of its value against the US$. However, Cardoso's strict adherence to his economic course, with the support of the International Monetary Fund (IMF), led in the end to an economic recovery. The Lula government too knew how to dispel the doubts of donor countries and managed to be given a favourable line of credit.

History

Indigenous way of life before the »discovery« of Brazil by the Europeans, colonization, declaration of independence. The monarchy and the Republic. The dictatorship of the Generals and return to democracy. An exploration of the chequered history of Brazil from the early days to the present time.

Brazil before Colonization

12,000 BC	First humans in America
8,000 BC	Oldest traces of human settlement in modern-day Brazil

The temporary fall of sea levels in the Pleistocene ice ages enabled people from Asia to reach the American double continent via the Bering land bridge. The oldest confirmed records of human settlement of America, dated to approx. 12,000 BC, were found in Alaska. Over the following two millennia, the **Paleo-Indians** moved south. The first undisputed traces of human settlement around modern-day Brazil – skeletal finds dated to around 8,000 BC – confirm the early human settlement of the Brazilian east. However, recent findings of skeletons and stone tools in North and South America have led scientists to assume that the settlement of America, and Brazil, happened up to 5,000 years earlier than previously thought.

Until 1500 AD the indigenous population of Brazil lived in tribal units, some of them with several hundred members, along the coastal strip and in the forests of the interior. The Indians, dwelling in large houses made from tree trunks and covered with leaf roofs, engaged in agriculture, at least near the coast, complementing their food supply with hunting and gathering. The periodical exhaustion of the soils resulting from agricultural cultivation hindered a permanent settlement of humans at any one place. The social structure was characterized by **flat hierarchies**, with strictly observed division of labour between men and women: men would hunt and gather, as well as clear the land of trees, whilst the women were in charge of working the soil, processing the agricultural produce and preparing meals.

Indigenous way of life before 1500

Early Colonial Development

1494 AD	Treaty of Tordesillas
1500	Portuguese seafarer Pedro Álvares Cabral lands on the Brazilian coast
from 1530	The Portuguese crown takes the first steps towards establishing a colonial administration

← *Pedro Álvares Cabral »discovered« Brazil.*

Treaty of Tordesillas

Following arbitration by Pope Alexander VI, with the signing of the Treaty of Tordesillas between Spain and Portugal in 1494, i.e. before the Portuguese »discovery« of Brazil, the two countries agreed to a demarcation line running 370 leagues (around 2,000km) west of the Cape Verde islands, dividing up both states' spheres of colonial influence in the New World. All known territories, as well as those still to be discovered, east of this line were awarded to Portugal, all those west of it to Spain. Today, this line would run more or less at a longitude of 48 degrees west.

Arrival of the Portuguese

The Portuguese landing on the South American Atlantic coast under the leadership of **Admiral Pedro Álvares Cabral** marks the biggest watershed in Brazilian history. 22 April 1500 saw the first – peaceful – encounter of Brazilian Indians with Portuguese seafarers. However, the first Portuguese in Brazil were quick to spot the land's wealth in dyewood. The French, Spanish and later the Dutch also recognized the economic importance of the territory conquered by the Portuguese and tried to seize a slice of it for themselves.

Feudal settlement policy

In order to underline and implement Portugal's colonial claims to Brazil, from 1530 onwards the Portuguese **King João III** took the first steps towards setting up a colonial administration with the establishment of capitanias. The coastal strip was divided up into 15 portions and granted as hereditary fiefdoms to Portuguese noblemen, who pledged to settle and defend the areas given to them. Thus, a series of large feudal estates with no central administrative authority were created.

Establishment of central government

This feudally-based settlement policy was not that fruitful however, as conflicts with European seafarers and the indigenous population, as well as a lack of settlers, threatened the Portuguese attempts at colonization. By 1548 the Portuguese crown felt obliged to establish a governor-general system. A central administration was set up, charged with military, civil, judicial and fiscal duties and with its seat in Bahia, today's Salvador da Bahia. At the same time that the government was established, predominantly Jesuit missionaries started converting the indigenous population groups to Christianity and introducing them to European ways of life.

Economic changes

The exploitation of dyewood formed the economic basis for the first colonial settlements in Brazil. With the political-administrative stabilization of the colony in the course of the establishment of the governor-general system, from 1570 onwards long-term agricultural methods gained ground, the **cultivation of sugar cane** in particular. The increasing demand in labour that went with it led to more recruitment of Indian plantation workers, most of whom refused this kind of work however, as tilling the land and harvesting – as opposed to clearing trees – traditionally fell to the women. The consequence was, on the one hand, the enslavement of Indians, on the other, the organized kidnapping and shipping of millions of African slaves to Brazil.

Venturing into the Interior

from 1635	Expeditions by the bandeirantes
1654	Battle of Recife, expulsion of Dutch colonists
1698/99	Gold found in Minas Gerais

By 1600, only the extended coastal area had been settled, somewhat sparsely: only Bahia, founded in 1549, Rio de Janeiro (1565) and Philipéia (1584) had the rights and privileges of a town, alongside a good number of smaller settlements. From 1635 onwards, there started to be more expeditions into the unknown Brazilian hinterland, in order to capture Indian slaves and to hunt for precious metals. The leaders of this kind of expedition into the interior – agricultural entrepreneurs, or adventurers sponsored by them – were called **bandeirantes** after the bandeira, the banner that they always carried with them. In the south, they pushed as far as the area that is today occupied by the federal states of Minas Gerais, Mato Grosso and Goiás, in the northwest to the source of the Amazon and, following the definitive expulsion of the Dutch colonists after the battle of Recife 1654, into the interior of the northeast.

Expeditions by the bandeirantes

The interests of the bandeirantes clashed vehemently with those of the Jesuits, who in the 17th century had founded numerous missionary settlements in the interior of the country as bases for peaceful conversion, »civilization« and integration of indigenous peoples. Military conflicts between extremely brutal bandeirantes and Jesuits did occur. In the meantime, even the crown took **measures for the protection of the indigenous population**;

Hunting Indian slaves

? DID YOU KNOW ...?

■ ... that Roland Joffé's award-winning 1986 film *The Mission*, with Robert de Niro and Jeremy Irons in the main roles, deals with the desperate fight for survival of a Jesuit mission in the Brazilian jungle? The film has a dramatic ending: missionaries as well as converted Indians are slaughtered by Portuguese soldiers.

however, economic necessities, namely demand for labour, prevented a consistent policy for the protection of indigenous peoples. The Jesuits for their part became the most staunch advocates of Brazilian Indians.

It was the discovery of gold in Minas Gerais in 1698/1699 that triggered a large-scale penetration of the Brazilian interior. The settlements created, amongst them **Ouro Preto**, required infrastructural links with the coastal centres. In this way, the discovery of precious metals not only heralded a phase of economic revival and the rise of Brazil to become the biggest suppliers of gold worldwide, but also brought about the opening up of the country's interior.

Imposed Modernization

from	Authoritarian modernization of Brazil according to the
1750	Marquês de Pombal's vision of enlightened absolutism
1759	Expulsion of the Jesuits from the entire Portuguese territories
1789	The Inconfidência Mineira conspirators demand independence from the mother country.

In the second half of the 18th century, enlightened absolutism in Portugal reached its peak under King José I. Informed by these ideas, the king's prime minister, **Marquês de Pombal** (1699–1782), immediately set a programme of reform under way, the radicalism of which would have far-reaching consequences for colonial Brazil. Part of his comprehensive reform programme were population-boosting measures designed to improve the defensive capabilities of Brazil. As a consequence, numerous cities were founded and the military, tax and finance systems reorganized. In the wake of the reorganization of the administration, Pombal ordered in 1763 the transfer of the capital from Bahia to Rio de Janeiro, the future seat of the central administrative authorities. The foundation of privileged, monopolistic trading companies, a mercantile policy favouring Portugal, the increasingly centralized administration, systematization of the legal system and strengthening of the authority of the state – the whole programme of authoritarian modernization led by the crown in favour of Portugal – actually increased Brazilian discontentment with the mother country and fostered the emergence of a Brazilian identity.

The expulsion of the Jesuit order from the entire Portuguese territories in 1759 reinforced the disassociation of Brazil from the mother country. The reason behind the expulsion of the Jesuits was Pombal's attempt to reduce the church's influence in state and society, as well as the critical attitude of the Jesuit order towards monarchic absolutism. The **Jesuits' strong commitment** to the educational sector, and the consequent fact that a considerable part of the Brazilian elite had passed through Jesuit educational institutions and felt loyalty to the order, caused discontent towards Portugal's policy among those parts of the population.

Expulsion of the Jesuits

After the death of José I, the reactionary politics of the Portuguese government under **Maria I** (1777 – 1792) resulted in new hostility towards Lisbon from the inhabitants of Brazil. In 1789, the feelings of discontent with Portugal culminated in the conspiracy of the **Inconfidência Mineira**. This conspiracy was instigated by a dozen influential citizens from Ouro Preto wanting to achieve independence from the mother country. The plot failed, and its leader, Joaquim José da Silva Xavier, named after his profession **Tiradentes** (= teeth puller), was sentenced to death, and his fellow conspirators forced to leave the country. Further anticolonial republican conspiracies, in Rio de Janeiro in 1794 and Bahia in 1798, initiated by various social groups, are evidence of the strong dislike felt by large parts of society towards the Portuguese crown.

Anticolonial movement

The Path to Independence

1807/08	The Portuguese court flees Napoleonic army to Brazil; Rio de Janeiro becomes capital of the Kingdom of Portugal.
1815	Proclamation of the United Kingdom of Portugal, Brazil and the Algarve
1822	Brazil becomes independent.

In the Portugal of 1792, João, son of Maria I, took over the Regency for his mentally ill mother and in 1816, after her death, was officially crowned **João VI**. In the face of the threat from Napoleonic France, the whole Portuguese court transferred to Brazil as early as 1807/08. Rio de Janeiro became the temporary capital of the Kingdom of Portugal. With the end of the Napoleonic wars in Europe, João VI decided – against his original intentions – to remain in Brazil, proclaiming in 1815 the **United Kingdom of Portugal, Brazil and the Algarve**. This meant political equality for Brazil and Portugal and the formal termination of Brazil's colonial status, the idea being to take the wind out of the sails of the separatist movement in the former colony.

The end of colonial status

DOM PEDRO

EMPEREUR DU BRÉSIL

The liberal movement in Portugal, which in 1821 demanded both the summoning of the state assembly (Cortes), last convened in 1697, as well as the establishment of a constitutional monarchy, thwarted – through the planned revision of equality for Brazil – the far-sighted appeasement policy of João VI. Increasing separatist unrest in Brazil was the logical consequence of this neo-colonial policy. Liberal activities in Portugal required the return of João VI and his government to Lisbon. Before returning, he appointed his son Pedro Regent of Brazil. Pedro was to make history by resisting the renewed colonial endeavours of his motherland with the rallying call of »Independência ou Morte!« (»Independence or Death!«), which was to enter the history books as the **»Cry of Ipiranga«**. On 1 December 1822, he was proclaimed Pedro I, Emperor of Brazil. Whilst the emancipation from Portugal spelled the end of Brazilian colonial history, the country's colonial economic and social structures – e.g. the practice of slavery – and the monarchic state system remained intact for a long time.

Declaration of Independence

From Monarchy to Republic

1824	Proclamation of Brazil's first constitution
1840 – 1889	Reign of Pedro II
1850	Prohibition of slave imports
1865 – 1870	War of the Triple Alliance against Paraguay
1888	Abolition of slavery

On 25 March 1824, Rio de Janeiro saw the solemn announcement of the first constitution of the Empire of Brazil, which was to remain in force until the proclamation of the Republic in 1889. This constitution established the hereditary monarchy, a constitutional and representative system, and the separation of powers, as well as the clear political dominance of the Emperor. The sovereign's centralized powers met with massive criticism from the country's liberal forces. Increasing domestic tensions and – following the death of João VI of Portugal – the prospect of the Portuguese throne led to the abdication of Pedro I in 1831 in favour of his son **Pedro de Alcântara**, who was only five years old at the time and therefore reigned with the help of a regency council.

The constitution of 1824

Until the accession and taking up of government business by Pedro de Alcântara as Dom Pedro II in 1840, the political situation in Brazil

The Second Empire

← »Independence or Death« was his motto: Dom Pedro.

was characterized by the parliamentary dispute between centralist conservative forces and supporters of liberal ideas looking to strengthen the **autonomy of the provinces** through a system of federal rule. In the 1840s, the conservatives were increasingly able to shape politics according to their wishes and consolidate their power, whereas the liberal movement expressed its opposition in several localized rebellions, which were all violently put down. In 1853, the simmering conflict ended when the liberals entered government, beginning a constructive phase of domestic cooperation.

Foreign affairs In its foreign policy, Brazil supported the Liberals of Uruguay against the Argentinian dictator Juan Manuel de Rosas and later – between 1865 and 1870 – fought on the side of Uruguay and Argentina against Paraguay, governed by Francisco Solano Lopez. This war entered the history books as the bloodiest conflict South America had seen. The Brazilians alone mourned over 50,000 dead, while the Paraguayans, who had fought superior armies with a courage born out of desperation, were practically annihilated. This war, called the **War of the Triple Alliance** was to have far-reaching consequences for Brazil. On the one hand, the dependence on foreign powers, Great Britain in particular, increased as war-related financial problems necessitated the borrowing of international credits, on the other hand, the military rose to become a significant force in politics.

Economy Over the course of the 19th century, the economic situation of Brazil underwent profound changes. From 1850 onwards, the states of São Paulo and Rio Grande do Sul in particular saw the blossoming of the coffee industry. The plantations cultivating this product multiplied in the shortest of times, creating a new moneyed class of major landowners (fazendeiros) and wholesalers, who were soon threatening the wealth and political influence of the old cotton and sugar barons in the north of the country. The rising demand for labour in the central and southern regions led to increasing social mobility and the selling of slaves from the sugar-producing northeast to the coffee-growing areas.

Abolition of slavery After the importation of new slaves from Africa was prohibited in 1850 following severe pressure from England, the view that slavery constituted an outdated relic of the past gradually took root in Brazilian society. The champions of the nascent **abolition movement** were a number of organizations, including masonic lodges and newspapers, but also the Republican Party, founded in 1870 in Itú in São Paulo province, which propagated the abolition of slavery and of the monarchy. The **»Lei do Ventre Livre«** (»Law of the Free Womb«) of 1871 guaranteed all newborn children from black slave families their freedom. The gradual restriction of slavery finally led to its definitive prohibition through the **»Lei Aurea«** (»Golden Law«) of 13 May 1888.

The ship journey to Brazil marked the beginning of the slaves' long ordeal.

In the late 19th century, the republican movement was not alone in its anti-monarchist attitude. The military, too, increasingly politicized following the War of the Triple Alliance, recognized in the monarchy a relic of the European colonial past. The conspiratorial collaboration of military and republican movement, with the goal of abolishing the monarchy, culminated in the siege of Rio de Janeiro through **General Deodoro da Fonseca** on 15 November 1889. Two days later, Pedro II left for exile in Europe.

Downfall of the monarchy

The First Republic

1889	Proclamation of the Republic
1891	The constitution of the United States of Brazil comes into effect.
1930	End of the Republic

The interim government under Deodoro da Fonseca immediately started to dismantle the empire's anachronistic structures: separating state and church, introducing freedom of religion and abolishing the nobility. The new constitution of 1891 was modelled on its US-American counterpart; the centralism practised for many years ended through the upgrading of the former provinces to federal

Consolidating the Republic

states with comprehensive powers. The Supreme Court as judicial, the parliament and Senate as legislative and the president as executive authority guaranteed the constitutional principle of the separation of powers. Voting rights, however, remained tied to the census. When, following violent domestic clashes, Fonseca was considering a coup, the military intervened again, deciding to back **Marshal Floriano de Peixoto**, who was to hold presidential office for only three years. Prudente de Morais, elected in 1894, was the first president of Brazil not to have come from the military.

Economic development

Up to 1930, the political arena was granted a period of relative quiet, leaving economic prosperity to consolidate itself. Countless immigrants from Europe and Japan provided the labour necessary for development and contributed to the growth of the larger cities. Four million people emigrated from European countries, and some 200,000 from Japan. Coffee and rubber were the pillars of the national economy; the coffee plantations expanded, not least thanks to the Italian immigrants, whilst the rubber plantations of the Amazon used mainly workers from the coastal areas of the northeast. Urban industrialization made São Paulo rise to become Brazil's most important economic hub. Towards the end of the 19th century, Belém and Manaus also blossomed ostentatiously, with the rubber boom helping the larger Amazon cities to achieve unimaginable wealth over a short period of time. The theatre and opera house of Manaus, erected at that time in the middle of the jungle, is a reminder of former prosperity and the resulting visionary sense of a new era, captured by Werner Herzog in his jungle epic *Fitzcarraldo*, starring Klaus Kinski as an enthusiastic Caruso fan. The monopoly in extracting and trading rubber did not last however: the English smuggled rubber tree seeds out of the country and started very successful rubber plantations in Southeast Asia. When the First World War broke out, this competition had already badly damaged the Brazilian rubber sector. Alongside coffee, rubber and sugar, Brazil began to export the meat of cattle reared in Minas Gerais, opening up a further economic sector.

From Vargas to Kubitschek

1930 – 1945	Presidency of Getúlio Vargas;
1942	Brazil enters the war on the side of the Allies
1951 – 1954	Second presidency of Vargas
1956 – 1961	Presidency of Juscelino Kubitschek; construction of Brasília
1960	Brasília becomes the capital.

The economic growth of the country was not, however, accompa-　**The Vargas era**
nied by a political maturation. By the time Getúlio Vargas took
power in 1930, supported by the military – following the dramatic
economic collapse of Brazil as a result of the worldwide economic
crisis – corruption and glaring social inequalities were widespread.
Vargas' presidency, which lasted 15 years, was in reality nothing more
than a dictatorship camouflaged by phoney constitutional guaran-
tees. Vargas was the first Brazilian statesman who tried to solve certain problems of the republic nationally, by weakening the local
centres of power in order to centralize government responsibility. He
managed for instance to transfer to the federal government all taxa-
tion rights that previously had been within the remit of the local authorities. Whilst Vargas used authoritarian methods to push through
his policies, they were successful too – in the labour and social sectors in particular. Vargas represented a new, rising economic force,
that of the entrepreneur who refused to accept the traditional **monopoly of the plantation owners**. Whilst his system of government
mixed democratic and fascistic ideas, his policies met with popular
support; breaking with the past and bringing progressive elements
into politics, he gained the support of the more dynamic economic
forces.

During the Second World War, Brazil joined the coalition against　**Second**
Hitler in 1942, sending troops to the Italian front. After the war　**World War**
ended, Vargas found himself confronted with the resistance of all the
domestic democratic movements claiming for Brazil those institutions and freedoms that they had defended in Europe. In 1945, this
paradoxical situation forced Vargas' resignation.

In 1946, Vargas' long-term war minister **Eurico Gaspar Dutra** became　**Post-war period**
his democratically-elected successor, running for a centre-right party.
Following a promising start it became clear, however, that the new
government was unable to come to grips with the country's problems, of economic and industrial development in particular. Due to
the failings of the Dutra government, Vargas returned to the presidential palace in 1951 – with democratic legitimization this time,
continuing the policy of import substitution and state-led industrialization initiated during his first presidency. His **National Plan**, which
provided for the nationalization of the oil industry, amongst other
things, leading in 1953 to the foundation of the state-owned oil company Petrobras, drastically increased external debt. Following an assassination attempt on a journalist critical of the government – initiated from Vargas' inner circle – which resulted in the death of the
person accompanying the journalist, a high-ranking military officer,
the army gave the president an ultimatum to resign. Vargas, unable
to withstand the political pressure, took his own life in 1954. His
successor, former vice president João Café Filho, called new elections
for 1955.

A capital is born: the construction of Brasília

The Kubitschek era

The elections were won by Juscelino Kubitschek de Oliveira, who held the office of president between 1956 and 1961. The new government steered a clever middle course, continuing the policy of combating the backwardness of the country – initiated by its predecessors – as well as taking into account foreign interests in Brazil. However, the concentration of investments in the industrial sector favoured already existing industrial agglomerations such as São Paulo, whilst industrially backward regions were not able to benefit from the success of the economic hubs. The regional imbalances deepened by this policy were to survive the Kubitschek era and last to the present day.

Construction of Brasília

It was during the presidency of Kubitschek that the aspirational ultra-modern federal capital of Brasília was created on the high plateau of Goiás state. This ambitious project, widely supported by the people as a symbol of progress and national justice, was remarkably successful. The new metropolis, designed mainly by the architects **Lúcio Costa and Oscar Niemeyer**, was built over a period of only five years.

The end of the Republic

Kubitschek's elected successor Jânio Quadros only remained in office for seven months. Quadros' successor, João Goulart, was boycotted by the military and the conservative forces because of his left-wing politics. Goulart's attempt, begun in 1964, to force through economic structural reforms, in particular **land reforms**, brought the generals back onto the political stage. Once again the military – in a move often repeated in South American contemporary history – ignored the rules of democracy and blocked fundamental reforms of land distribution, which to this day hinder the economic and social development of Brazil and provoke militant conflicts between the landless and large estate owners.

Dictatorship of the Generals

| 1964 – 1985 | Military dictatorship and the repeal of constitutional rights |
| 1982 | The outbreak of the debt crisis marks the end of the Brazilian economic miracle. |

Under Presidents Humberto Castelo Branco (1964 – 1967), Arthur da Costa e Silva (1967 – 1969), Emílio Garrastazu Médici (1969 to 1974), Ernesto Geisel (1974 – 1979) and João Baptista de Oliveira Figueiredo (1979 – 1985) – all generals of the Brazilian armed forces – the military dictated the politics of Brazil. By the »cleansing« of parliament, the administration and armed forces, by prohibiting parties and suspending constitutional rights, as well as the comprehensive censorship of all media, the military created the basis for authoritarian rule. The political opposition was eliminated by arbitrary arrest, torture and murder. During the presidency of Médici, **state-sponsored terrorism** reached its peak: the Marxist guerrilla movement was not only ruthlessly combated, but also served as an alibi for smashing the student opposition. With the presidency of Geisel, the hard stance of the military dictatorship began to relax, leading to a phase of tentative redemocratization under Figueiredo.

Elimination of the opposition

The end of the Republic: in 1964, the military takes over government. The generals' state terrorism was to last until 1985.

Prosperity and recession

The years of military dictatorship were, however, also the years of the economic miracle, in which Brazil grew to be the industrial giant of South America. At the same time the social divide grew disproportionately, as shown by the rampant growth of favelas, the slums at the edge of the big cities. The policy of industrialization on the back of international credits had multiplied external debt; a part of the foreign capital financed the construction of the Itaipu Dam, iron ore mining in Carajás and the exploitation of the Amazon. The oil price shocks of the 1970s, inflation and the debt crisis, as well as the accompanying end of the economic boom, heralded the decline of the tyrannical regime.

Return to the Republic

1985	Return to the Republic
1988	Proclamation of the constitution, still in force today
1994–2002	Term of office of President Fernando Henrique Cardoso
2003	Lula da Silva becomes President of Brazil.

New Republic

In terms of its protagonists, the eagerly awaited New Republic was not that new: in 1985, an electoral college chose a president, **Tancredo Neves**, who under Vargas had held the office of justice minister and had been prime minister under Goulart. Neves' death before taking office suddenly thrust the mantle of presidential office on the designated vice president **José Sarney** – until recently still chairman of the military regime's ruling party. Sarney's term in office was dominated by several failed attempts to stabilize the economy, but also saw the proclamation of the modern constitution of 1988, still in force today.

Corruption, inflation and poverty

With the election of **Fernando Collor de Mello** in 1990, for the first time in 29 years a directly elected head of state took the reins of government. When he took office the conditions were not exactly auspicious: annual inflation running at over 2,750% and 30 million Brazilians living below the poverty threshold were a heavy burden, which Collor de Mello aimed to lift by stabilizing the currency, privatizing and deregulating the economy as well as through liberalization of foreign trade – all to no avail. In the end however, Collor de Mello failed not through his unsuccessful policies, but because of numerous (bribery) scandals. In 1992, immediately before he was due to be removed from office, he stepped down, being replaced by vice president **Itamar Franco**, who finished Collor's term of office. After inflation had doubled again compared to 1990, Franco's finance minister and future president **Fernando Henrique Cardoso** succeeded

in establishing a nearly stable currency by introducing the real on 1 July 1994.

The currency stabilization initiated by **Cardoso** made him unbeatable at the presidential elections of 1994, running for the Partido da Social Democracia Brasileira. In 1998, he was confirmed in office following a change in the constitution allowing the president to be reelected for a second term. The sociology professor's first term in office saw a number of attempts at reform in the privatization of state-

Luiz Inácio da Silva, better known as »Lula«

owned enterprises, social security, the budget and land reform. The first half of his second term in office was overshadowed by the devaluation of the real, recession and unemployment, as well as by **accusations of corruption** in connection with the privatization of the telecommunications company Telebras. Cardoso's term in office ended on 1 January 2003.

At the presidential elections of 27 October 2002, the candidate of the Workers' Party, **Luiz Inácio »Lula« da Silva** achieved the best result that a person running for the highest political office in Brazil had ever reached. On 1 January 2003, Lula officially took over from his predecessor Fernando Henrique Cardoso. Worldwide, the government programme proclaimed by Lula da Silva as: **»Fome Zero«**, »Zero Hunger« was met with much applause. With prudence, sound arguments and by sending the right signals, the socialist also managed to gain the trust of both the industrial sector and the International Monetary Fund (IMF) for his economic policy. In late 2002, Brazil was given huge credit facilities to help stabilize the country's public finances long-term. In 2004, Brazilian gross domestic product rose 5.3 per cent compared to the previous year, and the balance of trade posted a surplus of 33 billion US dollars. Much less successful to date however has been the forest protection programme put forward by the Lula government. Greenpeace and the WWF have denounced the fact that in 2004, the large-scale destruction of the rainforest in Brazil had reached the second-highest level of all time. In mid-2005, accusations of massive electoral manipulation, systematic money laundering and corruption levelled at important officials of Lula's PT Workers' Party were substantiated. Feelings of indignation and deep disappointment ran through all levels of Brazilian society. Whilst Lula da Silva swore that he did not know anything about the scandalous wheeling and dealing, his political credibility took a major hit. Despite this, in late 2006, Lula was confirmed in office.

Lula da Silva becomes president

Art and culture

From Pre-Columbian art via Colonial Baroque to contemporary architecture. The characteristics of Brazilian music. The importance of Afro-Brazilian religions. A cross-section of the arts and culture of Brazil.

Arts and Architectural History

Pre-Columbian art

In thehistory of art of Brazil – as in the whole of Mesoamerica and South America – the appearance on the scene of the first Europeans marks a turning point. Unlike the Mesoamerican areas and the Andes, which show extraordinarily rich and very old pre-Columbian cultures, Brazil in this respect has a lot less to offer. The earliest evidence of artistic production is **rock and cave paintings**, often featuring animals and hunting scenes and estimated to be at most 8,000 years old. Of particular interest are the ornate urns discovered in raised burial cairns on the island of Marajó in the Amazon delta. These were decorated using various techniques; decorations – always stylized – show humans or animals, or intricate geometrical patterns.

Early colonial times

Very few monuments dating from the first one-and-a-half centuries of modern Brazil have been preserved. This is not just due to the fact that pirates destroyed many buildings along the coast, but also because Portugal initially did not express much interest in the colony, failing at the time to recognize its enormous resources. The churches erected by the first settlers were very simple. Initially built with bricks and covered with plant matter – hence the name **igrejas de palha** (Straw Churches) – these churches were soon replaced by buildings made from stone and lime mortar, with a ground plan formed by two rectangles. The larger one held the congregation, with the smaller one forming the chancel.

The entrances had porticos with stone or wooden pillars, accomodating members of the congregation that were not allowed inside the church. Interior and exterior walls were whitewashed, standing out against the red roof tiles. The façades were broken up by rectangular windows, above and between which were the round or oval windows also found in the tympanum. This marked tendency to fit out church buildings with many sources of natural light is characteristic for Brazilian architecture.

Two of the oldest surviving Brazilian churches are in **Porto Seguro**, on the coast south of Salvador, where Pedro Álvares Cabral is said to have first sighted Brazilian land in 1500. Building work on the Igreja da Misericórdia started in 1526, and on the Igreja de Nossa Senhora da Pena in 1535.

Churches in Porto Seguro

← *Brasília – showcase of the country's architecture, mainly designed by Lúcio Costa and Oscar Niemeyer*

Colonial Baroque

Jesuit church of Salvador

The heyday of Brazilian architecture began with the gold finds of 1696 and developed under the influence of the baroque style that was spreading in Europe in the 17th and 18th centuries. The second half of the 17th century saw the construction of one of the most important buildings, which went on to be a decisive influence on the later history of architecture: the Jesuit church of Salvador (1652–1672), today the city's cathedral. This, the fourth church erected by the Jesuit order in Salvador, remains the most monumental church in all of Brazil. The one-naved ground plan with the shallow interconnected side chapels is reminiscent of the Lisbon church of São Roque, which in turn is inspired architecturally by the first Jesuit church of Il Gesù (1568) in Rome. Like its model in Lisbon, the church of Salvador has no dome. Another example of lavish baroque is the **convent church of São Francisco in Salvador**, begun in 1709 and later restored, but there are also numerous other impressive baroque churches throughout the country. The 17th and early 18th centuries still saw the construction of large Jesuit buildings in the mission settlements and in the cities – just think of the fortress-like Jesuit college in Paranaguá Bay in Paraná state or the São Miguel Mission, one of the examples, now so few, of baroque Guaraní architecture in Rio Grande do Sul.

Civilian buildings

The number of baroque-style civilian buildings still standing is negligible, most serving representative or administrative purposes, e. g. the **Palácio do Rio Branco in Salvador**, destroyed during the war against the Dutch and later rebuilt, the 18th-century Câmara Municipal (city hall) of Salvador with its elegant arcades, the Paço Imperial in Rio de Janeiro, which served first as governors palace, then as royal residence and finally as post and telegraph office, and last but not least the **Palácio Cruz e Souza in Florianópolis** in Santa Catarina state, a mighty pink building dating from the years 1770 to 1780. Cities such as Recife, Olinda, Belém, Rio de Janeiro, São Paulo and several former gold mining settlements in Minas Gerais such as Sabará, Ouro Preto, Mariana, Congonhas, São João del Rei and Tiradentes have well-preserved Old Towns that have now been declared national cultural monuments or have been placed under UNESCO protection as World Cultural Heritage Sites.

Francophile art movements and art nouveau

French influence

The moment when João VI in 1816 called a group of French artists to Rio de Janeiro under the guidance of Joachim Le Breton marked Brazil's first contact with modern art movements, in particular from Paris. After the proclamation of the Republic in 1889, many cities were redesigned, which led to a veritable **flowering of art-nouveau works**. Some of the best examples of this construction phase of the late 19th and early 20th century are a whole series of unusual buildings in Manaus: the Mercado Municipal (Municipal Market) with its roof designed by Eiffel, the Alfândega (Customs House), delivered in individual parts from England, and the imposing Teatro Amazonas, the construction of which dragged on for 17 years. Also belonging to this period are the Teatro da Paz, the opera house of Belém, as well as the Municipal Theatre and Estação da Luz railway station in São Paulo, both dating from the first years of the 20th century.

Art and architecture in the 20th century

Held in 1922 in the Teatro Municipal of São Paulo, the **»Week of Modern Art«** became the clarion call for the Brazilian artistic and intellectual scene. The first landmark architectural work of the new modernist movement in Brazil was the palace built for the Ministry of Education and Health in Rio de Janeiro, between 1936 and 1943. Among the protagonists of the early modernist phase were the rationalist Gregori Warchavchik and the French-born **Lúcio Costa**. Costa was also given responsibility for the group of architects charged with designing the new ministry. In bringing in Le Corbusier as consultant, Costa not only connected with the Francophile tendencies of 19th-century Brazil, but also steered the culture of his country towards Le Corbusier's functional architecture. Even the

Brasília Cathedral: an Oscar Niemeyer masterpiece

ART FROM ADVERSITY

Considered the most important artist of the Brazilian colonial era, the architect and sculptor Antônio Francisco Lisboa (1730–1814), from Ouro Preto, owed his nickname »Aleijadinho« (little cripple) to his disfigurement after contracting leprosy.

Never showing himself in public, Aleijadinho, in the last years of his life, with some of his fingers mere stumps, had to have pencil and chisel strapped to his crippled wrists. His handicap did however secure him a special place in the hearts of Brazilians and was one of the reasons why his life and works were to become legendary.

Major works

Aleijadinho's most important works are the façade of the church of São Francisco in Ouro Preto, the façade of the Igreja do Carmo in Sabará and the

church of São Francisco in São João del Rei, as well as the façade sculptures and two side altars in the Igreja do Carmo in Ouro Preto, designed by his father. He also created the six groups of figures of the Stations of the Cross on the slope in front of the pilgrimage church of **Bom Jesus do Matosinhos** in Congonhas do Campo, which show a realistic, popular drama bordering on the grotesque. Along with his twelve statues of the prophets adorning a magnificent flight of stairs leading up to the façade, they count amongst the most fascinating sculptural groups that colonial Baroque produced. Alei-

The church of Bom Jesus do Matosinhos in Congonhas

jadinho's churches are noted less for their layout, usually a traditional rectangle, than for their façades. Here, the imagination of the artist transcends **strict geometric schemes**, employing sweeping lines and forms often resulting in original solutions, particularly for the transitions to the lateral bell towers. Typical examples are the churches of São Francisco in Ouro Preto and São João del Rei, commonly praised as his masterpieces.

Gold!

Aleijadinho designed original and ornate baroque and rococo churches on the coast which were entirely gilded, such as the church of the São Francisco convent in Salvador, the **Capela Dourada** in Recife and the chapel of the Third Carmelite order in

Chaoeira. Sharing a single artistic concept, their interiors are lined with gilded, colourfully composed sculptures covering walls, vaults, pulpits and altars. These sculptures kept scores of wood carvers, gilders, sculptors, painters and goldsmiths in work.

Expressive and compelling: Aleijandinho's Jesus Bound

master builders of the next generation remained true to Costa's concepts, which did however mean they neglected essential innovations such as those introduced by Wright, Gropius and Mies van der Rohe.

Costa, Niemeyer and Portinari

After this time, Brazilian architecture took a different direction, towards a more brilliant, more dynamic style, full of apparently irrational improvisations. The main exponent of this style is **Oscar Niemeyer** (► Famous People p. 71), born in 1907 in Rio de Janeiro. If Costa is regarded as the founder of the new Brazilian architecture, Niemeyer has to take pride of place as the most significant personality in the field. Niemeyer's signature features are powerfully sweeping ground plans and parabolically vaulted roofs. With wood hardly used due to the danger of termites, and little natural stone in the country, reinforced concrete has become the favoured material for construction, and walls are often clad with mosaics and colourful majolica tiles (azulejos). Good examples are the frescoes by **Cândido Portinari** (1903–1962; ► Famous People p. 72) in the Ministry of Education and Health in Rio and the mosaics in the church of São Francisco on the Pampulha reservoir. Through his use of loud colours and his untamed expressiveness, Portinari, one of the dominant figures of Brazilian painting, grasped the vital characteristics of his people.

Painting and sculpture

The influence of abstract art and the subsequent American art movements on the cultural life of Brazil lasted until the 1960s and 1970s. It had an effect on very varied artistic personalities, e. g. the painters Iberê Camargo, Arcangelo Ianelli, Maria Leontina, Antônio Henrique Valentin or the sculptors Sergio Camargo, Bruno Giorgi and Maria Martins. However, the chief representatives of the avant garde style are **Barrio and Hélio Oiticica**, with their unsettling compositions portraying urban living conditions. Ligia Pepe, Sergio Augusto Porto and Regina Vater also contributed to the development of the new style. Beyond that, Brazil boasts a broad movement of naive painters, whose work is much more authentic and connected with their people than that produced in other parts of the world.

New avenues in architecture

The creation of the city of Brasília is the outstanding event in the history of Brazilian 20th-century architecture. The urban layout thought up by Lúcio Costa is predicated on basic symbolic forms, and on traditional patterns of urban planning, the sign of the cross in particular. Alongside Costa and Niemeyer, **Afonso Reidy** (1909–1964) can take his place amongst the leading architects of Brazil. Reidy designed the residential complex of Peregulho at the edge of Rio de Janeiro, with a sweeping form that adapts perfectly to the curves of the hill on which it sits, following the model of Le Corbusier's apartment units in Algiers. The museum complex dedicated to modern art in Rio de Janeiro is the fruit of a successful collaboration by Reidy and Burle Marx. In the gardens and parks created by

Burle Marx – amongst them the Botanical Gardens of Petrópolis, as well as the Zoological and Botanical Gardens of Brasília – nature and functional architecture seem to acquire a human dimension through the imaginatively curving lines of the avenues, benches and borders as well as the recurring surfaces made up of ceramics and mosaics, mirroring the lively colours of the tropical flora.

Music: from Samba to Sepultura

Not every musician is Brazilian, but most Brazilians are musicians, and not just since samba conquered the world. Ballroom dances with decidedly ambiguous body language have always been a speciality of Brazil, and European parents at the end of the 18th century were as shocked by the enthusiasm of their well-bred daughters for the lundú, as they were, 100 years later, by the maxixe, and, more recently, the lambada.

Decidedly Brazilian ambiguities

To this day, the samba, omnipresent not only at carnival time, remains the music of the common people, having absorbed over time so many stylistic influences that it has become the musical **mirror image of the multicultural society of Brazil**. Whilst the modern samba of a Martinho da Vila, Beth Carvalho or Bezerra da Silva might occasionally sound completely different from the still popular compositions of the veterans from the 1930s, such as Ary Barroso, Ismael Silva or Noel Rosa, a contagious danceability and driving rhythms remain the trademark of the music of the favelas, where without samba there would often not be so much to laugh about.

Samba

 Baedeker TIP

Information on the Net

Lovers of Brazilian music should take note of the comprehensive website www.thebrazilian-sound.com, with links to the homepages of many famous Brazilian musicians and bands.

Whilst one of the roots of the bossa nova lies in the samba, it was considered by traditionalists for a long time as an intellectual counter movement and rejected as an »un-Brazilian« flirtation with US-American cool jazz. In Europe and the US however, the »new way« was acclaimed as a revelation, after *Orfeu Negro* **by Marcel Camus** – not least because of the film score recorded by Antonio Carlos Jobim and Vinicius de Moraes – won the 1959 Golden Palm of Cannes and the Oscar for Best Foreign Film. After the mambo and the cha cha cha, the bossa nova triggered the next Latin-jazz wave, which, alongside countless pseudo-exotic embarrassments – think Eydie Gorme's »Blame it on the bossa nova« – also produced masterpieces such as

Bossa nova

the 1962 *Jazz Samba* album by Stan Getz and Charlie Byrd or, probably the most famous collaboration of North American and Brazilian musicians, ***The Girl from Ipanema***. On this worldwide hit, Stan Getz and A C Jobim accompany Astrid and João Gilberto's (▶ Famous People p. 70) singing. Criticized for the blending of Brazilian rhythms with jazz harmonies, felt to be too off-beat, João Gilberto had countered as early as 1958 with the classic *Desafinado* (Out of Tune), which became the hymn of the Copacabana bossa nova high society, culminating in the following message, roughly translating as: »If you don't get it, you are free to call me anti-musical. I'll have the answer though: this is bossa nova and it is coming from me naturally.«

No dance!   Although eminently suitable for it, originally bossa nova was not a dance, but a form of song, where poetic lyricism counts for as much as musical composition. The most common theme is walking the tightrope between **euphoria and saudade**, a concept that could be characterized as a state of mind of indulgent melancholia, coupled with a small shot of masochism. Alongside de Moraes, Jobim and Gilberto, Carlos Lyra, Nara Leão, Roberto Menescal and the brothers Marcos and Paulo Sérgio Valle count amongst the most famous performers of the bossa nova. Musicians who became famous beyond the borders of Brazil are the guitar virtuoso Baden Powell (▶ Famous People p. 73), as well as Sérgio Mendes, who, with his interpretation of *Fool on the Hill* made the Beatles socially acceptable, and whose version of the Jorge Ben song *Mas que nada* has become a perennial favourite.

Tropicalismo and censorship

E proibido   National pride and increasing censorship after the military coup of
proibir   1964 ensured that the wishes of many parents around the globe – shocked by that music and its messages – became reality in Brazil. Despite such talented followers such as Os Jovens (The Young Ones), Os Aranhas (The Spiders) or The Brazilian Bitles (whose names seems to owe something to a phonetic slip), the beat boom of the 1960s remained a temporary and marginal phenomenon. At the time, it was left to Os Mutantes to play original Brazilian rock. Between 1968 and 1970, the band recorded three fabulous albums reminiscent of Frank Zappa in their delight in experimentation and, as co-founders of the Tropicália movement, managed to attract a lot of the wrong kind of attention with songs such as *E proibido proibir* (*It is prohibited to prohibit*) right into the 1970s.

Poetic criticism   The Tropicalistas counted Gal Costa, Torquato Neto, Julio Medaglia
of the system   and the Beat Boys amongst their number. The true stars of the poetic criticism of the system however were **Gilberto Gil and Caetano Veloso**, both from Bahia. Due to the particularly eager censorship of the

late 1960s, hardly any records have survived from the Tropicália era. However, Brazilians rolling with the spirit of 1968 used the music festivals held all over the country as a forum for their mixture of rock 'n' roll and folklore, dada and samba, kitsch and art, causing a generational divide between the fathers and sons of Brazil, comparable to the effect that Bob Dylan and Jimi Hendrix had in the West. The clever metaphors which left scope for various interpretations made the generals extremely nervous, seeing that the texts of Tropicália hymns such as Caetano Veloso's *Alegria, alegria* or Gilberto Gil's **Domingo no parque**, written to a capoeira rhythm and spread by word-of-mouth, had more currency with the increasingly rebellious youth than the national anthem. Both Gil and Veloso paid for this in 1969 with months of imprisonment and afterwards, until 1972, chose England as their country of exile. Gilberto Gil, who was incarcerated without having been charged, later commented: »They didn't know what to charge me with, apart from the fact that I was different: unpredictable, bold, cheeky, provocative hence danger-

Gilberto Gil in action

ous.« In truth, Tropicalismo, with its spontaneous artistic »happenings« that accepted no rules, not only scared the reactionary state power, but also the dogmatic left, who took to the hedonistic anarchism of the Brazilian hippies about as much as Chairman Mao did to the Rolling Stones.

Música popular brasileira

In a remarkable parallel with Anglo-American culture, the stormy waters calmed in the 1970s, and the repatriated Tropicalistas joined the MPB generation. MPB (Música popular brasileira) is the equivalent of what is called – with equal problems of definition – »pop music« elsewhere. Folklore, samba and bossa nova were blended with rock, jazz, reggae and electronic music, and the result was once again a typically Brazilian mixture of rousing rhythms, irresistible melodies and poetry, which occasionally probed the tolerance limits of the state censorship, which remained in place until 1984.

Calm after the storm

The most-famous representative of the MPB, and rightly so, did not grow up in one of the vibrant metropolises. Milton Nascimento's music is steeped in the meditative, restrained mentality of the people

Milton Nascimento

of his home province of Minas Gerais. Instead of exhibiting exuberant samba cheer, he prefers to blend traditional toadas from Belo Horizonte and Portuguese fados with Gregorian chants, panpipes, jazz and Bach, on a bossa nova base. The man responsible for discovering and promoting Nascimento in 1967 was **Eumir Deodato**, the legendary Brazilian composer and arranger, who shot to worldwide fame in 1970 when his version of Richard Strauss' *Also sprach Zarathustra* (Thus Spake Zarathustra), blending jazz and rock, was used as the soundtrack for Kubrick's film *2001 – A Space Odyssey*. Milton Nascimento continues to be one of the most celebrated Brazilian musicians on the international stage, often inviting celebrities such as Paul Simon, Quincy Jones, Pat Metheny or Herbie Hancock to join him in the recording studio. Other famous MPB artists, alongside Gilberto Gil and Caetano Veloso, are Chico Buarque, Gal Costa, Maria Bethânia, João Bosco, Luis Melodia and Djavan. These however are only the spearhead of the MPB generation, which includes hundreds of musicians combining samba and bossa nova with styles from all over the world. The results are so distinctive that most musical production in the 1970s and 1980s in the big cities may be subsumed under the MPB header.

Balanço – between improvisation and structure

The jazz of Brazil is not bound by either the indigestible excesses of free jazz or the meticulously detailed arrangements of Big Band swing, having found in the aptly-named concept of Balanço a path between improvisation and structure. As may be expected, samba and bossa nova are also elementary building blocks. Another influence is the **choro**, which became popular in Rio from 1870 onwards. Although born at a time when North America was still in thrall to ragtime, the style shows surprising parallels with the improvised instrumental music of the marching bands that were part of the street scenery of early 20th-century New Orleans. As with dixieland, choro is a symbiosis of classical western harmonies and African feeling for rhythm, even though the combination of flute, guitar and percussion of the legendary band leader Pixinguinha resulted in a more relaxed style than the frenetic wind section of a Kid Ory or King Oliver.

Brazilian jazz

Heavy metal, hip hop and acid house

In the recent past, the boundaries between Brazilian and European or American music have become blurred: in the 1990s, bands emerged who were far from defined by their Brazilian origins, amongst them the internationally successful, if since disbanded **Sepultura**, who, with their mixture of heavy metal, punk and grunge gave the best American and European hardrock bands a run for their

← *One of the great Brazilian musicians: Milton Nascimento*

money. **Xanando** have proven that hip hop with samba elements makes for an infectious sound combination, and **Vinicius Cantuaria and Bebel Gilberto** have demonstrated the surprisingly mellow sound that can be achieved by crossing acid house and bossa nova. Bebel Gilberto is now nearly as popular as her father João in her home country.

Afro-Brazilian religions

The slave trade resulted in the enforced deportation to Brazil of an estimated 5 to 10 million black Africans of various origins. The enslaved Bantu came from Mozambique, Angola and the Congo, whilst the Yoruba (Nagô), Gêgê and others were wrenched from their homelands in the Bay of Guinea and the Niger Delta. There were significant differences between the individual ethnic groups, both in terms of physical appearance and lifestyle, customs and traditions. These peoples exerted the strongest influence on Brazilian culture in the area of music, but their religious ideas were also to enter Brazilian society.

Candomblé

Candomblé has its origin in the religious traditions of the Yoruba (Nagô) in Nigeria and Benin. The Yoruba worship a supreme deity called Olorúm, which has traditionally not been embodied by an idol nor the subject of specific rituals. As Olorúm showed itself completely impervious to human appeals, the Yoruba turned to the **Orixás**, god-like beings functioning as mediators between the believers and the Supreme Being. According to Yoruba belief, the Orixás resided on the African coast, but could be summoned by song and the sound of drums, taking possession of the bodies of their disciples, called cavalos (horses), and using them to express their wishes. The Orixás represent the forces of nature. Each Orixá has its own day of the week, specific attributes, foodstuffs, colours, clothes, dedicated sacrificial animals, and even its own summoning call.

Daughters of the Saints These Afro-Brazilian deities have their filhas-de-santo, priestesses clad in their colours and dedicated to their personal cult, who wear specific bracelets and pearl necklaces and offer up ritual dishes. The Orixá taking possession of the filha-de-santo (Daughter of the Saint) is the purpose and at the same time the climax of the **queda do santo** ceremonial act, performed in a terreiro (ritual site for the Candomblé). Dance, chants and rhythmic drumming invoke the deities and impel the followers into a trance often accompanied by fits, a sign that the saint of Orixá has entered the body of its disciple. The highest-ranking priest of the Nagô is a woman, the **ialorixá or mãe-**

de-santo (Mother of the Saint). With the Bantu however, it is a man, the **babalorixá** (pai de santo), who determines the course of the Candomblé ceremonies; in this, he is always assisted by the mãe pequena (Little Mother). The Candomblé priests are also held in high esteem by their disciples as counsellors in everyday concerns, thereby fulfilling more than just a religious role.

Belief in the Orixás was passed on by the Yoruba (Nagô) to the Gêgê slaves from the region that today is Benin, and from the Gêgê-Nagô culture it passed on to the Bantu peoples following the cult of the ancestral spirits. As the large estate owners tried for a long time to suppress the religion of the Yoruba slaves, it camouflaged itself behind a Catholic façade, assigning to the Orixás the attributes and even the names of Christian saints, leading to an inextricable **syncretism** between the Catholic faith and the Afro-Brazilian religions. The very naming of the gods as santos (saints) stems from this. Each Orixá has two names: one African, one Catholic. Oxalá, the most powerful of all the Orixás, for instance, is identified with the most popular Catholic iconic figure of Bahia, the Nosso Senhor do Bonfim. His colour being white, the disciples of Candomblé wear white clothing on feast days.

Dissemination

Umbanda

The Umbanda religion has been practised by the Bantu settled in Rio de Janeiro since the time of slavery. It is clearly influenced by the Orixá rites, which can be seen for instance in the **Iemanjá Feast**, celebrated on the coast of Guanabara Bay on 31 December. All ceremonies are accompanied by ritual chants (pontos or toadas) and hypnotic atabaques (drums), inviting the santos (saints) or Orixás to descend, putting the disciples in a trance and setting the dance rhythm. In African society, the drummer fulfils an important function, as the person who knows the rhythm that will summon the gods, and is able to establish contact with them. The Umbanda religion is more distanced from the purely African tradition: whilst the worship of the Orixás remains an essential part of Umbanda rites, Christian-spiritualist elements and the integration of Indian spirits, the caboclos, occupy a more important position compared to the Candomblé.

Famous People

Personalities who have left their mark on Brazil: writer Jorge Amado, musician João Gilberto, architect Oscar Niemeyer, footballer Pelé, racing driver Ayrton Senna – and others from politics, the arts and literature.

Jorge Amado (1912 – 2001)

Jorge Amado is probably the best-known author in contemporary Brazilian literature. His childhood, spent in Ilhéus in Bahia state, provided him with material for many of his books. He started work as a journalist when only fifteen, publishing various contributions in *A Semana* and *Meridiano* magazines. In 1930 Amado moved to Rio de Janeiro, becoming a law student, and in 1932 made his literary debut with ***O País do Carnaval***. In 1945, Amado was elected as a federal parliament deputy for the Brazilian Communist Party, but soon after went into exile in Europe and Asia. Returning to his home country in 1952, Amado founded the *Para Todos* weekly journal in 1956. His works have been translated into over 30 languages and published in over 40 countries; many of his novels and short stories, mostly informed by a critical analysis of society, were filmed several times over or adapted for the stage, radio or television. Some of his most important works are *Mar Morto* (*Sea of Death*, 1936), *Capitães de Areia* (*Captains of the Sand*, 1937), *Gabriela, Cravo e Canela* (»Gabriela, Clove and Cinnamon, 1958) and *Dona Flor e Seus Dois Maridos* (*Dona Flor and her Two Husbands*, 1966).

The writer

Dom Helder Pessôa Câmara (1909 – 1999)

Helder Pessôa Câmara became a catholic priest in 1931 and in 1952 was made an auxiliary bishop of Rio de Janeiro, where he was much involved with housing and redevelopment programmes for the slums. Câmara's commitment, both in the Brazilian Bishops' Conference and in the Latin American Episcopal Council (CELAM), where he repeatedly and vehemently demanded both a fundamental change of policy from the catholic church and a targeted development policy in favour of Brazil's Northeast from the Brazilian state, was noted internationally.

Theologian

Under the military regime, Dom Helder Câmara, now **Archbishop of Olinda and Recife**, stepped up his attacks on imperialism, capitalism and oppression, publicly demanding a Brazilian socialism. He famously stated »When I give food to the poor, they call me a saint. When I ask why the poor have no food, they call me a Communist.« He held honorary doctorates from six Brazilian and 18 foreign universities, and received 14 international peace prizes, including the Martin Luther King Jr. Peace Prize in the US in 1970. In the same year, he was nominated for the Nobel Peace Prize by the Lutheran World Federation; in 1974 he was awarded the People's Peace Prize in Oslo and in 1983, in Tokyo, the Niwano Peace Prize.

In 1984, at the age of 75, Dom Helder Câmara resigned his post due to old age. The Vatican was quick to take the unconventional and in-

← *The tragic figure of Brazilian aviation:*
  Alberto Santos-Dumont was to commit suicide in 1932.

convenient churchman up on his offer, ordaining in Bishop Cardoso a conservative hardliner as his successor. Cardoso went on to either stop most of the projects initiated by Helder Câmara or to reverse them. Dom Helder Câmara died in Recife, at 90 years of age.

João Gilberto (born 1931)

Musician In 1949, João Gilberto moved to Rio de Janeiro, performing initially in the Plaza nightclub, a famous musicians' haunt in the city. In 1958, he recorded **Chega de Saudade** by Tom Jobim and Vinicius de Moraes and *Bim Bom*, composed by himself. Due to its style, running counter to musical fashions of the time, this record drew much attention. In the same year, Gilberto also released *Desafinado*, a kind of hymn to the bossa nova by Tom Jobim and Newton Mendonça, as well as his own composition *Oba La La*. In 1962, Gilberto performed in New York's Carnegie Hall and settled in the American city. An album recorded with Stan Getz in 1964 was awarded six Grammys. Some of his greatest successes are *Lobo Bobo*, *Samba da Minha Terra*, *Saudade da Bahia*, *O Barquinho* and *Falsa Baiana*.

Chico Mendes (1944 – 1988)

Union leader In 1980 Chico Mendes, union leader and holder of the Alternative Nobel Prize, took over from the assassinated Wilson Pinheiro as leader of the rubber tappers' union of Xapuri. The seringeiros (rubber tappers) were fighting the interests of the cattle farmers and settlers, in order to secure their own existence and to preserve the rainforest. Mendes managed to organize the seringeiros of Xapuri, who began to successfully resist the arbitrary actions of large landowners, local authorities and the police. Thanks to the increased worldwide interest in the preservation of the tropical rainforest, he gained a degree of popularity in his lifetime, outside Brazil in particular. On 22 December 1988, Mendes was shot dead in his hometown of Seringal Cachoeira in the federal state of Acre. The man who had ordered this cowardly assassination, the father of the killer, fazendeiro Darli Alvez da Silva, had not reckoned with the worldwide outrage over the murder of a union leader in remote Acre. Under pressure from the international press, in 1990 Alvez da Silva was put on trial – an uncommon occurrence given the state of the law, or lack of, in the extreme west of Brazil. Over the course of the proceedings, fif-

? DID YOU KNOW ...?

■ ... that Chico Mendes' spirit lives on in a new project to save the world's largest rainforest by making love? The government of the state of Acre is building a £10/$20 million factory in Xapuri to produce »Made in Amazonia« condoms from natural rubber. The project will not only improve the lives of local rubber tappers and their families, but also produce an environmentally sound product that will help save lives threatened by Brazilian's HIV/AIDS crisis.

teen more murders surfaced and were laid at the door of the Silva clan. Father and son were condemned to 19 years in jail; escaping from prison in 1993, they were recaptured only in 1996.

Vinicius de Moraes (1913 – 1980)

Poet

Born into a wealthy literary family, Vinicius de Moraes is one of Brazil's most important modern poets. Working as a film critic and journalist, he skilfully combined his diplomatic career with that of a writer. His most renowned work is *Orfeu da Conceição*, which inspired Marcel Camus' famous film **Orfeo Negro**. Not content with this, de Moraes was also an acclaimed guitarist, composer and performer of samba and bossa nova. Together with Tom Jobim, Baden Powell, Toquinho and Chico Buarque, he composed world-famous songs, such as *Chega de Saudade*, *Garota de Ipanema* (*The Girl from Ipanema*), *Canto de Ossanha* and *Gente Humilde*. As a poet he first went public in 1933 with *O Caminho para a Distancia*, influenced by the aesthetics of mysticism. He followed those with *Forma e Exegese* (1935) and *Cinco Elegias* (1943), amongst others. The anthologies published subsequently – *Poemas, Sonetos e Baladas* (1946), *Patria Minha* (1949) and *Antologia poética* (1954) – display a deliberately political character and refined metrical forms.

Oscar Niemeyer (born 1907)

Architect

Widely considered to be the most important personality in modern Brazilian architecture, Oscar Niemeyer's designs are recognizable by

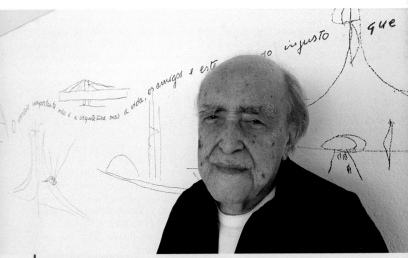

Without Oscar Niemeyer Brasília would look very different.

the strong curves of his buildings and their daring parabolic roofs. His most important creation is Brasília, the capital designed and constructed between 1956 and 1960 at the instigation of President Kubitschek: Niemeyer completed Lúcio Costa's Plano Piloto (Pilot Plan) and oversaw its execution, including his own dramatic layout for the eye-catching triangular **Praça dos Três Poderes** (Square of the Three Powers). The capital's theatre and cathedral were also designed by him. Before embarking on the mammoth task of Brasília, Niemeyer had collaborated on the new building for the Ministry of Education and Health in Rio de Janeiro in 1936, and the design of the Pampulha buildings in Belo Horizonte. In São Paulo, he was one of the main architects behind the Ibirapuera Park building (1954). In 1983 he designed the Sambódromo samba stadium in Rio, and in 1989 the *Monument to Latin America* in São Paulo. Outside Brazil he built, amongst others, the University of Constantine in Algeria (1969), the seat of the French communist party in Paris (1969) and, in the 1970s, the office building of the Mondadori publishing house in Milan.

Pelé (born 1940)

Football player Immensely popular to this day throughout Brazil, Edson Arantes do Nascimento, better known as Pelé, is considered the best footballer of all time. From 1956 onwards, for nearly 20 years he was the undisputed star of FC Santos and the Brazilian national team. In 1975 he signed with the New York Cosmos, playing the last match of his unique career in 1977 – against his old team FC Santos. In the 22 years of his playing career he won 53 titles, amongst them three World Cups with Brazil in 1958, 1962 and 1970, also twice winning the Intercontinental Cup with FC Santos in 1962 and 1963. In the 1,363 matches he took part in, Pelé scored 1,283 goals. Between 1995 and 1998, Pelé served as Brazilian sports minister. In 1999 he was crowned Athlete of the Century by the International Olympic Committee, and a year later FIFA proclaimed him its World Footballer of the Century.

Cândido Portinari (1903 – 1962)

Artist Influenced by Mexican muralism – a politically conscious, large-scale art form – Cândido Portinari gained recognition both in his home country and in the United States of America. In 1938, the New York Museum of Modern Art acquired his painting *O Morro*, conferring official recognition on the artist. Amongst his best-known paintings are *Primeira Missa no Brasil* (*First Mass in Brazil*, Banco Boavista in Rio), *Tiradentes* (Colégio Cataguases in Minas Gerais), *Descobrimento do Brasil* (*Discovery of Brazil*, Banco Português in Rio), the *Emigrantes* cycle (Museu de Arte in São Paulo), *Guerra e Paz* (*War and Peace*, UN building in New York), the frescoes in the Ministry of Ed-

Pelé's outstanding talent made him arguably the greatest footballer of all time.

ucation and Health in Rio and, last but not least, the mosaics of the church on the Pampulha reservoir.

Baden Powell (1937 – 2000)

Musician

Whether it really was Baden Powell de Aquino who invented bossa nova, his place amongst the founders of the new style, mixing the rhythmical elements of the samba with those of cool jazz, is assured. Born in 1937 as the son of amateur violonist Lino de Aquino near Rio de Janeiro, Baden Powell started to play the guitar at eight, and by the age of 15 was already a professional musician. Influenced by cool jazz musicians such as Gerry Mulligan and Chet Baker, and by classical guitarists such as Andrés Segovia, he had his first big success in 1956, with ***Samba triste***. The artistic collaboration with the poet Vinicius de Moraes resulted in bossa nova classics, amongst them *Só por amor*. Baden Powell died of pneumonia in Rio de Janeiro on 6 September 2000.

Glauber Rocha (1939 – 1981)

Film director

Glauber Rocha was the most important figure of the Brazilian Cinema Novo, gaining international recognition from 1964 as the most respected filmmaker of his country. His breakthrough came with *Deus e o Diabo na Terra do Sol* (Black God, White Devil, 1964), an era-defining film among the new generation of international directors. In this work, Rocha looks at the political problems of Brazil and the reasons behind its underdevelopment, combining social analysis with a cinematic perspective steeped in the folk myths of his country. The phrases coined by Rocha to express his convictions, such as »culture of hunger« or »aesthetics of violence« became famous, with one deriving from the other. In his 1967 film *Terra em Transe*, the director uncovers the contradictions in which Brazilian left-wing intellectuals, faced with an increasingly reactionary regime, had become enmeshed. In *Antônio das Mortes*, Rocha revisits one of his protagonists, to lead him towards a process of awakening conciousness. In exile he used new forms of expression and revolutionary metaphors, in such films as *O Leão de Sete Cabeças* (The Lion with Seven Heads, 1970) and *Cabeças Cortadas* (Severed Heads, 1971). He made his last film, *A Idade da Terra* (The Age of the Earth) in 1980.

Alberto Santos-Dumont (1873 – 1932)

Aviation pioneer The son of a coffee baron from Minas Gerais left Brazil for Paris at 18, with his share of the inheritance equivalent to three million dollars, to live an easy and aimless life – mostly chasing the city's beautiful women. Riding in impressive cars and taking champagne baths with his lover, Santos-Dumont rapidly became the most famous dandy in Parisian society, at the same time taking private lessons in physics, chemistry and »aerostatics«, i.e. the art of keeping oneself airborne using technical aids. Fascinated by the Swedish explorer Salomon August Andrée's balloon expedition to the North Pole, which ended tragically in 1897, Alberto Santos-Dumont went on to design a dozen different airships between 1898 and 1906, partly powered by internal combustion engine. At the same time he was working on the concept of hang gliders and propeller craft. After 1905, he dedicated himself to aircraft that were »heavier than air«. On 12 November 1906, the slight Mineiro with the trademark white carnation in his buttonhole did make aviation history. Aboard his machine *14 Bis*, he managed the first officially certified motor-powered flight – without the assisted start or headwind upon which the Wright brothers' early aircraft depended – witnessed by 300,000 euphoric spectators and a French Aeroclub jury. In 1907, Alberto Santos-Dumont designed and flew the **Demoiselle**, the world's first light aircraft. Three years later, however, he gave up

 ! *Baedeker* TIP

»Man Flies«

Do you want to learn more about Alberto Santos-Dumont? Then read Nancy Winter's biography »Man Flies. The Story of Alberto Santos-Dumont, Master of the Balloon« (Ecco, 1998).

The legendary 14-bis plane of aviation pioneer Santos-Dumont

flying completely, increasingly troubled by the military use of his invention already looming on the horizon. Aboard a steamer, the pioneer of flight returned to Brazil in 1928 depressed, down on his luck, nearly penniless and sick with incurable multiple sclerosis. As his ship was coming into Rio de Janeiro's Guanabara Bay, Alberto's prominent friends and a few journalists were approaching by plane, to welcome him back to his homeland in style. But the plane, baptized *Santos Dumont*, crashed – killing everybody on board. Alberto Santos-Dumont settled north of the Sugarloaf metropolis, in the former imperial summer residence of Petrópolis, writing books and studying the stars. Only four years later, on the morning of 23 July 1932, Santos-Dumont hung himself in the »La Plage« hotel in the Guarujá resort, São Paulo. When the French flight pioneer Louis Blériot heard about his old friend's suicide, he baptized his new plane *Santos Dumont*, but in a tragic duplication of events, the plane fell out of the sky shortly afterwards, killing the pilot.

Ayrton Senna (1960 – 1994)

65 pole positions, 41 Formula One victories and three World Championships – that is the highly impressive record of Ayrton Senna's

Racing driver

motor racing career, which ended tragically in 1994 at Imola. When Ayrton Senna da Silva celebrated his Formula One debut in 1984, he had already proven his exceptional talent by winning titles in the

European Formula Ford 2000 and the Formula 3 championships, amongst others. Displaying a combination of driving ability, technical know-how, perfectionism, a willingness to take risks and a controlled aggressiveness at the wheel, Senna matured within a few years to become the outstanding performer in Formula One. His first World Championship title in 1988 with McLaren confirmed his claim to be faster and better than everybody else. Further titles followed in 1990 and 1991. After two unsuccessful years in the now inferior McLaren team, Senna transferred to Williams-Renault in 1994. Tipped to win the World Championship title, Senna's 1994 season could not have started worse, with two no-shows and the arrival of the young, highly-gifted Michael Schumacher heralding a new generation in motoring's elite division. The Brazilian was not to survive his third race of the season at Imola: on the seventh lap, due to a technical fault, Senna lost control of his vehicle and crashed into a concrete wall. At Bologna University Hospital, he succumbed to major head injuries. Ayrton Senna was deeply mourned, not only in Brazil, where he was revered as a popular hero, but all over the world. His death meant not only the loss of one of the most exceptional racing drivers of all time, but also of a charismatic personality who with his work for the street children of Brazil added a humanitarian dimension to the glamorous racing profile. Today, a foundation named after him continues this work.

Heitor Villa-Lôbos (1887 – 1959)

Composer   At the tender age of twelve, Heitor Villa-Lôbos became a professional cellist. Later he was influenced by the traditional musicians and Brazilian folklore that he encountered from 1907 onwards on his travels into the interior of the country. Amongst his first compositions are *Danças Características Africanas*, *Amazonas* and *Uirapuru*. Between 1923 and 1930 he lived in Europe, where he wrote *Rudepoema*, an homage to Artur Rubinstein, and a cycle of fourteen »Chôros« compositions. On his return to Brazil, he taught choral music and even staged a performance with 40,000 pupils in a stadium. Villa-Lôbos created a whole repertoire of choral music and composed the *Bachianas Brasileiras* cycle (1930 – 1945), which combines Brazilian folk music with the spirit of Bach. Villa-Lôbos' far-reaching importance stems from his efforts to create a national style, with a musical language that, while drawing on European models, uses the typical motifs of Brazilian folklore, not merely as a token reference, but as an integral element.

Practicalities

WHAT'S THE BEST WAY TO
GET AROUND? WHERE ARE
THE MOST BEAUTIFUL
BEACHES? WHICH FESTIVALS
ARE UNMISSABLE? FINDING
YOUR FEET IN BRAZIL? READ
ALL ABOUT IT – BEFORE YOU GO!

Accommodation

Brazil provides a very wide range of accommodation. Large cities and the holiday resorts along the Atlantic coast offer a number of hotels with varying levels of comfort. Luxuriously appointed **resort hotels** can be found at some of the most beautiful beaches in the country, while apart-hotels (rental flats) are a particularly good-value alternative in the large urban centres. The plentiful **pousadas** (guest houses) found in smaller and historic places (usually) occupy the lower end of the price scale. Visitors will see motels lining the arterial roads; in Brazil, however, these are all hotels rented by the hour to couples. **Hotel fazendas**, where cattle herds are kept and sometimes horses hired out, are a form of accommodation typical of the swamps of the Pantanal. **Jungle lodges** are mainly found northwest of Manaus along the Rio Negro and are very expensive.

i	Price Categories

- The accommodation options recommended in the »Sights from A to Z« chapter are grouped into the following price categories (double room with breakfast):
- Luxury: from 460 reais
- Mid-range: 160 – 460 reais
- Budget: less than 160 reais

Classification

In towns and cities, the classification of the accommodation by stars (1 to 5) is displayed at the hotel entrance. The star rating is, however, not really comparable to European or US standards. As a rule of thumb, from a European/US perspective, most accommodation other than the top hotels and pousadas have at least one star too many.

Bed and breakfast

In most Brazilian hotels, the room price includes a simple breakfast. Outside the peak season, substantial discounts may be negotiated, whereas the costs for accommodation during carnival in Rio for example, can easily increase five-fold. In peak season in particular, a reservation is required and it is a good idea to ask for confirmation of the agreed rate by fax or email.

Camping

Brazil has a good number of camp sites; some are situated on the coast, others extend into the immediate vicinity of national parks. The level of facilities varies – in the south, standards are usually higher than in the northern half of Brazil. In peak season, however, many campsites are reserved for their paying members. For more information (in Portuguese), contact the Camping Clube do Brasil.

Youth hostels

Youth hostels are generally open to anybody. The Brazilian youth hostel associations are organized by state; the umbrella organization has its office in Rio de Janeiro, also running – at the same address – a very popular youth hostel.

⏵ IMPORTANT ADDRESSES

CAMPING CLUB

► **Camping Club do Brasil (CCB)**
Rua Senador Dantas 75
29° andar, Centro
20037-900 Rio de Janeiro
Tel. (021) 22 62-71 72
Fax (021) 22 62-31 43
www.campingclube.com.br

YOUTH HOSTEL-FEDERATION

► **Federaçao Brasileira de Albergues da Juventude (FBAJ)**
Rua Gal Dionisio 63, Botafogo
22271-050 Rio de Janeiro
Tel. (021) 22 86-03 03
Fax 22 86-56 52
www.hostel.org.br

Arrival · Before the journey

Scheduled airlines such as British Airways and the Brazilian airline **By air** TAM offer non-stop connections between London and Brazil to São Paulo, as the main hub, and increasingly, Rio de Janeiro, too. All major US airlines – American Airlines, Delta, Continental, United (plus Japan Airlines) – have scheduled flights to São Paulo; prices are relatively high. From the US East Coast, TAM, for instance, flies 14 times a week from JFK and also has a weekly NYC-Miami-Salvador service, Miami being the cheapest airport to fly from. A service from the West Coast is planned. For European travellers, enhanced competition from France means a good choice of flights from several French cities, with Air France, TAM and Varig. The European airline with most connections from Europe to Brazil, however, is TAP Air Portugal, offering non-stop services from Lisbon to Belo Horizonte, Brasília, Fortaleza, Natal, Recife, Salvador da Bahia, São Paulo and Rio de Janeiro, and onward connections with TAM to two dozen more cities. Former leading Brazilian carrier Varig, now, after financial struggles and a string of accidents, owned by new low-cost airline Gol, had introduced flights from Europe again, but is looking towards moving into US routes. From Canada, Air Canada connects Toronto non-stop with São Paulo. Visitors from Australia and New Zealand currently have to use either Buenos Aires (Quantas Sydney-Auckland), Tokyo (Japan Airlines) or one of the European hubs. From South Africa, the only direct connection is Johannesburg-São Paulo with South African Airways. For flights within Brazil, TAM has an extensive network, as well as the low-cost carriers Gol, Ocean Air (www.oceanair.com.br), and Web Jet (webjet.com.br). Since starting operations in 2001, Gol (www.voegol.com.br) has been particularly successful. www.holidayinbrazil.com is a useful site to keep abreast of new routes, but is not always up to date.

Non-stop to Brazil: many airlines fly direct to Rio or São Paulo.

Charter flights Charter airlines Fortaleza, Natal and Salvador are popular charter destinations from the UK. Between May and October, First Choice Holidays in the UK currently offer fortnightly connections between both London Gatwick and Manchester to Salvador da Bahia, while Thomsonfly flies to Natal and Salvador. www.charterflights.co.uk has the latest information. US charter traffic is hampered by the continuing visa obligation for US citizens.

By boat With the exception of a few cruise liners, there is little ship passenger traffic between Europe or the US and Brazil these days. There may be occasional opportunities to travel to South America aboard a freighter equipped with passenger cabins. However, as these are usually container ships with schedules depending on cargo movements, slight delays can occur. Prices are also far higher than an economy-class airfare, though what travellers pay for is not only a fortnight's en-suite cabin accommodation on a ship, but the whole experience, including dining with the officers. A full round trip on a German ship starting at Antwerp and Rotterdam docks at Rio de Janeiro, Santos, Rio Grande, Buenos Aires, São Francisco do Sul, amongst others. Another, using a French ship, docks at Tilbury, Essex, for the start of a trip lasting several weeks to North Brazil (Belém, Fortaleza, Natal) via the West Indies and French Guiana.

Entry and exit requirements

Visas and passports At the time of writing, UK, Irish and South African citizens did not require a visa for visiting Brazil (up to a stay of 90 days), thanks to a

► ARRIVAL

SCHEDULED AIRLINES

► British Airways
Reservations:
Tel. (08 44) 493 07-87
Sales office Brazil:
Tel. (011) 30 40-04 44-40
www.ba.com

► TAM Brazilian Airlines
Terminal 4, Zone D
London Heathrow Airport
Tel. (02 08) 897-1753

In Brazil:
Tel. (08 00) 123-100
www.tam.com.br

US Reservations:
Tel. (1 888) 235 98-26

► Varig
UK reservations:
Tel. (02 0) 76 60 03-41
Brazil reservations:
Tel. 40 03-70 00
www.varig.com.br

► TAP Portugal
Chapter House
22 Chapter Street
London SW1P 4NP
Tel. (08 45) 601-0932
In Brazil: Tel. (03 00) 21 0 60-60

► American Airlines
Reservations:
Tel. (1 800) 43 3 73-00 (toll-free)
Sales office São Paulo:
Tel. (0 11) 45 02-40 00
Outside SP: Tel. (03 00) 78 97-77 8
www.aa.com

► Continental
Reservations:
Tel. (8 00) 23 1 08-56
www.continental.com

► Delta
Reservations US/Canada:
Tel. (8 00) 22 1 12-12
In Brazil: Tel. 40 03 21-21
www.delta.com

► United
Reservations US:
Tel. (1 800) 86 48 33-1 (toll-free)
www.united.com

In Rio:
Av Rio Branco 89
17th floor Manhattan Tower
Centro, Rio de Janeiro 22420-040

In São Paulo:
Edificio Vikings Av Paulista 777
8th floor
Sales: Tel. (0 11) 31 45-42 25
Reservations:
Tel. (0 11) 31 45-42 00
www.united.com.br

► Air Canada
Reservations Canada/US:
Tel. (1 888) 24 7 22-62 (toll-free)
Sales office São Paulo:
Tel. (0 11) 32 54-66 00
Sales office Belo Horizonte:
Tel. (0 31) 33 44-83 55
www.aircanada.com

► South African Airlines
Reservations:
Tel. (08 61) 35 97 22
Sales offices São Paulo:
Tel. (0 11) 30 65 51-15 (city) and
Tel. (0 11) 64 45 41-51 (Guarulhos airport)
www.flysaa.com

► Gol Transportes Aéreos
Reservations:
Tel. (0 11) 55-04 44-10
www.voegol.br.com

CHARTER AIRLINES

▶ **First Choice Holidays**
TUI Travel House
Crawley, West Sussex, RH10 9QL
Tel. (08 71) 200-7799 and
Tel. (012 93) 560-777
www.firstchoice.co.uk

▶ **Thomsonfly**
Tel. (08 71) 23 1 46-91
www.thomsonfly.com

FREIGHTBROKERS

▶ **The Cruise People Ltd**
88 York Street
London W1H 1QT
Tel. (02 0) 77 23-24 50
www.cruisepeople.co.uk

▶ **Maris USA**
1320 State Route 9
Champlain, NY 12919
Tel. 1 800 99-Maris/-62747
www.freightercruises.com

reciprocal agreement, but citizens of the US, Canada, Australia and New Zealand did. Check the embassies' websites for details and downloadable forms.. A current passport valid for at least six months is required to enter the country, as well as a return or onward flight ticket. Generally, tourists may extend their stay for a further 90 days by applying to the Polícia Federal (federal police). This extension incurs a charge and applications should be made at least 14 days before the end of the original intended duration of stay.

Entry/exit forms   At entry, every visitor to Brazil has to complete a so-called **cartão de entrada/saída**, a form with basic personal information. The border police affix a carbon copy of this form into the passport. This copy must be kept safe, as it will need to be shown again when leaving the country. All passengers receive this form together with the customs declaration (see below) from airline staff during the flight.

Customs-declaration   In addition, entry to the country requires the completion of an **accompanied baggage declaration**, listing all items being brought into Brazil exceeding a value of US$3,000, as well as any animals, plants and seeds. Bringing currency (cash and cheques) over a value of 10,000 reais into the country requires authorization. Violating this rule may be classed as a currency offence. Electrical and electronic goods brought into the country must be taken out again. Any theft should immediately be reported to the police, who will issue a **boletim de ocorrência** certifying the incident; this has to be shown at customs.

Proof of identity   In Brazil it is common practice to carry an ID card (or copy) at all times. Foreigners are advised to carry a certified photocopy of the first five pages of their passport and to leave the original in the hotel safe. When cashing traveller's cheques, however, the original passport is required; a photocopy is not acceptable.

Beach holidays

According to Brazilian and international sociologists, the carnival and the beach are both essential release valves for a society that has to deal with extreme social divides and racial diversity. In bikinisand swimming trunks, Brazil's race and class differences literally melt in the tropical sun – the body is all that counts, the bathing bay becomes the place of national integration. The beach is both living room and meeting place, a place for commerce and work, a catwalk for hedonists and gym for fitness lovers, volleyball arena, surfer's paradise and football pitch – simply it is the sandy heart of life for the majority of the Brazilian population.

Caution should always be used on any long beaches open to the Atlantic, as very dangerous currents can occasionally develop here. Visitors with children should look for bathing bays protected from the swell by reefs. Ask locals or hotel reception for advice on which sandy beaches are most suitable for the youngsters.

Dangerous currents

 ## SWIMMING BEACHES

ALAGOAS

▶ **Praia da Gunga**
Beach suitable for swimming and diving. The pleasure boats departing for Lagoa do Roteiro from Barra de São Miguel stop here, docking – for lunch – right in front of the beach restaurants (▶ p. 277).

▶ **Praia do Francês**
Situated 24km/15 miles southwest from the provincial capital of Maceió in the district of Marechal Deodoro, a section of the Praia do Francês (www.praiadofrances.net) is considered the jewel in the surfing crown of Alagoas state. With its pousadas and bars, this beach is frequently noisy and crowded at weekends (▶ p. 277).

BAHIA

▶ **Itapoã**
Still the most highly rated swimming beach close to Salvador da Bahia. Kiosks and beach bars for the comfort of bathing guests. Overcrowded at weekends.

▶ **Praia do Forte**
Lined with coconut palms, this stretch of coast (www.praiadoforte.org.br) unfolds some 70km/44 miles north of Salvador da Bahia. On the sandy beach, TAMAR manages a rearing station for marine turtles, including an information centre (▶ p. 409).

CEARÁ

▶ **Canoa Quebrada**
In the 1970s, this beach near Aracati (www.canoa-quebrada.com), 167km/104 miles southeast of Fortaleza, was a hippies' paradise. No longer exactly an insider tip, the beach today has its own attractive infrastructure with pretty pousadas and rustic restaurants (▶ p. 161).

▶ **Jericoacoara**
This former fishing village (www.jericoacoara.tur.br) lies in a nature reserve with dunes of up to 30m/100ft high. Despite strict planning regulations, however, the town, 72km/45 miles from Camocim and 305km/190 miles from Fortaleza, has grown steadily in recent years (▶ p. 201).

▶ **Morro Branco**
Crafts and colourful sands arranged into pictures in small glass bottles, have made the beaches of Morro Branco and Praia das Fontes, situated near Beberibe, 85km/53 miles southeast of Fortaleza, famous far beyond the confines of Ceará state (▶ p. 244).

FERNANDO DE NORONHA

▶ **Baia do Sancho**
When Brazilian travel magazines choose the ten most beautiful beaches in the country, Praia do Sancho on Fernando de Noronha usually occupies one of the top places (▶ p. 231).

PERNAMBUCO

▶ **Porto de Galinhas**
Porto de Galinhas (www.portode-galinhas.com.br), 70km/44 miles south of Recife, has become »the« top beach destination. However, with one new hotel following another, the charm of this stretch of coast could soon be smothered by concrete (▶ p. 350).

RIO DE JANEIRO

▶ **Armação dos Búzios**
Situated 177km/110 miles east of Rio de Janeiro, this resort has grown enormously over recent years, without however denting the charm and beauty of the

The coast of Bahia – here Itapoã beach near Salvador – is a picture of beauty.

neighbouring beaches. Our tip: Praia Azeda, reachable on foot via Praia dos Ossos (► p. 164).

► Praia de Ipanema

Rio de Janeiro's 1.3km/0.8-mile city beach was immortalized in the 1960s by the bossa nova *Garota da Ipanema* (*The Girl from Ipanema*). Today it is a better bet for swimming than the neighbouring Copacabana (► p. 382).

RIO GRANDE DO NORTE

► Genipabu

Situated 24km/15 miles north of Natal, in the district of Extremoz, this coastal resort is considered »Brazil's Buggy Capital« due to the popularity of beach buggy trips through the magnificent dune scenery. Another option is simply to enjoy a great swim, either at Praia Genipabu or Praia Pitangui (► p. 291).

► Praia da Ponta Negra

The busiest swimming beach south of Natal has long since surpassed the capital of Rio Grande do Norte, only 14km/ 9 miles away, in terms of popularity, building boom and property prices (► p. 292).

► Praia da Pipa

Praia da Pipa (www.pipa.com.br) lies near Tibau do Sul, almost 90 km/60 miles from Natal. There is hardly another stretch of coast in Brazil where property prices have skyrocketed as much as they have around the beaches of Praia da Pipa, do Amor, do Moleque and Praia das Minas (► p. 292).

SANTA CATARINA

► Praia Joaquina

Located on the eastern half of Ilha de Santa Catarina off the provincial capital of Florianópolis, are the beaches of Praia Joaquina, Praia da Armação and Praia dos Ingleses. However, temperatures here are only suitable for swimming from December to February (► p. 240).

SÃO PAULO

► Praia de Pernambuco

Praia de Pernambuco is one of the most popular swimming beaches off Guarujá, with a good infrastructure providing a wide selection of sports such as jet-skiing, kayaking, sailing and surfing (► p. 252).

Electricity

Mains voltage in Brazil differs between states. Households in the conurbations of Rio and São Paulo receive electricity from two-pin powerpoints (110 Volts/60 Hertz alternating current); only up-market hotels here offer power points with 220 Volts. Brasília and Recife are supplied with 220 Volts/60 Hertz. British three-pin or US round two-pin appliances will not fit – so a travel adaptor and/or transformer will be necessary.

Emergencies

- ► **Military police**
  Tel. 190

- ► **First aid**
  Tel. 192

- ► **Fire service**
  Tel. 193

- ► **Civilian police**
  Tel. 194

Etiquette and customs

Brazilians are very hospitable, relaxed and easy-going. Even people you meet for the first time will smile and give the thumbs up, which means (and is often accompanied by the question) **»tudo bem?«** (»All OK?«). Visitors to the country who are able to at least repeat these words alone are already half there with the locals! It is not rare for travellers to be invited into a Brazilian's house or family home.

Small and large families

Brazilian families in the south are similar in size to European and Western countries. Children remain at »Hotel Mama« for as long as possible, especially as salaries at the beginning of young people's careers are significantly lower than those in the US or Europe. In the north, however, there are still plenty of families with 10 siblings – as for a long time, having many children was the only »old-age pension« available.

Dress sense

Even in five-star hotels, visitors to Brazil are hardly ever expected to sport more than **casual sports dress**. While ties are not exactly popular with Brazilians (outside São Paulo), some restaurant owners might react badly to flip-flops/thongs, locally called »chinelas«. In Rio de Janeiro's São Bento monastery church, male visitors are not allowed entry in shorts (women never have access to this Benedictine monastery, except on its annual »Open Day«). Though Brazil may appear liberal, topless bathing in this Catholic country is a sacrilege punishable if necessary by the police. There are very few nudist beaches along the 7,500km/4,600-mile coastline of Brazil.

Safety and security

To keep out of trouble as much as possible, travellers' choice of clothing should be governed by the need not to signal wealth; expensive watches and jewellery should be left at home (or at least in the hotel safe). Police checks accept a visitor's **photocopy of passport or ID card** without question. And if something should go missing, it helps if all the relevant documentation, vouchers and flight tickets have been photocopied. Travellers should always take a note of the serial numbers of camera and lenses. A travel insurance policy covering the loss of luggage can do no harm in Brazil either.

Festivals · Holidays · Events

In colonial times, cattle ranching was concentrated in the Northeast, though today it includes the South, Southeast and Midwest of Brazil. As the cattle industry has always played a very important role, a separate culture has risen up around it, finding expression in its own festivals.

Cattle-cycle festivals

A myriad names – Boi Bumbá, Boi Calemba, Três Pedaços, Folguedo do Boi, Reis de Boi and Bumba Meu Boi – hide a **satirical and dramatic folk dance**, probably the most sparkling and significant of all the traditional Brazilian festival dramas. Bumba is a Congolese concept mimicking the muffled sound made by the thrusting of the bull. The most important protagonist of this dramatic folk play is the Bumba Meu Boi, a dancing bull that is exposed to all kinds of humiliations. Its origins can be traced back to the 18th century, to the time of the so-called »cattle cycle«. First emerging in the Northeast, the Bumba Meu Boi went on to spread into the other cattle regions. The main theme is the **sacrificial death of the bull** and his resurrection. The performance, lasting up to eight hours, is staged in the streets, quickly turning passers-by into an appreciative audience for this musical play's generous servings of irony and mockery. The main protagonists are people, animals and mythical creatures such as Pai Francisco, Mãe Catarina (Francisco's pregnant wife), Capitão Boca Mole (the policeman), Mateus, Bastião and Fidelis (African slaves), Arlequim (the Harlequin), Padre (the priest), Pastorinha (a little girl) and of course the Boi, the bull. The Boi is represented by a framed structure featuring a real or replica bull's head and covered with printed calico or embroidered velvet, sometimes set with pearls, depending on the finances of the troupe. The main centre for the Bumba Meu Boi spectacle is **São Luís**, the capital of Maranhão.

Bumba Meu Boi

Festas de Peão de Boiadeiro (rodeos) are held in several towns in midwestern, southeastern and southern Brazil. The cowboys and horsemen, some of them real pros, earn their living by travelling from one contest to the next. First they have to catch the animals, wild horses or bulls, with the lasso, then mount them and stay in the saddle for as long as possible. Depending on their performance at each rodeo, they receive a certain number of points. Music shows and folklore complement the spectacle.

Rodeos

Glitter and glamour: carnival in Rio de Janeiro is a massive party, with dancing, music and the prestigious contest of the samba schools.

COLLECTIVE INTOXICATION OF THE SENSES

There is no European celebration that can match the sheer fanatical enthusiasm generated by carnival in Brazil. Once a year, a whole nation seems to leave behind all the norms, institutions and hierarchies of society.

Millions celebrate their collective joy in colourful parades, and wear themselves out in an all-night grand frenzy. The huge numbers of have-nots and the uneducated in particular use carnival as a welcome outlet to suspend for a short time the glaring injustices of wealth distribution and the invisible yet immovable race barriers within Brazilian society, in a phantom utopia of opulence, luxury and extravagance.

Samba non-stop

Officially, the duration of the carnivalesque activities that go under the name of Brincadera Carnavalesca, are restricted, even in Rio de Janeiro, to the manageable short time just before Ash Wednesday. However, accompanied by the non-stop samba on all radio stations and TV channels, the Sugarloaf megalopolis reaches its festive boiling point much earlier. A never-ending sequence of balls, from formal to risqué, and public rehearsals of the famous samba schools whip up the crazed abandon of the »cariocas«, the inhabitants of Rio, to fever pitch.

Rio: an orgy of opulence

Since 1984, the spectacular climax of carnival in Rio, the prestigious competition of the samba schools, has been celebrated in the Sambódromo carnival arena, which can hold 50,000 spectators. The parade of the famous samba schools is an opulent orgy of colour, naked skin and music, attracts thousands of tourists every year and is billed as the »greatest show on earth«. The concrete Sambódromo complex, designed by Oscar Niemeyer, is not

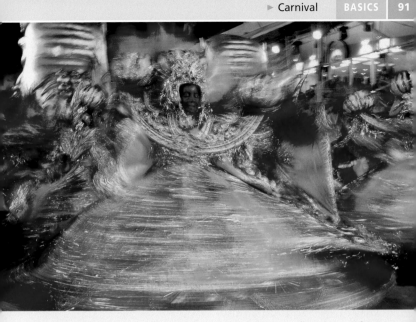

much loved by the cariocas, as tickets for seats in the stands have long been beyond the means of average Brazilian earners. The 1,700m/1860-yd parade ground allows samba schools to make the most of their colourful displays. Representatives of record companies and TV stations interested in recording here have to pay steep fees to be allowed in. »Bicheiros«, the clan chiefs of the illegal »jogo-de-bicho« lottery, as well as commercial sponsors and Rio's smart set now use the former party of the poor favelados for their own celebration, to the point where many cariocas choose to turn their backs on their own town.

Salvador

The first street carnival was organized in Salvador da Bahia as early as 1884, i.e. before slave emancipation, which Brazil only implemented in 1888, the last country in the world to do so. Bahia's carnival to this day has retained strong African connections;

the parades usually start with a religious ceremony. As opposed to Rio, and despite its popularity increasing year on year, the costumed parades are held on the squares and streets of the historical old town. All carnival groups – afoxés, blocos afros, blocos indios and the noisy trios eléctricos – may be admired between Good Friday and Ash Wednesday on a street circuit between Campo Grande and the Castro Alves square, as well as in Salvador's modern Barra neighbourhood. Blocos afros such as Olodum or Ilê Aiyê and afoxés such as the Filhos de Gandhi are the traditional elements of the carnival of Bahia, whilst the noisy trios eléctricos are particularly popular with young people. Their infectious axé and samba-reggae rhythms get entire neighbourhoods dancing, not least thanks to their massive amplifiers that need heavy-duty articulated lorries to move through the streets. In the early hours of the morning of Ash Wednesday, all the groups of carnival revellers make their way, one by one, to the Praça Castro Alves, where live music and dance conclude the still relatively authentic and emphatically Afro-Brazilian street carnival of Bahia.

Frevo in Olinda

Olinda, the historic neighbouring town of Recife, only sheds its all-year-round sleepy atmosphere at carnival, when some 600,000 daily visitors pass through the narrow lanes of the 500-year-old town. Since the early 20th century, carnival here has been raging between the Convento São Bento and the Sé cathedral, to the beat of loud frevo sounds. For decades, the stick puppets (bonecos), such as the Mulher do Dia or the Meninho da Tarde from the workshop of Mestre Julião have been part of the exuberant throng. The climax of carnival in Olinda is marked by the processions of the traditional costumed maracatú groups from the back-country of Pernambuco. Wearing lavishly ornate robes, hung with heavy, hand-cast bells, these groups perform traditional dances that have their origin in Africa.

Micareta

Finally, fifteen days after Easter, the small Recôncavo town of Feira de Santana hosts the regional carnival celebration of Micareta. Some two months after the carnival activities in Salvador da Bahia, trios eléctricos, afoxés and blocos afros get together for a five-day street party – a good opportunity for lovers of dance and hot rhythms to treat themselves to a second helping.

▶ CALENDAR OF EVENTS

PUBLIC HOLIDAYS

▶ **1 January**
Int. Peace Day
(New Year)

▶ **6 January**
Epiphany

▶ **2 February**
Festa da Yemanjá in Salvador
(honouring the Afro-Brazilian sea
goddess Yemanjá)

▶ **21 April**
Tiradentes Day

▶ **1 May**
Labour Day

▶ **29 June**
St Peter and St Paul Day

▶ **7 September**
Independence Day

▶ **12 October**
Nossa Senhora da Aparecida
(Our Lady of Aparecida, literally
»appeared«, patron saint of Brazil)

▶ **1 November**
All Saints

▶ **2 November**
All Souls

▶ **15 November**
Proclamation of the Republic

▶ **25 December**
Christmas

Movable feasts and public holidays
are: Shrove (»Fat«) Tuesday, Ash
Wednesday, Palm Sunday, Good
Friday, Easter Saturday, Easter
Sunday, Ascension Day, Whit
Sunday and Corpus Christi.

FESTIVALS IN JANUARY

▶ **Angra dos Reis**
On 1 January, the New Year is
greeted by a regatta involving over
600 boats.

▶ **Aracaju**
The estuary of the Rio Sergipe
hosts the most famous marine
procession of Sergipe state (1
January).

▶ **Conceição da Barra**
Centred on a bull, the popular
Bumba Meu Boi drama is celebrated here as Reis de Bois (King
of the Bulls), a variant particular
to Espírito Santo blending the
Epiphany festival with that of the
Boi Santo, the holy bull. As part of
this festival, various traditional
dances and plays are performed,
such as congadas, cheganças, fan-
dangos and lapinhas (5/6 January).

▶ **Natal**
On 5/6 January, the Reisado
(Dance of the Three Kings) is a
resurrection of a festival dating
back to the founding of the city.

▶ **Salvador da Bahia**
On 1 January, a huge maritime
procession with hundreds of
boats, festively decorated in honour of Bom Jesus dos Navegantes
(Christ of the Seafarers) makes its
way around the Baía de Todos os
Santos (All Saints' Bay) to the
beach of Boa Viagem, where the
party continues with sambas, local
drinks and food.

On 5/6 January, Salvador celebrates the Festa dos Santos Reis (Feast of the Three Holy Kings) with the terno dos reis and the ranchos (traditional processions and dances).

In the second half of January, Salvador celebrates the Festa do Bonfim, where worship of the Catholic Nosso Senhor do Bonfim is blended with African Candomblé rites. At the centre of festivities is the Lavagem, the ritual washing of the outer steps of the Bonfim church. Countless Baianas, dressed in white, gather in Salvador's Lower Town in front of the Nossa Senhora da Conceição church, before making the pilgrimage to the Bonfim church, accompanied by the local populace in a 12km/7.5-mile long beach procession, where they proceed to wash the steps and to decorate the façade of the church with colourful flowers and garlands. On the following six nights, the inhabitants of Bahia dance until daybreak. On the Monday following the end of the festival the Mudança das Barracas begins: the stalls are taken down and moved to the Ribeira district where the next and no-less convivial festivity of the Festa da Ribeira is ready to kick-off.

IN FEBRUARY

► **Itamaracá**
Off the island of Itamaracá, jangadas, canoes and tugs decorated with flowers and colourful bunting bear the image of the Nossa Senhora do Pilar as part of a maritime procession, the »Buscada de Itamaracá«. As part of this festival, lasting deep into the night, traditional ciranda (a form of round dance) and Bumba Meu Boi are performed alongside modern rhythms. A banda de pífanos (pipe band) also makes an appearance (1 February).

► **Porto Alegre**
On 2 February, the Feast of Nossa Senhora dos Navegantes (Our Lady of the Seafarers) takes place, including a procession on the Rio Guaíba river.

IN MARCH

► **Nova Jerusalém**
In Easter week, in the town of Nova Jerusalém (182km/113 miles from Recife), part of the municipality of Brejo da Mãe de Deus, several hundred local actors perform the dramatic and lavish Paixão de Cristo passion plays.

IN APRIL

► **Jaboatão**
On the mountain of Guararapes, the Festa de Nossa Senhora dos Prazeres (Feast of Our Lady of the Pleasures) dates back to the 17th century. The festival is celebrated with Mass honouring Our Lady in gratitude for the victory once gained by the inhabitants of Pernambuco against the Dutch invaders. Around the baroque churches, food and drink typical to this region, mainly pitomba juice, are available for sale (8–14 April).

IN MAY

Whitsun, 40 days after the end of Lent, is the time for one of the most popular Brazilian festivals, which celebrates the Divino Espírito Santo (Festival of the Holy Spirit). Of Portuguese origin, it was introduced during the

16th century in Brazil and is observed in numerous cities of the Amazon states, including Espírito Santo, Goiás, Maranhão, Minas Gerais, Paraná, Rio de Janeiro, Santa Catarina and São Paulo. The festival has a special significance in the following places:

► **Alcântara**
Alcântara still preserves the old rituals with figures from the colonial era.

► **Parati**
Here the festival is celebrated in the Boi do Divino form, including the feeding of the poor. Its highlight is the Folia do Divino (a procession of singing adolescents dressed in white asking for alms) with High Mass, fireworks, a puppet theatre, equestrian contests, bands and the crowning of the Imperador do Divino, the festival king. The processions with the bandeira do divino, the banner depicting a white dove on a red background, last for about ten days and end on Whit Sunday.

► **Pirenópolis**
This is where the most colourful festival devoted to the Holy Spirit takes place. The main attractions are the cavalhadas, one of the most beautiful traditional spectacles that Brazil has to offer. These equestrian contests symbolize the fight between the Christians of the occidental emperor Charlemagne and the Moors conquering the Iberian Peninsula. The festival lasts three days.

IN JUNE

Festas Juninas (June festivals) are held across nearly all of Brazil. In reality they comprise a whole series of feast days, including those for St Anthony (13 June), St John (24 June) and St Peter and St Paul (29 June). In the Northeast, the festivals of Campina Grande and João Pessoa, Maceió, Aracaju, São Luís and in some cities of Pernambuco are famous far and wide. In Cachoeira (BA), St John's Day is of particular importance, while Fortaleza holds a quadrille dance competition. In the Midwest, the June festivals in Dourados and Corumbá are the most interesting, in the Southwest the main festivals are in Cabo Frio, Rio de Janeiro and Ubatuba.

► **Parintins**
In recent years, the popular Boi Bumbá festival celebrated in Parintins at the end of June has become increasingly important and is now Brazil's second-largest fancy-dress festival after the Rio carnival.

IN JULY

► **Campo Grande**
On 10 July, Campo Grande (MS) celebrates the solemn procession of Nossa Senhora da Aparecida.

► **Serrita**
On the third weekend in July, Serrita (PE) hosts the Missa dos Vaqueiros, an open-air service held by sertão cowboys. Here, too, firewater and piety are not mutually exclusive: alcohol and forró music dominate the secular part of this festival observed since 1971.

IN SEPTEMBER

► **Alter do Chão**
At the end of September, the inhabitants of Alter do Chão near

Santarém celebrate the three-day Festa do Çairé with processions and plenty of music and dance, as well as with çairés, litters laden with local flowers and fruit. The festival, ending with the destruction of the çairés, used to be celebrated in July; for commercial reasons, however, it was moved back at the end of the 1990s.

▶ **São Paulo**
From 14 to 29 September, Móoca, a heavily Italian district of São Paulo, celebrates the Festa do Padroeiro San Genaro (feast of the San Genaro patron saint) with a procession, Mass, Italian songs and Italian food dishes.

IN OCTOBER

▶ **Aparecida do Norte**
The feast day of Nossa Senhora Aparecida (Our Lady of Aparecida), patron saint of Brazil, is celebrated on 12 October. On this day, there are many pilgrimages to Aparecida do Norte, one of the biggest Catholic pilgrimage sites in the world.

▶ **Belém**
On the second Sunday of October, Belém celebrates the Círio de Nazaré festival, lasting several days and including the largest Catholic festive procession in Brazil. Beginning in early morning at the baroque cathedral, the procession lasts around four hours and moves for 6km/3.7 miles through the city, to the neo-classical Basílica de Nazaré. At the same time, the dock workers of Belém worship Our Lady of Nazareth in their own way, shooting thousands of rockets into the air from decorated boats.

IN DECEMBER

▶ **Salvador da Bahia**
For the Festa de Conceição da Praia in Salvador, a procession bearing a likeness of Nossa Senhora da Conceição (Our Lady of Conception) moves through the streets of the Lower Town.

Food and drink

Rather than a national cuisine, Brazil has several widely differing regional culinary traditions. There is, however, one simple meal that is served in every restaurant, eating house, snack-stall and bar, which comes close to representing the national dish of Brazil, namely **feijão com arroz, bife, batata frita e salada** (black beans with rice, beef, chips/fries and salad), also known under the abbreviation PF (prato feito = ready-made dish) or as refeição comercial (budget fast food).

Meat dishes

Churrasco   The Brazilian South, Southeast and Midwest count amongst the largest cattle-rearing regions on earth, making them naturally the place to enjoy excellent churrasco (spit roast): juicy beef (but also pork and poultry) roasted over embers or on the barbecue. In the South-east and Midwest, the cattle are mainly zebus from India; visitors to the area should try churrasco de cupim, the roast hump meat of these animals. Usually, alongside cupim and cutlets, barbecue restaurants, known as churrascaria all over the country, offer a selection of particularly choice cuts at good-value fixed prices as **rodízio**. Visitors should be sure to try maminha de Alcatra (the mayor's cut), fraldi-nha (thin flank, literally 'little nappy/diaper') or the famous finely sliced picanha (rump). However, it's also perfectly acceptable to stick to more familiar cuts such as contra filé (a central cut of chine) and filé mignon (filet mignon). A churrasco is often served with farinha (manioc flour), rice and a vinaigrette sauce.

A barreado is prepared using fatty beef, braised with lard and spices for around twelve hours in a sealed clay pot dug into the earth, above which a fire is lit. The barreado is most popular in Paraná state.

Barreado

Restaurant in the narrow streets of Parati

Carne de sol, carne seca, charque
In the Northeast, the three terms carne de sol, carne seca and charque cover a variety of similar meat dishes. Their main ingredient is sun-dried beef or goat meat preserved with sea salt.

Feijoada
Originally, feijoada provided cheap food for slaves: the ears, feet, snouts and curly tails of slaughtered pigs not used by the main household, the Casa Grande. These scraps found their way into the pots of the slave huts, the senzalas, where the daily ration of black beans was already simmering away. Today, the recipe for feijoada remains basically the same, although slightly more refined: black beans cooked with minced pork or lard, salted pork meat, sun-dried beef, and sausages such as lingüiça or paio. The meat is served with manioc flour, rice and steamed couve (kale); this dish is particularly popular in Rio de Janeiro and São Paulo and is traditionally eaten on a Friday or a Saturday.

Fish and seafood

Brazil has some 7,500km/4,600 miles of Atlantic coast and a dense network of inland waterways. This means that in many parts of the country, freshwater and seawater fish, as well as all kinds of seafood – from the most sophisticated recipe to the most basic method of preparation – form an essential part of the region's gastronomic culture. The most commonly used edible fishes are cod, perch, garoupa (a kind of perch), bonito, roach and mullet. Amongst seafood and crustaceans, lobsters, crabs, prawns and squid are the most popular.

Freshwater fish
Menus in the big cities usually feature cultivated fish such as carp and trout, as well as golden bream, the most common riverine fish from the Paraná Basin and the São Francisco Basin. In the interior, near the large rivers, fish typical for the region are offered. Fish such as the tucunaré, tambaqui and pacu living in the major rivers of the Amazon region, around Goiás, Tocantins and the two Mato Grosso states, may reach a considerable size in adulthood. The mightiest riverine fish in Brazil is the pirarucu; living in the Amazon Basin, it can reach a length of nearly two metres/six-and-a-half feet and weigh up to 300 kilos/650 pounds.

? DID YOU KNOW …?

■ … that piranhas, infamous with Europeans, quite frequently end up in Brazilian frying pans? They are, however, generally considered by restaurants to be a low-quality food.

Tacacá no Tucupi
Tacacá no Tucupi, a dish of Indian origin, is typical for Amazonia and Pará. Tacacá is prepared from manioc starch, tucupi sauce, jambu (an aromatic herb with supposed aphrodisiac effects), dried and puréed shrimps and plenty of malagueta pepper. Tucupi is a sauce characteristic of Amazonian dishes, made from fresh manioc juice

and heated over the fire for long enough to neutralize the prussic acid contained in the raw manioc root until the stock becomes syrupy and honey-coloured.

Afro-Brazilian cuisine

Today, Afro-Brazilian cuisine is chiefly associated with Bahia state, though several dishes originate from other Northeastern states and have by now spread across Brazil. A characteristic image in Salvador in particular is that of dark-skinned Baianas splendidly dressed and bedecked with jewellery, selling original ritual dishes on the roadside. This gastronomic culture, traditionally linked to Afro-Brazilian religions, uses a lot of dendê oil (palm oil), coconut milk and pimenta (hot pepper).

Ritual origins

Drinks

Thanks to the countless numbers of tasty fruits thriving in Brazil, lanchonetes, bars and the fairly common juice bars offer an incredible choice of fruit juices. Blended with sugar and ice in the mixer, they make very pleasant refreshing drinks. In addition to juices, fruits are also made into tasty ice cream.

Juices

> ## ? DID YOU KNOW …?
>
> ■ … that coffee is drunk much less in Brazil than would be expected from a country with such a long tradition in cultivating the crop? Coffee is served strong, hot and extremely sweet – for breakfast, after meals and all day long in the office.

In Brazil, large breweries produce a relatively light beer that locals order on the beaches as »estupidamento gelado« (»frozen stupid«). Tasty wines produced in the south of the country have only regional importance. The usual alcoholic drink of choice is **cachaça or pinga**, distilled from sugar cane. Hardened drinkers take them either neat, distilled with fruit juices (batida), or mixed with crushed lemon, ice and sugar to become the famous **caipirinha**.

Eating out

Brazilian towns and cities feature a growing number of fast-food restaurants, which always offer a large selection of snacks and sandwiches including hamburgers, X burgers (mincemeat with cheese), cachorro quente (hot dog), misto quente (warm sandwich with cheese and ham), baurú (like misto quente, but with tomatoes) and americano (like misto quente, but with a fried egg and salad).

Fast food

As well as the international snack chains, at every street corner hungry visitors to Brazil will encounter a bar or a lanchonete, a sort of cross between a stand-up snack bar and a European café. These pla-

Lanchonetes and bars

Not a bad selection here!

ces sell drinks, sandwiches, cigarettes and coffee and sometimes serve light snacks too.

Padarias Padarias (bakeries), usually attached to lanchonetes, also sell various salgadinhos (small savoury appetizers) such as empadinhas (a small pastry with a filling of meat, palm hearts or prawn), coxinhas (a small cake made from a potato flour dough, filled with chopped chicken), pão de queijo (literally »cheese bread«; pastry made from fine manioc flour and fresh Minas cheese baked in the oven) and small bites from Arab cuisine such as baked quibe made from wholegrain wheat with mincemeat.

Pastelarias Pastelarias (cafés) serve pastéis (fine white dough filled with mozzarella cheese, mincemeat or palm hearts and deep-fried), served with a caldo de cana or garapa (freshly-squeezed sugar cane juice, sometimes diluted with lemon juice).

Pizzerias All medium-sized and larger towns now have numerous pizzerias – nearly as many as bars and lanchonetes. They vary from the most basic budget shack to up-market speciality restaurants and offer pizzas thin or thick with every conceivable variation of topping. Most common are pizzas with mozzarella, Margherita (with basil and tomatoes), Calabreza (with the fatty sausage of the same name), Quatro Queijos (four cheeses: mozzarella, provolone, catupiry cream cheese and gorgonzola), Portuguesa (mozzarella, egg, olives and onions). A pizza rodízio, where small pizza portions may be sampled in varying combinations, may offer up to 40 different types. Most pizzerias are only open in the evening and, like lanchonetes, often serve as popular meeting places for young Brazilians.

The cariocas, the inhabitants of Rio, in particular enjoy frequenting their local botequim. Whilst quite a few botequims offer very good food, in these traditional places eating tends to take a back seat: botequims are first and foremost meeting places where thirst is quenched with a chope (draught beer), accompanied by a chat. The local pub in England or Ireland, or an old-style diner for regulars, comes closest to the botequim's traditional function. As botequims become increasingly popular, other restaurants – with a bit of judicious rebranding – are also attempting to jump on the bandwagon. As a rule of thumb, a proper botequim is never chic and will certainly not have a bouncer!

Meeting place botequim

Nearly all restaurants offer a starter/appetizer (that is charged separately), ranging from simple bread and butter with olives through to small pâtés, cheese pastries, strips of carrot, anise and cucumber, radishes, tomatoes, and so on. Visitors not intending to consume or pay for the offered starter/appetizer should make it clear that they have declined. Apart from top restaurants, where servings tend to be smaller, portions are usually generous everywhere, often feeding two people.

Restaurants

i Price Categories

- The restaurants recommended in the »Sights from A to Z« chapter are grouped according to the following price categories (main dish):
- Expensive: from 55 reais
- Moderate: 28 – 55 reais
- Inexpensive: up to 28 reais

São Paulo, which grew through waves of immigration, is said to be the city in Brazil offering the most international cuisine: diners can choose from Italian, Japanese, Arab, Portuguese, Spanish, French, German, Chinese, Hungarian, Swiss, Indian, kosher and vegetarian restaurants. Locations in Santa Catarina state such as Blumenau, Treze Tílias, Pomerode or Joinville are particular strongholds of German and Austrian cuisine.

Health

As a general rule, only use boiled water or bottled mineral water (also for teeth-brushing), especially outside of the big cities. In the interior, sterilizing tablets or manual filters are recommended. In cheap restaurants or hotels, always ask for drinks sem gelo (without ice), as it is probable that in those places no sterilized or boiled water is used to make the ice cubes. Caution should be exercised when enjoying ice cream and salads; fruit should be peeled or at least washed before consumption. During trips into the interior it is a good idea to take single-use syringes to have some handy if a hospital stay should become necessary.

The sun's rays are strong in Brazil, so visitors should take care to minimise exposure. Sun screens with a high protection factor and a hat or protection for the head are indispensable.

Vaccinations Visitors travelling from Europe do not need any mandatory vaccinations. Travellers who in the six days before entering Brazil spent time in a country at risk of yellow fever are obliged to show the relevant vaccination. In the view of Brazilian authorities, many African states, as well as Bolivia, Peru, Ecuador and Colombia carry the risk of yellow fever infections. In any case, for visitors planning to travel to the Amazon Basin, a yellow fever vaccination is recommended. It is a wise precaution to further immunise against Hepatitis A and typhoid – especially for independent travellers likely to encounter poor hygiene.

! *Baedeker* TIP

Don't forget your vaccination documents!

Travellers on boat and bus journeys into the interior should carry their vaccination documents with them at all times. At some borders between Brazilian states, passengers unable to prove their vaccination status are summarily inoculated.

Malaria Malaria is still widespread in many parts of the Amazon region. It is recommended therefore to obtain the relevant information from a travel clinic or an institute of tropical diseases well ahead of departure. Standard malaria prophylaxis, which provides at least some protection, has to be started as early as one week before departure and continued for about four weeks after returning. Most doctors recommend packing supplementary stand-by medication. For emergencies, there are SUCAM malaria stations over the whole of Amazonia that can provide effective treatment. In order to minimize the risk, pack a mosquito net and, at dusk, try and wear proper socks, long trousers and long-sleeved tops in light colours. Parts of the body left uncovered may be effectively protected with mosquito repellent. As incubation time may last up to several months, visitors to Brazil should seek medical advice if flu-like symptoms develop after their return.

Chagas' disease Chagas' disease (doença de Chagas), named after the Brazilian bacteriologist who discovered it, is an additional risk occurring in some areas of the Northeast and Amazonia. Whilst rare, it can cause serious heart and kidney complications. Transmission occurs by the prick of the barbeiro, a nocturnal blood-sucking bug nesting in the cracks of simple clay huts. The main symptoms are fever, swollen lymph nodes and a rapid pulse.

Dengue fever, popularly called five-day or seven-day fever, has repeatedly claimed victims in various regions of Brazil, most recently in early 2008 in Rio de Janeiro. At dusk, travellers should protect themselves from the Aedes mosquitoes that transmit the dengue virus by wearing long trousers and long-sleeved blouses/shirts.

Dengue fever

The infective potential of the immune deficiency syndrome AIDS (sida) is extremely high, especially in the urban areas of Brazil. HIV positive diagnoses and AIDS victims can be found across the entire population, not only in the alleged high-risk groups. Taking the relevant precautions is recommended.

AIDS

Medical help and pharmacies

If medical help is needed, visitors should avoid the inevitably overcrowded public hospitals. The private sector provides excellent medical and dental care. If the need arises, ask in hotels or travel agencies for a list of doctors that speak foreign languages. All costs of treatment will need to be paid in cash. It is recommended to take out additional travel health insurance cover for medical and hospital costs before departure.

Medical help

Most common medicines can be obtained without a prescription in farmácias and drogarias. Some medicines, such as antibiotics – their packaging shows a red border – are prescription-only. Farmácias de manipulação sell both allopathic and homeopathic remedies. Pharmacies in Brazil are often open till late in the evening, some even round the clock.

Pharmacies

Information

USEFUL ADDRESSES

Note that not all offices are open to the public, or only by appointment. For travel planning, start with the website (see below); brochures may be requested from the relevant embassies/consulates.

► **Brazilian Tourist Information London**
Tel. (020) 73 96-55 51
Fax (020) 73 96-55 99
www.braziltour.com

► **Brazilian Tourist Information US East Coast**
Tel. (646) 37 82-12 6
Fax (646) 37 82-03 4

► **Brazilian Tourist Information US West Coast**
Tel. (310) 34 18-39 4
www.braziltour.com

EMBASSIES IN BRASÍLIA

► **British Embassy**
SES – Avenida das Nações

Quadra 801
Conjunto K, Lote 8 70408-900
Brasília, DF
Tel. (061) 33 29-23 00
Fax (061) 33 29-23 69
www.britishembassy.gov.uk/brazil

► **Irish Embassy**
SHIS QL 12
Conjunto 05, casa 09 – Lago Sul,
71630-255 Brasília, DF
Tel. (061) 32 48-88 00
Fax (061) 32 48-88 16
brasiliaembassy@dfa.ie

► **US Embassy**
SES – Avenida das Nações
Quadra 801
Lote 03 70403-900 Brasília, DF
Tel. (061) 33 12-70 00
Fax (061) 32 25-91 36
www.embaixada-americana.gov

► **Canadian Embass**
SES – Avenida das Nações Quadra
803
Lote 16, 70410-5400 Brasília, DF
Tel. (061) 34 24-54 00
Fax (061) 3443-54 90
www.dfait-maeci.gc.ca/brazil

► **Australian Embassy**
SES – Avenida das Nações
Quadra 801
Conjunto K, Lote 7 Brasília, DF
Tel. (061) 32 26-31 11
Fax (061) 32 26-11 12
www.brazilembassy.gov.au

► **New Zealand Embassy**
SHIS
QI 09
Conjunto 16, casa 01, 71625-160
Brasília, DF
Tel. (061) 32 48-99 00
Fax (061) 32 48-99 16
www.nzembassy.com

► **South African Embassy**
SES – Avenida das Nações
Quadra 801
Lote 6 70406-900 Brasília, DF
Tel. (061) 33 12-95 00
Fax (061) 33 22-84 91
www.africadosulorg.br

BRAZILIAN EMBASSIES

► **in the UK**
32 Green Street
London, W1K 7AT
Tel. (020) 73 99-90 00
Fax (020) 73 99-91 00
www.brazil.org.uk

► **in Ireland**
HSBC House, 5th floor, 41-54
Harcourt Street
Dublin 2
Tel. (01) 475 60 00
Fax (01) 475 13 41
www.brazil.ie

► **in the US**
3006 Massachusetts Avenue, NW
Washington, DC, 20008-3634
Tel. (202) 238 27-00
Fax (202) 238 2827
www.brazilemb.org

► **in Canada**
450 Wilbrod Street
Ottawa, Ontario, K1N 6M8
Tel. (613) 237 10-90
Fax (613) 755 51-60
www.brasembottawa.org

► **in Australia**
19 Forster Crescent
Yarralumla ACT 2600
Tel. (02) 62 73-23 72
Fax (02) 62 73-23 75
www.brazil.org.au

► **in New Zealand**
Level 9, Deloitte House 10
Brandon Street, Wellington 6011

Tel. (04) 473 35-16
Fax (04) 473 35-17
www.brazil.org.nz

► **in South Africa**
Hillcrest Office Park, Woodpecker

Place, 1st floor
177 Dyer Road, Hillcrest
Pretoria 0083
Tel. (012) 366 52-00
Fax (012) 366 52-99
www.brazilianembassy.org.za

Language

Portuguese is the official and everyday language throughout Brazil. The difference between Brazilian Portuguese and European Portuguese is mainly one of pronunciation. Brazilian Portuguese, however, also uses numerous words and expressions from Indian and African languages. There are no dialects, only regional accents.

In hotels and restaurants within main tourist centres, English will usually be spoken. Beyond destinations heavily frequented by tourists some basic Portuguese is vital for communication.

Communication

PORTUGUESE LANGUAGE GUIDE

At a glance

Yes	Sim
No	Não
Mrs	Senhora
Mr	Senhor
Maybe	Talvez
Please	Se faz favor
Thank you	Obrigado (male speakers)/ Obrigada (female speakers)
You're welcome/No problem	De nada/Não tem de quê
Sorry!	Desculpe! (formal)/ Desculpa! (informal)
OK/agreed!	Está bem/De acordo!
When?	Quando?
Where?	Onde?
What?	Que?
Who?	Quem?
Excuse me?	Como?
Excuse me!	Com licença.
How much?	Quanto?
Where to?	Aonde? Para onde?
What's the time?	Que horas são?

Olá! Como vai? Hello! How's it going?

I don't understand.	Não compreendo.
Do you speak English?	Fala inglês?
Could you help me please?	Pode ajudar-me, se faz favor?
I would like …	Queria …
I (don't) like it.	(Não) Gosto disto.
Do you have …?	Tem …?
How much is it?	Quanto custa?

Greetings

Good morning/afternoon!	Bom dia!/Boa tarde!
Good evening/night!	Boa tarde!/Boa noite!
Hi! Hello!	Oi! Olá!
How are you?	Como está?
How's it going?	Como vai?
Fine, thanks. And you?	Bem, obrigado/obrigada. E o senhor/a senhora/você/tu?
Goodbye!/See you later!/See you again!	Adeus!/Até logo!/Até à próxima!

Directions

Left	a esquerda
Right	a direita

Straight ahead	em frente
Near/far	perto/longe
Where is .., please?	Se faz favor, onde está ...?
How far is it?	Quantos quilómetros são?

Breakdowns

My car has broken down	Tenho uma avaria
Would you tow me to the nearest garage please?	Pode rebocar-me até a oficina mais próxima?
Is there a garage nearby?	Há alguma oficina aqui perto?

Petrol/Gas stations

Where is the nearest petrol/ gas station please?	Se faz favor, onde está a bomba de gasolina mais próxima?
I would like ... litres ...	Se faz favor ... litros de ...
...Normal petrol.	...gasolina normal.
...Super.	...super.
...Diesel.	...gasóleo.
...Unleaded/leaded.	...sem/com chumbo.
...octane.	...octanas.
Full tank, please.	Cheio, se faz favor.

Accidents

Help!	Socorro!
Watch out! / Careful!	Atenção! / Cuidado!
Quick, call ...	Chame depressa ...
...an ambulance!	...uma ambulância!
...the police!	...a polícia!
...the fire service!	...os bombeiros.
It was my/your fault.	A culpa foi minha/sua!
Would you give me your name and address please?	Pode dizer-me o seu nome e o seu endereço, se faz favor?

Food

Is there a ... here, please?	Pode dizer-me, se faz favor, onde há aqui ...
...a good restaurant?	...um bom restaurante?
Is there a bar/café here?	Há aqui um bar/um café?

Could you please book a table for four people for tonight?	Pode reservar-nos para hoje à noite uma mesa para quatro pessoas, se faz favor?
Could I please have ...?	Pode-me dar ..., se faz favor?
Knife / Fork / Spoon	faca / garfo / colher
Glass	copo
Plate/dish	prato
Napkin	guardanapo
Toothpick	palitos
Salt / Pepper	sal / primenta
Cheers!/Your good health!	À sua saúde!
The bill/check please!	A conta, se faz favor.
Did you enjoy it?	Estava bom?
The food was excellent.	A comida estava êcelente.

Accommodation

Could you please recommend ...?	Se faz favor, pode recomendarme
...a good hotel?	...um bom hotel?
...a guesthouse?	...uma pousada/pensão?
Do you have a room available?	Ainda tem quartos livres?
a single room	um quarto individual
a double room	um quarto de casal
en-suite	com casa de banho
... for one night.	...para uma noite.
... for one week.	...para uma semana.

Doctors

Can you recommend a good doctor?	Pode indicarme um bom médico?
It hurts here.	Dói-me aqui.

Banks

Where can I find ...	Onde há aqui ...
...a bank?	...um banco?
...a cash point/ATM?	...uma caixa automática?

Post

stamp	selo
How much is ...	Quanto custa ...
...a letter ...	...uma carta ...
...a postcard ...	...um postal ...

to England?	para a Inglaterra?
to Ireland?	para a Irlanda?
to the United States?	para os Estados Unidos?
to Canada?	para o Canada?
to Australia?	para a Australia?
to New Zealand?	para a Nova Zelândia?
to South Africa?	para a África do Sul?
Could I send a fax/an email to ... ?	Posso mandar aqui um fax/ email para ...?

Numbers

0	zero
1	um, uma
2	dois, duas
3	três
4	quatro
5	cinco
6	seis
7	sete
8	oito
9	nove
10	dez
11	onze
12	doze
13	treze
14	catorze
15	quinze
16	dezasseis
17	dezassete
18	dezoito
19	dezanove
20	vinte
21	vinte e um
22	vinte e dois
30	trinta
40	quarenta
50	cinquenta
60	sessenta
70	setenta
80	oitenta
90	noventa
100	cem
101	cento e um
200	duzentos
1,000	mil
2,000	dois mil

10,000	dez mil
1/2	um meio
1/3	um terço
1/4	um quarto

Ementa/Menu – Sopas/Soups

Açorda	Bread and garlic soup
Caldo verde	Portuguese cabbage soup
Sopa de legumes	Vegetable soup
Sopa de peíe	Fish soup
Sopa alentejana	Garlic soup with egg

Entradas/Starters/Appetizers

Amêijoas	Clams
Azeitonas	Olives
Caracóis	Snails
Espargos frios	Cold asparagus
Melão com presunto	Melon with ham
Pão com manteiga	Bread and butter
Salada de atum	Tuna salad
Salada à portuguesa	Mixed salad
Sardinhas em azeite	Sardines in olive oil

Peixe e mariscos/Fish and seafood

Amêijoas ao natural	Clams in half shell
Atum	Tuna
Bacalhau com todos	Dressed cod
Bacalhau à Bráz	Cod, roast potatoes and scrambled egg
Caldeirada	Fish stew
Camarão grelhado	Grilled shrimps
Cataplana	Mussels, fish or meat, paprika, onions, potatoes
Dourada	Golden bream
Ensopado de enguias	Stewed eel
Espadarte	Swordfish
Filetes de cherne	Silver perch fillets
Gambas na grelha	Grilled prawns
Lagosta cozida	Boiled lobster
Linguado	Sole
Lulas à sevilhana	Baked squid
Mêilhões de cebolada	Mussels with onions
Pargo	Sea bream

Peixe espada	Silver needle fish
Perca	Perch
Pescada à portuguesa	Haddock Portuguese-style
Salmão	Salmon
Sardinhas assadas	Roasted sardines

Carne e aves/Meat and poultry

Bife à portuguesa	Portuguese beefsteak
Bife de cebolada	Onion steak
Bife de peru	Turkey steak
Cabrito	Kid goat
Carne de porco à Alentejana	Pork with cockles
Carne na grelha/Churrasco	Meat from the (charcoal) grill
Coelho	Rabbit
Costelata de cordeiro	Lamb cutlet
Costeleta de porco	Pork cutlet
Escalope de vitela	Veal escalope
Espetadas de carne	Meat kebab

A few words of Portuguese and you'll make friends!

Fígado de vitela	Veal liver
Frango assado	Roast chicken
Frango na pucara	Clay pot chicken
Iscas	Braised liver
Lebre	Hare
Leitão assado	Roasted suckling pig
Lombo de carneiro	Saddle of mutton
Pato	Duck
Perdiz	Partridge
Pimentões recheados	Stuffed peppers
Porco assado	Pork roast
Rins	Kidneys
Tripas	Tripe

Legumes/Vegetables

Batatas	Potatoes
Beringelas fritas	Fried aubergines/eggplants
Bróculos	Broccoli
Cogumelos	Mushrooms
Espargos	Asparagus
Espinafres	Spinach
Feijão verde	Runner/string beans
Pepinos	Cucumbers

Sobremesa/Pudding/Dessert

Arroz doce	Rice pudding
Compota de maçã	Stewed apples
Gelado misto	Mixed ice cream
Leite creme	Egg and milk custard
Maçã assada	Baked apple
Pêra Helena	Pear Hélène
Pudim flan	Caramel custard
Sorvete	Fruit sorbet
Tarte de amêndoa	Almond tart

Lista de bebidas/Drinks menu

Aguardente	Spirit/Brandy
Aguardente de figos	Fig brandy
Aguardente velho	Aged brandy
Bagaço	Sugar cane liqueur
Ginjinha	Cherry liqueur
Madeira	Madeira wine

Medronho	Strawberry (Arbutus unedo) brandy
Porto	Port wine

Cerveja e vinho/Beer and wine

Cerveja	Beer
Imperial	Draught beer
Vinho branco	White wine
Vinho tinto	Red wine

Bebidas não alcoólicas/Non-alcoholic drinks

Água mineral	Mineral water
Bica	Espresso coffee
Café (com leite)	Coffee (with milk)
Chá com leite/limão	Tea with milk/lemon
Galão	Milky coffee in a glass
Meia de leite	Half coffee, half milk
Garoto	Espresso with a shot of milk
Sumo de laranja	Orange juice

Days of the week

Segunda-feira	Monday
Terça-feira	Tuesday
Quarta-feira	Wednesday
Quinta-feira	Thursday
Sexta-feira	Friday
Sábado	Saturday
Domingo	Sunday
Feriado	Public holiday

Literature

Amado, Jorge: Dona Flor and Her Two Husbands (Vintage, London   Novels
2006)
The story of how the Bahian Dona Flor manages her life with two
husbands is told in an ironic and entertaining way, garnished with
the light touch of machismo typical of the author's work.

Ribeiro, João Ubaldo: An Invincible Memory (Harper Collins, London 1989)
Ribeiro's mighty epic, translated by the author himself, gives deep insights into the history and mentality of the Brazilian nation and uses the history of a family clan to illustrate the social and political development of Brazil. The setting for the novel, which spans several generations, is Ribeiro's island home of Itaparica, off Salvador.

O'Hanlon, Redmond: In Trouble Again – A Journey Between the Orinoco and the Amazon (Penguin, London 1989)
The Thames is not the Amazon. This much the valiant Brit Reymono, as his local companions call him, knew before his expedition into the jungle. What he finds there exceeds his worst fears: parasites and wild animals, heat and humidity. He does however also encounter Indians that stubbornly refuse to live up to their reputation as violent monsters. Redmond's troubles make for a travelogue full of suspense and entertainment.

Zweig, Stefan: Brazil – Land of the Future (Ariadne Press, Riverside/CA, USA 2000)
While Europe was living through the darkest chapter of humankind's history, Zweig's 1941 homage to the South American country that he believed to be a model example of a peaceful and tolerant nation was published in Portugal, Brazil and the USA. The moral strength of the Brazilian nation kept alive the author's hopes for a humane future. The idolization of Brazil may have been Zweig's last attempt to overcome his inner demons and depression. In 1942 he took his own life in Petrópolis.

Ethnology **Lévi-Strauss, Claude:** Tristes Tropiques (Atheneum, New York 1973)
This ethnological classic by the French structuralist Lévi-Strauss is less of an objective, rigid, scientific analysis than a subjective homage to the culture of the Brazilian Indians.

Non-fiction **Taylor, Gerard:** Capoeira 100: An Illustrated Guide to the Essential Movements and Techniques (Frog, Berkeley, CA, USA 2007)
A practical introduction to the Afro-Brazilian martial dance.

Money

Currency The name of the Brazilian currency is real. One real is divided into 100 centavos. Bank notes in circulation are to the values of 1, 2, 5, 10, 20, 50 and 100 reais. There are two versions of the 10 reais note, both valid. Coins come in denominations of 1, 5, 10, 25 and 50 centavos, as well as 1, 2, 3, 4, 5 and 20 reais. The 1 real note and 1 centavo coin have both been discontinued but remain legal tender.

One pound sterling is worth approximately 3.3 reais, one euro approx. 2.6 reais, one US dollar approx. 1.6 reais, one Australian dollar 1.5 reais, one New Zealand dollar 1.3 reais and one South African rand just over 20 centavos.

US dollars – either as cash, or better traveller's cheques – are recommended for travelling in the country. In the past, other currencies have been undervalued in Brazil; in addition it is not possible to change money in the interior. As credit cards are not accepted everywhere, travellers should carry sufficient dollars with them.

i **Lost credit card?**

■ Before departing, visitors planning to use their credit card while travelling should take a note of relevant service numbers for reporting its loss or theft. Most card companies have a toll-free emergency number to ring from abroad.

There is no limit on the amount of foreign currency that may be imported or exported by non-Brazilian residents. The import and export of Brazilian currency is also unlimited, although amounts over 10,000 reais must be declared. However, there is no advantage in bringing in large amounts of national currency as local rates of exchange are more advantageous.

Currency regulations

Casas de câmbio (bureaux de change), as well as some car-hire firms at the airports, usually change money at better rates of exchange than Brazilian banks, which charge a handling fee. Visitors wanting to change cash will need to show their passport.

Changing money

Visitors cashing traveller's cheques are also required to show their passport. Monies are only paid in real and a handling fee of 10 % of the cheque's nominal value is kept by the bank making the transaction.

Traveller's cheques

In Brazil, credit cards are only accepted by shops, hotels and upmarket restaurants in the big cities. The most-widely accepted card is VISA, followed by American Express. Away from the urban hubs, cash payments are the norm. Not all bank branches offer the facility to withdraw money at ATMs using credit cards. Often, ATMs are automatically shut down late at night, to deter crime.

Credit cards

National Parks

Brazil now has more than 40 recognized national parks managed by the **IBAMA environmental protection agency** and serving the primitive regions and habitats. Some national parks offer modest accommodation for longer stays. However, by no means all protected areas

are accessible to the public. The national parks, in northern Brazil in particular, are situated far from the usual tourist tracks and are often inaccessible during the rainy season or only with considerable effort. The popular favourites amongst the Brazilian national parks are Iguaçu (▶ p. 244), Itatiaia (▶ p. 261), the eponymous nature reserve near Brasília (▶ p. 198) and the Pantanal (▶ p. 310).

Post · Communications

In every main town and all Brazilian federal capitals there is a main post office and several smaller correios (branches) distributed across individual districts. Some post offices carry signs saying ECT (Empresa de Correios e Telégrafos = post and telephone company). Letter boxes can be found mainly along busy streets. It is however a good idea to hand in post at the counter of a post office, as some letter boxes are only emptied sporadically. Letters and postcards from Brazil usually take 12 to 14 days to reach Europe or the US, allow longer for destinations further afield.

Public telephones

The Brazilian telephone network is modern and functions well. All parts of the country can be reached by direct dialling. The dialling codes can be found under the DDD section in the listas telefônicas (telephone books). Alongside the **orelhões** (open telephone booths, nicknamed »big ears« for their shape), spread all over towns and cities, airports, post offices, railway stations, hotels, restaurants and bars have public card and coin phones. Orelhões bearing the word **»Interurbana«** are only suitable for local calls, while those marked **»Nacional«** permit long-distance calls within Brazil, and public phones marked **»Internacional«** can be used to call abroad.

Telephone cards

Telephone cards can be bought in units of 20, 50, 75 and 90, usually at the nearest kiosk or shop. For visitors making reverse charge/collect

DIALLING CODES FROM BRAZIL

- ► **to call Britain**
  Tel. 00 21 44

- ► **to call Ireland**
  Tel. 00 21 353

- ► **to call the USA/Canada**
  Tel. 00 21 1

- ► **to call Australia**
  Tel. 00 21 61

- ► **to call New Zealand**
  Tel. 00 21 64

- ► **to call South Africa**
  Tel. 00 21 27

- ► **to call Brazil from abroad**
  Tel. 00 55

calls, Brazil offers the ligação a cobrar (call-collect) option. For calls inside Brazil, dial 9 before the local area code; international collect calls require the relevant dialling code for the country (see below).

Visitors calling other networks should always dial the number of a prestadora (provider) of telephone services before the local area code. The providers' dialling codes, which differ between states, are listed in the operating manuals of public telephones. Currently, two telephone companies operate in all Brazilian states: Embratel, with the provider number 021, and Intelig/Bonari with the provider number 023. To make a long-distance call within Brazil, these provider numbers need to be dialled before the local area codes (omitting the first zero), i.e. for a call from Rio to São Paulo with Embratel dial 021 + 11 + the number of the person you want to call, for a call the other way round dial 021 + 21 + the number of the person you want to call. Only a few luxury hotels spare their guests this procedure.

Dialling codes

Prices

WHAT DOES IT COST?

Cup of coffee
2.50 reais

Main course
8–15 reais

3-course meal
from 25 reais

Double room
60–1,200 reais

Shopping · Souvenirs

Brazil produces particularly tasteful ceramics, partly made using Pre-Columbian patterns. Decorative objects carved from soapstone or steatite are also a popular type of souvenir. There is a particularly good choice of textiles, hammocks, braid and knotwork. **Leather goods** are a speciality of the traditional cattle-rearing areas of the Midwest, Northeast and South. When buying Indian crafts, visitors should make sure that no protected species or their carapaces, skin, feathers, hides or teeth, have been used. In Britain and the US, for instance, alongside the Washington Convention, the regulations of HM Customs and federal law for protected species apply. Explicitly prohibited, for instance, is the importing of parrot feathers, wildcat teeth, carapaces, skins and hides or their by-products. Antiques, precious stones, fossils, sacred artworks and weapons may not be taken out of Brazil.

Opening hours Shop opening hours vary; in general, visitors may expect shops to be open Monday to Friday from 9am to 6pm. In some towns, even cities, most shops close in the afternoons for about two hours. On Saturdays, many only open in the morning. Undeterred, the large shoppings (shopping centres) often open seven days a week between 9am and 10pm, and in many tourist places, local produce and souvenirs are also available for sale on Sundays.

Sport and Outdoors

The Brazilian Atlantic coast is a mecca for sun seekers and beach lovers. Sandy beaches unfolding for miles can be found in nearly all of the Brazilian states bordering the sea (▶ beach holidays) and are equally popular with locals and holiday-makers. Unlike those in the Brazilian interior, the nature reserves and national parks near the coast are usually fairly well explored by **hiking trails and trekking routes**. In national parks with suitable topography, visitors will find ideal conditions for mountain hikes and walks close to nature, as well as for extreme sports and the latest crazes.

Sailing Sailing has become ever more popular in Brazil, especially in recent years, and can also enrich foreigners' beach holidays at their chosen destination.
One of the country's most sought-after sailing spots lies off the town of **Angra dos Reis**, which is home to several yacht clubs. There's something for every sailor here – aside from the time available and the distance that they and the crew are looking to cover. The only formal requisite is a skipper with a coastal sailing licence and a sec-

ond crew member with a sailing licence. Further information can be found at: www.sailing-brazil.com and www.infohub.com.

Golfing facilities and courses exist in numerous states. The 18-hole courses in Trancoso (www.terravistabrasil.com.br), on the Ilha da Commandatuba peninsula (www.transamerica.com.br) and, in particular, in Costa do Sauípe (www.costadosauipe.com.br) all conform to international standards. Other leading facilities can be found in Angra dos Reis (www.hoteldofrade.com.br), Armação dos Búzios (www.buziosgolfe.com.br) and Foz do Iguaçu (www.bourbon.-com.br). For more information on golf and a list of further facilities, see www.brasilgolfe.com.br and www.golfebrasil.com.br. *Golf*

Diving in Brazil is still in its infancy, mainly because the only diving spots with really good underwater visibility, such as off Cabo Frio or Fernando de Noronha, have relatively cool water. **Fernando de Noronha** however, commands the same respect from Brazilian divers as Hawaii from American surfers. One reason is the number of diving spots off this volcanic island, but there are also 18 different types of coral living here, along with marine turtles and dolphins and ten types of shark raising their young here. Last not least: Fernando de Noronha is the only Brazilian diving spot that boasts not only a PADI-certified diving school, but also a decompression chamber. For more information, see www.atlantisdivers.com.br. *Diving*

Palm trees, sand and sea – Brazil's beaches don't exactly make it hard for visitors to enjoy them.

DEMIGODS IN YELLOW

If Brazilian football started out as a sport of the elites, it opened itself over time to a broader public and gradually became an essential part of Brazilian culture. In society, football's contribution to integration should not be underestimated, and the results of the Brazilian national team unmistakably have a strong impact on the confidence of the whole nation.

It is said that English sailors were the first to play football on Brazilian soil in 1884 in the harbour of Rio de Janeiro. Ten years later, the São Paulo Athletic Club founded the first football team in Brazil, and the early 20th century saw the first local championships in São Paulo and Rio de Janeiro. In its beginnings, the English import of »football« was a sport of the white elites, but unlike cricket, which also came from England and was able to

in the favelas, the city slums, and the poorest rural regions of Brazil, that the talents lay hidden that were to make the South American country the leading football nation and winners of five World Cup titles.

Football as opportunity

With the establishment of a national league and the professionalization of football, the playful leisure activity of the back yards, lanes and beaches

»Football became the common denominator of all Brazilians, across all barriers of society.«

hold on to its elitist aura in Brazil, football became the national sport. The leather sphere came to occupy the heart of leisure activities in the poor areas in particular, as it was a cheap sport to play. And it was there,

became a chance to escape the daily misery. Great teams such as Flamengo, Corinthians, Palmeiras or Vasco da Gama have always depended on new talents, for whom even the lowest entry salary means a better

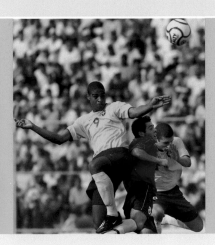

From up-and-coming player to superstar: Adriano

quality of life, but most of all the opportunity to become a star in the firmament of Brazilian football.

There is no shortage of role models: Arthur Friedenreich, the first black star player of Brazil, who scored the goals that propelled the country's Seleção to the 1919 South America title against Uruguay; Pelé, Jairzinho, Romario or Ronaldo, who all rose up to wealth and fame from the depths of the slums. Some of them returned to where they had come from: for instance Garrincha, the master dribbler of the World Cups from 1958 to 1962, was idolized in Brazil, but died, in 1983, in isolation and poverty. Football had been Garrincha's big chance. But with fame, he became hooked on alcohol and other vices, leaving, on his death, three wives, 13 of his own and six adopted children, as well as more mistresses than wives and children added together.

Uniting the nation: Pelé

As the former key player of the Brazilian national side, whom he led to victory in three World Cups (1958, 1962 and 1970), Pelé in particular became the figure to unite a whole, extremely heterogeneous nation. Regardless of ethnic or regional origin and social class, Pelé and his team were admired and cheered by everybody. Football went on to become the common denominator of all Brazilians, the binding element even across the barriers of society. The defeat of the Brazilian national team is the defeat of the whole nation, hence the sadness after losing and the effusive joy after a victory. An original manoeuvre by a player, a successful trick, and the deed is rewarded with a collective samba in the stands. And as the demigods in yellow are not exactly short of originality and variety, the rhythm of the samba is an integral part of Brazilian football – on the pitch, too. In the words of the Brazilian sociologist Gilberto Freyre: »Brazilian football is a dance full of irrational surprises and Dionysian variations.«

Spectator sports

Football
Amateur football is played everywhere in Brazil: city kids kick the ball about more or less anywhere, factory workers play impromptu games during their lunch break in backyards and on the streets. This is why »futebol« is considered the top Brazilian national sport. Brazil is the only country in the world to have won five football World Cup titles. The football stadiums here are huge. Some of them, such as the **Maracanã in Rio de Janeiro**, which is the world's largest, the Morumbi in São Paulo and the Mineirão in Belo Horizonte hold mostly euphoric crowds of over 100,000. Championships are held at regional, state and national level. Various states can boast several famous teams, supported by fanatic away supporters and often riven by ancient rivalries: in Rio de Janeiro, these are Flamengo, Fluminense, Botafogo and Vasco da Gama; in São Paulo they are Corinthians, Palmeiras, Santos, Portuguesa and Guarani; in Rio Grande do Sul Grêmio and Internacional; in Belo Horizonte Atlético Mineiro; in Bahia Salvador and Bahia; in Recife Sport and in Belém Remo and Paisandu (▶Baedeker Special p. 120).

Futebol de salão
In the big cities, a variant of traditional football called futebol de salão has spread. This is a five-a-side match using a smaller, but slightly heavier ball on a volleyball pitch. Some Brazilian states stage proper championships for this sport.

Basketball and volleyball
In recent decades both basketball and volleyball have reached a high level of popularity in the country. At championships and international competitions, the Brazilian national teams have been able to gain many medals and titles. Brazil's (beach) volleyball players, male and female, also count among the best in the world.

Motor sports
The international triumphs of Brazilian Formula 1 drivers such as Emerson Fittipaldi, Nelson Piquet and Ayrton Senna (▶Famous People p. 75) and the Grand Prix races on the track of **Interlagos near São Paulo** have brought many fans to automobile sports in Brazil. However, since the death of Ayrton Senna in 1994 in Imola, enthusiasm has markedly waned.

Sailing
Amongst over twenty types of sailing sports, Brazil prefers windsurfing and dinghy classes such as Optimist, Laser, Snipe, Star, Hobie Cat, Tornado, Finn, etc. The most important locations for regattas and contests are Araruama, Búzios, Guanabara Bay (Rio de Janeiro), Ilha Bela (São Paulo), Praia do Canto (Vitória), Florianópolis (Santa Catarina) and Praia do Forte (Bahia).

Time zones

Brazil has four different time zones, all behind Greenwich Mean Time (GMT), roughly in line with US time zones. The following time differences refer to GMT: Fernando de Noronha: two hours behind; the east of Pará state, the entire Brazilian coastal area, the Northeast, the Interior (Brasília time) and the South: three hours behind; Amazonia (apart from Acre state and the southwest of Amazonas state), the west of Pará, the states of Mato Grosso and Mato Grosso do Sul: four hours behind; the southwest of Amazonas state and Acre state: five hours behind. During European **summer time**, one hour has to be added to the time differences.

Time Zones

Tipping

Nearly all hotels and restaurants in Brazil add a 10 % service charge to the bill/check. Whether this really finds its way to staff is not always clear. Some restaurants put on the bill »serviço não incluído« (gratuities not included); in this case, around 10 % should be added. Tips above this are not necessary, although it is of course always a nice gesture to show appreciation of good service. Maids in hotels, as well as hotel porters expect a small tip; hairdressers about 10 % of the bill. Baggage porters at airports either charge according to their own tariffs, depending on the amount of luggage, or expect about 50 US cents per item. Taxi drivers do not commonly receive a proper tip; usually, the amount requested is just rounded up.

Transport

By air

Inland flights The most important Brazilian conurbations are linked by the regular passenger jets of the big national carriers – TAM and Varig. For tourists looking to cover large distances within Brazil, the **Brazil Airpass** offered by both airlines comes recommended: the TAM Brazil Airpass allows four inland flights within Brazil and is valid for 21 days. Every further flight coupon – up to nine are allowed – incurs an extra charge. Sales of the Airpasses are not conditional on the purchase of a TAM transatlantic flight. Varig offers four kinds of Airpass. For more information on the Airpass, contact travel agencies or the airlines direct.

Air taxis Those towns not connected to a scheduled flight network can be reached by air taxi, as scarcely one of Brazil's 4,000 communities is without at least a small untarmacked landing strip.

By bus · By rail · By river

A fleet of scheduled buses takes on the main burden of inter-Brazilian private traffic. Long-distance routes are often made by state-of-the art three or four-axle luxury coaches, whereas the shorter routes and those in the interior are plied by much older vehicles. Most **long-distance coaches** have comfortable seating, air conditioning and on-board toilets. Leading companies have even started equipping their top coach class with satellite telephones. Long-distance coaches depart from bus stations called **estações rodoviárias**. The coaches are on the road day and night, with two drivers taking it in turns at the wheel. Every three or four hours, the coaches stop at a petrol station

Reliable and cheap: the donkey has its advantages compared to modern means of transport.

with a snack bar where passengers can have a bite and a drink. Luggage is stowed from outside in the luggage compartments below; when travellers hand it over they are given a receipt which has to be shown again at arrival. In the interior of the country in particular it is a good idea to protect luggage against dust during the journey. Travellers are also advised to keep a close eye on their hand luggage and not to leave any valuables or documents on the bus during stops.

The scheduled services of the **»Itapemirim«** company operate in 21 Brazilian states, covering 70 % of the Brazilian mainland. The yellow »Itapemirim« buses connect towns and cities along the entire Atlantic coast of Brazil. For instance, a trip from Rio de Janeiro to Belém takes approx. 50 hours. In general, even for journeys in the up-market bus classes, tickets will never cost more than a quarter of the air-fare. The long-distance buses of the **»Ouro Branco«** company commute between São Paulo and numerous cities and towns of neighbouring Paraná state, including the provincial capital of Curitiba. The **»Rede Brasil de Viagens«** is an association of various companies operating buses throughout Brazil. **Bus companies**

While Brazil has an extensive rail network for freight transport, the passenger sector is not very well developed. Passenger trains are also slow and more expensive than buses. The exceptions are railway lines used exclusively for tourism in the states of Minas Gerais, Paraná and Santa Catarina. **Rail**

River travel
As Amazonia has only a very sparse road network, river boats here account for the lion's share of transportation, especially in Belém, Manaus and Santarém. There are options to either take one of the low-cost **scheduled ships or boats** or to hire a motorboat (▶Baedeker Special p. 170). A regular boat service also serves passenger traffic on the Rio São Francisco (Minas Gerais, Bahia, Pernambuco) and a few sections of the Rio Paraná (Mato Grosso and Mato Grosso do Sul). On most of these boats, a second-class ticket allows the holder to sleep in hammocks on deck, a solution that is usually preferable to the cramped first-class cabins and permits contact with the locals.

By road

Brazil has a well-developed network of trunk roads. In the rainy season, however, landslips may occur, blocking the streets and temporarily disrupting traffic. This does not affect most roads in the states with a more moderate climate: São Paulo, Paraná, Santa Catarina and Rio Grande do Sul.

Traffic regulations
In Brazil, traffic drives on the right. Signs follow international norms. Because of the frequently bad state of the streets and the lack of regard for traffic discipline, visitors should always drive cautiously and defensively. At night people often drive without adequate lights, so driving after dark is not advised. Front-seat passengers are obliged to wear a seat belt. Children must travel in the back. It is prohibited to drive under the influence of alcohol.

Speed limits
Outside built-up areas, the top speed limit is usually 50mph/80kmh, apart from some motorways and major roads in São Paulo state, where 60mph/100kmh is allowed.

Road tolls
As some stretches of rural roads in Brazil have been privatized, their use incurs a road toll. So far federal roads can still be used free of charge.

Car hire

Avis and Hertz are the two main international car rental companies in Brazil and are represented alongside national companies such as Interlocadora, Localiza, Mega and Unidas in nearly all larger towns and cities. At some locations smaller firms often offer more competitive rates. Renting a car is particularly recommended for day trips outside of cities, as public transport can turn a short day trip into a long journey. The above-mentioned car rental companies usually maintain a desk in airport arrivals areas.

Requirements
In order to hire a rental car in Brazil, drivers require a valid national driving licence (international documents are not usually requested),

USEFUL ADDRESSES

BUS COMPANIES

▶ **Empresa de Ônibus NS da Penha/Viação Itapemirim S.A.**
Tel. (08 00) 992-627
www.itapemirim.com.br

▶ **Viação Ouro Branco S.A.**
Tel. (043) 33 29-10 36
www.rbv.com.br/associados.htm

BY AIR

▶ Transport p. 124

CAR HIRE

▶ **Avis**
in the UK:
Tel. (08 445) 81 81 81
in Ireland:
Tel. (021) 428 11 11
in the US:
Tel. (1 800) 331 10 84
in Canada:
Tel. (1 800) 879 28 47

in Australia:
Tel. 136 3 33
in New Zealand:
Tel. (08 00) 65 51 11
in South Africa:
Tel. (011) 923 36 60
Internet: www.avis.com

▶ **Hertz**
in the UK:
Tel. (08 708) 44 88 44
in Ireland:
Tel. (01) 676 74 76
in the US/Canada:
Tel. (1 800) 65 43 13 1
in Australia:
Tel. (0 3) 96 98 25 55
in New Zealand:
Tel. (08 00) 65 43 21
Internet: www.hertz.com
(also for South African customers)

which they must have held for at least two years, need to be 21 years or older and require a valid credit card. Visitors renting a car should not only enquire about the rate, but also the covered risks (accident/theft). For legal as well as for insurance reasons it might make sense to book the hire car from the head office of one of the leading companies before leaving home.

Urban transport

The bus network within towns and cities usually works quite well; at peak times, however, it can get very crowded. At these times pickpockets in the big cities redouble their efforts. Entry to buses is normally from the rear.

Buses

São Paulo, Rio, Belo Horizonte and Recife all have modern underground systems. Rio's Metrô in particular is suitable for tourist exploration especially since the recent construction of the Cardeal Arcoverde station in Copacabana district, linking the existing network with the main Sugarloaf tourist centre.

Metrô

Taxis Taxi fares arelow by European and US standards and are calculated by the kilometre. The meter, which the driver is requested to set by law, shows the fare in reais. Tariffs at weekends, public holidays or at night are significantly higher than the day rate. Regulations governing the times of day at which the higher tariff applies differ between states, as do the basic meter rates.

Radio taxis Most airports and some bus stations work with taxi cooperatives. Company staff display price lists with the fares for the various districts; the agreed fare for the radio taxi is paid in advance at the counter. The driver receives part of the receipt, if necessary, with the destination written on it. Tips, whilst not mandatory, are certainly welcome.

Travelling with children

For adults, Brazil undoubtedly provides a fascinating and varied travelling experience. As a general rule, Brazilians are very child-friendly, and in many hotels and restaurants, families with children enjoy sometimes quite substantial discounts. However, the choice of leisure activities on offer for children and adolescents wanting more than just museum visits (some free of charge), beach and sun, is not overwhelming. A number of **theme parks** provide at least a measure of child-friendly entertainment in Brazil.

▶ THEME PARKS

▶ **Terra Encantada**
Avenida Ayrton Senna 2800
Barra da Tijuca, Rio de Janeiro
Opening times:
Tue–Sat 2–9pm, Sun 12–9pm
www.terra-encantada.com.br

▶ **Playcenter**
José Gomes Falcão 20
Barra Funda, São Paulo
Tel.: (011) 33 50-01 99
Opening times:
Thu–Fri 10am–5pm, Sat
10am–9pm, Sun 10am–10pm
www.playcenter.com.br
Children up to the age of 5, senior citizens over 60 and anybody who has a birthday in the current week, enjoy free entry.

▶ **Parque da Mônica**
Avenida Rebouças 3970
Shopping Eldorado, Pinheiros
São Paulo
Tel. (011) 30 93-77 66
Opening times:
Thu–Fri 10am–5pm, Sat
10am–9pm, Sun 10am–8pm
www.parquemonica.com.br
Entertainment includes carousels and theatre

▶ **Hopi Hari**
Rodovia dos Bandeirantes, km 72, Vinhedo
São Paulo state
Tel.: (019) 38 36-90 00
Opening times:
Wed–Fri 10am–6pm,

Sat – Sun 10am – 8pm; opening times vary according to the month
www.hopihari.com
Includes Ferris wheel, catapult and a rollercoaster with top speeds of over 100kmh/60mph – more suitable for teenagers than young children

► **Ski Mountain Park**
Rodovia Livío Tagliassachi/Estrada da Serrinha
São Roque, São Paulo state
Tel: (011) 47 12-32 99
Opening times:
Thu – Sun 10am – 6pm
www.skipark.com.br
Offers a summer ski piste and chair lift

► **Kinder Park**
Rua João Negrão 1100
Rebouças, Curitiba, Paraná
Tel. (041) 30 29-74 74
Opening times:

Tue – Sun 2 – 8.30pm
www.kinderpark.com.br
Ideal for visitors with babies and children up to 14 years of age

► **Beto Carrero World**
Rua Inácio Francisco de Sousa
Balneário de Penha
Santa Catarina state
Tel. (047) 32 61-23 54
Opening times:
Wed – Sun 9am – 7pm
www.betocarrero.com.br

► **Parque Walter World**
Avenida Vereador Edmundo Cardillo 3131
Poços de Caldas, Minas Gerais
Tel. (035) 37 22-22 20
Opening times:
Thu – Sun 10am – 6pm
www.walterworld.com.br
Amusement park with around 30 rides

When to go

When choosing the best time to travel to Brazil it is a good idea to take into account the regional climatic differences (► p. 22). As a general rule: the further from the Equator the greater the seasonal fluctuations. As most of Brazil is situated south of the Equator, the seasons are the opposite of those in the northern hemisphere. This explains why most Europeans visit Brazil between December and February, the Brazilian summer, in order to escape the winter at home. However, in Amazonia south of the Equator, this is the rainy season. In the extreme south, the period between June and September can bring cool temperatures sometimes going below zero at night. On the coast between Rio Grande do Norte and São Paulo states, visitors can avoid the highest temperatures, which can reach up to 40 °C/104 F.

Tours

TOURS THROUGH BRAZIL.
ALONG THE COAST AND INTO THE
BACKCOUNTRY. FROM EASY ROUTES BY
CAR OR TRAIN TO CHALLENGES FOR
HARDCORE OFF-ROADERS, WE REVEAL
THE BEST ROUTES.

TOURS THROUGH BRAZIL

Not sure yet exactly where to head? Our suggested tours offer a selection of particularly scenic roads within Brazil, as well as giving numerous tips to help you get the most out of each region.

━━ **TOUR 1**   **Along the Costa Verde**
A classic route, counting amongst the most beautiful stretches of road that Brazil can offer drivers.   ▶ **page 136**

━━ **TOUR 2**   **Estrada Real**
It might only run for 34km/21 miles, but this route from Ouro Branco to the baroque town of Ouro Preto – used in colonial times by mule treks crossing the Serra do Espinhaço – has extraordinary scenic appeal.   ▶ **page 138**

━━ **TOUR 3**   **Estrada Parque**
From Ilhéus to Itacaré, through the Atlantic rainforest and the traditional area of cocoa cultivation of Bahia, running parallel to the Atlantic coast – and hopefully leaving enough time to linger on the magnificent beaches along the way.   ▶ **page 139**

━━ **TOUR 4**   **Estrada do Coco/Linha Verde**
With its good trunk road, the northern coast of Bahia is great for self-drive adventures – offering visitors arguably the most beautiful beaches of the Brazilian mainland.   ▶ **page 140**

━━ **TOUR 5**   **Estrada Parque do Pantanal**
Leading through the unique natural landscape of the southern Pantanal, this tortuous track between Corumbá and Buraco das Piranhas is a challenge for hardcore off-roaders.   ▶ **page 144**

━━ **TOUR 6**   **Estrada da Graciosa**
With its hairpin bends the Estrada da Graciosa road is not to be tackled in a hurry, as it clears the coastal mountains of the Serra do Mar and winds its way through the thick Atlantic rainforest. No car? No problem, the scenery may also be experienced aboard a unique train.   ▶ **page 145**

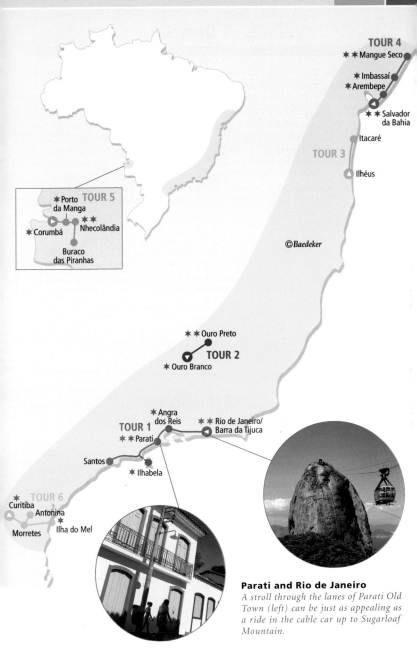

TOUR 4
✳ ✳ Mangue Seco
✳ Imbassaí
✳ Arembepe
✳ ✳ Salvador da Bahia
Itacaré
TOUR 3
△ Ilhéus

©*Baedeker*

✳ Porto **TOUR 5**
da Manga
✳ ✳ Nhecolândia
✳ Corumbá
Buraco
das Piranhas

✳ ✳ Ouro Preto
TOUR 2
✳ Ouro Branco

✳ Angra
dos Reis
✳ ✳ Rio de Janeiro/
Barra da Tijuca
TOUR 1
✳ ✳ Parati
Santos
✳ Ilhabela

✳ **TOUR 6**
Curitiba
△ Antonina
Morretes   ✳ Ilha do Mel

Parati and Rio de Janeiro
A stroll through the lanes of Parati Old Town (left) can be just as appealing as a ride in the cable car up to Sugarloaf Mountain.

Travelling in Brazil

In many ways, Brazil defies the imagination. Its territory comprises over 8.5 million sq km/3.2 million square miles, which represents 42 % of the South American land mass. Even making a conscious effort to visualize the extent of this giant – Britain, for instance, would fit into Brazil over 36 times – only goes a little way towards making the distances within the country more tangible. Looked at in European dimensions, a trip from Belém in the north to Porto Alegre in the south of Brazil can be compared with epic continental journeys such as Lisbon-Moscow or Spitsbergen-Palermo. In the same way, whilst mention of Brazil's **7,400km/4,600-mile Atlantic coast** might be met with polite wonder, it is difficult to comprehend what this really means.

From air passes to open-jaw flights
The two major cities of São Paulo and, to a lesser degree, Rio de Janeiro, are the most important gateways to Brazil. These days, travellers can also, via Portugal, book scheduled flights to the Brazilian northeast – to Fortaleza, Natal, Recife and Salvador – or catch a charter flight to these destinations from London or Miami. Scheduled services fly to São Paulo from Atlanta, Chicago, Dallas, New York, Houston, Miami, Newark, Toronto and Washington DC in North America, from Amsterdam, Frankfurt (also non-stop to Rio), Madrid and Rome in Europe, and from Johannesburg or Cape Town

A journey through Brazil is also a journey into the past: Ouro Preto's Old Town

in South Africa. Given Brazil's size, the scheduled airlines have an advantage that should not be underestimated, offering the opportunity to book an open-jaw ticket (allowing the traveller to enter and leave the country via different airports). The Brazilian scheduled airlines also offer a **Brazil Airpass** (a domestic ticket valid for 21 days with coupons for four to nine trips) which makes more than just economic sense. However, this ticket doesn't allow visitors to just fly where the fancy takes them, as the Airpass may only be purchased outside Brazil and individual legs must be specified – another reason, apart from the size and diversity of the country, to plan a trip to Brazil properly.

Large swaths of the Brazilian north are covered in tropical rainforest. This exotic and unusual environment exerts a particular fascination on many people from North Europe and America. But beware, as this landscape, criss-crossed by the tributaries of the **Amazon**, follows its own laws, demanding a much more intensive preparation than most other parts of the country. While on the coast of Brazil it might be a moot point whether or not a traveller has been vaccinated against Yellow Fever, in the states in the Amazon area – Amapá, Acre, Maranhão, Mato Grosso, Rondônia, Tocantins, Pará in north and western Brazil – and in Piauí too, malaria prophylaxis, water purification tablets and clothing suitable for the tropics can be essential lifesavers. | **Be prepared**

Travelling in the rest of the country requires less preparation. Visitors who don't speak any Portuguese may feel safest joining an organized tour. However, those who want to explore on their own and can muster even the most basic Portuguese will experience the accommodating **friendliness and hospitality** with which Brazilians – outside the big cities in particular – react to visitors to their country. And visitors from other football-mad countries such as »Inglaterra« will be given a warm welcome from most brasileiros, not least because of the shared love for the Beautiful Game. | **Exploring the country**

Most foreign visitors to Brazil take the plane to get around this huge country. The coach alternative is a lot more time-consuming but normally costs only a quarter of the air fare for the same route. Going it alone by (hire) car opens up many possibilities, but is not completely devoid of risk. In the big cities in particular, foreign drivers will soon form the impression that there are a high number of wannabe racers going at crazy speeds. It is also a fact that most accidents happen at weekends – after the odd caipirinha too many. Country roads outside the major urban areas might be easier to deal with, but because of huge potholes that could easily accommodate a VW Gol (the Brazilian version of the Golf), night drives at least make no sense. Despite the challenges outlined above, Brazil has incredibly beautiful routes for self-driving – six of which we have put together here. | **Touring by car**

Tour 1 Along the Costa Verde

Length of tour: approx. 490km/305 miles

Duration of tour: 3 to 6 days

This route – amongst the most beautiful drives in the country – may also be started in Rio de Janeiro. However, the drive only really becomes interesting beyond the city of the Sugarloaf, once the skyline of the wealthy Barra da Tijuca suburb is left behind and the multi-lane highway turns into the old windy and pothole-strewn Rio– Santos (BR-101) coastal road, which always hugs the bays and beaches along the Costa Verde (Green Coast).

Recreio dos Bandeirantes

Going west from ❶**Barra da Tijuca**, the next stop is Recreio dos Bandeirantes. Drivers not in a hurry may wish to visit – a few kilometres further inland – the Casa do Pontal (►p. 384) museum of folk art. As the coast continues, a hill initially blocks the view of ✳ **Prainha Beach**, only 150m/492ft long.

Grumari

Next comes the bay of ✳✳ **Grumari**, 4km/2.5 miles long and today a nature reserve. Framed by hills, its yellow, sandy beach (Praia de Grumari) is absolutely beautiful. There is a simple campsite nearby, as well as a few snack stalls. The next coves that follow – ✳ **Praia do Inferno**, ✳ **Praia Funda**, ✳ **Praia do Meio** and ✳ **Praia Perigosinha** – are not connected with each other and are only accessible via steep paths. It is likely they owe their unspoilt state only to these difficult approaches, dictated by the rocky hill of Morro de Guaratiba. There is no shade on these beaches, so they are not a good proposition on very hot days.

Itacuruçá

Some 90km/56 miles beyond Rio de Janeiro, the real Costa Verde, owing its name to the green of the Atlantic coastal rainforest, truly begins at ❷**Itacuruçá** (pop 3,500). The coastal mountain range, covered in dense tropical vegetation, charming bays and islands with unspoilt sandy beaches, as well as the azure Atlantic mark the rest of the drive as much as the chronic bad state of this old road between Rio and Santos, today mostly avoided by long-distance traffic.

Ilha Grande

Just over 90km/56 miles from Barra da Tijuca, the coastal town of ❸**Mangaratiba** is the launching point for boats to ❹✳ **Ilha Grande**. Most of the islands in the Baía da Ilha Grande, such as the Ilha da Gipóia, are blessed with beautiful sandy beaches, with the tourist infrastructure to go with them. From ❺✳ **Angra dos Reis**, boats take a good half-hour to reach the ❻✳ **Ilha da Gipóia**.

Mambucaba

In the colonial era, the next large town on the BR-101, ❼ **Mambucaba**, was, just as Angra dos Reis and Parati, a port of exit for the

Islands ...
... *off Angra dos Reis*

Parati
Charming colonial town

gold brought here on muleback from Minas Gerais. A reminder of those times to this day is the Trilha do Ouro, a trekking trail (manageable in three days) from Mambucaba to the ✳ **Serra da Bocaina** national park, established in 1971. This protected area harbours the largest surviving patch of Mata Atlântica (Atlantic rainforest). Running parallel to the Trilha do Ouro, the Rio Mambucaba river is ideal for rafting.

Parati

Just before reaching the border with the neighbouring state of São Paulo, the BR-101 road leads to the beautifully situated small colonial town of ❽ ✳ ✳ **Parati**. Do try and include a few days' stay in the listed baroque town – there is no shortage of pousadas – to explore the magnificent beaches by car or aboard a schooner.

Ubatuba

The stretch of coast between Parati and ❾ **Ubatuba** offers many fine swimming options. The well-known holiday resort of Ubatuba, with its numerous beaches, coves and off-shore islands, is not only an ideal playground for sun worshippers, but for divers and snorkellers too.

To Santos

Carry on southwest from Ubatuba along the coast, for just under 80km/50 miles, to reach the popular resort of ❿ **São Sebastião**. The offshore Ilha de São Sebastião, commonly known as ⑪ ✳ **Ilhabela** (Beautiful Island), does indeed live up to its name. The beaches, coves and numerous waterfalls are often only accessible via fairly difficult hiking trails. From São Sebastião, it is another 125km/78 miles to ⑫ **Santos**, where this tour ends.

Tour 2 Estrada Real

Length of tour: 64km/40 miles   **Duration of tour:** 1 to 2 days

The route from Ouro Branco to Ouro Preto was already known in colonial times. This is where once caravans of mules laden with gold transported the coveted precious metal across the Serra do Espinhaço mountain range. Today, the first stretch of road, starting from the small town of Ouro Branco, with its 30,000 inhabitants, is, for 11km/7 miles, closed to trucks and coaches – which adds to the appeal of driving this route.

From Ouro Branco to Cristais Even in the dry months (March to September), the going is never very fast on the MG 129 road from ❶ ✳ **Ouro Branco**, whilst before reaching the 19th-century bridges of ✳ **Pé do Morro** and **Ponte da Biquinha** it is best to slow down to a crawl. As early as the village of ❷ **Cristais**, a stop to visit the ✳ **Mirante da Serra de Ouro Branco** viewpoint is worth the effort as, from up here, the magnificent mountain scenery can be appreciated to the full.

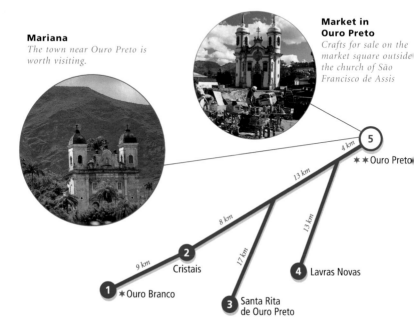

Mariana
The town near Ouro Preto is worth visiting.

Market in Ouro Preto
Crafts for sale on the market square outside the church of São Francisco de Assis

✳ ✳ Ouro Preto

4 km

13 km

8 km

13 km

❺

9 km

❷ Cristais

17 km

❹ Lavras Novas

❶ ✳ Ouro Branco

❸ Santa Rita de Ouro Preto

After another 8km/5 miles on the Estrada Real, a dirt road turns off to ❸**Santa Rita de Ouro Preto**, a small village where soapstone is made into all kinds of crafts. Another route, taking drivers right across the natural beauties of the Serra do Espinhaço, begins past ❹**Lavras Novas**, where a few waterfalls make a good stopping point or place for a break.

Through the Serra do Espinhaço

The closer one gets on the Estrada Real to the baroque town of ❺ ✶ ✶ **Ouro Preto**, the less spectacular the landscape becomes. The treat waiting at the end of the journey is, however, well worth the effort, in particular its historic Old Town, which was listed as a UNESCO World Heritage site in 1980 – the first of all Brazilian World Heritage sites! The beginning or end of the Estrada Real is particularly appealing in carnival season; the carnival of Ouro Preto counts amongst the most colourful the Brazilian interior.

> ! *Baedeker* TIP
>
> **One night at the manor**
> Seven of the 18 rooms of the Fazenda Pé do Morro near Cristais are located in a listed manor house. Amenities for the guests include restaurant, bar, sauna and lake, as well as horse-riding (tel. 031/37 41-81 81).

Tour 3 Estrada Parque

Length of tour: 72km/45 miles   **Duration of tour:** 1 to 2 days

Bahia's well-signposted tarmacked BA-001 country road – particularly on the stretch between the Cocoa Coast city of Ilhéus and the Itacaré community of 18,000– is one of the Brazilian driving routes that take the adjacent ecosystems into consideration. Thus, within the sections bordered by Atlantic rainforest, there are specially marked areas for the crossing of wild animals.

Despite following the Atlantic coast, the Estrada Parque does not have many bends. At ❶**Ilhéus**, birthplace of world-famous Brazilian writer Jorge Amado (► Famous People p. 69), , the road initially seems fairly urban, but just a few kilometres further north out of town, there are several worthwhile stopping points on the 50km/31-mile sandy beach of ❷ ✶ **Praia do Norte**. Over a long stretch, the Rio Almada flows parallel to the road towards the beach, flanked by palm trees and Atlantic rainforest. Some sections – Ponta do Ramo for instance, or Ponta da Serra Grande – are particularly popular with surfers and anglers.

Strung out off Itacaré like pearls in the ocean, one more beautiful than the other, are the bathing bays of ❸**Itacarezinho** and

Beaches, beaches …

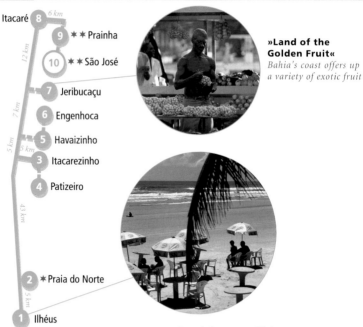

Itacaré **8** 6 km

9 ＊＊Prainha

10 ＊＊São José

7 Jeribuçaçu

6 Engenhoca

5 Havaizinho

3 Itacarezinho

4 Patizeiro

2 ＊Praia do Norte

1 Ilhéus

12 km

7 km

5 km 5 km

43 km

5 km

»Land of the Golden Fruit«
Bahia's coast offers up a variety of exotic fruit

Beach bar near Ilhéus
Sipping a caipirinha while gazing into the wild blue yonder

4 **Patizeiro**, **5** **Havaizinho**, **6** **Engenhoca**, and **7** **Jeribuçaçu** as well as two beaches which may only be reached on foot from **8** **Itacaré**: **9** ＊＊ **Prainha** and, a bit further south, **10** ＊＊ **São José** – all pleasingly remote from the centre of Itacaré. In terms of the beaches, the time between August and February is the ideal half of the year, as there is less rain.

Tour 4 Estrada do Côco/Linha Verde

Length of tour:
approx. 280km/174 miles

Duration of tour: 3 to 7 days

From the excellent BA-099 trunk road – the Estrada do Côco, later called Linha Verde – small access roads lead to the beaches north of Salvador da Bahia.

The starting point of this very worthwhile route is **1** ＊＊ **Salvador da Bahia**. **2** ＊ **Arembepe**, a coastal town owing part of its reputation to the Aldeia de Caratingui on the Rio Capivara – a hippy encampment set up in the 1960s and 1970s – marks the beginning of the string of possibly the most beautiful swimming bays on the coast of Bahia. At the town of ❸✳ **Barra do Jacuípe** the BA-099 changes its name to Estrada do Côco, and there is a toll booth where drivers have to pay a toll. The beach, of the same name, has coconut palms, light sand and strong waves.

Praia do Forte

❹✳✳ **Praia do Forte** has not one but several popular sights. Directly on the beach is the area covered by the »Tamar« conservation project – in various open-air enclosures with seawater pools, a variety of marine turtles, as well as rays, sharks, piranhas, sea stars and water snakes may be observed. Between September and March, the baby turtles hatch in a fenced-off area, and between August and October, tourists can go whale-spotting off the coast aboard a schooner leaving from here. The ruined 16th-century Castelo Garcia d'Avila is another tourist attraction.

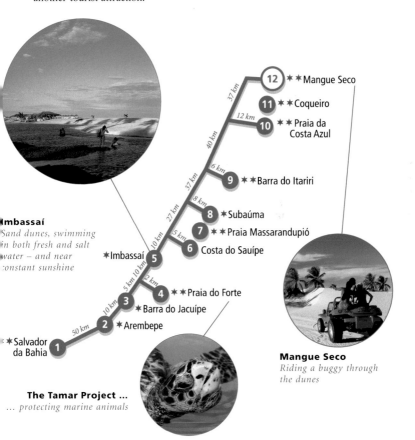

Imbassaí
Sand dunes, swimming in both fresh and salt water – and near constant sunshine

12 ✳✳ Mangue Seco
11 ✳✳ Coqueiro
10 ✳✳ Praia da Costa Azul
37 km
12 km
40 km
6 km
9 ✳✳ Barra do Itariri
37 km
8 km
8 ✳ Subaúma
27 km
7 ✳✳ Praia Massarandupió
5 km
6 Costa do Sauípe
10 km
5 ✳ Imbassaí
5 km 10 km
2 km
4 ✳✳ Praia do Forte
10 km
3 ✳ Barra do Jacuípe
2 ✳ Arembepe
50 km
1 ✳ Salvador da Bahia

Mangue Seco
Riding a buggy through the dunes

The Tamar Project ...
... protecting marine animals

Imbassaí and Costa do Sauípe

At the town of ❺ ✳ **Imbassaí**, the Rio Barroso flows parallel to the Atlantic. Visitors wanting to alternate between swimming in fresh-water and salt water only have to cross a small sand dune; the side facing the river is also suitable for small children. Over the past few years, ❻ ✳ **Costa do Sauípe** has seen the birth of a large-scale tourist complex with five international chain hotels, half a dozen informal pousadas, a broad range of sports and leisure facilities (including a first-rate golf course), as well as restaurants and boutiques. The palm-fringed beach in front of the resort offers fine sand, dunes and a strong swell.

Praia Massarandupió

More unspoilt is the ❼ ✳✳ **Praia Massarandupió**. The distance from the straight-as-a-die beach to the Linha Verde is 10km/6 miles and the approach road is in a bad state. Fine light-coloured sand, a fishing village, slim coconut palms and the strong surf make the effort worth while however.

Further north, at ❽ ✳ **Subaúma**, the Projeto Tamar has a further base for the protection of the marine turtles laying their eggs here and in Massarandupió. With its fine white sand, palm trees and holiday cottages, the beach of Subaúma is popular with visitors in high season. At low tide, natural pools form offshore, and on the beach, »jangadas« (simple sailing boats) may be rented.

❾ ✳✳ **Barra do Itariri** lies 9km/5.5 miles from the Linha Verde and has all the hallmarks of a fabulous beach, as it is here that the palm-fringed Rio Itariri makes a grandiose sweep past dunes to the sea. The beaches further to the north, ❿ ✳✳ **Praia da Costa Azul** and ⓫ ✳✳ **Coqueiro**, are best reached using off-road vehicles or buggies. Crystal-clear waters, dunes and fine sand reward the drive, which, given enough time, may be continued on to ⓬ ✳✳ **Mangue Seco**, an over 30km/18.5-mile stretch of coast in the extreme north of Bahia. Since the aiting of a Brazilian soap opera that was filmed here Mangue Seco is becoming more and more popular among Brazilians. Drivers choosing the Linha Verde to get to Mangue Seco have to go to Indiaroba, which lies in the neighbouring state of Sergipe. Here, an intermittently tarmacked dirt road turns off to the fishing village of Pontal, which has secure parking. To reach Mangue Seco on the other bank, travellers have to cross the Rio Real aboard one of the motor launches; the trip takes around 30 minutes.

The beach of Mangue Seco →

Tour 5 Estrada Parque do Pantanal

Length of tour: approx. 130km/81 miles

Duration of tour: 3 to 4 days

This classic route from Corumbá to Buraco das Piranhas promises adventure and challenge. However, the road is only navigable in the dry season between May and October and, to avoid unnecessary risks, should only be attempted using a four-wheel drive. Even then, with gravel and dirt tracks, sandy stretches and narrow wooden bridges, as well as a ferry ride across the Rio Paraguaí, there are plenty of thrills on this section of the MS-228 and MS-184.

The Estrada Parque do Pantanal was laid out at the end of the 19th century by the pioneer battalions led by the legendary general and protector of the Indians Cândido Rondon, and for a long time was the only access to ❶ ✳ **Corumbá**. With its promenades and rows of houses from the colonial era, the border town's old river port, the Porto Geral, has its charms, but most tourists only use the town as the point of entry and exit for trips into the unique, unspoilt natural wonders of the southern Pantanal.

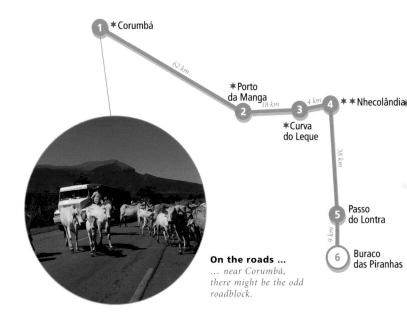

1 ✳ Corumbá

62 km

✳ Porto da Manga

2 — 18 km — 3 — 4 km — 4 ✳✳ Nhecolândia

✳ Curva do Leque

38 km

5 Passo do Lontra

9 km

6 Buraco das Piranhas

On the roads ...
... near Corumbá, there might be the odd roadblock.

Drivers on the Estrada Parque do Pantanal to ❷ ✶ **Porto da Manga**, are already in the middle of the rich flora and fauna of the world's largest freshwater wetland system. Parrots, toucans, caymans and capybaras gather around the water-holes, which become rarer the longer the dry season goes on. It is not unusual for a herd of anteaters to cross the track; sometimes wild boar and deer have been spotted too.

In the Pantanal

Drivers wishing to continue beyond Ponta da Manga have to take a ferry (between 6am and 6pm) across the Rio Paraguaí. Back behind the wheel, carry on to ❸ ✶ **Curva do Leque**. During the rainy season (October to March), vast areas of the region surrounding ❹ ✶ ✶ **Nhecolândia** sink nearly completely underwater. Especially in the transitional period from May to July, this area is considered one of the most rewarding places for photo safaris. Drivers who have used up more than half of their tank of petrol, have to hold out till ❺ **Passo do Lontra**. At ❻ **Buraco das Piranhas**, the hardship is over, when the track eventually becomes the better-maintained BR-262 federal road.

> # ! Baedeker TIP
>
> **Bathing lake, boats and beds**
> The pousada (and fazenda) Bela Vista near Porto da Manga has 13 air-conditioned rooms and offers its guests, amongst other amenities, boats, a lake to swim in and horses. Excursions by jeep are another option (tel. 067/99 87-36 60, www.pousadabelavista.com).

Tour 6 Estrada da Graciosa

Length of tour: approx. 150km/93 miles

Duration of tour: 1 to 2 days

The hairpin bends of the Estrada da Graciosa have led across the Serra do Mar coastal mountains, with their dense cover of Atlantic rainforest, since 1646, although the road was only paved about 200 years later (following many serious accidents). Despite the tarmac cover on most stretches, this extremely scenic but rather narrow road still requires a fair bit of concentration, as well as reduced speed, as this mountainous region often receives heavy precipitation.

After approx. 40km/25 miles, the Régis Bittencourt (BR-116) trunk road from ❶ ✶ **Curitiba** city in the direction of São Paulo, leads to the Estrada da Graciosa access road, turning towards the coast. It is not a good idea to just zoom along the Estrada da Graciosa – although only a short stretch, it invites many stops, even if only to breathe in the fresh mountain air or admire the begonias growing on either side of the road.

Through the valley of Gruta Funda

Just before the turn off the BR-116, near ② ✳ **Engenheiro Lacerda**, there is an inviting first viewpoint, from where, on a clear day, there are sweeping views all the way to the coast. Another worthwhile place for a break is the waterfall of the Rio Cascata river, and just a little further on the valley of Gruta Funda opens up, before another viewpoint is reached at ③ ✳ **Bela Vista**.

Morretes and Antonina

At ④ **São João da Graciosa** the road forks, leaving two options: either driving to Antonina first, or driving – via Ponta de Cima, a mecca for extreme sports enthusiasts – to Morretes. A community of 15,000 inhabitants, ⑤ **Morretes** was founded in 1721 on the Rio Nhundiaquara. The town, boasting numerous colonial buildings, lies on the Curitiba – Paranaguá train line. ⑥ **Antonina** (pop 19,000) was founded even earlier, in 1643, by settlers from the neighbouring state of São Paulo. Today however, it's a bit out on a limb, since the railway to the port was dismantled in 1977.

Detour to Honey Island

Ferries and water taxis ply the stretch of water between ⑦ **Paranaguá** and the protected island of ⑧ ✳ **Ilha do Mel**. Up to now at least, the 2,700-ha/6,670-acre island in Paranaguá Bay has managed without cars. Despite attempts at limiting the number of visitors, such as the environmental tax (»taxa ambiental«), between December and April in particular, »Honey Island« is a favourite destination not only with surfers. One time when the Ilha do Mel should definitely be avoided however is November, when swarms of »mutucas« come out, extremely annoying insects that make light of practically all the insect repellents on the market.

By train to Paranaguá

Another option to travel the Serra do Mar to Morretes or Paranaguá is a narrow-gauge railway starting in the provincial capital of Curiti-

Engenheiro
Lacerda

② ③ ✳ Bela Vista

⑥ Antonina

São João
da Graciosa

④ ⑤ Morretes

✳ Ilha do Mel

⑧

By train …

*… from Curitiba
to Paranaguá*

① ✳ Curitiba

⑦ Paranaguá

No stone throwing please: Curitiba's botanical gardens

ba – the most spectacular rail journey in Brazil. Over 110km/68 miles, the trains hurtle through no less than 13 tunnels, clatter over 67 bridges and clear a difference in elevation of 951 metres/3,120 feet. The regular trains leave Curitiba Tuesdays to Sundays at 8am, whilst the more touristy xxxLitorinayyy railcar starts its journey Fridays and Sundays at 9am from the same place. The seats on the left-hand side have the better views. For further information, call Serra Verde Express: tel. 041/33 23 40 07.

Sights from A to Z

THE VIBRANT CITY LIFE OF
RIO DE JANEIRO OR SÃO PAULO.
FASCINATING NATURE ALONG
THE AMAZON OR IN THE
PANTANAL. AND ALONG THE
COAST OF BRAZIL ARGUABLY THE MOST BEAUTI-
FUL BEACHES ON THE PLANET AWAIT.

✳ Angra dos Reis

Sc 57

State: Rio de Janeiro (RJ)   **Population:** 120,000
Altitude: 6m/20ft

Angra dos Reis is the largest town on the Costa Verde. Mainly Brazilian tourists come here, powering the economy of the town; the best sites have nearly all been filled with private villas belonging to wealthy city dwellers from São Paulo or Rio. Angra dos Reis is a good base for day trips to the nearby islands of the Baía da Ilha Grande.

The importance of the town, founded in the 16th century and limited on one side by the Atlantic Ocean, on the other by the Serra do Mar coastal mountains, grew with the expansion of the port. In colonial times, Angra dos Reis was – alongside Parati – the prime trading post for gold from Minas Gerais and coffee from the Paraíba valley. At the end of the 20th century, the controversial construction of two nuclear reactors brought the town its share of dubious fame.

What to see in Angra dos Reis

Colonial buildings

Amongst the most impressive colonial buildings in town are the **convent of Nossa Senhora do Carmo** on Praça General Osório, dating from 1593, the **Capela de Santa Luzia**, built in 1632 in Rua do Comércio, and the former **convent of São Bernardino de Sena**, which was erected in 1653 on the Santo Antônio hill. From this height, there is a splendid view of the entire area. The parish church of Nossa Senhora da Conceição in the centre of town, and the Nossa Senhora da Lapa church on the Largo da Lapa, date from 1749 and 1752 respectively.

✳ Beaches

Angra's town beaches are Praia do Anil, do Jardim, do Café and Praia do Oeste; further north in **Jacuecanga Bay**, 15km/9.5 miles to 20km/12.5 miles out of town, stretch the bays of Camdorim Grande, Monsuaba and Paraíso, but the water here is said to be polluted. However, continuing northeast on the BR¬-101 brings you to the swimming beaches of Biscaia, Praia da Fazenda and Praia da Espia. On the Morro da Espia hill, an obelisk commemorates the mariners who lost their lives in the sinking of the warship ***Aquidabã*** in 1906 in the Baía da Ilha Grande. The most popular beaches around Angra dos Reis however, lie to the southwest, in the direction of Parati. To discover some of the most beautiful spots – only accessible by sea or trails – head for the bay of the Praia da Freguesia da Ribeira (10km/ 6.2 miles from Angra dos Reis), as well as Praia Grande do Frade (33km/20.5 miles), Praia do Saco (39km/24 miles), Brava (45km/28 miles), and Praia Mambucaba (50km/31 miles) at the mouth of the river of the same name.

▶ VISITING ANGRA DOS REIS

INFORMATION

Avenida Júlio Maria
Cais de Santa Luzia
Tel. (024) 33 65-11 75
www.angra-dos-reis.com

GETTING THERE

Bus station
Praia da Chácara
Tel. (024) 33 65-20 41

EVENTS

On 1 January and on the second Sunday in May, the feast day of the Senhor do Bonfim, lavishly decorated boats turn up in Angra dos Reis, to take part in one of the most spectacular sea processions in Brazil. The fame of the boat parade in carnival time also extends far beyond the town limits.

WHERE TO EAT

▶ Expensive

Chez Dominique
km 514 on BR-101
Condomínio Porto Frade
35km/22 miles outside Angra dos Reis
Tel. (024) 33 69-54 58
Fine dining, French-style; credit cards are accepted.

ACCOMMODATION

▶ Luxury

Hotel do Frade & Golf Resort
km 513 on BR-101
Praia do Frade
Tel. (024) 33 69-95 00
www.hotel-do-frade.com
Beach hotel halfway between Angra dos Reis and Parati. Guests may avail themselves of: 162 apartments, 16 houses, six restaurants, 15 tennis courts, a private beach with service, boat hire, diving school, horses for hire, kayaks, sailing trips by catamaran and the hotel shuttle bus (taking 150 min to/from Rio).

▶ Mid-range

Hotel do Bosque
km 533 on BR-101 in the direction of Parati
Mambucaba
Tel. (024) 33 62-31 30
www.hoteldobosque.com.br
Beach and business hotel with 96 apartments, some of which are accessible to wheelchair users. Private beach with service, bar, restaurant, swimming pool, sauna and boat pier. Rental of sailing boats, water-skis, kayaks, diving equipment and horses.

▶ Budget

Pousada do Alemão
Estrada dos Marinas 991
Marinas, Angra dos Reis
Tel. (024) 33 65-15 93
www.pousadadoalemao.com.br
Seven double rooms with sea view, air conditioning, TV and fridge

✱ Ilha Grande

Ilha Grande (large island), a state-protected nature reserve which has belonged to Angra dos Reis since 1978, is a 1.5-hr boat trip from

Ilha Grande Map

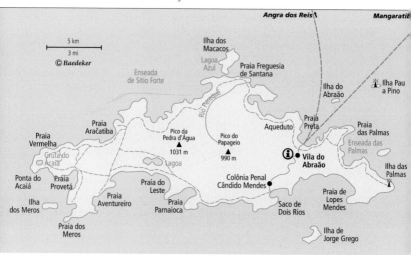

town. Its lovely fishing villages, lagoons, waterfalls and beaches attract many visitors. It was not always so: originally settled by Tupinambá Indians in the 16th century, the island became a **pirate's lair** in the 19th century; later, a leper colony was established on the island, whilst from 1903 to 1994, it served as a penal colony. So it is not surprising that, over the centuries, people stayed away from Ilha Grande as much as they could!

Vila do Abraão The pier for the boats coming from the mainland is in Vila do Abraão, seat of the island's administration and at the same time its only settlement, which has a modest tourist infrastructure. Not far from here rises the 1,000m/3,280-ft **Pico do Papagaio**, and further west the **Pico da Pedra d'Água** (1,031m/3,382 ft). The remains of a 19th-century aqueduct to the northwest of the settlement are worth seeing, as well as the ruin of the infamous former Cândido Mendes penitentiary near the bay of Saco de Dois Rios.

★ ★
Beaches In the north, at Vila do Abraão, lie the beaches of Abraão, Preta and do Morcego; to the east don't miss Praia Lopes Mendes – one of the most beautiful swimming bays in Brazil and an ideal surfing spot –, whilst further to the south, in the **Bay of Dois Rios**, lie the beaches of Parnaioca (with a waterfall), do L'Este (with monazite sand and lagoons), do Sul and Aventureiro. To the west and southwest of Ilha Grande the beaches of Vermelha, Provetá (with fishing village) and the diving spots off Praia dos Meros are recommended. The bays can be reached by narrow trails or by boat.

The rich marine fauna of Ilha Grande, but also the remains of the
ships that sank in these waters, are a strong draw for sports divers.
The wreck of the ***Pinguino***, sunk in 1959, lies 21m/69 feet under the
sea to the southwest of Ilha
Grande; the wreck of the ***Califórnia***
lies a bit further south, 15m/49ft
deep, while in the far south, at a
depth of 7m/23ft, the underwater
cave of Acaiá is famous for its colourful fish life.

✳ Diving spots

> ### ! *Baedeker* TIP
>
> **A two-masted boat off Angra dos Reis**
>
> An estimated 2,000 beaches ring Angra dos Reis,
> if you add the 360 islands of the Baía da Ilha
> Grande to the coastal strip. Visitors interested in
> exploring the islands can book trips on a
> schooner (Escuna) or other watercraft at Santa
> Luzia quay, at the town's port or directly with the
> hotels. For more information, contact the
> Associação dos Barqueiros on tel. (024) 33 65-
> 31 65.

It is a 20-min boat trip from Angra
dos Reis to the smaller neighbouring island **Ilha do Bonfim**. In 1780
the hermitage of Senhor do Bonfim was built on the island. The islands of **Sandri and Comprida**, situated at the level of the closed-off
beach of Itaorna, are particularly
popular with divers. The **Ilha da Gipóia** lies opposite Angra dos Reis,
30 minutes away by boat. The island has famous beaches, including
Praia Jurubaíba, Armação, Fazenda, Morcego, Oeste, Flechas, and a
varied marine fauna and flora. Near the port rises the Laje dos
Homens. At the foot of this rock rest the remains of the *Bezerra de
Menezes*, a ship which sank in 1890.

✳ ✳ Aparados da Serra ·
Serra Geral

Rk 60

States: Rio Grande do Sul (RS) and Santa
Catarina (SC)

**Together with the Parque Nacional da Serra Geral, the Aparados
da Serra National Park forms the most scenic region of the Brazilian southeast, preserving one of the largest araucaria forests in
Brazil, with trees of over 40m/130ft in height. Hunting is prohibited
to protect the indigenous fauna, including ocelots, otters, tapirs,
deer and hares, as well as the few remaining pumas and wolves.**

One of the national park's major sights is the Itaimbézinho Gorge, a
canyon traversed by the Perdiz and Preá rivers. At nearly 6km/3.5
miles long and up to 900m/2,950 ft high, the Itaimbézinho Gorge,
rich in araucaria forests, counts amongst the largest canyons in South
America. The **Véu da Noiva waterfall** plunges some 720m/2,360ft
down the virtually vertical rock walls.

**✳ ✳
Cânion de
Itaimbézinho**

⏵ VISITING APARADOS DA SERRA

PARK ADMINISTRATION

Cambará do Sul
Tel. (054) 32 51-12 77
Praia Grande
Tel. (048) 35 32-01 32

WHEN TO VISIT

The Parque Nacional de Aparados da Serra is only open to visitors Wed–Sun 9am–6pm. The nature reserve has a cool climate in June and July, and gets particularly hot in January.

WHERE TO STAY

Accommodation can only be had outside the national park – which is patrolled by rangers – in the town of Cambará do Sul 22km/13.5 miles away.

Parque Nacional da Serra Geral Serra Geral, which was only declared a national park in 1992, adjoins directly the Aparados da Serra nature reserve and reaches up to altitudes of around 1,100m/3,600ft above the sea. The Parque Nacional da Serra Geral includes four more canyons, furrowed as deep as 990m/3,250ft into the basalt: Churriado, Fortaleza and Malacara in the north, as well as Faxinalzinho in the south. The Serra Geral National Park has no tourist infrastructure.

It's all about the journey: mountain road through the Serra Geral

✳ Aparecida

Sc 57

State: São Paulo (SP)
Altitude: 542m/1,778ft

Population: 35,000

The foundation of Aparecida goes back to the year 1717, when local fishermen salvaged a Black Madonna from the Rio Paraíba river, which was said to have worked miracles over the course of time. Nossa Senhora Aparecida even became the patron saint of Brazil, making the town the most important centre of pilgrimage in the country.

What to see in Aparecida

The New Basilica (Basílica Nova Nossa Senhora Aparecida), built in 1939, houses a **Museum of Sacred Art** and a historical museum documenting the economic and social development during the coffee and sugar boom in the Paraíba Valley. The 18th floor of the main tower is used as a viewing terrace. Pilgrims visit the pilgrimage church the whole year round, in particular on 12 October and 8 December, the two feast days of the patron saint of Brazil, the 42cm/17-inch clay figure of whom is revered here.

✳ **Basílica Nova**

The construction of the Old Basilica (Basílica Velha Nossa Senhora Aparecida) was begun in 1745, on the exact site where earlier the first oratory of the saint had stood, in today's Praça Nossa Senhora

Basílica Velha

▶ VISITING APARECIDA

INFORMATION

Centro de Apoio do Romeiro
Rua Joaquim Prado 369
Tel. (012) 31 05-18 06
www.aparecida.com.br

GETTING THERE

Bus station
Praça Antônio Francisco Julianeli
Tel. (012) 31 06-22 85

WHERE TO EAT

▶ **Inexpensive**
Arco-Íris
km 75.6 on Via Dutra
in the direction of São Paulo
Tel. (012) 31 05-32 47

Brazilian and international cuisine. Both à la carte and buffet (priced per kilo) are available.

ACCOMMODATION

▶ **Mid-range**
Estância Porto dos Milagres
Avenida Itaguaçu/
Praça São Geraldo 2
Tel. (012) 31 05-56 44
www.portodosmilagres.com.br
Opened in 2003, this hotel has 15 well-appointed rooms, a bar, restaurant, natural swimming pool, playground and football field.

Aparecida in the centre of town. Over the centuries, the church was extended and refurbished several times, and in 1909 recognized as a Minor Basilica by Pope Pius X.

✳
Festa das Congadas

Alongside the Old and New Basilicas, the town also has several other churches, amongst them **São Benedito parish church**, where every year, straight after Easter on the feast day of St Benedict, there is a celebration known as the Festa das Congadas (congadas are dramatic ceremonial dances of African origin). Over 40 groups perform dances and play in honour of the Virgem do Rosário, the Rosary Madonna, and Saint Benedict.

Aracaju

Sg 51

State: Sergipe (SE)
Altitude: 5m/16ft

Population: 462,000

Aracaju, founded in 1592 by the Portuguese, has been the capital of Sergipe state since 1855. The city is located between Salvador and Maceió, where the Rio Sergipe flows into the Atlantic.

In 1855, the seat of government of Sergipe state was transferred from São Cristóvão to the old settlement of Santo Antônio de Aracaju, which boasted a good deepwater port. The new capital was the first systematically planned city in Brazil, using the layout of a chess board.

What to see in Aracaju

Ponte do Imperador

On the banks of the Rio Sergipe lies the Ponte do Imperador (Emperor's Bridge), a jetty that was erected for a visit of Emperor Dom Pedro II to the town.

✳
Ilha de Santa Luzia

The nearby Avenida Rio Branco coast road leads directly to the port and the boat pier for Santa Luzia island. The islet, where the beach of **Atalaia Nova** stretches for kilometres, is a 15-min boat ride away.

Museu do Homem Sergipano

Walking through the city centre from the Emperor's Bridge leads to Rua Itabaianinha and the Museu do Homem Sergipano (Praça Camerino 227). The collection includes items from archeological finds to folkloric exhibits from Sergipe.

Catedral Metropolitana

Standing proudly on Praça Olímpio Campos, west of the Ponte do Imperador, the Catedral Metropolitana was built between 1862 and 1875. Northeast of the cathedral, look for the tourist information centre (Centro de Turismo), offering traditional crafts for sale.

▶ VISITING ARACAJU

INFORMATION
Praça Olímpio Campos
Rua 24 Horas
Tel. (079) 31 79-19 47
www.aracaju.com.br

GETTING THERE
Bus station
Avenida Presidente Tancredo Neves
Tel. (079) 32 59-28 48

EVENTS
Celebrated on 1 January, the most impressive event in town is the annual Festa de Bom Jesus dos Navegantes, a boat procession on the Rio Sergipe with fireworks and numerous music groups. Aracaju celebrates the high point of carnival time (Pré-Caju) 15 days before carnival. Apart from this, the city is famous all over Brazil for its June festivities with traditional quadrille dances and shows on Praça Fausto Cardoso and in Rua São João.

WHERE TO EAT
► Moderate
O Miguel
Avenida Antônio Alves 340
Tel. (079) 32 43-14 44
The most prestigious restaurant in town, with Carne de Sol a speciality.

ACCOMMODATION
► Mid-range
Resort Hotel da Ilha
Praia da Costa
Ilha de Santa Luiza
Tel. (079) 32 62-12 21
Beach hotel with boats, bikes and horses for hire. The hotel can only be reached by ferry.

► Budget
Pousada Costa do Mar
Rua Niceu Dantas 325, Atalaia
Tel (079) 32 43-13 49
www.costadomar.com.br
21 air-conditioned rooms with telephone, TV and swimming pool

To the south, out of the city centre, on the Avenida Beira Mar coast road, an extensive leisure centre in the Parque dos Cajueiros (named after the cashew nut trees) offers relaxation. The area has water slides and playgrounds for children and includes the lake called **Mare Apicum**.

Parque dos Cajueiros

Detour to São Cristóvão

The small colonial town of São Cristóvão, founded in 1590 and now a listed monument, was the seat of the government of Sergipe up to 1855. Situated only 25km/15.5 miles southwest of Aracaju, the town of 65,000 inhabitants has not lost its old-time charm. Many of the winding roads, centuries-old churches and houses have preserved their characteristic aspect to this day.

★
Townscape

The church and monastery of São Francisco on Praça São Francisco date back to the year 1693. The monastery houses the **Museum of**

Praça São Francisco

Sacred Art with exhibits from the 17th to 19th centuries. The Historical Museum of Sergipe in the former governor's palace and the Misericórdia church can also be found here. The Historical Museum in the Palácio do Governo contains paintings, ceramics and furniture from the era of the Brazilian Empire.

✳
Senhor dos Passos

The Senhor dos Passos church, built between 1739 and 1743 on the Praça Senhor dos Passos houses the **Museu dos Exvotos**. The collection shows a large selection of offerings by people who were healed or hoping to be healed. Other churches are the Nossa Senhora da Vitória on the 17th century Praça Getúlio Vargas square and the ruins of the Igreja dos Capuchinhos, built in 1746 and destroyed during the Dutch invasion, situated 10km/6.2 miles from São Cristóvão.

Laranjeiras

NS da Comandaroba

Laranjeiras, founded in 1605 and situated 24km/15 miles north of Aracaju, was razed to the ground during the occupation by the Dutch but reconstructed in the 18th century by the Jesuits. The Nossa Senhora da Comandaroba church 4km/2.5 miles outside the town, with its baroque altar, was also built by the Jesuits. Tradition has it that a tunnel connected the high altar with the **Gruta da Pedra Furada**, a cave lying 3km/1.8 miles from Laranjeiras on the same road as the church. In an emergency, the monks were meant to flee to safety via this subterranean escape route.

Museu Afro-Brasileiro

Visitors can learn about the culture of the black African slaves forcibly brought to Brazil, in the Afro-Brazilian Museum in the Palácio Accioles Ribeiro in Rua José do Prado Franco.

✳ ## Beaches on the coast of Sergipe

South of Aracaju

Along the coast, extending for some 200km/125 miles there are still some fine sections that haven't been built-up yet. Stretching out south of Aracaju are the beaches of Coroa do Meio (7km/4.3 miles from Aracaju) and Atalaia Velha (9km/5.5 miles). The latter is well-known for its huge crabs called caranguejos, who can attain a diameter of up to 25cm/10 inches.

✳
Praia do Saco

The BR-101 trunk road leading south to the neighbouring state of Bahia leads to the beaches of Praia dos Náufragos, Caueira and Abaís, that in parts have preserved an unspoilt beauty.
Further on, in Estância Bay on the border with Bahia, and crossing the Rio Real river, the huge sand dunes of Praia do Saco suddenly appear.

Largely unspoilt: the Sergipe coast →

Beaches north of Aracaju On the coast in the north of Aracaju and Barra dos Coqueiros stretch extensive, mostly unspoilt sandy beaches. Near the border with Alagoas, on the mouth of the Rio São Francisco, lies the **Ponta do Arambipe**, and before that the northernmost beach of Sergipe, Praia de Arambipe. Boats connect the Piraçabuçus river harbour with the beach, taking 40 minutes.

Aracati

Sg 48

State: Ceará (CE)
Altitude: 5m/16ft

Population: 60,000

In colonial times, cattle from all parts of Ceará state were herded to Aracati or other ports in the region for slaughter. The meat was salted and hung up in the »charqueadas« farms to dry. The export of animal hides and dried meat laid the foundation for Aracati's prosperity.

Towards the end of the 18th century, the methods of work pioneered here were introduced in the Gaúcho region of Pelotas in the far south, which subsequently developed into the most important centre for dried meat production in Rio Grande do Sul. Fine **colonial buildings** bear witness to the former economic prosperity of Aracati. The town, situated near the coast on Rio Jaguaribe became particularly popular as a base for trips to the famous beaches of southeastern Ceará.

▶ VISITING ARACATI

GETTING THERE
Bus station
Avenida Coronel Alexandrino
Tel. (088) 34 21-30 47

WHERE TO EAT
▶ **Inexpensive**
Natural Bistrô
Rua Dragão do Mar
Tel. (088) 34 21-71 62
Regional and international cuisine

WHERE TO STAY
▶ **Mid-range**
Pousada Long Beach
Rua Quatro Ventos

Praia da Canoa Quebrada
Tel. (088) 34 21-74 04
www.lonelybeach-village.com
This pousada offers 7 apartments and 20 chalets, bar, pool and car parking.

▶ **Budget**
Refúgio Dourado
Rua Refúgio Dourado
Praia de Majorlândia
Tel. (088) 34 21-80 85
The 12 chalets can each accommodate up to 3 people. With restaurant, internet access, carparking, pool and playground.

What to see in and around Aracati

Aracati still has fine buildings from the 18th century, amongst them the townhouse of the Baron of Aracati (Sobrado do Barão de Aracati) in Avenida Alexandrino Lima, housing the **Museu Jaguaribano** with exhibits featuring arts & crafts and sacred art, the Senhor de Bonfim church, dating from 1774, and the main church of Nossa Senhora do Rosário in the Rua Dragão do Mar, built in 1785.

Colonial architecture

The beach of Canoa Quebrada with its impressive dunes, the emerald-green surf of the Atlantic and its laterite-red cliffs is famous all over the world. There are few reminders left in this small fishing village 9km/5.5 miles southeast of Aracati of the time when this was a hippies' paradise, as it has long been opened to commercial tourism. However, Canoa Quebrada still has the traditional crafts and folklore of the northeast: delicate lacework made by the wives of the local fishermen and little glass bottles containing landscapes crafted – with the utmost precision – from coloured sand are for sale.

★ ★
Canoa Quebrada

Jangada fishing boats on the beach of Canoa Quebrada

Majorlândia

The coastal town of Majorlândia, 12km/7.5 miles southeast of Aracati and famous for its embroidery and laces, is a **stronghold of the »jangadeiros«**, as the fishermen of northeastern Brazil are called. To this day, these coastal dwellers live off lobster fishing. The large beach of Majorlândia is the next one along going southeast from Canoa Quebrada beach, and has a strong swell which draws surfers in particular. However, it only gets really crowded at weekends.

Ponta Grossa

A few kilometres before the BR-304 reaches the coastal town of **Icapuí**, a good 50km/31 miles southeast of Aracati, an access road branches off, leading to the gently curved swimming beach of Praia da Ponta Grossa. The bay is framed by rocks and coconut palms, although due to the steep drop of the coast here, with reefs and underwater rocks, diving is only recommended for experienced scuba divers. At low tide, take a walk to the neighbouring beaches of **Redondas and Mutamba** with their multicoloured dunes. Behind Icapuí, discover the unspoilt beach of Tremembé, fringed with coconut palms and famous for its lobsters. In this bay's little fishing settlement, finely-wrought lacework is for sale.

✴ Armação dos Búzios

Se 57

State: Rio de Janeiro (RJ)
Altitude: 3m/10ft

Population: 18,500

The resort Armação dos Búzios started life as a fishing village. »Discovered« in the 1960s by Brigitte Bardot and other representatives of the international jetset, it has become one of the most fashionable and expensive beach resorts of the country, a kind of Brazilian St Tropez.

What to see in Armação dos Búzios

Rua das Pedras

The majority of the more exclusive shops and top restaurants of Búzios cluster around Avenida José Bento Ribeiro Dantas, also called Rua das Pedras (Street of Stones). Most buildings follow the architectural model of the old indigenous fishermen's houses: one or two-storey gabled houses, painted in blue or white, with tile roofs in colonial style and transom windows. With the more recent buildings also blending in well with the landscape of the city, Búzios has been able to preserve at least some of its village character despite the bustle.

Beaches near the city centre

Near the city centre, the beaches of Armação (with the Rua das Pedras), Ossos, Canto, Amores and Virgens have numerous pousadas. From the first three beaches, boats runs to the islands of Ancora, Gravatá, Branca, Rasa and Feia. The church of Sant'Ana – built in

▶ VISITING ARMAÇÃO DOS BÚZIOS

INFORMATION
Pórtico de Búzios
Trevo de Entrada
Tel. (08 00) 249-999 (free of charge)
or (022) 26 23-20 99
www.visitbuzios.com.br

GETTING THERE
Bus station
Estrada da Usina Velha 444
Tel. (022) 26 23-20 50

BOAT TRIPS
On offer are sailing trips, taking
2.5hours, that stop at the beaches of
João Fernandes, Tartaruga and in
front of Ilha Feia island. Boats leave
from the central pier on Praia do
Canto.
For more information:
Interbúzios: tel. (022) 26 23-64 54
Queen Lory: tel. (022) 26 23-11 79
Lady Gabi: tel. (022) 26 23-23 12

WHERE TO EAT
▶ Expensive
Satyricon
Av José Bento Ribeiro Dantas 500
Praia da Armação
Tel. (022) 26 23-15 95
Exclusive Italian restaurant with
Mediterranean-inspired cuisine and
excellent fish dishes

▶ Moderate
Estáncia Don Juan
Rua das Pedras 178
Tel. (022) 26 23-21 69
House speciality: grill and meat
dishes. Tuesday nights tango shows.
Reservation recommended.

▶ Inexpensive
Bar dos Pescadores
Associação dos Pescadores de Man-
guinhos, 3km/1.8 miles out of town,
on the Estrada da Usina next to
Búzios hospital, right on the seafront
Tel. (022) 26 23-74 37
Nowhere in Búzios serves fresher fish.

WHERE TO STAY
▶ Luxury
Galápagos Inn
Praia João Fernandinho
João Ferandez, 2 km/1.2 miles out of
town
Tel. (022) 26 23-61 61
www.galapagos.com.br
This complex has 37 apartments with
verandas. Bloco 3 has the best views.

Vila Boa Vida
Ferradura
Rua Q, Lote 12
Tel. (022) 26 23-67 67
www.vilaboavida.com.br
German-run hotel with splendid
views over the horseshoe-shaped bay
of Praia da Ferradura.

▶ Mid-range
Pousada João Fernandes
Rua João Fernandes 100
2km/1.2 miles outside the city centre
of Armação dos Búzios
Tel. (022) 26 23-22 99
www.pousadajoaofernandes.com.br
Pousada with 20 rooms, parking,
restaurant, swimming pool and sauna

Pousada San Francisco
Rua 9, Quadra B, Lote 44
João Fernandes
Around 2km/1.2 miles outside Ar-
mação
dos Búzios
Tel. (022) 26 23-63 17
www.sanfrancisco.com.br
Pousada with 15 rooms, parking, bar
and swimming pool

gratitude for the rescue of a slave ship in distress – rises on an elevation of the **Praia dos Ossos**. The Praia dos Ossos probably owes its name – Beach of the Bones – to a 16th-century massacre, where Goicataz Indians were incited by the Portuguese to kill the Tupinambá.

★ ★
Beaches around town

North of this small touristic town lies a string of beaches starting at Azeda (1.3km/0.8 miles from Armação dos Búzios), Azedinha, João Fernandez (2km/1.2 miles) and João Fernandinho, and to the west Praia do Criminoso and Praia Brava (2km/1.2 miles). On the Ilha Rasa, the beaches of Lua and Ancora are recommended. The crossing to the island from Porto Búzios, reached via the street leading to Baía Formosa, takes about 15 min. Some of the local hotels offer sailing yachts and motor boats for hire.

Most beaches south of Armação dos Búzios are located in **Búzios Bay and Manguinhos Bay**. Amongst the most beautiful swimming beaches are Forno, Foca, Tartaruga, Ferradura, Manguinhos and Baía Formosa. The fairly light swell of the first three beaches makes them ideally suited for swimming, whilst the near-circular Ferradura Bay is popular with both sailors and divers.

Cabo Frio

The town of Cabo Frio (pop 127,000) was founded in 1615 on the eastern end of the Lagoon of Araruama. This stretch of coast has been known since the discovery of the continent; in 1503, **Amerigo Vespucci** had a small fort built near Cabo Frio, and in 1504 production of pau brasil, the dyewood which lent Brazil its name, started here. Its historic centre still preserves numerous colonial buildings, and whilst the town is only 24km/15 miles from Armação dos Búzios and 163km/100 miles from Rio, it hardly ever seems overrun with tourists. Although with its fine sandy beaches, dunes and various offshore islands, the town today counts amongst the most-visited beach resorts in Brazil.

!
Baedeker TIP

The coast from above

The Guia hill, topped by the Nossa Senhora da Guia chapel, dating from 1740, can be reached on foot by parking the car at Largo Santo Antônio and walking from here. The reward for all the effort is a far-reaching panoramic view of Cabo Frio and the surrounding coast.

Convento e Igreja NS dos Anjos
🕐

The Franciscan monastery of Nossa Senhora dos Anjos was built between 1686 and 1696 on the Largo Santo Antônio. The monastery church houses the **Museu de Arte Religiosa e Tradicional**. The collection consists of sacred artworks from the Baroque era. Opening times: Wed–Fri 2–8pm, Sat/Sun 4–8pm.

★
Forte São Mateus

Dominating the coast, the Forte São Mateus is one of the landmarks of Cabo Frio. It was built in 1616/17 under the supervision of the fa-

The white-washed Forte São Mateus is considered a symbol of Cabo Frio.

mous military engineer **Francisco de Frias da Mesquita**, who also designed the coastal fortresses of Forte do Mar in Salvador, Forte dos Reis Magos in Natal and the first drafts for the abbey of Mosteiro de São Bento in Rio de Janeiro.

Praia do Forte with its fine sand is near the centre of Cabo Frio; from here, visitors can hire kayaks or take a trip on a schooner. Nudists have a refuge at Praia Brava, which is difficult to access. North of the town stretch the beaches of Praia das Conchas (2.5km/1.5 miles from the town centre) and do Peró (6km/3.5 miles). To the south, on the road leading to Arraial do Cabo, lie the swimming beach and high dunes of Praia das Dunas (2km/1.2 miles). Its largest dune is known as **Dama Branca** (White Lady). Praia do Foguete is considered Cabo Frio's most beautiful beach.

Beaches

Arraial do Cabo

Arraial do Cabo (24,000) lies 14km/8.5 miles south of Cabo Frio. In 1503, Amerigo Vespucci had a fort erected here. Today, the main attractions of this small town are its beautiful beaches, sand dunes and islets.

Ilha do Cabo Frio On the city beach of Praia dos Anjos, the 16th-century Nossa Senhora dos Remédios church and the museum of the Brazilian Navy's Institute of Oceanography (Museu Oceanográfico) are worth a visit,
whilst from the nearby harbour master's office (Capitania dos Por-
tos), boats leave for Cabo Frio island off the coast, with the **Gruta
Azul**, a 15m/50-ft lagoon with shimmering blue water – the Brazilian counterpart to Capri's Blue Lagoon. Similarly enchanting, if a
bit smaller, is the **Gruta do Ora-tório**.

! **Baedeker TIP**

Calling all divers!

The water temperatures off Arraial do Cabo are relatively low, giving this section of the Atlantic Ocean the clearest water – ideal for scuba divers. The best dive sites are Pedra Vermelha (Red Stone), Ponta d'Água and the wreck of the *Teixeirinha*. Equipment and wetsuits may be hired from: Arraial Sub (Tel. 26 22-19 45), Deep Trip (26 22-18 00) and Sandmar (26 22-13 56).

Around Arraial do Cabo, beach lovers can choose between the beautiful **Praia do Forno** with the ruins of Fortaleza do Marisco, a
somewhat inaccessible bay with the Praia do Pontal do Atalaia, and
the tiny Prainha beach. In the west, towards the coastal lagoon of
Araruama, lie the heavily duned and very popular beaches of Praia
Grande and Restinga da Massambaba.

✶✶ Belém

Sa 46

State: Pará (PA)   **Population:** 1.2 million
Altitude: 11m/36ft

**Alongside Manaus, Belém do Pará is the most important metropo-
lis in the Amazon basin and at the same time the world's largest
city in the immediate vicinity of the Equator. Belém, situated on
the Baía de Marajó, the river mouth of both the Rio Tocantins and
Rio do Pará, is the capital of Pará state.**

The town was founded in 1616 as a fortified river port, soon after
the French were chased out of São Luís. The defensive settlement
was intended to block, or at least make more difficult, any foreign
invasion in the north of Portuguese America. Over time, Belém
turned into a commercial hub and important port of departure for
caoutchouc (India rubber) and tropical hardwood. In 1751, Belém
became capital of Grão-Pará state, which comprised Maranhão and
the entire Brazilian north. Until the end of the caoutchouc boom the
town was very wealthy, and the **buildings from colonial times** that
remain give an idea of the former splendour of Belém. The architectural styles range from the colonial baroque of the Italian Antônio
Giuseppe Landí via rococo to classicism.

▶ VISITING BELÉM

INFORMATION

Solar da Beira
At the Ver-o-Peso market
Tel. (091) 32 12-84 84

Paratur
Inside the airport terminal
Tel. (091) 32 10-63 30 and
32 57-48 60
www.belem.pa.gov.br

GETTING THERE

Airport
Aeroporto Internacional Val de Cans
Tel. (091) 32 10-60 39

Bus station
Praça do Operário
Tel. (091) 32 66-26 25

EVENTS

Círio de Nazaré
Every year, on the second weekend of October, this procession brings a million pilgrims to the town. On the Saturday one week before the Círio, a boat procession honours the Virgem de Nazaré, the patron saint of mariners. On the following Saturday, tens of thousands of people accompany the statue of the Virgin from the Basilica de Nazaré to the Catedral da Sé. On the Sunday, the area around the basilica turns into a huge funfair. During the Círio candle festival most hotels in Belém are booked up, so early booking is advised.

Feira do Açaí
On the quays below the Forte do Castelo, the Feira do Açaí takes place – a market which in the early hours of the morning takes delivery of, amongst other things, the fruits of the local açaí palm, which are used in ice cream or soft drinks.

WHERE TO EAT

▶ Expensive

① Capone
Estação das Docas do Pará
Boulevard Castilhos França
Tel. (091) 32 12-55 66
Italian restaurant with terrace and air-conditioned bar

② Hatobá
Estação das Docas do Pará
Boulevard Castilhos França
Tel. (091) 32 12-31 43
Japanese restaurant with terrace

③ Lá em Casa
Av Governador José Malcher 247
Nazaré district
Tel. (091) 32 23-12 12
Excellent regional cuisine. When it rains, the transparent roof covers the inner courtyard.

WHERE TO STAY

▶ Luxury

① Hilton Belém
Avenida Presidente Vargas 882
Praça da República
Tel. (091) 40 06-70 00
www.hilton.com
Best hotel in town

▶ Mid-range

② Equatorial Palace
Avenida Braz de Aguiar 612
Nazaré district
Tel. (091) 31 81-60 00
www.equatorialhotel.com.br
Business hotel with 126 rooms

▶ Budget

③ Itaoca Belém
Avenida Presidente Vargas 132
Tel. (091) 32 41-34 34
www.pousadadosguaras.com.br
36 rooms in a central location

Belém Map

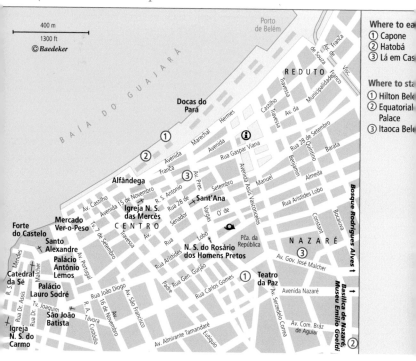

400 m
1300 ft
© Baedeker

Porto de Belém

Where to ea
① Capone
② Hatobá
③ Lá em Cas

Where to sta
① Hilton Bele
② Equatorial Palace
③ Itaoca Bele

REDUTO

BAIA DO GUAJARÁ

Docas do Pará

Alfândega

Mercado Ver-o-Peso

CENTRO

Forte do Castelo

Santo Alexandre

Palácio Antônio Lemos

Catedral da Sé

Palácio Lauro Sodré

São João Batista

Igreja N. S. do Carmo

Igreja N. S. das Mercês

Sant'Ana

N. S. do Rosário dos Homens Pretos

Pça. da República

NAZARÉ

Teatro da Paz

Bosque Rodrigues Alves

Basílica de Nazaré, Museu Emilio Goeldi

Port area

Ver-o-Peso

The first thing visitors coming ashore at the port of Belém see on the quay is probably the lively Ver-o-Peso market (literally »check the weight«), where indigenous products, spices, plant oils, medicinal herbs and fresh fish, but also mysterious Umbanda amulets and various souvenirs are for sale. The **market hall**, crowned by small iron towers, was imported in the 19th century from England in individual parts and is one of the landmarks of Belém; the covered meat market opposite rests on fine cast-iron supports. Unfortunately, the area around Ver-o-Peso is a favourite hunting ground for gangs of young thieves.

Forte do Castelo

Southwest of the Ver-o-Peso market, where the Rio Guamá river runs into the Baía de Guajará, rises the Forte do Castelo fortress, erected in 1616 to protect the port. The fort, built using beaten clay and gravel, formed the core of the original settlement and has the nickname **Forte do Presépio de Belém** (Fort of the Bethlehem Nativity). The mighty stone walls that visitors see today are much more recent, built in 1878 as part of the reconstruction of the fort, heavily fought over during the Cabanagem Rebellion (1835/36).

✳ Old Town

The steeply rising Ladeira do Castelo, connecting the fort with the Old Town, is the oldest street in Belém and is lined by houses panelled with Portuguese azulejo tiles and picturesque, weather-beaten churches. Many buildings in the Old Town date from the mid-18th century, when Belém attracted artists from various European countries.

✳
Ladeira do Castelo

The best example of the tropical Baroque style is provided by the large **Jesuit college** immediately south of the fort, begun, along with the Santo Alexandre church, in the late 17th century,. The church, consisting of only one nave with side chapels, conforms to the basic layout of Jesuit churches and is – after the Catedral Basílica in Salvador – the largest preserved building of this once so important religious order. The lavishly decorated pulpits are attributed to the Aus-

✳
Santo Alexandre

Colonial architecture in Belém Old Town

Many passengers, little space: luxury is rare on the riverboats plying the Amazon.

WATERWAY TO THE WEST

Together with its tributaries, the Amazon forms by far the largest river system on the planet. Visitors can get the best idea of the gigantic scale of this unique tropical waterway, the lush vegetation covering its banks and the conditions of life along the mighty jungle river from aboard a riverboat or steamer.

The three large headwaters of the Amazon – Rio Huallaga, Rio Marañón and Rio Ucayali – contribute muddy brown water from the Andes, which on its way to its Atlantic outlet covers a distance of over 6,500km/4,040 miles. With the **Ilha de Marajó**, the Amazon delta fits in a river island the size of the Netherlands. These days, the five to six-day trip upriver to the previously thriving India rubber metropolis of Manaus, is made even by large freight ships.

Starting point: Belém

East of Manaus, the Amazon is, in most places, over 5km/3 miles wide. Bearing this in mind, any boat trip should be taken upriver, as only vessels heading in that direction avoid the strong currents in the middle of the river and stay, of necessity, closer to the banks. An ideal starting point is the port city of Belém. However, in recent years, the passenger catamarans operated by the **ENASA** state-owned shipping company have been running at a loss on the stretch of river between Belém and Manaus; currently, this company only runs a modest ferry service between Belém and the Ilha de Marajó. For reservations, call (091) 32-57-68 68.

Small shipping companies

Small and medium-sized operations handle the lion's share of the cargo and passenger trade – for instance, the Marques Pinto Navegação Ltda shipping company, Av Bernardo Sagāo 3012, Belém, tel. (091) 32 72-38 47, fax (091) 32 72-38 47. Their boats operate several times a month from Belém via Santarém to Manaus using,

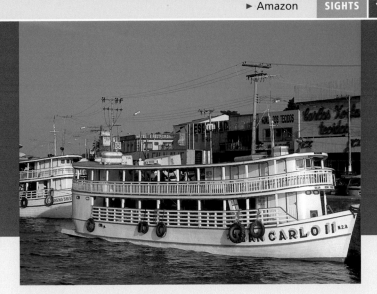

for instance, the modern *Nélio Corrêaô*, which is designed to take over 300 passengers and has climatized cabins. The boat leaves every other week on a Tuesday evening. The *Rodrigues Alves*, owned by the Alves e Rodrigues Ltda shipping company, Av Maréchal Hermes, Cia. Docas do Pará, Portão 15, Belém, tel. (091) 32 41-75 08 and 32 12-24 25, fax (091) 32 12-24 24, also regularly heads towards Santarém and is able to transport up to 340 passengers in hammocks and cabins. However, travellers should always get the latest up-to-date information on all boats waiting at berth and their expected departure times. The Macamazônia agency, Boulevard Castilho França 730, Belém, tel. (091) 30 86-01 07, fax 32 22-56 04, sells tickets for all the steamers commuting betwen Belém, Macapá, Santarém and Manaus.

Gaiolas

For an Amazon trip aboard the gaiolas (bird cage) boats, travellers should stock up in Belém with hammocks and ropes. The most interesting stretches are around Breves and Óbidos. Near Breves, the boats pass through a narrow tidal canal, and at **Óbidos** the Amazon narrows again. Here, only 2.5km/1.5 miles separate the two river banks, and compared to the rest of this stretch, it is possible to get a fairly good idea of the flora and fauna of the Amazon. Aboard the river steamers, travellers should however be prepared for very basic food indeed and toilets that may or may not work. It is also advisable to carry a private supply of drinking water. And after the shortest time spent on the river, any kind of games – dominoes, cards or a chess set – will provide an extremely welcome distraction. In any case, the occasionally monotone journey will be regularly disrupted by the afternoon showers. When the large drops drum on the boat, colouring the planks dark, the boat suddenly springs to hectic life, in an attempt to shelter the intermediate decks against the downpour coming in at diagonal angles.

trian priest **Father Johannes Xaver Traer**, a painter and sculptor from Tyrol, who worked in the college from 1723 onwards. Next to the Jesuit college, the **Archbishop's Palace** is not open to visitors, but the collection of the attached **Museu de Arte Sacra** gives at least some idea of the Jesuit monastery's former glory. Opening times: Tue – Fri 1 – 6pm, Sat/Sun 9am – 1pm.

Catedral da Sé

The foundation stone of the Cathedral of Belém, opposite the Jesuit college on Praça Frei Caetano Brandão, was laid in 1748 on the order of **Dom João V of Portugal**; the works were only completed in 1771. The belltowers and gables in the neoclassical style were designed by Antônio Giuseppe Landí (1708 – 1790), an architect from Bologna, who settled in Belém in 1753. Landí also designed the reredos (altarpiece) on the original altar. The reredos visitors see today was specially made in Rome and given by Pope Pius XI (1922 – 1939). It features a painting with the figure of the Madonna Full of Grace created by the Lisbon painter Pedro Alexandrino de Carvalho (1730 – 1810).

The Catedral da Sé has weathered many storms already.

The neoclassical Teatro da Paz (Theatre of Peace), inaugurated in 1874 during the rubber boom in the Amazon area, seats 1,100 people. The curtain, with an **allegory of the Republic**, was made in Paris. The theatre's entrance, supported by pillars, opens onto the Avenida da Paz on the central Praça da República. In the late 19th and early 20th centuries, this imposing edifice was the scene of important performances; stars such as the Russian prima ballerina Anna Pavlowa trod the boards here. Today, the theatre is only rarely used for its original purpose. Guided tours: Tue – Sat by appointment; tel. (091) 32 24-73 55.

✶ ✶
Teatro da Paz

The Basílica de Nossa Senhora de Nazaré (Our Lady of Nazareth), east of the Praça da República on the Praça Justo Chermont and designed in 1909 following the example of the Roman San Paolo fuori le mura church, has colourful stained-glass windows and is lined with gold and marble from Carrara. Next to the basilica, the **Museu do Círio** gives an insight into the long tradition of the Círio de Nazaré (Nazareth Taper). The basilica and its surrounding Praça Justo Chermont square, provide the starting point of the famous Círio de Nazaré candlelit procession.

✶
Basílica de Nazaré

The park and exhibits of the Museu Paraense Emílio Goeldi at 376 Avenida Magalhães Barata, illustrates the flora and fauna of the Amazon area. This is also the site of **archaeological and ethnographic exhibitions**, botanical and zoological collections, and a rainforest park with indigenous amphibians, freshwater fish, mammals and birds. Opening times: Tue – Sun 9am – 11.30am and 2 – 5pm, Fri 9 – 11.30am, Sat/Sun 9am – 5pm.

✶
Museu Emílio Goeldi

The Public Market of São Bráz, built in 1616 to the east of the Museu Emílio Goeldi on the Praça Lauro Sodré is one of the oldest and most impressive colonial buildings in Belém. The former market hall has been refurbished several times – and defaced by graffitti an equal number of times– and houses a cultural centre, as well as a restaurant.

Mercado Público de São Bráz

The Bosque Rodrigues Alves city park on Avenida Almirante Barroso leading northeast from the centre to the Belém-Brasília trunk road is one of the oldest botanical gardens in Brazil. Also containing a mini zoo and a turtle enclosure, the gardens serve as a recreational area – as a consequence, they get fairly overrun with visitors at weekends.

Bosque Rodrigues Alves

Around Belém

In the village of Icoaraci, 23km/14.5 miles north of Belém on the Cruzeiro river beach in Marajó Bay, many artisans live and work, recreating the famous **Marajoara ceramics** once made by the indige-

Icoaraci

A scene from the backcountry of Pará state

nous Indian population. From Icoaraci, visitors can take a boat across to the **Ilha do Outeiro** with its forests and river beaches; the latter, however, are contaminated by industrial waste, chemicals and sewage.

Ilha do Mosqueiro

The river island of Mosqueiro, 86km/53 miles north of Belém, has numerous freshwater beaches popular with weekend visitors, all in all 17km/11 miles long. Some of the best bays for swimming are **Baía do Sol, Ariramba, die Praia do Chapéu Virado and Praia Grande**. However, during the school holidays (July and the second half of December) and at weekends, the beaches are usually overrun with people and littered accordingly; also, at such times, a long line of traffic often blocks the access roads.

✳ ✳ Ilha de Marajó

Occupying just under 50,000 sq km/19,300 sq miles – a surface area larger than the Netherlands – the Ilha de Marajó, surrounded by the waters of the Amazon, the Tapajó and the Atlantic Ocean, is one of the largest river islands in the world. During the dry season, the island is characterized by two completely different types of landscape: in the east, a plain stretching for about 23,000 sq km/8,880 sq miles is covered by shrubs and grass, whilst the lower-lying remainder of the island is taken up by forests. From January to June, i.e. in the rainy season, the forested areas are flooded by the Amazon, turning them into an extensive swamp – ideal **pasture for large herds of water buffalo**. Marajó Island is also home to caymans, sloths, monkeys, capybaras, deer, turtles and a variety of species of snakes and birds, not to mention the countless species of fish, such as the pirarucus and the tucunarés – freshwater fish belonging to the cichlid family – as well as tambaquis and the feared piranhas. To get to Marajó, either take a plane (air taxi from Belém to Soure), a boat (6hr from Belém) or a bus from Belém, crossing Marajó Bay by ferry and carrying on to Salvaterra, connecting with a ferry to Soure.

Soure

The 250,000 inhabitants of Marajó Island are spread across seven municipalities, the most important town being Soure. Situated on Marajó Bay, Soure has several river beaches. Wooden handcarts drawn by buffaloes are an integral feature of the town. Hotels and fazendas with rooms offer trips into the surrounding area, as well as performances of carimbó and landú, two indigenous dances that should not be missed. Several fazendas where buffaloes are bred rent out rooms to visitors. They may be reached by air taxi from Soure or directly from Belém. Hunting is prohibited, but the trip is worth doing for the photo safaris and the fishing in the Igarapés and lakes alone.

Beaches on the Ilha de Marajó

For good swimming, try the beach of Araruna, just under 2km/1.2 miles outside Soure, as well as the Pesqueiro and Caju Una beaches, 13km/8 miles and 15km/9 miles outside town respectively. In the northwest of the Ilha de Marajó lies the sandy beach of Chaves, 6km/3.5 miles long and lined by trees, some of which are 100 years old. **Praia Joanes** is considered the most beautiful river beach on Marajó Island. It is a six-hour boat trip via Soure, but in the time of the school holidays it does get very busy.

Marajoara ceramics

Around 2,500 years ago, an Indian culture flourished on Marajó Island, whose elegant ceramics decorated with geometric patterns became famous outside Brazil too. The oldest preserved pieces were made in around 980 BC, the most recent in the 17th century. Examples of Marajoara ceramics are on display at Belém's Emílio Goeldi Museum. According to numerous experts, the birth and flowering of this highly developed craft can be ascribed to the cultural influence of the Incas or other Andean peoples. However, finds of burial urns in the shape of humans in Amapá state, north of the Ilha de Marajó and assigned to the Indian people of the **Maracá** – alongside further archeological finds illustrating the high cultural level of

! Baedeker TIP

Short trips to Ilha de Marajó

Three-day excursions from Belém to Ilha de Marajó are organized by Iara Turismo, Rua Jerônimo Pimental 82, Umarizal, Belém, Tel. (091) 4006-3850, Fax (091) 4006-3851, www.iaraturismo.com.br.

the Indian peoples on the Amazon – support the thesis that it was not the Andean peoples that influenced the culture of the Amazon Indians, but rather the other way round: that the culture of the Andean peoples might have its origin in the culture of the rainforest-dwelling Indians.

✳ Belo Horizonte

Sd 55

State: Minas Gerais (MG)
Altitude: 858m/2,815ft

Population: 2.2 million

Belo Horizonte, capital of Minas Gerais, is surrounded by the hills of the Serra do Curral and was planned using a grid layout rather like a chess-board, for which the urban planners took their inspiration from the US capital Washington DC.

The original plans for Brazil's first artificially created city predicted that around 200,000 people would be living here after the first 100 years. Belo Horizonte has long since become a huge conglomeration comprising 20 cities, with a population surpassing all predictions. Tourists usually use Belo Horizonte only as a springboard for visiting the historic baroque towns of Minas Gerais.

What to see in Belo Horizonte

✳ Palácio das Artes

On the southwestern edge of the central city park (Parque Municipal), at 1537 Avenida Afonso Pena, rises the Palácio das Artes (»Palace of the Arts«), housing a cinema, a theatre, a library, conference rooms, an art gallery and the Minas Gerais arts and crafts centre. The latter sells rustic fabrics and crafts made from soapstone, wood, clay, pewter, silver and other materials.

Museu Mineiro

Housed in the former Senate building, the Museu Mineiro – incorporating the **Minas Gerais art museum** – is situated at 342 Avenida João Pinheiro, which leads from the Parque Municipal to Praça da Liberdade. Opening times: Tue – Fri 10am – 5pm, Sat/Sun to 4pm.

Praça da Liberdade

Lined by the Palácio do Governo (government palace) and the Biblioteca Pública (municipal library), as well as numerous palm trees, the Praça da Liberdade (Freedom Square) in the city centre was designed to be the seat of the state administration. There are regular markets selling crafts, flowers, antiques and food.

✳ Museu Histórico Abílio Barreto

West of Praça da Liberdade, the Abílio Barreto Historical Museum at 202 Avenida Prudente de Morais, shows a rich **photographic docu-**

▶ VISITING BELO HORIZONTE

INFORMATION

Belotur
Aeroporto da Pampulha
Tel. (031) 32 77-74 00
Aeroporto de Tancredo Neves
Tel. (031) 36 89-25 57
www.belotur.com.br

Secretaria de Turismo
Praça Rio Branco
Tel. (031) 32 72-85 67
www.pbh.gov.br

GETTING THERE

Airport
Aeroporto International Tancredo
Neves, Confins
Tel. (031) 36 89-27 00
Aeroporto de Pampulha
Praça Bagatelle 204
Tel. (031) 34 90-20 01

Bus station
Praça Rio Branco
Tel. (031) 32 71-30 00

WHERE TO EAT

▶ Expensive
① *Taste Vin*
Rua Curitiba 2105
Lourdes district
Tel. (031) 32 92-54 23
Prestigious French restaurant with
outstanding wine list

▶ Moderate
② *Haus München*
Rua Juiz de Fora
Agostinho district
Tel. (031) 32 91-69 00
German cuisine.

▶ Inexpensive
③ *Sushi Thai*
Rua Grão-Mogol 564 Carmo district
Tel. (031) 32 81-65 69

Good Asian restaurant. All credit
cards accepted.

Baedeker recommendation

▶ Inexpensive
④ *Vecchio Sogno*
Rua Martim de Carvalho 75
Santo Agostinho district
Tel. (031) 32 92-52 51
First-class restaurant with French-influ-
enced cuisine. Seafood, meat and pasta are
turned into imaginative dishes.

WHERE TO STAY

▶ Mid-range
① *Mercure*
Avenida do Contorno 7315
Santo Antônio district
Tel. (031) 32 98-41 00
www.accorhotels.com.br
Business hotel, opened in 2001, with
370 rooms and a fine swimming pool

② *Royal Savassi*
Rua Alagoas 699
Funcionários district
Tel. (031) 32 47-69 99
and (08 00) 704-00 22
www.royaltowers.com.br
This hotel in an excellent location is
the flagship of the Savassi chain of
hotels, with 84 generously appointed
rooms, bar, restaurant, sauna and
gym.

▶ Budget
③ *Savassi*
Rua Sergipe 893
Funcionários district
Tel. (031) 32 61-32 66
85 rooms in a central location. Good
standard.

mentation of the development of the city over the course of the 20th century, with old and modern views of Belo Horizonte. The museum is housed in the Fazenda do Leitão's former manor house, built in 1883. Opening times: Tue – Sun 10am – 5pm.

Pampulha district · Cidade Universitária

The north of Belo Horizonte is home to the Cidade Universitária university district and the Pampulha district, where Brazilian star architect **Oscar Niemeyer** realized some of his avant-garde construction projects. Pampulha, one of Belo Horizonte's most important recreation areas, is connected with the city centre by the Avenidas 21 de Abril, Presidente Carlos Luz and Presidente Antônio Carlos.

Museu de Arte da Pampulha
On Avenida Otacílio Negrão de Lima, touching the reservoir of Pampulha and alongside the zoo, two famous buildings by Oscar Niemeyer can be found: the Museum for Modern Art and the São Francisco de Assis church. The museum, originally built as a casino in 1940, houses paintings, sculptures, engravings, ceramics and video films by various artists, amongst them Di Cavalcanti, Volpi and Portinari. Opening times: Tue – Sun 9am – 7pm.

São Francisco de Assis
The church, built in 1942/43, holds the 14 Stations of the Cross and azulejo tiles by Candido Portinari. Initially, the shape of the roof, reminiscent of a parabola, and the unusual belltower, resembling a stake tapering towards the bottom, were so disliked by the clergy that years had to pass – allowing Niemeyer to achieve worldwide fame as the architect of Brasília – before the decision was taken to consecrate the church dedicated to St Francis after all.

Around Belo Horizonte

Parque das Mangabeiras
The extensive Mangabeiras Park – situated 6km/3.5 miles outside the town in the Serra do Curral, where the headstreams of the Rio das Velhas come together – includes a piece of primitive forest, a lake, several springs, an arena and an amphitheatre. Look on the immediate left behind the two entrance gates (Avenida Anel da Serra and Avenida Bandeirantes) for the point of departure for a round trip through the park by bus. The **Mirante da Mata** viewpoint, a 20-minute walk from the entrance, gives a fine view of Belo Horizonte.

Santa Luzia
The thermal spa town of Santa Luzia (pop 186,000) is situated 26km/16 miles northeast of Belo Horizonte and has preserved its historic town centre. This is where visitors can find the **Fonte dos Camelos** bubbling away – an alkaline, iron-rich spring. The most interesting of the colonial buildings are the Igreja Nossa Senhora do Rosário (Rosary Church; 1755) and the parish church of Matriz Santuário de Santa Luzia (1744 – 1778), as well as the palaces of Solar

Belo Horizonte Map

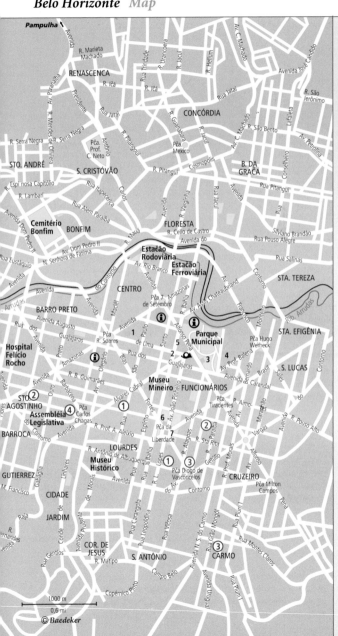

Where to eat
1. Taste Vin
2. Haus München
3. Sushi Thai
4. Veccio Sogno

Where to stay
1. Mercure
2. Royal Savassi
3. Savassi

1. Mercado Central
2. Museu de Mineralogia
3. Palácio das Artes
4. Hospital
5. Prefeitura
6. Biblioteka Pública
7. Palácio do Governo

© Baedeker

Teixeira da Costa (1745) and Solar da Baronesa (now the city hall), which all line the Rua Direita. The Convento de Macaúbas convent (1714–1733) is 14km/8.5 miles outside town on the road leading to Jaboticatubas.

Caeté

Matriz de NS do Bom Sucesso

Caeté, 60km/37 miles east of Belo Horizonte, was founded in 1713 as Vila Nova da Rainha. The town retains several historic buildings and churches from the 18th century. Construction of the Nossa Senhora do Bom Sucesso main church was started in 1757 as one of the first churches in Minas Gerais to use quarrystone. The wooden carvings inside the church were made between 1758 and 1765 under the supervision of **José Coelho de Noronha**, one of the masters who taught Antônio Francisco Lisboa, better known as Aleijadinho (»little cripple«). The parish church stands on the Praça João Pinheiro, with the Pelourinho (pillory), a well dating from 1800 (Chafariz da Matriz) and the public library all housed in the former city hall (1772).

Solar do Tinoco

The Solar do Tinoco mansion used to be the residence of two former governors of Minas Gerais: João Pinheiro da Silva and his son Israel Pinheiro. The house, redesigned as a museum, shows furniture, photos and documents (Praça Paulo Pinheiro da Silva).

Rio Vermelho

Rio Vermelho, 9km/5.5 miles outside Caeté, was the scene of a battle in the War of the Emboabas (1708–1709) between the Portuguese on one side, and on the other the bandeirantes from São Paulo, plus numerous other adventurers flocking from other parts of Brazil to the **»region of the mines«**. At that time, »emboabas« was the name given to all gold prospectors not from São Paulo, amongst them many escaped slaves of African origin. The egalitarian force of the gold rush in Minas Gerais overthrew Brazil's traditional hierarchy, many years before the official abolishment of slavery in 1888.

Santa Bárbara · Parque Natural do Caraça

Matriz Santo Antônio

The historic town of Santa Bárbara (pop 25,000) is situated about 110km/68 miles east of Belo Horizonte. The town's parish church of Santo Antônio, built in 1724 on Praça Cleves de Faraia, has paintings by Manuel Rebelo e Sousa from around 1752. At the beginning of the 19th century, **Manuel da Costa Athayde** executed one of his most famous paintings on the ceiling of the chancel chapel, a representation of the Ascension of Christ.

Matriz de São João Batista

The church of São João Batista, completed in 1764, is considered the first major project by Aleijadinho. Standing in the part of town called Barão de Cocais, on the Praça Alencar Peixoto, the church is, however, not usually open to visitors.

Just 14km/8.5 miles south of the small town of Santa Bárbara lies the village of Catas Altas, with 4,000 inhabitants in the Parque Natural do Caraça. This small village and its historic buildings share the magnificent nature reserve hugging the slopes of the Serra do Caraça with several waterfalls, lagoons and lakes. The centre is dominated by the parish church of NS Mãe dos Homens, built between 1876 and 1883 – its extensive library, French windows and large organ are particularly impressive.

Parque Natural do Caraça

On the plateau of the Caraça park in the municipality of the same name, 26km/16 miles from Santa Bárbara, stands the former Lazarist college and seminary. The institution's history began with the foundation of the **Nossa Senhora dos Homens** sanctuary, erected between 1770 and 1774 by a Franciscan monk by the name of Lourenço. In 1819, it was given over to the congregation of the Lazarists; two years later followed the completion of the college, one of the first in the whole of Brazil, incidentally, to offer a complete grammar school cycle. In the 19th century, even the Brazilian Emperor Dom Pedro I stayed in the prestigious college. It was closed only when, in 1968, an entire wing of the building burned to the ground. The college consisted of several wings and the church, erected in 1880 as the first neogothic church in Brazil, with twelve granite pillars, twelve side altars made from Minas marble, and French stained-glass windows. The catacombs below hold the tombs of the monks. Today, after extensive renovation works, the natural stone and mortar blend in with modern materials such as reinforced concrete and aluminium – with the old walls reflecting in the frosted glass of the new parts of the building. Several wings of the Colégio do Caraça have been turned into the attractive Hospedaria do Caraça hotel. Tel. (031) 38 37-26 98.

★
Colégio do Caraça

Lagoa Santa

Famous for its prehistoric sites, Lagoa Santa (pop 38,000), lies 42km/26 miles north of Belo Horizonte. Cave paintings, human skeletal remains and other traces of prehistoric people of the area – called **»Lagoa Santa Man«** – date back some 10,000 years.

13km/8 miles north of Lagoa Santa, on the road leading to Conceição do Mato Dentro, explore Lapinha Cave, 511m/1,676 ft long and 40m/131ft deep. Next to the cave, the **Museu Arqueológico de Lagoa Santa** documents the research on »Lagoa Santa Man«. Opening times: daily 9am – 4.30pm.

Rock paintings near Lagoa Santa

✳ **Parque Nacional da Serra do Cipó**

The Serra do Cipó National Park is situated in the Serra do Espinhaço mountain range, 72km/45 miles northeast of Lagoa Santa and
just 110km/68 miles from Belo Horizonte. In the park, numerous
canyons and caves with prehistoric rock paintings may be explored.
Highland steppe is the predominant terrain, with gallery forests and
mountain meadows adding to the varied aspect of the park's landscape. This is the best place for visitors to spot up to 60 different species of mammals, such as ocelots, otters, anteaters, maned wolves
and red deer as well as 150 bird species. The waterways of the São
Francisco and Rio Doce basin form fine beaches and waterfalls, such
as the **Cachoeira da Farofa** which plunges 80m/260ft, as well as the
waterfalls of Braúnas, Grande, Usina, Véu da Noiva and Cachoeira
do Congonhas.

Tourist
infrastructure
⏱
The Serra do Cipó National Park has several campsites and a simple
restaurant, as well as horse and bike rental. The best times to visit
are the months of March and November, when it rains least. Opening times: daily 8am – 5pm.

Blumenau · Itajaí Valley

Sa 59

State: Santa Catarina (SC)
Altitude: 21m/69ft

Population: 262,000

**This town, founded on 2 September 1850 by Hermann Otto Blume-
nau, was the first German settlement in the Itajaí Valley. To this
day, those 40 % of Blumenau's citizens who claim German descent
celebrate German folklore and traditions in a romantic alpine-
style, timber-framed setting.**

At the same time, the town has a fair amount of industry and is considered not only the economic and touristic focal point of the Itajaí
Valley, as well as of the whole northeast of Santa Catarina, but also
an important cultural centre: its chamber orchestra, founded in
1981, counts among the best in the country.

What to see in and around Blumenau

Museu da
Família Colonial
⏱
The Museu da Família Colonial at 78 Av Duque de Caxias is housed
in a timber-framed building once inhabited by the founder of the
town, Hermann Otto Blumenau (1819 – 1899). The museum exhibits
personal items that belonged to Blumenau, collections of books and
utensils used by the indigenous Indians. Opening times: Tue – Fri
8am – 5.30pm, Sat 9.00 – noon and 2 – 4.30pm, Sun 9.30am to noon.

▶ VISITING BLUMENAU • ITAJAÍ VALLEY

INFORMATION
Rua Quinze de Novembro 1050
Tel. (047) 33 26-69 31
www.blumenau.com.br

GETTING THERE
Bus station
Rua 2 de Setembro 1222
Tel. (047) 33 23-06 90

EVENTS
Oktoberfest
Blumenau's beer-fuelled Oktoberfest, adapted from the famous Munich model, has become one of the biggest mass events in southern Brazil. Starting on the first Friday in October, the town enters 18 days of exuberant party mode; visitors – their numbers breaking the one-million mark in 1992 for the first time – are entertained by traditional combos from Germany or the Itajaí Valley, as well as folkloric dances. During the lederhosen-heavy spectacle, visitors may also sample German food and drink and admire the passage of horse-drawn beer carts in the streets. Needless to say that rivers of beer are consumed during these folksy festivities.

WHERE TO EAT
▶ Moderate
Frohsinn
Rua Gertrud Sierich, Morro do Aipim
Access via Rua Itajaí
Tel. (047) 33 22-21 37
German specialities.

WHERE TO STAY
▶ Mid-range
Plaza Blumenau
Rua Sete de Setembro 818
Tel. (047) 32 31-70 00
www.plazahoteis.com.br
Best hotel in town, 131 spacious rooms, gym, pool and restaurant.

▶ Budget
Steinhausen
Rua Minas Gerais 53,
Tel. (047) 33 29-24 37
www.hotelsteinhausen.com.br
Simple hotel with pool

The natural history museum, established in a timber-framed house built in 1860, preserves geological and natural history finds, as well as precious stones from the region and the personal collection of the German natural scientist Fritz Müller (1821–1897), a pupil and collaborator of Charles Darwin who died in Blumenau. The museum can be found at 2195 Rua Itajaí. Opening times: Mon – Fri 8am to 6pm, Sat/Sun 8 – 11.30am and 2 – 5pm.

Museu de Ecológia Fritz Müller

🕐

Some 15km/9.5 miles from the centre of Blumenau town, discover the Spitzkopf nature reserve, with waterfalls, small rivers and a number of inviting hiking trails around the **Pico da Ponta Aguda** (936m/ 3,070ft).

Ecológico Spitzkopf

The small town of Pomerode (pop 22 000), founded by Pomeranian settlers 31km/19 miles northwest of Blumenau, is considered in the

★
Pomerode

Time seems to be standing still in this shed near Pomerode.

whole of Brazil as the archetype of a German town, thanks mainly to the many still preserved timber-framed houses. The overwhelming majority of the inhabitants of Pomerode are the descendants of German-speaking immigrants, holding on not just to their linguistic roots, but also to the customs and traditions of their ancestors. Have a look at the **Museu Pomerano** (Museum of Pomerania), 3 km/1.8 miles south of the town in the direction of Blumenau on the BR-418 federal road, which shows the tools used by the first settlers. Also worth a visit – for visitors looking for a beery party atmosphere – is the annual Festa Pomerana in January, with German and Brazilian music and dancing.

Boa Vista

State: Roraima (RR)
Altitude: 85m/279ft

Population: 200,000

Tourists use Boa Vista, the capital of Roraima state, most of all as a cheap stop-off on the way to Guyana and Venezuela.

On the continuation of the BR-174 connecting Manaus with Boa Vista, a bus can take travellers to Santa Elena de Uairén (Venezuela), and on the BR-401 to Guyana, as long as they have the relevant valid visas – these cannot be obtained at the border.

What to see in and around Boa Vista

The Museu de Roraima in Parque Anauá, on Avenida Eduardo Gomes, displays the weapons, clothing and crafts of Roraima's various indigenous groups.

Museu de Roraima

Access to the nature reserve – covering 92,000 ha/227,300 acres on Maracá Island, situated in the Rio Uraricoera river 100km/62 miles north of Boa Vista – is via the BR-174 federal road (in the direction of Aparecida). For a visit to the island, a permit has to be obtained from the IBAMA environment agency, tel. (095) 36 23-93 84 – hunting and fishing are prohibited. The indigenous fauna is rich in herons, red wolves and buffaloes. Visitors wanting to see the beach called **Boca do Inferno** (Mouth of Hell) with its dark, loamy sand, have to cross the Igarapé do Inferno (Channel of Hell) that divides the island in two. As the name suggests, this is not something to be undertaken lightly.

Ilha Maracá

The fort of São Joaquim, built in the 18th century at the point where the Tacutu and Uraricoera rivers become the Rio Branco, is today only ruins. Several agencies based in Boa Vista, 40km/25 miles to the southwest, offer day trips to the crumbling stronghold. These trips include a visit to the Fazenda São Marcos as well as a 2.5-hr boat trip to the fort.

São Joaquim

The Monte Roraima National Park occupies the extreme north of the Brazilian state, bordering Venezuela and Guyana. At its centre, the nature reserve has the table mountains (tepuís) of the Serra de Paracaíma, the largest part of which extends into the two bordering states. The **Monte Roraima** (2,875m/9,432ft) and **Monte Caburaí**

Parque Nacional Monte Roraima

▶ VISITING BOA VISTA

GETTING THERE

Airport
Aeroporto Internacional
Tel. (095) 36 23-04 04

Bus station
Avenida das Guianas 1627
Tel. (095) 36 23-22 33

WHERE TO EAT

▶ **Moderate**
Ver o Rio
Rua Floriano Peixoto 116
Tel. (095) 36 24-16 83

Speciality: freshwater fish. All credit cards accepted.

WHERE TO STAY

▶ **Budget**
Itamaraty Palace
Avenida Nossa Senhora da Consolata 1957
São Vicente
Tel. (095) 32 24-97 57
www.hotelitamaraty.com.br
Servicable hotel with 32 air-conditioned rooms, restaurant, bar and swimming pool

(1,456m/4,777ft) are the highest peaks in the national park. The area does not have any tourist infrastructure, but Roraima Adventures – Tel. (095) 32 24-16 68, www.roraima-brasil.com.br – offer tours there.

Bonito

Rg 56

State: Mato Grosso do Sul (MS)   **Population:** 15,500
Altitude: 315m/1,033ft

Bonito, in the southwest of Mato Grosso do Sul state is completely given over to ecotourism. While the place itself has no sights as such, it is a good base for numerous guided excursions into the surrounding area.

The clear rivers in the area are a mecca for anglers, while the multitude of caves makes it a paradise for anyone interested in the Brazilian »underworld«; however, these are only accessible for visits with a local guide who knows his way around. All access roads – only a few of them tarred – are in a bad state, making every journey to the widely scattered scenic attractions hard and time-consuming.

What to see around Bonito

Ilha do Padre, Aquário Natural

Situated in the Rio Formoso, the Ilha do Padre (Priest Island) with its waterfalls and good fishing, lies 12km/7.5 miles east of Bonito. After another 8km/5 miles, the area where Rio Mimoso runs into Rio Formoso has excellent fishing in crystal-clear water. Only 7km/4.5 miles outside Bonito, one of the sources of the **Rio Formoso** forms the Aquário Natural, with a rich marine life that snorkellers may experience at close quarters. Even from the outside, the clarity of the water allows an impressive view of the luxuriant underwater world. The Aquário Natural may only be visited accompanied by a local guide.

> ! *Baedeker* TIP
>
> **A dive into the underworld**
> The »Atlantic Sport« diving operator runs several diving bases in Brazil and also organizes dives in the underwater caves of Bonito. For more information, call the central telephone number: (081) 33 41-10 97.

★
Gruta do
Lago Azul

20km/12.5 miles southwest of Bonito, the 156m/512ft deep Gruta do Lago Azul cave features a lake of over 70m/230ft depth, giving the light coming in a blueish tinge. The cave may only be visited as part of a guided tour.

► VISITING BONITO

INFORMATION
Rua Cel. Pilad Rebuá 1780
Tel. (067) 32 55-18 50
www.portalbonito.com.br

GETTING THERE
Bus station
Rua Pedro Álvarez Cabral
Tel. (067) 32 55-16 06

WHERE TO EAT
► Budget
Cantinho de Peixe
Rua 31 de Março 1918
Tel. (067) 32 25-17 13
House special: freshwater fish.

WHERE TO STAY
► Mid-range
Zagaia Eco Resort
Rodovia Três Morros
in the direction of Campo dos Índios
Tel. (067) 32 55-12 80
www.zagaia.com.br
100 spacious rooms and suites, bar,
restaurant, pool

► Budget
Recanto dos Pássaros
Rua Marechal Rondon 549
Tel. (067) 32 55-10 48
www.hotelrecantodospassaros.com.br
Horses and mountain bikes for hire,
as well as 20 air-conditioned rooms

*The underwater world around Bonito is unique. Snorkellers and divers get their money's worth –
partly thanks to the clear water.*

★ ★ # Brasília

State: Distrito Federal   **Population:** 2.1 million
Altitude: 1,172m/3,845ft

Brasília rose out of nothing in little more than three years – between 1956 and 1960 – and was carved out of Goiás state, together with the surrounding 5,814 sq km/2,245 sq miles of Federal District. The artificially-created residential and government districts are situated on the 900–1,170m/2,950–3,840ft Planalto Central lowlands, surrounded by the extensive bush of the cerrado steppe.

Whilst Brasília was only built in the mid-20th century, first considerations on transferring the Brazilian capital to the interior of the country date back to the supporters of the 1789 Inconfidência Mineira resistance movement. Its leader, Tiradentes (►History p. 43) intended to counteract the neglect of the interests of Brazilians living far from the coast. Over the course of the 19th century, the idea of establishing a new Brazilian capital was never forgotten, even being enshrined in the constitution in 1891. In the end, it fell to president **Juscelino Kubitschek** to make history through the committed implementation of an idea carried by the will of the people. Brazil's third capital – after Salvador da Bahia and Rio de Janeiro – was inaugurated on 21 April 1960 – the 168th anniversary of the death of Tiradentes – with a good dose of national pathos.

Brasília's monumental avant-garde buildings seem to defy the laws of statics and, in the early 1960s, caused quite a stir worldwide. The city, intended to express its planners' visionary faith in the future, has long taken its place in architectural history. Accordingly, in 1987, »Brasília«, the fantasy-turned-reality, was given UNESCO World Heritage status. Brazil's new capital was intended to be progressive, car-friendly and built in an orderly way, with a lot of open spaces – a seat of government unburdened by industry and annoying exhaust fumes.

Visionary ideas

Beyond that, Brasília's ambitious concept of urban space included an **»egalitarian coexistence of poor and rich«**. However, from the beginning the city suffered from the lack of a viable strategy for coping with the mass immigration from the surrounding areas; today the contemporary reality of Brazil has long caught up with this idealistic project. Instead of the planned 500,000 inhabitants, over two million people now live here, and a belt of faceless suburbs is growing unchecked around the artificially created city, which was planted onto

← *At the Praça dos Três Poderes: with the buildings housing the country's executive, legislature and judiciary*

● VISITING BRASÍLIA

INFORMATION

Setur (Secretaria de Turismo)
Aeroporto International
Tel. (061) 34 29-76 35

Centro de Convenções
Eixo Monumental
Tel. (061) 33 25-57 30
www.dicasdebrasilia.com.br

GETTING THERE

Airport
Aeroporto Internacional
Tel. (061) 33 64-90 00

Bus station
Setor Noroeste, Cruzeiro
Tel. (061) 33 63-22 81

CITY TOURS

Due to the large distances involved,
an exploration of the city on foot is
near-impossible. Visitors may see
the sights by hire car or as part of
an organized tour. For more information, contact the Secretaria de
Turismo.

GOING OUT

Pubs with live music, clubs and trendy
restaurants cluster in the Centro
Comercial Gilberto Salomão on Lago
Sul. Going out is absolutely no problem here: Brasília is amongst the safest
cities in the country.

WHERE TO EAT

► Expensive

① **Babel**
Comércio Local Sul
Quadra 215
Bloco A, Loja 37
Tel. (061) 33 45-60 42 Upmarket
western cuisine, mixed with Far East-
ern and Brazilian ingredients

② **Villa Tevere**
Comércio Local Sul
Quadra 115, Bloco A, Loja 2
Tel. (061) 33 45-55 13
Excellent Italian restaurant – with
fountain and veranda – which also
makes use of local ingredients, such as
plantains and sweet potatoes

► Moderate

③ **Bragaço**
Comércio Local Sul
Quadra 405, Bloco D, Loja 36
Tel. (061) 34 43-80 98
One of the leading restaurants in town
for years, specializing in the cuisine of
Bahia

④ **Dom Francisco do Lago**
c/o Clube Asbac
Setor de Clubes Esportivos Sul
Trecho 2
Conjunto 31
Tel. (061) 32 26-21 25
International cuisine, right on the
Lagoa do Paranoá
reservoir

⑤ **Lagash**
Comércio Local Norte
Quadra 308/309, Bloco B, Loja 11/17
Tel. (061) 32 73-00 98
Good Arabic restaurant, with goat
dishes a speciality.

WHERE TO STAY

► Mid-range

① **SIA Park**
Setor de Indústia e Abastecimeto
Quadra 2-C, Bloco D
Tel. (061) 34 03-66 55
www.siapark.com.br
Particularly suited to guests wanting
an overnight stop on the outskirts of
Brasília

► **Budget**

② *Saan Park*
Setor de Armazenamento e
Abastecimeto Norte
Quadra 3, Bloco D
Tel. (061) 33 61-00 77
www.saanpark.com.br
72 rooms, parking spaces, restaurant
and sauna

③ *Brasília Park*
Setor de Indústia e Abastecimeto
Quadra 1-C
Bloco D
Tel. (061) 32 47-00 00
www.brasilia-park.com.br
Simple accommodation with 65
rooms and restaurant. All credit cards
accepted.

the plateau straight from the urban planners' drawing board. Within
Brazil, Brasília still seems out of place – not helped by the enormous
distances to the country's most important economic centres: Belo
Horizonte is 714km/444 miles from the capital, Rio de Janeiro
1,140km/708 miles, São Paulo 1,027km/638 miles, and Porto Alegre
as much as 2,111km/1,312 miles.

The urban core of the Brazilian capital is mainly dominated by the **Niemeyer**
architectural creations of two men. Lúcio Costa (1902 – 1998) was **and Costa**
responsible for the urban design concept and the **Superquadras**,
blocks of flats inspired by Le Corbusier and Bauhaus, while Brazil's
most famous architect, Oscar Niemeyer, designed the most striking
functional buildings, whose concrete defiance of the forces of gravity
still impresses today.

What to see in the city centre

Lúcio Costa's »Plano Piloto« gave Brasília's city centre a striking lay- **Axes of urban**
out, characterized by two main thoroughfares in the shape of a large **planning**
cross. The two central road axes are **Eixo Rodoviário** and **Eixo Monumental**. The sweeping Eixo Rodoviário north-south city motorway is
lined by blocks of flats grouped in sectors, whilst the Eixo Monumental, running from east to west, is lined by a phalanx of hotels,
ministries and government buildings.

Clustered around the **»Square of the Three Powers«** are the most **✶ ✶**
important buildings of the executive, legislative and judicial powers **Praça dos**
in the country. Amongst them are also some of the most significant **Três Poderes**
buildings designed by Oscar Niemeyer, such as the Supremo Tribu-
nal Federal supreme court and the Palácio do Planalto, the official
residence of the Brazilian president, whose pillars Niemeyer shaped
like lateen sails. Niemeyer also designed the Congresso Nacional
building, with the Câmara de Deputados (Chamber of Deputies –
the parliament's lower house) and the Senado (Senate), as well as the
two adjoining high-rise towers housing the deputies' offices.

Brasília Map

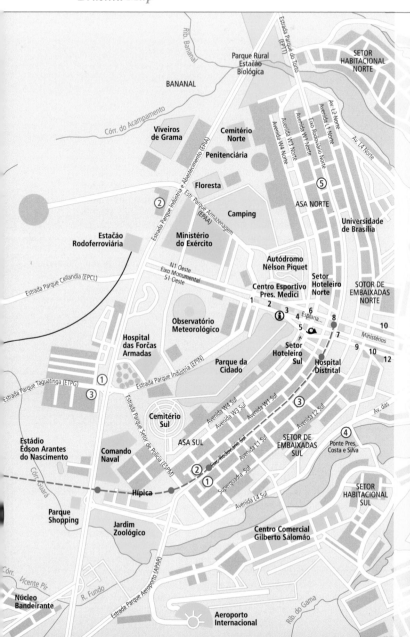

Where to eat
① Babel
② Villa Tevere
③ Bragaço
④ Dom Francisco do Lago
⑤ Lagash

Where to stay
① SIA Park
② Saan Park
③ Brasília Park

1 Monumento Juscelino Kubitschek
2 Centro de Convenções de Brasília
3 Planetario
4 Torre de TV
5 Santnário Dom Bosco
6 Fonte Sonora Luminosa
7 Shopping do Conjunto Nacional
8 Teatro Nacional
9 Catedral
10 Ministérios
11 Congresso Nacional (Câmera e Senado)
12 Palácio dos Arcos (Itamaraty)
13 Palácio da Justiča
14 Palácio do Planalto
15 Museu Histórico da Brasília
16 Panteão da Liberdade
17 Supremo Tribunal Federal

Highlights Brasília

Praça dos Três Poderes
The heart of the city and of Brazilian political life
▶ page 191

Jardim Botânico de Brasília
A great stop for visitors interested in the region's fauna and flora.
▶ page 198

Catedral Metropolitana
Famous cathedral designed by star architect Oscar Niemeyer
▶ page 194 and 196

Parque Nacional de Brasília
Unspoilt nature in close vicinity to the capital
▶ page 198

Panteão da Pátria

This complex is completed by the Panteão da Pátria Tancredo Neves temple honouring both the 1789 Inconfidência Mineira revolt against the Portuguese crown, and the Brazilian president Tancredo Neves, who died in 1985, shortly before taking office. Pride of place in the centre of the Praça dos Três Poderes square is given to the famous sculpture *Os Candangos* by Bruno Giorgi, in honour of the 40,000 workers who built Brasília.

Esplanada dos Ministérios

West of the Praça dos Três Poderes, the Esplanada dos Ministérios opens up, the buildings on both sides of the boulevard housing the Brazilian federal ministeries. The original architectural line has since been broken by several extensions and alterations.

✳

Palácio dos Arcos

The Palácio dos Arcos, also known as Palácio do Itamaraty and serving as the Foreign Ministry, was also designed by Oscar Niemeyer. The palace is surrounded by a park and a pond created by the legendary landscape gardener **Roberto Burle Marx** (1909 – 1994).

✳ ✳

Catedral Metropolitana

Even visitors with only a passing interest in modern architecture cannot fail to be impressed by Oscar Niemeyer's famous cathedral. The church, topped by a crown of thorns and inaugurated in 1967, is situated near the crossing of Eixo Monumental and Eixo Rodoviário. Access to the **light-filled interior** of arguably the most fascinating church created by the convinced atheist Niemeyer, is only through an underground passage. Inside the church, look for works by Emiliano Di Cavalcanti, Athos Bulcão and of course the angels by Alfredo Ceschiatti that appear to be floating below the conical ceiling. Opening times: daily 8am – 5pm.

Teatro Nacional

Across from the cathedral, near the Rodoviária bus station, rises the national theatre, practically on the intersection of these two traffic-plagued arteries. The theatre's lavishly structured façade has the shape of an Aztec pyramid.

osks shaded by awnings on the northern shore of the Lago do Paranoá are called Calcadão do Lago by the locals; after sunset, they are a popular meeting point. Also lining the shores of the reservoir are the northern and southern residential quarters, Brasília University, the Olympic Centre and Palácio da Alvorada, the official residence of the president. The 'Dawn Palace' is not open to visitors, but the Changing of the Guard (daily 10am and 6pm) is worth seeing.

Ermida Dom Bosco

The Ermida Dom Bosco pilgrimage chapel lies on the eastern shore of the Paranoá lake, directly opposite the Palácio da Alvorada. The small triangular pyramid of white marble, erected exactly on the 15th parallel, was dedicated to the Italian Salesian priest (1815–1888), who in 1883 prophesied the creation of a humane society in the region of today's Brasília. From the terrace around the monument there is a splendid view of the silhouette of Brasília and the presidential palace on the opposite bank of the reservoir. The memorial site does not have many visitors these days, since in its immediate vicinity, the Villa da Alvorada, illegally built, blocks the way to the lake's originally freely accessible shore.

Jardim Botânico de Brasília (JBB)

The Botanic Gardens of Brasília, with their car-friendly layout, some 20km/12.5 miles from the city centre, have a small visitor centre and a well-labelled **collection of medicinal plants**. The gardens give a quick idea of the flora and fauna of the cerrado tropical savannah landscape surrounding Brasília and its satellite towns. The park lies on the southern bank of the Paranoá lake, in the Setor Mansões Urbanas Dom Bosco, Conjunto 12, Lago Sul. Opening times: Tue – Sun 9am – 5pm.

Jardim Zoológico

Brasília's Jardim Zoológico zoo is one of the best-run zoos in South America and famous worldwide for its big cats (jaguars, ocelots and pumas) kept in relatively spacious enclosures. Alongside indigenous animals, other species, such as monkeys and elephants from Africa are also on display. The extensive area (Avenida Nações Unidas) can be reached by foot or by private car. The zoo lies about 9km/5.5 miles southwest of the city centre of Brasília on the airport road.

✱ Parque Nacional de Brasília

This national park was established in the early 1960s and today extends over 30,000ha/74,100-acres of cerrado savannah landscape, beginning 10km/6 miles outside Brasília, on the (Rodovia) BR-040 country road. The locals appreciate having a splash in its swimming and paddling pools – which are fed by spring water – and usually only know it by its nickname, **Parque da Água Mineral**. The less-visited area of the park in particular displays a large num-

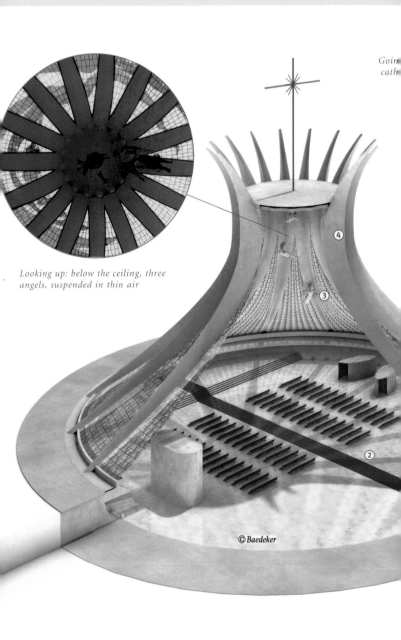

Looking up: below the ceiling, three angels, suspended in thin air

©Baedeker

...own: access to the ...al is via a tunnel.

⑤

①

CATEDRAL METROPOLITANA

✶✶ **Suspended angels animate the light-filled interior of a cathedral that from the outside resembles a crown of thorns. Here, pain and redemption are portrayed symbolically by convinced atheist Oscar Niemeyer: a masterpiece of modern architecture!**

🕐 Opening times:
8am–5pm

① Entrance
A subterranean entrance leads into the Catedral Metropolitana.

② Interior
The light-filled interior of the cathedral lies below ground level. A red carpet leads through the rows of seats to the altar. Consecrated in 1970, the church can accommodate some 4,000 people.

③ Suspended angels
Three bronze angels, sculpted by Alfredo Ceschiatti and modelled on the baroque angels in the churches of Congonhas, hang suspended from the ceiling of the church. Ceschiatti also created four larger-than-life bronze figures, representing the four evangelists, at the entrance to the cathedral.

④ Concrete columns
Tapering concrete columns support the central conical rotunda. Seen from the outside, the columns may be interpreted as a crown, a chalice or a flower that is opening up.

⑤ Bell tower
The bell tower was erected in 1977 in close proximity to the cathedral, with its four bells donated by Spanish immigrants. The tower has the shape of the letter T.

The futuristic cathedral of Brasília. To the right the bell tower, erected in 1977.

This television tower, 75m/246ft high, was erected at the highest point of Eixo Monumental; take the elevator to its **viewing platform** for a good view across the extensive city centre of Brasília. Right behind the television tower, helicopters lift off for panoramic flights over the city. Opening times television tower: Mon 2–5.45pm, Tue to Sun 9am–5.45pm.

Torre de Televisão

West of the television tower, the sweeping building of the Centro de Convenções Ulysses Guimarães and the much smaller planetarium catch the eye. The conference centre, named after the deputy U Guimarães (one of the leading forces behind the movement to oust president Collor from office) has two conference rooms and a theatre, as well as a restaurant.

Planetário, Centro de Convenções U Guimarães

In the adjoining recreational sector to the north, level with the conference centre, spreads the Presidente Médici sports centre, with the Autódromo Nelson Piquet racing track, a cycling track, a swimming pool, a gym, an athletics track, a playground, sports and tennis courts as well as the Mané Garrincha stadium.

Centro Esportivo Pres. Médici

Standing on the Praça do Cruzeiro (Eixo Monumental), the memorial dedicated to president Juscelino Kubitschek includes a small museum with photos and documents related to the pioneer of Brasília, who lost his life in 1976 in a car accident – probably a victim of the military regime of the time. Opening times: Tue–Sun 9am–6pm.

Memorial J Kubitschek

The Parque da Cidade Sarah Kubitschek, created by Roberto Burle Marx, stretches out to the south of the city centre. Access is also via the Eixo Monumental, opposite the Presidente Médici sports centre. Here, city dwellers looking for respite can find numerous sports facilities, a go-kart track, lanes for rollerbladers and cyclists, as well as playgrounds and a lake.

★ Parque da Cidade Sarah Kubitschek

Behind the city park, on the Avenida W-3 Sul, Quadra 702, Bloco B, look for the Santuário Dom Bosco sanctuary. The façade of this angular church, which was inaugurated in 1980, is dominated by 76 tapering arcade arches, each 18m/59ft high. Daylight falling into the interior of the spacious church is muted by blocks of blue glass. Inside, next to the statue of Dom Bosco, the huge wooden sculpture of the Redeemer on the Cross hanging above the altar catches the eye.

★ Santuário Dom Bosco

★ Lago do Paranoá

East of the city centre, the Rio Paranoá has been dammed to form an artificial lake. The lake has a circumference of 80km/50 miles and is spanned to the south by Niemeyer's white **Ponte Costa e Silva**. The best sites on its banks are shared between embassies and consulates, upmarket sports clubs and restaurants and new hotels. The ki-

Inside the Santuário Dom Bosco

ber of the plants typical for midwestern Brazil: from the low trees of
the cerrado bush steppe, mostly gnarled and crooked – amongst
them primarily the pau-terra and the gujak tree – to the gallery forests thriving along the rivers and lakes, with Ipês roxos (yielding dyewood) and jataís. The national park also includes numerous fields
with shrubs and grass, as well as marshy plains with buriti palms.
The headstreams within the nature reserve provide Brasília with
drinking water. On quiet days, visitors making their way to the viewing tower within the park may – with a little luck – discover anteaters (tamanduás) and armadillos (tatus) in the undergrowth, as well
as numerous bird species including nandus. Opening times: daily ⏲
8am–4pm.

✳ Parque Nacional da Chapada dos Veadeiros

The establishment in 1961 of the Chapada dos Veadeiros National Park, on the initiative of President Juscelino Kubitschek, was closely connected with the building of the capital. Located 230km/143 miles north of Brasília in the federal state of Goiás, the nature reserve forms the watershed between the Amazon, Rio Paraná and Rio São Francisco rivers. The landscape of the plateau is dominated by the canyon of the Rio Preto – with its many waterfalls amongst the park's most important attractions – and by the varied cerrado woodland savannah.

Hiking
Hikers may discover the Chapada dos Veadeiros park on two trekking routes beginning near the town of **São Jorge**. This is also where some local guides offer their services. They know the places where visitors can admire anteaters, armadillos, cerrado deer, emus, capybaras and toucans in the wild. The best time for visiting the national park is in the dry season, here lasting from April to November. Simple accommodation can be found in the small town of **Alto Paraíso de Goiás**, 36km/22 miles away. 300 visitors are allowed inside the park every day, and there is a small information centre.

Camocim

Se 47

State: Ceará (CE)	**Population:** 55,500
Altitude: 8m/26ft	

Camocim is the starting point for day trips to the attractive coastal landscapes of the northwestern part of Ceará state. The town's chief attraction is its proximity to the varied landscapes of the nearby coastal strip.

Despite – or maybe because of – the area's remoteness from the large cities, the huge shifting dunes, lagoons, steep cliffs, mangrove vegetation and splendid swimming beaches attract many tourists, both domestic and foreign.

✳ Beaches around Camocim

The Praias das Barreiras and do Farol lie 2km/1.2 miles and 4km/2.5 miles outside the town centre. Lying between 10km/6 miles and 70km/43 miles from Camocim, the most attractive beaches of Bitupitá, Imburana, Tatajuba, Mangue Seco, Guriú, Preá and Formosa are difficult to access by land. The most famous amongst them, said to be one of the most beautiful in the world, is the swimming beach of Jericoacoara.

A toucan in Chapada dos Veadeiros National Park

Only accessible on horseback or with a 4x4 vehicle, the designated nature reserve of Praia de Jericoacoara, 72km/45 miles east of Camocim, is a sandy beach, 23km/14 miles long, with golden sand and white, golden and pink dunes that reach over 30m/98ft. The beach's landmark feature is the **Ponte de Jericoacoara**, a rock portal hollowed out by the sea. Package tours of three or more days to Jericoacoara are offered by nearly all travel agencies in Fortaleza.

✳ ✳
Jericoacoara

Campinas

State: São Paulo (SP)　　　　　　**Population:** 969,500
Altitude: 854m/2,802ft

Founded in 1774, Campinas is the second-largest city in São Paulo state. Today's city centre started out as a bandeirantes encampment.

As early as the 18th century, the fertile soil of the area started to attract farmers, too; the first crop to be cultivated here was sugar cane. Around 1842, when there were already over 100 sugar cane plantations here, the coffee boom started. The discovery and exploitation of mineral resources then drove the industrialization of a city that today has grown into a significant commercial and industrial centre.

▶ VISITING CAMPINAS

INFORMATION
Avenida Anchieta 200, Centro
Tel. (019) 37 35-05 55
www.campinas.sp.gov.br

GETTING THERE
Airport
Aeroporto Internacional de
Viracopos
Tel. (019) 37 25-50 00

Bus station
Rua Br de Parnaíba 690
Tel. (019) 32 32-13 55

WHERE TO EAT
▶ **Expensive**
① *Matisse*
The Royal Palm Residence
Rua Conceição 450
Tel. (019) 37 31-42 03
www.royalpalmhoteis.com.br
The cuisine of this hotel is Far Eastern
style: shrimps come with curry sauce
and fried goat with mango chutney.

▶ **Moderate**
② *Bellini*
Hotel Vitória
Avenida José de Souza Campose 425
Cambuí district
Tel. (019) 37 55-80 20
Restaurant with Italian cuisine and
extensive drinks list

③ *La Parrilla del Cambuí*
Avenida Cel Silva Teles 755
Cambuí district
Tel. (019) 32 52-53 44
Argentinian cuisine indulging in a
variety of beef dishes

WHERE TO STAY
▶ **Mid-range**
① *Vitória*
Avenida José de Souza Campos 425
Cambuí
district Tel. (019) 37 55-80 00
www.vitoriahotel.com.br
Over 140 air-conditioned rooms, car
parking, a restaurant (see above), bar,
pool, sauna and gym

② *Meliá Confort*
Rua Severo Penteado 140
Cambuí district
Tel. (019) 37 53-80 00
www.solmelia.com
308 air-conditioned rooms, conference centre, restaurant, bar, pool,
gym and sauna

▶ **Budget**
③ *Opala Barão*
Rua Barão de Jaguará 1136
Tel. (019) 32 32-49 99
www.hoteisopala.com.br
Simple accommodation with
restaurant

What to see in Campinas

Museu Histórico Campos Salles, Museu Carlos Gomes — Branching off from the railway station – built in 1887 southwest of the city centre on Praça Marechal Floriano Peixoto – are various boulevards, amongst them the Avenida Dr Costa Aguiar running across the city to Praça José Bonifácio. The Avenida Campos Salles and Rua Bernardino de Campos run northwest parallel to Costa Aguiar. In Campos Salles, look for the Historical Museum Campos

Campinas Map

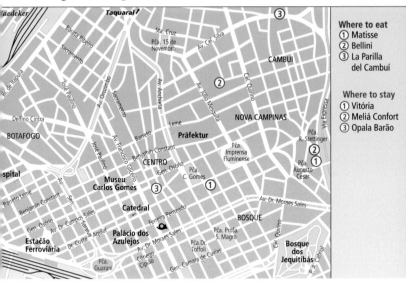

Where to eat
① Matisse
② Bellini
③ La Parilla del Cambuí

Where to stay
① Vitória
② Meliá Confort
③ Opala Barão

Salles, in Rua Bernardino de Campos for the Museu Carlos Gomes **Centre for Sciences, Literature and the Arts**. The centre takes its name from the Campinas-born composer Carlos Gomes (1836 to 1896); his monument and grave can also be visited in the city centre, on Praça Bento Quirino.

The city hall lies immediately beyond the intersection of Benjamin Constant and Avenida Anchieta. The former city hall building, the Palácio dos Azulejos (1870) in Rua Regente Feijó, is one of the most attractive buildings in the city.

Palácio dos Azulejos

In and around Campinas there are extensive parks and forests. The city's largest green space is the Bosque dos Jequitibás in the **Bairro do Bosque** district southeast of the city centre, in Rua Coronel Quirino. This nature reserve boasts a small zoo, an aquarium, springs and lakes. The park also contains the Carlos Maia children's theatre and the Folklore Museum, the Indian Museum, Historical Museum, as well as the Natural History Museum.

★ Bosque dos Jequitibás

The Parque Portugal with Lake Taquaral spreads out in the Bairro Parque Taquaral district in the north of Campinas. The entrance to the park is at 1671 Avenida Heitor Penteado. Visitors can hire pedalo boats, take a tram or try out the go-kart track. Among the attractions of the park is a replica of the caravel captained by Cabral, who »discovered« Brazil, as well as a planetarium.

Parque Portugal

Campo Grande

Rh 56

State: Mato Grosso do Sul (MS)
Altitude: 532m/1,745ft

Population: 664,000

Campo Grande, the capital of Mato Grosso do Sul state, is an ideal base for tours into the Pantanal. Founded around 1889, the city's fortunes rose with the opening of the railway line to Corumbá in 1914.

As the most important centre for commerce, industry, agriculture and livestock farming of the old state of Mato Grosso, Campo Grande benefited from good road and rail links with São Paulo and the southern states of Brazil. For decades, the city harboured separatist ambitions, culminating in 1924 and 1932 in the support of São Paulo's rebellions against the federal government. In 1932, the paulistas were promised help only on condition that São Paulo would later work towards independence for the southern part of Mato Grosso. Decades later these hopes were to be fulfilled, with the establishment in 1977 of the state of Mato Grosso do Sul.

What to see in Campo Grande

✳
**Museu
Dom Bosco**

The Dom Bosco Museum, also known as **Museu do Índio**, can be found at 1843 Rua Barão do Rio Branco. The museum's natural history collection is impressive: alongside 5,000 items made by the Bororó, Moro, Carajá and Xavante Indians, there are 7,000 shells from all the world's oceans, 7,000 prepared butterflies and 3,000 other insects, as well as 1,600 stuffed birds, reptiles, mammals and fish (most of them from the Pantanal). Opening times: Tue–Sat 8am–6pm, Sun 8am–noon and 2–6pm.

View of Campo Grande

The **Casa do Artesão** (House of Crafts), at the corner of Avenida Calógeras and Avenida Afonso Pena, exhibits items made by local craftspeople from leather, raffia, wood, straw and other materials.

▶ VISITING CAMPO GRANDE

INFORMATION

Morada do Baís
Av Afonso Pena/Av Noroeste 5140
Tel. (067) 33 24-58 30
www.campogrande.ms.gov.br/cidade-morena

GETTING THERE

Airport
Aeroporto Int. do Campo Grande
Tel. (067) 33 68-60 93

Bus station
Rua Joaquim Nabuco
Tel. (067) 33 83-16 78

WHERE TO EAT

▶ **Expensive**
Fogo Caipira
Rua José Antônio Pereira 145
Tel. (067) 33 24-16 41
Typical recipes from the Pantanal and other Brazilian dishes; don't come in a rush, as the preparation seldom takes under 30 minutes.

▶ **Moderate**
Fogão de Minas
Rua Dom Aquino 2200
Tel. (067) 33 25-52 87
Calorific food from the self-service buffet, cooked to recipes from Minas Gerais

WHERE TO STAY

▶ **Mid-range**
Jandaia
Rua Barão do Rio Branco 1271
Tel. (067) 33 21-70 00
www.jandaia.com.br
City hotel with 140 rooms, pool, gym, restaurant and bar

Bristol Exceler Plaza
Avenida Afonso Pena 444
Tel. (067) 33 12-28 00
www.bristolhoteis.com
80 apartments, as well as sauna, swimming pool, tennis courts, bar and restaurant

Campos do Jordão

Sc 57

State: São Paulo (SP)
Altitude: 1628m/5,341ft

Population: 44,500

Campos do Jordão in the Serra da Mantiqueira, 167km/104 miles northeast of São Paulo, is one of the most elegant spa and health resorts in Brazil. Both the alpine aspect of the town's architecture and the rural surroundings seem more European than South American.

What to see in Campos do Jordão

The boulevard running from the Praça de Capivari is lined with timber-framed houses and elegant shops. Close to the boulevard, the   **Praça de Capivari**

Capivari Park has a chair lift travelling nearly 600m/650yd to the peak of the 1,800m/5,905-ft **Morro do Elefante** (Hill of the Elephant), with views across the whole city. The park comprises a lake, where pedalo and rowing boats plus horse-drawn carts may be hired, and there is also a go-kart track.

Trams and trains
Other visitor attractions are the small Bonde trams covering the entire city between Capivari and Pórtico, and the **narrow-gauge railway** leading from the Emílio Ribas railway station situated near the park on the highest railway tracks in Brazil, right across the Serra da Mantiqueira to Santo Antônio do Pinhal. Local guides accompany visitors on the 2.5-hour trip. For more information, contact: tel. (012) 36 63-15 31.

▶ VISITING CAMPOS DO JORDÃO

INFORMATION
Pórtico
(on the access road into town)
Tel. (012) 36 64-35 25
www.camposdojordao.com.br
www.pmcg.ms.gov.br

GETTING THERE
Bus station
Avenida Dr Januário Miraglia
Tel. (012) 36 62-19 96

WHERE TO EAT
▶ **Expensive**
Ludwig
Rua Aristides de Souza Melo 50
Vila Capivari
Tel. (012) 36 63-51 11
Traditional international cuisine, plus fondue and German dishes. Booking a table in advance is recommended. All credit cards accepted.

▶ **Moderate**
Harry Pisek
Avenida Pedro Paulo 857
Estrada do Horto, km 2.5
Tel. (012) 36 63-40 30
For Brazilians, the menu is exotic: six kinds of German sausage, Emmental cheese, pickled knuckle of pork and Bavarian meat loaf.

WHERE TO STAY
▶ **Luxury**
Grande Hotel
Campos do Jordão
Av Frei Orestes Girardi 3549
Tel. (012) 36 68-30 00
www.grandehotelcampos
dojordao.com.br
This upmarket hotel, surrounded by extensive, park-like gardens, was built in the 1940s. There are 95 rooms and, alongside many other amenities, an excellent restaurant.

▶ **Mid-range**
Orotour Garden
Rua Engenheiro G Kaiser 165
Tel. (012) 36 62-28 33
www.orotour.com.br
The complex comprises 61 rooms, as well as 4 chalets each sleeping up to 4 people. The hotel guests have access to several sports facilities, a pool and a sauna. A children's playground and chauffeur service round off the experience.

The Palácio Boa Vista, winter residence of the governors of São Paulo, was erected between 1938 and 1963 high up in the Serra, towering above the districts of Capivari, Abernéssia and Jaguaribe. The palace houses one of the largest permanent art exhibitions in the country. The collection comprises works by, amongst others, Tarsilo de Amaral, Portinari, Volpi, Anita Malfati and Di Cavalcanti.

Palácio Boa Vista

> **! Baedeker TIP**
>
> **Festival do Inverno**
> The annual Campos do Jordão winter festival, which has been taking place in July since 1970, has over the years evolved into one of the most interesting cultural events in São Paulo state. It has been so successful that now another 14 municipalities take part. Today, the concerts of classical music are complemented by films, shows and sports performances. For more information, contact: tel. (012) 36 62-60 00.

The concert hall of Campos do Jordão, the **Auditório Cláudio Santoro**, was purpose-built for the musical performances of the winter festival (► Tip see right). Built entirely of exposed concrete and glass, the concert hall stands 2km/ 1.2 miles from Palácio Boa Vista, in the middle of a park. In the immediate vicinity, lok for one of the few open-air museums in Brazil, the **Museu Felícia Leirner**, established in 1978. The museum's avenues and hills are decorated with 78 animal and human sculptures of various sizes donated to the museum by the artist.

Caravelas

Sf 54

State: Bahia (BA)
Altitude: 10m/33ft

Population: 20,000

In the 17th and 18th centuries, the charming small fishermen's town of Caravelas in the extreme south of Bahia, with its numerous nearby beaches, was an important trading post. Today, tourism is the most important economic factor, in particular as Caravelas is the gateway to the Abrolhos National Marine Park.

What to see in and around Caravelas

North of Caravelas lie the beaches of Zeloris, Praia da Ponta da Baleia, Praia de Yemajá and Barra de Caravelas, as well as the Praias Grauçá (9km/5.5 miles) and Quitongo. South of the town lie the beaches of Pontal do Sul (only accessible by boat, taking 20 min), Barra Nova and Ponta do Catueiro. The island of Coroa da Barra is a 20-min drive, the island of Coroa Vermelha a two-hour drive from Caravelas.

★
Beaches and islands

Alcobaça The main attraction of Alcobaça (pop 16,000), 27km/16.5 miles north of Caravelas, are the fine beaches, including Barra, Farol and Alcobaça. Visible at low tide, the **Timbebas Cliffs** (an hour and a half away by boat) are a further attraction. The small town can also be reached from Caravelas by ferry (passenger transport only).

★ Parque Nacional Marinho dos Abrolhos

The Parque Nacional Marinho dos Abrolhos (National Marine Park), situated 80km/50 miles southeast of Caravelas in the Atlantic, covers an area of 91,300ha/225,600 acres. The park comprises four of the five volcanic islands that make up the Abrolhos archipelago: Redonda, Sueste, Siriba and Guarita. These are grouped around the main island of **Santa Bárbara**, which serves as a naval base and is closed to visitors. From Caravelas, Alcobaça and Nova Viçosa, situated southwest of Caravelas, ferries run to the Abrolhos islands – from Caravelas, the crossing takes six hours. Visitors may only go ashore on Ilha Redonda and Ilha Siriba; overnight accommodation is provided aboard the schooners used for the crossing. Before travelling, visitors have to apply for a permit with the IBAMA Brazilian environmental protection agency (tel. (073) 32 97-11 11). Fishing, both above or under water, is prohibited in this unique nature reserve.

Up close and personal with the marine turtles in Marinho dos Abrolhos National Park

The name of Abrolhos goes back to Amerigo Vespucci, who on his nautical chart noted »Abre os Olhos« (»Keep your eyes open«). How dangerous these waters are is evidenced by numerous shipwrecks, such as the one of the Italian freighter *Rosalina*, which sank only a few kilometres off the main island of Santa Bárbara, despite the erection of a lighthouse there – on orders of Emperor Dom Pedro II and imported from France – as early as 1861. In the 17th century, the decisive battle between the Portuguese navy and the Dutch invaders took place off Abrolhos. In 1830, during his circumnavigation of the earth aboard the research vessel *Beagle*, the islands were visited by **Charles Darwin**. Needless to say, **Jacques Cousteau** is also amongst the scientists who have investigated the unique flora and fauna of Abrolhos.

»Keep your eyes open«

In Abrolhos National Marine Park, fairly rare corals form a 910 sq km/351 sq mile reef around the islands. Alongside diverse underwater fauna, visitors can observe a great variety of sea birds, such as frigate birds, divers, dippers and rabos-de-palha (red-beaked, pelican-like tropical birds). Between July and November, the very plankton-rich waters of the archipelago are regularly visited by whales for mating, and marine turtles lay their eggs on the beaches of the volcanic islands.

Plants and animals

Caxambu

Sc 56

State: Minas Gerais (MG)   **Population:** 22,000
Altitude: 895m/2,936ft

The mountainous environment of Caxambu, in the extreme south of Minas Gerais, lends the spa resort with mineral springs and elegant hotels pleasant temperatures of 15 to 25 °C/59 to 77 F all year round, making the small town a favourite with the Brazilian emperor's family in the 19th century.

Caxambu's springs, which by that time were already used to treat stomach, liver and kidney complaints, were also much appreciated by Emperor Dom Pedro II. Today, Caxambu is a quiet resort popular mainly with older people.

What to see in and around Caxambu

The statue of the Redeemer (Cristo Redentor), dominating the peak of the 1,050m/3,444ft Caxambu Hill, is visible for miles around. It can be reached either by the road winding its way up the hill or – more comfortably – by cable car.

Cristo Redentor

CAXAMBU

INFORMATION
Rua João Carlos 100
Tel. (035) 33 41-12 98
www.descubraminas.com.br

GETTING THERE
Bus station
Praça José de Castilho Moreira
Tel. (035) 33 41-55 66

The magnificent **Parque das Águas** (Water Park) in the city centre, dating from 1912, comprises eleven pavilions built in oriental style, with mineral springs containing magnesium, sulphur, iron, alkali and carbonic acid, as well as opulently decorated **Turkish Baths**, and several saunas and massage rooms. Opening times: daily 7am – 6pm.

São Tomé das Letras lies 61km/38 miles north of Caxambu, at an altitude of nearly 1,300m/4265ft in the **Serra da Mantiqueira**. Many of the town's 6,000 inhabitants belong to alternative religious movements, for whom this little town is one of the mystic centres of South America. São Tomé das Letras is considered a prime location for UFO spotting, inscriptions in the surrounding caves are believed to be of extraterrestrial origin, whilst the caves themselves are thought to offer access to civilizations living under the surface of the earth! Whether these slightly odd ideas owe more to some of the townsfolk's esoteric otherworldliness or their considerable consumption of stimulants, they lend the town an unusual flair.

São Lourenço   A large part of the centre of São Lourenço (pop 37,000), 25km/15.5 miles southwest of Caxambu, is taken up by the **Parque das Águas** (Water Park) on Praça Brasil. This nature reserve has walking trails and extensive gardens, including an imposing ensemble of art-déco pavilions dating from the 1940s. There are six mineral springs in the park, a fine lido as well as a lake with an artificial island.

Near the lake there is a daily **craft market**, selling items made from bamboo, leather or straw, as well as knitted goods.

★ Chapada Diamantina

Se 52

State: Bahia (BA)

Around 430km/267 miles west of Salvador unfold the table mountains and canyons of the Chapada Diamantina National Park, which was established in 1985 in the Serra de Sincorá.

This nature reserve, most of which lies at an altitude of over 800m/ 2,625ft, boasts lush vegetation, nourished by mountain streams, with many species of orchids and bromelias. Deer, capybara water pigs and anteaters may still be seen here. The most noteworthy amongst the birds is the exceedingly rare Beija Flor Gravata Vermelha, a species of hummingbird with a red throat. The bizarre sandstone mountains – formed by wind erosion with some of them up to 1,200m/ 3,937ft high – plateaus, valleys, mountain streams and waterfalls make the national park a popular area for hiking. Recommended trekking and riding tours can be organized in the town of Lençóis (► p. 213), the eastern gateway to the Chapada Diamantina. This is also the place to find accommodation.

What to see in and around the national park

Within the park, 4km/2.5 miles from Lençóis, look for the Gruta do Lapão, at over 1km/0.6 miles long the largest quartzite cave in Brazil and probably one of the largest in the whole of South America.

Gruta do Lapão

One of the spectacular sights of the park is the Fumaça Waterfall, with a descent of 340m/1,115ft the highest in the country. At the foot of the rock wall, its waters dissolve into a veil of mist moments before hitting the ground. The waterfall is 12km/7.5 miles outside Lençóis; when there is no rain for a while, the Cachoeira da Fumaça disappears.

✷ ✷
Cachoeira da Fumaça

The luminous red glow of evening playing on the table mountains of Chapada Diamantina

▶ VISITING CHAPADA DIAMANTINA

INFORMATION
Lençóis
Tel. (075) 33 34-14 25
www.guialencois.com

HIKING TOURS
Eco trekking
Praça Horácio de Matos 656, Lençóis
Tel. (075) 33 34-14 91

WHERE TO EAT
▶ **Moderate**
Cozinha Aberta
Rua da Baderna 111, Lençóis
Tel. (075) 33 34-10 66
International and regional dishes, extensive drinks menu. No credit cards.

▶ Budget
A Picanha na Praça
Praça Otaviano Alves 62, Lençóis
Tel. (075) 33 34-10 80
Barbecued beef a speciality.

WHERE TO STAY
▶ **Mid-range**
Portal Lençóis
Rua Chácara Grota
Altina Alves, Lençóis
Tel. (075) 33 34-12 33
www.portalhoteis.tur.br
Best hotel in town. 69 rooms and 15 chalets, good restaurant, children's play area, pool, gym, sauna and car parking.

Morro do Pai Inácio

On the northern border of the Parque Nacional da Chapada Diamantina, 30km/18.5 miles northwest of Lençóis, rises the Pai Inácio mountain (1,120m/3,674ft), the symbol of the region and an ideal destination for climbers. According to legend a slave called Inácio, pursued by his colonial masters, threw himself off the peak of the mountain, but survived. The African heritage of this region survives in ceremonies such as the **Festa do Jaré**, Jaré being a local variation of the Candomblé.

Caves

Some 50km/31 miles north of Lençóis, some very interesting caves can be explored around the the municipality of Iraquara. The **Gruta Lapa Doce** – 13km/8 miles long in total, but with only 1.3km/0.8 miles open to the public – is the fourth-largest cave in Brazil, attracting many visitors keen to see its magnificent stalactite and stalagmite formations. The **Gruta da Pratinha**, with a crystal-clear river of the same name winding its way through it, shelters a lake with wonderfully clear green water. Close by there is another cave, the **Gruta Azul**. The access road for all three caves branches off from the BR-242 federal road. Between late April and early September, in the **Poço Encantado** cave, situated southeast of the national park, the slanted morning light hits the surface of an underground lake (42m/138ft) in such a way that it turns a magical blue. South of the Serra do Sincorá, in the valley of the Rio de Contas, the **Gruta da Mangabeira** is illuminated in August with candles lit by pilgrims. Traversing the Morro do Chapéu, the **Gruta de Brejões** is the sixth-largest cave in Brazil. Huge limestone formations create a natural altar, decorated with a cross and images of saints. The cave is located near the Rio Jacaré, a tributary of the São Francisco river.

Lençóis

Lençóis (pop 10,000), on the northeastern edge of the national park, experienced a big upturn in fortunes in 1844, with the discovery in the nearby Serra de Sincorá of a rich vein of diamonds, enabling it to evolve into the third-largest city in Bahia. The town's former wealth is still reflected in splendid buildings. But with the diamond deposits being completely exhausted after only 50 years, the boom had an abrupt ending. Reminders of this brief but glorious phase in the development of the town are the stone-built church of **Bom Jesus dos Passos**, with finely-wrought portals and baroque paintings, as well as several houses dating from the 18th and 19th centuries – an architectural heritage that was given listed status in 1973.

Taking a break in the searing heat of the Chapada Diamantina

Running through a rocky landscape and reflecting the light in a variety of colours, the Rio Lençóis river has carved out many hollows and potholes to be filled with iron-rich dark water. Two kilometres/1.2 miles upriver from the town centre, the Salão de Areias is a cave famous for its sand, shimmering in over 100 different colours. Local artists use this to create clever and colourful sand pictures in transparent glass bottles.

Rio Lençóis, Salão de Areias

> **? DID YOU KNOW …?**
>
> ■ … that the name Lençóis has its origin in the years of the diamond boom? Lured by the prospect of making a quick buck, adventurers settled here in droves, finding accommodation in miserable tents that were no more than patched-up bedsheets; the Portuguese word for bedsheet (lençol) eventually giving the town its unusual name.

1km/0.6 miles outside Lençóis, the **Rio Serrano** river boasts a natural waterslide made from smooth stones, with a charming water basin at its end. There are more waterfalls to discover in the area, such as the Cachoeira Primavera and the Cachoeirinha.

✦ Chapada dos Guimarães

Rh 53

State: Mato Grosso (MT)

With its archaeological sites, petroglyphs and some 200 waterfalls, as well as dramatic rock faces, canyons – amongst them the Portão do Inferno (Hell's Gate), some 50m/164ft deep – and huge rock formations carved out by erosion, the Parque Nacional Chapada dos Guimarães, situated in the transitional zone between the Amazon lowlands and the cerrados in central Brazil, is Mato Grosso's second-most important tourist attraction after the Pantanal.

What to see in the national park

Particularly impressive are the Salgadeira cascade near Hell's Gate, next to reddish rocks carved into bizarre forms by the forces of erosion, the waterfalls of Cachoeirinha and Salto das Andorinhas, and the famous **Cachoeira Véu da Noiva** (Bride's Veil Cascade), plunging 86m/282ft down to the valley. The Cachoeira da Salgadeira waterfall is situated near the national park visitor centre immediately next to the MT-251 country road cutting straight through the nature reserve; both the Véu da Noiva and Hell's Gate are equally easy to reach from the road.

✦ Waterfalls

← *Pretty creepy: Mucugê cemetery in the Chapada Diamantina*

▶ VISITING CHAPADA DOS GUIMARÃES

INFORMATION

In the park's visitor centre
Tel. (065) 33 01-11 33
www.chapadadosguimaraes.com.br

WHEN TO VISIT

The months between August and November are considered the best time to visit the national park, as the rains have stopped, but the cascades still carry enough water.

WHERE TO STAY

Accommodation can be found in the small town of Chapada dos Guimarães, a few kilometres south of the national park.

Morro São Jerônimo
A hiking trail leads up to the Salto das Andorinhas waterfall and past the Morro São Jerônimo, at 850m/2,789ft the park's highest peak. The mighty cave, called **Casa de Pedra** (House of Stone) also lies on this hiking route.

Cidade de Pedra
Around 15km/9.5 miles off the through road, some 25km/15.5 miles north of the town of Chapada dos Guimarães, look for bizarre rock formations carved out by the wind and the elements, known as Cidade de Pedra (Stone Town). The individual rocks have been named after their shape: Cabeça de Rei (Head of the King), Camelo (Camel) or Dedo de Deus (Finger of God).

Caverna Aroe Jari, Gruta da Lagoa Azul
Outside the Chapada dos Guimarães National Park, on the road to **Campo Verde**, lie the 1,100m/1,200-yd long Caverna Aroe Jari (41km/25 miles' drive from the park on a dirt road, plus an hour's trek) and the Gruta da Lagoa Azul (20 min on foot from the Caverna Aroe Jari), whose vault harbours crystal-clear water.

Chapada dos Guimarães (town)
The small town of Chapada dos Guimarães, with just under 16,000 inhabitants, was founded by bandeirantes from São Paulo, who had discovered veins of gold on the plateaus and the mountains north of Cuiabá. A few 18th-century buildings remind visitors of the town's history, such as the baroque church of **Nossa Senhora Santana**, built in 1779 on Praça Wunibaldo. Today, the small town mainly serves as the gateway to the national park of the same name. During the winter festival of the last week of July however, Chapada awakens from its slumber, making it difficult to find accommodation around that time.

Mirante do Centro Geodésico
Just under 10km/6.2 miles from the town of Chapada dos Guimarães – at the edge of the Mirante do Centro Geodésico panoramic terrace, from where visitors can enjoy an excellent view of the surrounding cerrado landscape – don't miss the geodesical centre of South America (Centro Geodésico).

Congonhas

✶✶

Sd 56

State: Minas Gerais (MG)   **Population:** 40,000
Altitude: 871m/2,858ft

Without the famous pilgrim's church of Bom Jesus de Matosinhos, Congonhas would hardly warrant a second glance. With this site of pilgrimage however, the town – situated 81km/50 miles south of Belo Horizonte amidst the once highly productive gold deposits of the Rio Maranhão river – can boast one of the most significant masterpieces of Minas Baroque.

In addition, the group of sculptures in front of the church, executed by Aleijadinho (►Baedeker Special p. 58), is considered probably the most expressive work of the artist.

✶✶ Bom Jesus de Matosinhos

The construction of the famous pilgrimage church of Bom Jesus de Matosinhos has its origins in the vow taken by gold prospector Feliciano Mendes, seriously ill at the time, to build a church should he be cured. The adventurer from Braga in northern Portugal was true to his word, putting up his own fortune for the construction and also collecting donations in order to realize his promise. In 1757, the

Bom Jesus de Matosinhos, with a group of sculptures by Aleijadinho

foundations were laid, and in 1771 – six years after Mendes' death – the edifice, resembling the Bom Jesus do Monte church near Braga, was completed. Declared a **World Heritage** site by UNESCO in 1985, the Basílica do Senhor Bom Jesus de Matosinhos has two outstanding sculpture groups by Antônio Francisco Lisboa, called **Aleijadinho** (little cripple): the soapstone statues of the twelve prophets and the wooden carvings of the Stations of the Cross, some of which were given colour by Manuel da Costa Athayde in 1818.

Twelve prophets In their interplay of gestures, the sculptures of the biblical prophets, created between 1800 and 1805 and now dominating the various levels of the church square, form a highly expressive ensemble. Some have interpreted them as an allegory of mute protest, other experts have seen the figures with their Latin scrolls as an **allusion to the Inconfidência Rebels**. In front of the stairway the visitor is welcomed by Jesaiah and Jeremiah, followed by Baruch and Ezekiel, and, on the terrace of the courtyard, Daniel, Hosea, Jonah and Joel. At the corners of the wall stand Obadiah and Habakuk, whilst Amos and Nahum can be seen at the outside edges. The statues of the four great prophets, Isaiah, Jeremiah, Ezekiel and Daniel, are larger than the other eight. The representations of Daniel and Jonah were sculpted from a single block. Daniel is represented as a confident young man, in the manner of a Renaissance David, whilst Jonah is given the face of a dead man, who, freed from the belly of the whale, comes to life again.

Stations of the Cross The life-size figures of the Stations of the Cross, carved between 1796 and 1799, lead to the terrace with the sculptures of the prophets. Spread over six chapels, they illustrate the following scenes: the Last Supper, Christ on the Mount of Olives, the Arrest of Christ, the Mocking of Christ, the Crown of Thorns, Calvary and Crucifixion. The face of Jesus in the crucifixion scene is considered to be one of Aleijadinho's most sublime creations.

Corumbá

Rg 55

State: Mato Grosso do Sul (MS) **Population:** 97,000
Altitude: 118m/387ft

This port on the Rio Paraguai in the western Pantanal, was once a Brazilian-Portuguese outpost in the midwest, founded following the 1750 Treaty of Madrid, which gave the Portuguese dominion over this area.

The original core of the town, a military garrison by the name of Albuquerque, came into being in 1778. In 1853 the commercial port

▶ VISITING CORUMBÁ

INFORMATION
Rua Manuel Cavassa 275
Porto Geral
Tel. (067) 32 31-73 36
www.corumba.com.br

GETTING THERE
Airport
Aeroporto Internacional
Rua Santos-Dumont
Tel. (067) 32 31-33 22

Bus station
Esplanada da Estação
Tel. (067) 32 31-20 33

WHERE TO EAT
▶ **Moderate**
Ceará
Rua Albuquerque 516
Tel. (067) 32 31-19 30
Specialities from the Pantanal

WHERE TO STAY
▶ **Mid-range**
Gold Fish
Avenida Rio Branco 2799
Tel. (067) 32 31-51 06
www.candelas.com.br
City hotel with 84 air-conditioned
apartments, bar, restaurant and pool

was inaugurated, marking the beginning of regular shipping on the Rio Paraguai. Today, Corumbá is considered an ideal starting point for tours into the southern ►Pantanal. Alongside trips to the Pantanal, photo safaris to Nhecolândia, Nabileque and Paiaguás can be organized too.

What to see in and around Corumbá

On the Praça da República stands the **Instituto Histórico Luiz de Albuquerque**, which houses the Museu do Pantanal, exhibiting stuffed animals as well as tools and weapons of the region's indigenous population. Handicrafts made by the indigenous Indians and regional crafts are for sale in the **Casa do Artesão** (Crafts House), the former prison at 405 Rua Dr Aquino Corrõa.

Museu do Pantanal

The Pantanal Museum lies very close to the Rio Paraguai river, where the quays and harbour with residential houses built in the 19th century and now listed, may be visited. Further east, also on the Rio Paraguai, the 18th century Forte Junqueira in Rua Cáceres occupies a prominent position.

Forte Junqueira

Visitors wanting to see the Forte de Coimbra – the Portuguese crown's largest fort in the area and a once strategically important defensive stronghold of Portugal in western Brazil – must apply to the Brigada Mista in Avenida General Rondon in Corumbá for a permit: contact tel. (067) 32 31-27 01. Built in 1776, the fort can only be accessed by a seven-hour boat trip on the Rio Paraguai.

Forte de Coimbra

Cuiabá

Rg 53

State: Mato Grosso (MT)   **Population:** 483,500
Altitude: 176m/577ft

In 1718, the bandeirantes Pascoal Moreiro Cabral and Miguel Sutil from São Paulo discovered rich gold deposits near the Cuiabá and Coxipó rivers. The following year, this settlement of gold prospectors under the administration of Moreiro Cabral became Arraial de Cuiabá.

However, the town had to wait until 1727 to be elevated to the status of a vila, and until 1818 to become a town, but in 1823 Cuiabá was finally declared the capital of Mato Grosso province. Cuiabá is an excellent base for day trips into the ►Pantanal and the ►Chapada dos Guimarães National Park.

What to see in Cuiabá

Fundação Cultural de Mato Grosso   Situated on the Praça da República, the Fundação Cultural de Mato Grosso (Cultural Foundation of Mato Grosso State) houses two interesting museums: the **Historical Museum** and the **Museum of Natural History and Anthropology** (Museu de História Natural e Antropologia) with numerous items of Indian daily life plus weapons and archaeological finds, as well as stuffed animals from the region.

▶ VISITING CUIABÁ

INFORMATION
Praça da República 131
Tel. (065) 36 13-93 00
www.cuiaba.mt.gov.br

GETTING THERE

Airport
Marechal Rondon
Varze Grande
Tel. (065) 36 14-25 10

Bus station
Avenida Marechal Deodoro
Tel. (065) 36 21-10 40

WHERE TO EAT
▶ Expensive
Al Manzul
Cachoieira das Garças

Tel. (065) 36 63-22 37
Lebanese specialities

WHERE TO STAY
▶ Mid-range
Eldorado Cuiabá
Avenida Isaac Póvoas 1000
Tel. (041) 36 24-40 00
www.hoteiseldorado.com.br
The best hotel in town. 147 air-conditioned rooms plus restaurant.

▶ Budget
Fazenda Mato Grosso
Rua Antônio Dorileo 1100
Tel. (041) 36 61-12 00
www.hotelmatogrosso.com.br
Country estate in attractive surroundings

The Rondon Museum in Avenida Fernando Corrêa da Costa, also called **Museu do Indio** (Indian Museum), exhibits weapons, crafts and tools of the indigeneous Indians living in the Mato Grosso, which offer the visitor an excellent insight into the daily life of the indigeneous population. Opening times: Mon – Sat 7.30 to 11.30am.

✳ **Museu Rondon**

🕓

✳ Curitiba

Sa 58

State: Paraná (PR)
Altitude: 934m/3,064ft

Population: 1.6 million

Curitiba, the capital of Paraná state in the south of Brazil, stretches across the plateau of the same name west of Serra do Mar.

Owing to its well-conceived, modern public transport system, an extensive network of cycle lanes, and its generously laid-out green spaces, Curitiba enjoys a reputation all over Brazil as a city with human dimensions and an above-average quality of life. Its pioneering urban planning, complemented by a progressive environmental and waste management policy, has earned Curitiba the title of »Ecological Capital of Brazil«.

What to see in Curitiba

In the western part of the city, 6km/3.5 miles from the city centre, the green spaces of Barigui Park contain a forest with a large lake, sports facilities, a playground, a track for model cars and an automobile museum.

✳ **Parque do Barigui**

Going northwest from the city centre via Avenida Jaime Reis leads to the Santa Felicidade neighbourhood which was established in the 19th century and is mainly inhabited by Italians. Italian restaurants, frequented mainly by the city's wealthy inhabitants, line the main road, called from this point onwards **Avenida Manoel Ribas**. Every year, this neighbourhood celebrates a wine festival in February, and, at varying dates, the Quattro Giorni in Italia (Four Days in Italy) event.

Santa Felicidade

The Park Jardim Botânico with its araucaria forests, gardens and flower borders laid out in the French style, as well as a hothouse, lies in Rua Ostoja Roguski and is worth seeing for its unusual construction alone. The green spaces and flowerbeds are looked after by street children as part of a pilot scheme.Opening times: daily 6am to 8pm.

✳ **Jardim Botânico**

🕓

⏵ VISITING CURITIBA

INFORMATION

Rua 24 Horas
Tel. (041) 33 52-80 00
www.curitiba.pr.gov.br

GETTING THERE

Airport
Aeroporto Afonso Pena
Av Rocha Pombo
Tel. (041) 33 81-15 15

Bus station
Avenida Presidente Afonso
Camargo 330
Tel. (041) 33 20-30 00

VISITING THE CITY

Linha Turismo
Visitors can tick off the 22 most important city sights by taking the specially provided Jardineira buses. These open-topped tours run Tue to Sun 9am – 5.30pm every half-hour on a circular route. A coupon system allows travellers to break the journey three times.

WHERE TO EAT

▶ **Expensive**

① *Boulevard*
Rua Voluntários da Pátria 539
Tel. (041) 32 24-82 44
Best restaurant in town, overseen by renowned chef Celso Figueiredo Freire Filho. The exquisite wine list is fairly priced.

▶ **Moderate**

② *Durski*
Rua Jaime Reis 254
Tel. (041) 32 25-78 93
Expertly prepared specialities from Poland, Russia and the Ukraine – such as borscht, platzki potato pancakes and holopti (rice and beef wrapped in cabbage)

③ *Zea Mais*
In the San Juan Palace Hotel
Rua Barão do Rio Branco 354
Tel. (041) 32 32-39 88
International cuisine in a central location. Closed for lunch.

WHERE TO STAY

▶ **Mid-range**

① *Bourbon & Tower*
Rua Cândido Lopes 102
Tel. (041) 32 21-46 00
www.bourbon.com.br
Business hotel with 175 apartments and suites, bar, restaurant, swimming pool, sauna and gym. Partly accessible for wheelchair users.

② *Lancaster*
Rua Voluntários da Pátria 91
Tel. (041) 33 22-89 53
www.lancaster-hoteis.com
Traditional hotel with 106 spacious rooms with air-conditioning and heating, private car parking, good restaurant and fitness centre

▶ **Budget**

③ *San Martin*
Rua João Negrão 169
Tel (041) 32 22-52 11
www.sanmartin.com.br
Alongside its 94 rooms, this hotel offers a swimming pool and a sauna, but no restaurant.

④ *Deville Express*
Rua Amintas de Barros 73
Tel. (041) 33 22-85 58 und
(08 00) 703-18 66
www.deville.com.br
Hotel with 114 rooms, car parking, restaurant and gym

Curitiba Map

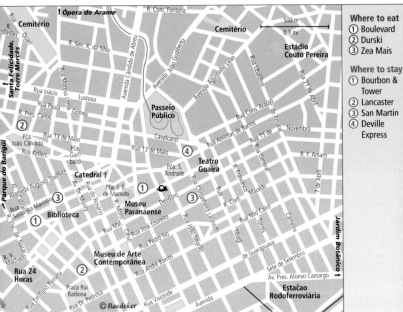

The fine Tingui Park lies on Avenida Fredolin Wolf. The monumental wooden cathedral topped by an onion dome in the park was built to honour the immigrants from the Ukraine.

Parque Tingui

Built in the 1960s, the Teatro Ópera de Arame (Wire Opera) is not only of architectural interest; it was built in a former quarry (Pedreira Paulo Leminski) north of the city centre on Rua João Gava, which was redesigned as a fine leisure park. The opera house, constructed in artistic simplicity from glass and tubes, bears the hallmarks of the architect and former town mayor **Jaime Lerner**.

★
Teatro Ópera de Arame

The view from the Torre Mercês telecommunications tower is most impressive at sunset. The 110m/360-ft high**viewing tower** at 191 Rua Professor Lycio de Castro Veloso also includes a small telephone museum. Opening times: Tue–Fri 11am–8pm, Sat/Sun 10am to 8pm.

Torre Mercês

On the border of the Largo da Ordem rise some of the oldest buildings of Curitiba: the **São Francisco de Chagas** church of the Franciscan lay order, erected in 1737 with the adjacent Museum of Sacred Art, the Nossa Senhora do Rosário church from the same century, as

Largo da Ordem

well as the 18th century Casa Rosário Martins, the second-oldest house in Curitiba, which houses the Historical Archive of the city.

Rua 24 Horas

As its name suggests, the glass-covered shopping centre in Rua Visconde de Nacar does actually stay open for near enough 24 hours every day. The numerous bars, bistros, pizzerias and restaurants are busy with the constant comings and goings of night owls well into the early hours.

Passeio Público

Rua Carlos Cavalcanti leads to the Passeio Público, laid out in 1866. The city park, of around 7ha/17 acres, is one of the most popular meeting points for the locals strolling around the tree-lined avenues and lake with its small islands, or visiting the zoo and the aquarium. Occasionally there are music performances on the promenade.

Bosque Papa João Paulo II

In the north of Curitiba are the Centro Cívico (civic centre) and the park named after Pope John Paul II with the **Immigrants' Museum**, dedicated mainly to the Polish settlers. Their story is brought to life by photos, household effects and tools.

Oscar Niemeyer Museum

Opened in 2002, the museum (Rua Marechal Hermes 999, Centro Cívico district) consists of two buildings, realized independently of each other – 35 years separate the two parts – and connected by one of the spiral staircases characteristic of Niemeyer's work, ie underground. The more recent wing measures 3,000 sq metres/32,300 sq feet and is designed – following Niemeyer's architectural symbolism – in the shape of a huge eye. Alongside occasional **changing exhibitions**, the inside so far has only a few drawings and photos illustrating the life's work of Oscar Niemeyer. Opening times: Tue–Sun 10am–8pm.

Around Curitiba

Parque Regional Iguaçu

The Avenidas Floriano Peixoto, das Torres and Centenário lead to the Iguaçu Regional Park, lying 13km/8 miles south of the city centre between the municipalities of Curitiba and São José dos Pinhais. This nature reserve (3.1 sq km/4.8 square miles) has lakes with beaches, a fish farm, orchards and a small zoo.

Estância Ouro Fino

Apart from its mineral springs, the Estância Ouro Fino thermal spa – in the municipality of **Campo Largo** (pop 92,000), 46km/28 miles west of Curitiba – offers visitors a lake, forest, extensive green spaces and a swimming pool with water rich in alkali and iron. Opening times: Tue–Sun 7am–6pm.

Caves

Around Curitiba, several caves are open to visitors; the nearest of which are the caves of **Bacaetava** on the road to Rio Branco do Sul. A little further on, look out for the cave of **Lancinhas**, at 1,700m/

1,860yd in length the largest in Paraná state. The cave of **Campinhas**, with three different entrances, can be found in the state park of the same name, 72km/45 miles past Curitiba on the BR-476.

✳ Parque Estadual da Vila Velha

90km/56 miles northwest of Curitiba, near the town of **Ponta Grossa**, rise the rock formations of Vila Velha, which in the past have been erroneously taken for a ruined town. In reality, these bizarre rock formations were created by tectonic shifts and erosion over millions of years.

From the park entrance, a walk or a ride on the visitor bus leads directly to the overhanging rocks; signposted trails lead to the other rock towers named after their shape. Easy to identify are the Chalice, Camel, Indian and Sparrowhawk rocks.

✳ Rock formations

Around 20km/12.5 miles outside Ponta Grossa, the Caldeirões do Inferno (Cauldrons of Hell) are round openings of up to 107m/351ft depth and an average diameter of 80m/262ft.

Caldeirões do Inferno

A climber tackling the bizarre rock formations of Vila Velha

Lagoa Dourada

Lined by trees and a veritable paradise for the water fauna of the area, the Lagoa Dourada (Golden Lagoon) is fed by a subterranean river, whose erosive action caused the collapse of the rocks and thus the formation of the caves. The bottom of the lake is covered in mica, which makes the water take on a golden shimmer in the sunlight. The Lagoa lies near the Caldeirões do Inferno.

✶ ✶ Diamantina

Sd 55

State: Minas Gerais (MG)
Altitude: 1,113m/3,600ft

Population: 44,000

The little town of Diamantina was founded on the banks of the Tijuco river by prospectors hunting for precious stones in the Jequitinhonha valley, in the heart of the sertão of Minas Gerais. It is also the birthplace of Juscelino Kubitschek de Oliveira (1902 – 1976), the former president of Brazil and founder of the artificially created capital of Brasília. The town, characterized by colonial architecture, is a UNESCO World Heritage Site.

In the 18th century, this small settlement evolved into the central hub of the Serra do Espinhaço, the central mountainous region of Minas Gerais. At the time, Diamantina – the clue is in the name – was so rich in diamonds that the town was placed under the direct administration of the Portuguese crown. The town's inhabitants were deprived of all usual civil liberties and for a long time, people could only enter or leave Diamantina with a royal permit. The **exploitation of the deposits of precious stones** had top priority, with even gold prospecting prohibited here.

João Fernandes, the administrator appointed to Diamantina by Portugal's king, was the richest man in Brazil at the time. His lasting fame however, is due to his passionate relationship with the mulatto Chica da Silva, his beautiful domestic slave. At his side, Chica was to achieve a position of power that no other woman in her time had ever reached, residing in Diamantina in the style of a baroque princess.

100 years of isolation

In Diamantina, precious stones and immense wealth are now a thing of the past as much as the courageous Chica, who all her life worked for the rights of the slaves sweating in the diamond mines. Due to the isolation of Diamantina that lasted a good century, the colonial settlement stayed preserved – and with it the memories of Chica and João.

Within the state of Minas Gerais, Diamantina may be the furthest historical town from Belo Horizonte, but the trip here is worthwhile,

▶ VISITING DIAMANTINA

INFORMATION
Rua Antônio Eulálio 53
Tel. (038) 35 31-16 36
www.diamantina.com.br

GETTING THERE
Bus station
Largo Dom João
Tel. (038) 35 31-16 43

EVENTS
Festa de Corpus Christi
During the Festa de Corpus Christi,
the streets of Diamantina undergo a
colourful transformation, becoming
elaborately carpeted with sawdust,
coloured sand and azalea petals, and
bicos de papagaio, a type of cactus
blossom reminiscent of a parrot's
beak.

Mercado Municipal
On a Saturday, the municipal market
on Praça Barão do Guaicuí in the
covered market hall (dating from
1835) has crafts from the Jequitinho
valley, liqueurs, cheese and typical
sweets for sale.

WHERE TO EAT
▶ **Inexpensive**
① *Trattoria*
La Dolce Vita
Rua da Caridade 147
Tel. (038) 35 31-84 85
Pasta and traditional dishes from
Minas Gerais, with an Italian
twist

② *Grupiara*
Rua Campos Carvalho 12
Tel. (038) 35 31-38 87
Simple but filling regional dishes.
Some of the recipes used date back to
the time of slavery

WHERE TO STAY
▶ **Budget**
① *Tijuco*
Rua Macau do Meio 211
Tel./fax (038) 35 31-10 22
This place was designed by the
Brazilian star architect Oscar Nie-
meyer in 1953.

② *Pousada dos Cristais*
Rua Jogo da Bola 53
Tel. (038) 35 31-28 97
www.diamantinanet.com.br
Small pousada in a central location;
19 rooms with TV

Baedeker recommendation

▶ **Budget**
③ *Pousada Jardim da Serra*
Estrada do Cruzeiro Luminoso
(accessible via the BR-367 to Araçuaí)
Tel. (038) 91 06-85 61 and
91 06-85 62
www.jardimdaserra.com.br
This is the place for nature lovers: this
pousada lies in the mountains of the Serra
dos Cristais, surrounded by forest and
meadows, offers an unobstructed view of
the Pico de Itambé peak and has a natural
lake.

not least because of the charming and varied scenery, in particular
on the stretch between Curvelo and the slopes of the Serra do Espinhaço.

What to see in Diamantina

Colonial buildings

The roads of Diamantina, paved with Pés-de-moleque, a kind of cobblestone, are lined by houses from the colonial era, while their central reservations, the capistrana, are formed by large smooth stones. Of particular interest is the group of buildings in the historical core of the **Arraial do Tijuco**, the Rua do Burgalhau, leading to the Praça Barão do Guaicuí, where the Mercado dos Tropeiros city market is held. Also worth seeing are the Casa de Chica da Silva and the Casa da Glória (both see below).

Baedeker TIP

A touch of Arabic architecture

The Casa do Muxarabiê, at 48 Rua da Quintanda, houses Diamantina's public library, named after Antônio Torres. The library has a remarkable collection of books and manuscripts from the 18th century. No less interesting is the house's finely-wrought veranda and its faintly Arabic-inspired façade. Opening times: Mon – Fri 7.30am – noon and 1.30 – 5pm.

Erected in 1728, the church of **Nossa Senhora do Rosário dos Pretos** (Our Lady of the Rosary of Black People) – the oldest church in Diamantina – towers above the Praça do Rosário, with the Chafariz do Rosário fountain and the Cruz da Gameleira cross, around which a tree has grown. The interior of the choir chapel was painted in 1779 by **José Soares de Araújo**, who was active in the Diamantina area from 1765 onwards. In the first half of October, the Festa do Rosário is celebrated here.

NS do Carmo

The Carmelite church of Nossa Senhora do Ordem Terceira do Carmo was built between 1760 and 1784 south of the Praça do Rosário in Rua Bonfim. The church became famous throughout Brazil as Chica's Church, as João Fernandes' capricious mistress demanded that the bell tower of the church be moved. The most noteworthy feature in the nave is the **ceiling fresco** painted between 1778 and 1784. The painting seems crammed into a small space and is carried out in sombre colours: both typical characteristics of painting in the Diamantina area. According to some experts, they symbolize the total oppression the town was suffering at the time, and the stifling feeling shared by its inhabitants. This masterpiece of José Soares de Araújo represents the prophet Elijah being carried up to heaven on a chariot of fire.

Palácio Episcopal

Built by the Portuguese governor João Fernandes de Oliveira, the Palácio Episcopal (Bishop's Palace) in Rua do Contrato also dates from the 18th century.

Casa de Chica da Silva

Between 1763 and 1771, this house on the Praça Lobo Mesquita was the home of João Fernandes and Chica da Silva, who at his side rose from being a slave to become the most powerful woman in Diamantina. The Casa de Chica da Silva has a spacious veranda, several balconies, 18 rooms and a small courtyard chapel. Opening times: Tue – Sat noon – 5.30pm, Sun 9am – noon.

The former residence of Padre Rolim, who took part in the uprising of the Inconfidentes, today houses the diamond museum (Rua Direita 14). Alongside 18th-century furniture, exhibits include Chinese and English porcelain, tabernacles, documents on mining in Diamantina, as well as **instruments of torture** used on the slaves of the time. Opening times: Tue – Sat noon – 5.30pm, Sun 9am – noon.

★ Museu do Diamante

At 241 Rua São Francisco stands the childhood home of President Juscelino Kubitschek, who died in a car accident in 1976. Here, photos and documents are preserved, alongside a small library.

Casa de J Kubitschek

Without a doubt one of the most beautiful churches in Diamantina is the Franciscan church of São Francisco de Assis, dating from 1766. Its entrance opens on to the Rua São Francisco, and the entire main altar is gilded.

★ São Francisco de Assis

The Casa da Glória (Rua da Glória 298), consisting of two wings – one erected in the 18th century and the other in the 19th – connected by a wooden bridge, houses the Institute of Geology and an impressive collection of old maps. Opening times: Tue – Sun 1 to 6pm.

Casa da Glória

Diamantina Map

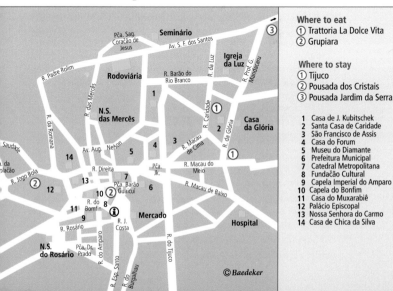

Where to eat
① Trattoria La Dolce Vita
② Grupiara

Where to stay
① Tijuco
② Pousada dos Cristais
③ Pousada Jardim da Serra

1 Casa de J. Kubitschek
2 Santa Casa de Caridade
3 São Francisco de Assis
4 Casa do Forum
5 Museu do Diamante
6 Prefeitura Municipal
7 Catedral Metropolitana
8 Fundação Cultural
9 Capela Imperial do Amparo
10 Capela do Bonfim
11 Casa do Muxarabiê
12 Palácio Episcopal
13 Nossa Senhora do Carmo
14 Casa de Chica da Silva

© Baedeker

Around Diamantina

Caminho dos Escravos
✴ The once important paved road connecting Diamantina and the north of Minas Gerais takes its name, Caminho dos Escravos, from those who were forced to build it. The Slave Way begins about 5km/ 3 miles outside the town on the BR-367, near the Araçuaí exit.

Cruz da Serra
Some 6km/3.5 miles from Diamantina, on an elevation on the road to Araçuaí, rises the »Cross of the Serra«. From here, there are views over the entire surrounding region.

Gruta do Salitre
Salitre Cave, situated 9km/5.5 miles east of Diamantina on the road to Curralino, boasts four halls, the largest of which reaches 5m/16ft in height and 64m/70yd in length.

Vila de Biribiri
The village of Biribiri, situated 10km/6.2 miles from Diamantina at an altitude of 1,300m/4,265ft in the Serra do Espinhaço, was founded around 1876 at the same time as a weaving mill. Since the factory shut down in 1973, Biribiri seems a **ghost town**: 30 settlers' homes, a church dating from 1890, a store, a school and other buildings stand empty, providing an ideal backdrop for films such as *Chica da Silva*.

Serro
The small colonial town of Serro (pop 21,000), 82km/51 miles south of Diamantina, is the birthplace of Chica da Silva, who went on to become the **»Lady of Diamantina«**. Serro still has a good number of colonial buildings, amongst them the Casa dos Otonis on the Praça Cristiano Otoni. On the same square rises the Senhor Bom Jesus de Matosinhos church, with a ceiling painted by Silvestre de Almeida Lopes in 1796. Other churches worthy of note are Nossa Senhora da Conceição, Nossa Senhora do Carmo and Santa Rita. One important event in the life of the town is the Festa do Rosário (Rosary festival), celebrated on the first Sunday in July. For this event, the streets of Serro are decorated with colourful creations of sand and flowers.

✴ ✴ Fernando de Noronha

Sj 47

State: Pernambuco	**Population:** 1,750
Altitude: 0–322m/0–1,056ft	

The archipelago of Fernando de Noronha, situated around 350km/ 217 miles northeast of Cabo São Roque, comprises the main island of the same name, as well as 20 surrounding islets. Since 1988, 11,270ha/27,850 acres of the archipelago have been placed under strict environmental protection.

Amerigo Vespucci and Gonçalo Coelho discovered this group of islands in 1503; Dutch, English and then French settlers were later attracted to its favourable strategic location. In the mid 19th century, Fernando de Noronha was turned into a prison island – even during the military dictatorship (1964–1985), opposition politicians disliked by the regime were banished to this remote archipelago. During World War II, the main island served as a base for Allied pilots. The runway, established for fighter planes, is today used by propeller aircraft transporting tourists.

What to see on Fernando de Noronha

The main island, the only one of the archipelago to be inhabited, is of volcanic origin and reaches its peak in the 322m/1,056-ft rock pinnacle of **Morro do Pico**. Today, a large part of the island and the coastal waters have been placed under environmental protection as the Parque Nacional Marinho de Fernando de Noronha; the state environmental protection agency carries out on-the-spot checks to ensure that the regulations are adhered to.

✳ ✳
National Marine Park

Alongside unspoilt bays with fine sandy swimming beaches – such as **Baía do Sancho**, Baía dos Porcos and Praia da Atalaia – unique diving spots make a trip to Fernando de Noronha worthwhile. The crystal-clear waters are home to 18 different types of coral; and as well as various species of shark, dolphins raise their young off Fernando de Noronha. Between January and July, marine turtles lay their eggs in the sand of Praia do Leão; during this time, the beach is off-limits for swimmers.

Underwater world

No crowds to avoid on the beaches of Fernando de Noronha

▶ VISITING FERNANDO DE NORONHA

INFORMATION

Vila dos Remédios
Palácio São Miguel
Tel. (081) 36 19-13 52
www.noronha.com.br

GETTING THERE

There are no boats between the Brazilian mainland and the archipelago, but scheduled Varig/Nordeste services fly to Fernando de Noronha from Recife (Pernambuco), and TRIP charter services from Natal (Rio Grande do Norte).

ENTRY GUIDELINES

Only a limited number of tourists are allowed onto the main island. Alongside the relevant regulations, a progressive conservation fee – rising with each additional day – and the low number of accommodation options and incoming flights help to further limit tourism. Straight after arrival at the airport, all passengers are checked by a civil servant of the IBAMA environment agency. Travellers arriving at this checkpoint without a confirmed accommodation reservation are going to lose time at least; if all pousadas are full, the worst-case scenario involves an early flight back.

TRIPS • DIVING

Boat trips and dives, as well as accommodation, transfers and gear may be arranged through the diving school: Atlantis Divers, Vila dos Remédios, tel./fax (081) 36 19-13 71 and tel. (084) 32 06-88 40, www.atlantisnoronha.com.br

WHERE TO STAY

▶ Luxury
Pousada Maravilha
BR-363, Sueste
Tel. 36 19-00 28
www.pousadamaravilha.com.br
The best-appointed and most expensive pousada on the island, with a good restaurant.

▶ Mid-range
Pousada Monsieur Rocha
Rua Dom Juquinha 139
Vila do Trinta, Tel. 36 19-12 27
Well established and under French management, with 14 air-conditioned apartments. Visa, Diners and Mastercard are accepted, but not American Express.

▶ Budget
Pousada Alamoa
Alameda das Acácias 2
Floresta Nova, Tel. 36 19-18 39
www.pousadaalamoa.com
This guesthouse offers 7 air-conditioned rooms, TV, Internet and (for a fee) transfers.

Nature Conservation Water temperatures average 25 °C/77 F all year round. The dry season (Aug – Jan) offers ideal conditions for snorkelling and diving, as underwater visibility reaches up to 50m/165ft. Off the beaches of Fernando de Noronha, surfers find the best waves in December. Boat trips along the west coast of the main island are offered all year round, and usually the cutters will have an escort of dolphins. The conservation of these intelligent marine mammals is one of the concerns of the Parque Nacional Marinho de Fernando de Noronha. For information on the various other projects, visit one of the multimedia shows – run by scientists and conservationists of the **Projeto Tamar** project – every evening around 9pm in the centrally located visitor centre. As there are few events here, and only a single bar, these presentations are fairly popular, managing to bring home the importance of the protection of the sensitive coral habitat to almost every visitor to the islands.

Vila dos Remédios

In the main settlement on the archipelago, the small village of Vila dos Remédios, the ruins of the **Forte dos Remédios** fort, built by the Portuguese colonizers in 1737, are a reminder of the islands' strategic importance. In order to reinforce their claim to the archipelago, in the 18th century the Portuguese built further defensive structures, of which little remains today, along with the well-preserved baroque church of **Nossa Senhora dos Remédios** and the governor's palace of **São Miguel**, as an ostentatious symbol of their secular rule.

Florianópolis /
Ilha de Santa Catarina

Sa 59

State: Santa Catarina (SC)
Altitude: 25m/82ft

Population: 342,500

Partly situated on Ilha de Santa Catarina island, Florianópolis is the capital of Santa Catarina state. In the summer, the island's magnificent beaches and fishing villages attract tens of thousands of tourists. Many of the houses, painted in blue and white and covered with steep lean-to roofs, clearly show their origins in the Azores.

Other visitors are attracted by the possibility of whale-watching; between July and November, the marine mammals can be seen on the southern coast of Ilha de Santa Catarina, now declared a protection zone for whales, without moving from the beach. Florianópolis is connected with the mainland by the 821m/898-yd **Hercílio Luz suspension bridge**, designed by Gustave Eiffel and built in 1906, but no longer usable by cars, and a pair of bridges – Colombo Sales and Pedro Ivo Campos – only inaugurated in 1975.

History

The historical core of the city, the village of Nossa Senhora de Desterro, was founded in 1673 by the bandeirante Francisco Dias Velho from São Paulo. On 23 March 1726, it was made a vila, representing the most-fortified settlement on the entire southern coast, an indispensable rear cover for the Portuguese colonizing the areas of Gaú-

The Hercílio Luz bridge connecting the Ilha de Santa Catarina with the mainland

cho and La Plata. In 1738, it was elevated to the seat of government of Santa Catarina. From 1748 onwards, immigrants from the Azores who had come ashore in the south of Brazil settled here. This explains how the city continued to preserve its Portuguese flair, despite the few years from 1777 when the whole island was occupied by the Spanish, who in the end swapped Santa Catarina for Uruguay.

What to see in Florianópolis

Forts   The fort of Sant'Ana was erected in 1750, near the place where today the Hercílio Luz Bridge starts. The fortress, accessible via Avenida Beira Mar Norte, houses the **arms museum of the military police**. Additional forts protect the city, such as the Fortaleza da Nossa Senhora da Conceição, built between 1742 and 1744, and the Fortaleza de Santo António dos Ratones, dating from 1641, on Ratones

▶ VISITING FLORIANÓPOLIS

INFORMATION
Praça Quinze de Novembro
Tel. (048) 32 23-77 96
www.florianopolis.sc.gov.br

GETTING THERE
Airport
Aeroporto Hercílio Luz
Av Deomício Freitas
Tel. (048) 33 31-40 00

Bus station
Terminal Rita Maria
Avenida Paulo Fontes
Tel. (048) 32 12-31 00

EVENTS
From 25 to 28 July, the town of Barra
da Lagoa on Ilha de Santa Catarina
celebrates the Festa da Tainha, a
festival of Azorean origin. The main
dish consumed during these days is
the tainha (grey mullet), which is
caught with large dragnets in the
colder months. However, another
big draw of this event is the music
and dance from various regions of
Portugal.

WHERE TO EAT
▶ Expensive
Bistrô d'Acampora
SC-401 in the direction of Canasviei-
ras, km 10, Santo Antônio de Lisboa
Tel. (048) 32 35-10 73

Seasonal menu with dishes that
change daily; fish and duck can be
had practically all year round. One
of the best restaurants in Greater
Florianópolis.

▶ Moderate
Gugu
Rua Antônio Dias Carneiro 147
Sambaqui
Tel. (048) 33 35-02 88
Here, diners can find mussels and
fresh fish prepared to recipes from the
Azores.

WHERE TO STAY
▶ Luxury
**Costão do
Santinho Resort**
Rodovia Vereador
O. Lemos 2505
Tel. (048) 32 61-10 00
www.costao.com.br
Beach hotel with 270 well-appointed
apartments, and a swimming and
thermal pool.

▶ Mid-range
Coral Plaza
Rua Felipe Schmidt 1320
Tel. (048) 32 25-60 02
www.westcoral.com.br
This city hotel has 72 air-conditioned
rooms.

Grande island. The Santa Cruz do Anhatomirim fort, built between
1739 and 1744 on an island northeast of Ilha Santa Catarina, is particularly worth seeing. This is where, in 1891, two years after the
overthrow of Emperor Dom Pedro II and the proclamation of the republic, the last remaining royalists were incarcerated and executed.
This coastal garrison is best visited by schooner from Canasvieiras
beach.

Florianópolis • Ilha de Santa Catarina

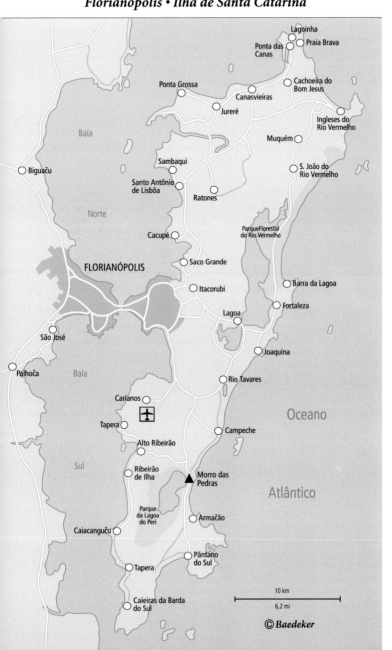

© Baedeker

No shortage of opportunities for bathing on the Ilha de Santa Catarina

The neo-classical customs house, rebuilt in 1898 in Rua Conselheiro Mafra, is one relic of the old port. The previous building, dating from colonial times, burned to the ground in 1866. Not all citizens of the city were too sorry about this, as the fire also destroyed the files of the tax office, which at the time was housed in the customs building. Today, artists have set up studios in the Alfândega.

Alfândega

The cathedral, completed in 1773 and totally renovated in 1922, stands in the city centre on the Praça Quinze de Novembro, near the Palácio Cruz e Sousa. The church houses, amongst other things, the life-sized wooden sculpture *Flight to Egypt*, a pipe organ dating from 1924 and some interesting stained-glass images.

Catedral Metropolitana

Only a few steps from the cathedral, the former government building houses the pink Museu Histórico, built between 1770 and 1780 and displaying arms, furniture and documents of historical significance to Santa Catarina state. More interesting than the exhibits is the building's interior: parquet floors made from canela and piroba wood, magnificent stucco ceilings supported by cast-iron pillars, and fine wrought-iron bannisters make the Palácio Cruz e Souza the most beautiful building in Florianópolis. Opening times: Tue–Fri 10am–6pm, Sat/Sun 10am–4pm.

★
Palácio Cruz e Souza

☉

A southern right whale off the coast of Santa Catarina: once hunted, they are now only observed.

SLOW, GOOD-NATURED, ENDANGERED

Southern right whales are slow swimmers. They are considered good-natured and come surprisingly close to the mainland, up to 30 metres/33 yards off the coast of Santa Catarina. This makes the mammals, which can grow up to 17m/56ft in length and weigh up to 50 tons/50,000kg, easy prey for whalers.

They are an enticing target too, as southern right whales in particular store their energy in a mighty layer of fat, which not only guaranteed that hunters made a good profit, but even made the bloody business easier, as harpooned southern right whales were borne to the surface by their blubber.

Whaling ban

In Brazilian waters southern right whales were hunted until 1973, when the last whaling station, near Imbituba in the southern Brazilian state of Santa Catarina closed down. Stocks were so decimated that it was to take nearly a decade until the mighty black mammals were sighted again off Santa Catarina. In 1995, Santa Catarina's government placed southern right whales under state protection. Five years later, the entire stretch of coast (156,000ha/385,500 acres) between the provincial capital of Florianópolis and the seaside resort of Balneário Rincão, some 25km/15.5 miles south of the Cape of Santa Marta, was declared a **whale and environment protection zone**. Late 2001 saw the foundation of the Instituto Baleia Franca (IBF). Together with its partner Vida Sol e Mar Resort in Praia do Rosa, the institute aims to research the whales and to alert the public to the necessity of protecting these

marine mammals, who are now back in the southern Brazilian conservation area in large numbers, to mate, breed and raise their young.

Whale Watching

As part of this conservation effort, dinghies measuring nine metres/30 feet and holding up to 20 people, are employed for whale watching. The cruises, lasting up to two hours, are led by specially trained skippers and always accompanied by a biologist from the Instituto Baleia Franca. Along the 80km/50-mile stretch of coast between **Praia da Pinheira and the Cape of Santa Marta**, these teams are supported by whale spotters posted onshore, who report each appearance of the mammals, mostly cows with calves, to the boat by radio.

Between July and November

Whale watching tours all over the world are adapted to the behaviour of the whales, the sea and the weather. The marine mammals visit the coast off Santa Catarina between July and November, i.e. outside the tourist peak season and during a time period

The whales come close to the shore, sometimes as near as 30m/33yd.

that in the southern hemisphere encompasses winter and spring. For more information, contact the Instituto Baleia Franca/Vida Sol e Mar Resort, www.vidasolemar.com.br, fax/tel (048) 33 55-61 11 and telephone (048) 32 54-41 99.

Casa de Victor Meirelles
At 59 Rua Victor Meirelles, near Praça Quinze de Novembro, the birthplace of the painter Victor Meirelles has been turned into a museum, showing a collection of documents, sketches and studies of the local artist. Some of his paintings hang in the **São Francisco da Ordem Terceira** church (1803), which can also boast several baroque altars.

Other sights on Ilha de Santa Catarina island

Santo Antônio de Lisboa
Situated in the north of the island, the village of Santo Antônio de Lisboa, with the church of Nossa Senhora da Necessidade (1750) and the Casa Açoriana arts centre, gives a good idea of Azorean architecture.

Barra da Lagoa, Lagoa da Conceição
The small blue-washed houses of Barra da Lagoa, a village near Lagoa da Conceição in the east of the island, also appear to be directly transplanted here from the Azores. The church of **Nossa Senhora da Conceição** dates from 1730.

Today, the population makes a living from fishing, tourism and the elaborate bone lace made by the local women. The Lagoa da Conceição, a protected lake, is one of the most popular sights on the island.

Jesuit monastery
Built on the top of the Morro das Pedras, this Jesuit monastery offers a generous view of the nature reserve of **Parque da Lagoa do Peri** 36km/22.5 miles outside Florianópolis, as well as the beaches of Morro das Pedras (not suitable for swimming) and Armação, both in the southeast of the island.

✳ ✳ Beaches on Ilha de Santa Catarina island

Nearby, north of Florianópolis, the beaches of Cacupé, Santo Antônio de Lisboa, Sambaqui and Santinho all attract many visitors during the Antarctic summer (Dec – Feb). Just as popular are the beaches of Canasvieiras and Praia de Jurerê that stretch opposite the Ilha do Francês in the northwest of the island, with its ruined São José da Ponta Grossa fort, built in 1741.

Surfers prefer the busy **Praia dos Ingleses** (Beach of the English), turned towards the Atlantic on the northeast flank of the Ilha de Santa Catarina. Near this stretch of coast, visitors can find two of the oldest churches on the island: São João Batista, dating from 1740 in the parish of Rio Vermelho, and São Francisco de Paula, erected in 1750 just behind the beach of Canasvieiras. Also facing the Atlantic are the extensive fine sands of the swimming beaches of Joaquina and Moçambique, as well as – further south – the bays of Campeche, Morro das Pedras and Armação. On **Praia Joaquina**, 17km/10.5 miles from Florianópolis, important national and international surf contests are held.

✳ Fortaleza

State: Ceará (CE)   **Population:** 2.1 million
Altitude: 21m/69ft

Fortaleza, the capital of Ceará and an important port and centre of tourism, is the fifth-largest city in Brazil. The city started life around the fort of Schoonenborch, erected by the Dutch in 1649 at the point where the Pajeú river flows into Mucuripe Bay.

The fort fell to the Portuguese soon afterwards in 1654, becoming the seat of a capitania under its new name of Fortaleza de Nossa Senhora da Assunção. Today, shortened to Fortaleza, the city is known all over Brazil as the place to get good-value leather goods and textiles. The fine beaches around Fortaleza are popular with both Brazilian and foreign tourists, as are the lively forró bars. Here, forró, a folk dance similar to foxtrot, is danced by young and old alike.

What to see in Fortaleza

In the former prison (Casa da Detenção), built between 1850 and 1856 in Rua Senador Pompeu 350, today numerous shops offer local crafts for sale.

Museu de Arte e Cultura Populares

Gaming room in Fortaleza

⏵ VISITING FORTELEZA

INFORMATION

Rua Senador Pompeu 350
Tel. (085) 32 31-35 66
www.ceara.com.br/fortaleza

GETTING THERE

Airport
Aeroporto Pinto Martins
Ferinha
Tel. (085) 34 77-12 00

Bus station
Avenida Borges de Melo 1630
Fátima
Tel. (085) 32 56-10 25

GOING OUT

Pirata Bar
This night club in Iracema has cult
status – across all generations! Opening from 8pm to 5am on Mondays
only, it is always full to bursting point.
Excellent live bands get things going
with forró and axé sounds (Rua dos
Tabajaras 325, Praia de Iracema,
www.pirata.com.br).

WHERE TO EAT

▶ **Moderate**
Cantino de Faustino
Rua Delmiro Gouveia 1520
 Varjota district
Tel. (085) 32 67-53 48
Simple restaurant, but where attentive
service complements the creative
preparation of regional specialities.
The highlights of the menu are fish
and lobster, along with goat.

▶ **Inexpensive**
Colher de Pau
Rua Frederico Borges 204
Varjota district
Tel. (085) 32 67-37 73
Cuisine of northeastern Brazil. House
speciality is Carne de Sol.

Picanha do Raul
Rua Joaquim Alves 73
Iracema district
Tel. (085) 32 19-65 00
Simple restaurant, but serving good
barbecued beef

WHERE TO STAY

▶ **Luxury**
Marina Park
Avenida Presidente Castelo
Branco 400
Tel. (085) 34 55-95 95
www.marinapark.com.br
The most beautiful hotel in the city is
located a little off the tourist trail. 315
air-conditioned apartments, a bar and
an excellent restaurant, four tennis
courts, swimming pool, sauna and
gym, as well as a children's playground, are all included in the
amenities. Partly suitable for wheelchair users.

▶ **Mid-range**
Lisboa Praia
Avenida Dioguinho 2860
Praia do Futuro district
Tel. (085) 34 86-40 00
www.lisboapraiahotel.com.br
Beach hotel with 145 rooms; some
also wheelchair-accessible.

▶ **Budget**
Pousada Feitiço do Ceará
Rua Hildebrando Pompeu 255
Praia do Futuro district
Tel. (085) 32 34-69 29
www.pousadafeiticodoceara.com.br
Small and simple: 5 apartments and 9
chalets (sleeping max. 5 guests), no
restaurant

In the city centre, facing Praça José de Alencar, sits the Teatro José de Alencar, a splendid iron construction in art nouveau style that opened in 1910. The courtyard, opening out to a garden, separates the entrance hall and foyer from the auditorium. The boxes are named after works by José de Alencar (1829–1877), the most famous writer of Ceará and author of the **Indian epic *Iracema***. The landscaped gardens surrounding the theatre was designed by Roberto Burle Marx (1909–1994).

★ ★ Teatro José de Alencar

Fortaleza's **automobile museum**, at 70 Avenida Desembargador Manoel Sales de Andrade, has a collection of vintage cars that is well worth seeing, with over 50 vehicles to admire, from the Thin Lizzy, a 1917 Ford Model T, to the 1959 VW Beetle.

As part of a comprehensive restoration of the old district of Iracema, the **Ponte Metálica** (Metal Bridge) was also given a facelift. Since then, a stretch of much-frequented bars and kiosks has been occupying the pier, constructed by a British company in 1925 and jutting out 130m/142yd into the Atlantic. Whilst the illumination of the pier, growing dimmer the further out to sea you get, makes Fortaleza's iron landmark a popular meeting point for courting couples, the listed building of the Estoril restaurant serves as a reminder of the 1950s, when the Iracema district was the centre of bohemian culture.

★ Iracema

> ! **Baedeker TIP**
>
> **Day trip to Baturité**
>
> A day trip from Fortaleza to Baturité, around 100km/160 miles southwest, is recommended – the buses leave in the morning from the bus station in Avenida Borges de Melo. This small mountain town preserves several buildings from colonial times, amongst them the main church of Nossa Senhora da Ralma (1764). From Baturité, regular buses go to the mountains of the Serra de Guaramiranga, 20 km/12.5 miles away. Alongside the numerous waterfalls, the Pico Alto (1,115m/3,658 ft), Ceará's highest peak, ranks among the most popular destinations for a day trip in the Serra.

None of Fortaleza's city beaches – Praia Formosa, Praia de Iracema, do Ideal, do Diário, do Meireles, do Mucuripe – have the best water quality (which doesn't seem to put the locals off), but there is a rich choice of the most varied restaurants and night clubs. **Praia do Meireles** and Mucuripe Beach, famous for its jangadas (flat sailing boats), are both in the eastern part of town, and act as starting points for day trips with larger boats that access even remote stretches of coast. From Praça Castro Carneiro (near the Fortur tourist information pavilion), a bus can take visitors easily to the **Praia do Futuro**, which offers dunes up to 30m/100ft high and relatively clean water.

Beaches

Around Fortaleza

Northwest and southeast of Fortaleza stretch fine beaches, interspersed with dunes and palm groves: in the northwest, between For-

★ Beaches near Fortaleza, Porto das Dunas

taleza and Camocim lie the Praias de Taíba, de Lagoinha, de Flechei-
ras, de Mundaú, de Icaraí, Cumbuco, Jericoacoara (▶ Camocim
p. 201) and many more. A little over 20km/12.5 miles southeast of
Fortaleza, the resort of Porto das Dunas has a Beach Park and Aqua
Park, where visitors can rent buggies, boats and watersports gear.

Aquiraz Near Porto das Dunas and 31km/19 miles southeast of Fortaleza, the
coastal town of Aquiraz (pop 60,500) has preserved some notable
colonial buildings. In the town, founded in 1699, the ruined Jesuit
college and the buildings on Praça Cônego Araripe – the church of
São José de Ribamar (1756) and the Museum of Sacred Art, also
dating from the 18th century and also named after Ceará's patron
saint São José de Ribamar – are particularly worth seeing.

✳
Beberibe The area around Beberibe (83km/51 miles southeast of Fortaleza)
has some of the most beautiful beaches in the northeast, including
Morro Branco (4km/2.5 miles from Beberibe), the Praia das Fontes
(10km/6.2 miles away) with a small rock cave – **Mãe d'Água** – which
becomes visible at low tide, Marambaia (15km/9.5 miles), Barra de
Sucatinga (18km/11 miles) and Pirajuru (42km/26 miles). The first
two beaches feature cascades of freshwater rushing down from the
hills.

Foz do Iguaçu

Rh 58

State: Paraná (PR)   **Population:** 259,000
Altitude: 164m/538ft

**Lying in the triangle formed by the three countries of Brazil, Para-
guay and Argentina, the town of Foz do Iguaçu might not have a
lot of charm, but is still one of the most important tourist centres
in the whole of Brazil.**

The main attractions in the area are the famous waterfalls of Iguaçu
in the national park of the same name, and the Itaipu hydroelectric
power plant.

✳ ✳ Cataratas do Iguaçu

The Rio Iguaçu rises at an altitude of some 1,300m/4,265ft, 500km/
310 miles east of the falls, in the Serra do Mar. Just before the stream
– here spanning 4km/2.5 miles at the border between Brazil and Argentina – flows into the **Rio Paraná** it narrows, forming through re-
gressive erosion a basalt plateau a good 80m/262ft in height, from
which its watery mass plunges down thunderously in a semicircle
2.7km/1.6-mile wide. In the rainy season, up to 6,500 cubic metres/

▶ VISITING FOZ DO IGUAÇU

INFORMATION

Informação Turística
Airport: tel. (045) 35 21-42 76

Bus station (Avenida Costa e Silva):
tel. (045) 35 22-10 27
www.fozdoiguacu.pr.gov.br

Parque Nacional do Iguaçu
Tel. (045) 35 21-44 00
www.cataratasdoiguacu.com.br

GETTING THERE

Airport
Aeroporto Internacional
Rodovia das Cataratas
Tel. (045) 35 21-42 00

Bus station
Avenida Costa e Silva
Tel. (045) 35 22-36 33

GOING OUT

Brazilians love gambling, but in order
to bet on black or red, odds or evens
at night, the inhabitants of Foz do
Iguaçu have to cross the border into
Argentina or Paraguay. Most of the
regional nightlife happens in and
around the local casinos.

WHERE TO EAT

▶ Moderate

Búfalo Branco
Rua Eng Rebouças 530
Tel. (045) 35 23-97 44
Well-established churrascaria (steak-
house) with rodízio (spit-grilled meat)

Tempero da Bahia
Rua Marechal Deodoro 1228
Tel. (045) 35 72-91 87
Afro-Brazilian cuisine from Bahia.

WHERE TO STAY

▶ Luxury

Tropical das Cataratas
Rodovia das Cataratas, km 24.5
Parque Nacional do Iguaçu
Tel. (045) 35 21-70 00
www.tropicalhotel.com.br
The only hotel right on the falls.
Excellent restaurants.

▶ Budget

Royal Park
Rodovia das Cataratas, km 11.7
Tel. (045) 35 29-60 70
www.hotel-royalpark.com.br Good-
sized hotel with 72 rooms and fine
swimming pools.

8,500 cubic yards of water per second form up to 272 cascades – the
most impressive natural spectacle in Brazil.

Numerous Indian legends surround the cataracts of Iguaçu. In the
worldview of the **Caingangues Indians**, the falls are the work of the
betrayed serpent god M'Boi. M'Boi was courting the Indian girl Naipi, who preferred the love of her fellow mortal Tarobá. The couple's
escape on a canoe along the Rio Iguaçu river was thwarted by the
jilted god with a lethal sweep of his tail, creating the canyon that to
this day receives the full force of the deluge of water. The lovers
drowned in the suddenly raging floods of the river that had previously calmly taken its course. After death, Tarobá turned into a palm

**Legend of the
Caingangues**

tree towering above the falls, Naipi into a rock at their foot – doomed to all eternity to be close to each other but not close enough. Today, by listening carefully, the mocking laughter of M'Boi may still be heard resounding; however, it is usually drowned out by the roaring mass of water.

Viewpoints

This symphony of spray, cascades, swaths of mist, iridescent rainbows and bubbling waters can be seen best from aboard a helicopter – or from one of the numerous viewpoints around the waterfalls. Several gangways have been built right up to the places where the waters gush over the plateau to plunge down into the abyss in a great roar. An elevator has made the viewing platform of the **Floriano Falls**, near the Tropical das Cataratas hotel, particularly easy to access.

Garganta do Diabo

A spectacular eye-catcher of the falls of Foz do Iguaçu is a place that bears the revealing name of Garganta do Diabo (Devil's Throat). This V-shaped cleft in the rock plateau receives 14 waterfalls in the tightest of spaces– making for a truly infernal scenario.

✳ ✳ Parque Nacional do Iguaçu

🕓
Opening times:
April – Sept
Tue – Sun
8am – 5pm,
Mon 1 – 5pm;
Oct – March
to 6pm

The Iguaçu Falls are enclosed by two national parks – one on each side of the border between Argentina and Brazil. Argentina's **Parque Nacional del Iguazú** (55,000ha/135,900 acres) was designated as early as 1934; five years later Brazil followed suit, giving environmental protection to 185,265 ha/457,800 acres of rainforest of the **Parque Nacional do Iguaçu**. In 1986, the entire area was given UNESCO World Natural Heritage status.

Flora and fauna

On the Brazilian side, the entrance to the Iguaçu Park lies just under 25km/15.5 miles east of Foz do Iguaçu town on the Rodovia das Cataratas. Alongside the world-famous falls, the nature reserve comprises the course of the Rio Floriano and – as the **largest forest protection area in southern Brazil** – the most varied vegetation zones, in parts even featuring plants that are now extinct elsewhere. Whilst in the north of the national park it is mainly pines and araucarias that thrive, at lower levels deciduous trees dominate the gallery forests along the rivers. The park is also home to around 1,100 types of bird, 700 species of butterfly and numerous smaller and larger mammals, amongst them deer, otters, ocelots and capybaras. From town, a major trunk road (Rodovia das Cataratas) leads past the airport and the Convention Center, through the park to the falls.

Coming from Argentina

There is an alternative access point to the national park on the Argentinian side. From the visitor centre there, the **Paseo Superior** (Upper Path), just under 1,000m/1,093yd long, leads to the Salto

The Iguaçu Falls →

Mbiguá, opening up the view to the Isla San Martín and the waterfall of the same name. The Paseo Inferior (Lower Path) follows the course of the falls at a lower level.

Parque das Aves

Extending over 4ha/10 acres immediately on the border of the Iguaçu National Park, the Parque das Aves features over 800 types of bird from all over the world, kept in cages and spacious aviaries, some of them open to walk into. The entrance to the bird park is on the Rodovia das Cataratas. Opening times: daily 8.30am–5.30pm.

> ## ! *Baedeker* TIP
>
> ### On safari
>
> Within the Iguaçu national park, Macuco Sáfari (Rodovia das Cataratas) organizes combined jeep and boat tours for groups of up to 25 people. Lasting about two hours, these trips by off-road vehicle lead for 3km/1.8 miles through the gallery forests, then on foot for 600m/1,970ft to the Macuco Falls, as well as by rubber dinghy to the cascades of the Garganta do Diabo. Tel. (045) 35 74-42 44, www.macucosafari.com.br

The **Ecomuseu de Itaipu** exhibits photos, Indian tools and stuffed animals. It lies on the Itaipu access road, on the Avenida Tancredo Neves, around 10km/6.2 miles outside the town of Foz do Iguaçu.

The Avenida General Meia leads from Foz do Iguaçu to Porto Meira and the **Marco das Três Fronteiras**, the boundary stone marking the triangle where the three countries (Brazil, Argentina and Paraguay) meet. At this spot, about 7km/4.3 miles outside town, the Rio Iguaçu flows into the larger Paraná river; the Marco das Três Fronteiras boundary stone also offers an excellent view over the borders of Argentina and Paraguay, as well as the surrounding region.

Around Foz do Iguaçu

In the Argentinian border town of **Puerto Iguazú**, connected with Brazil by the Tancredo Neves Bridge, many Brazilians buy up good-value Argentinian products such as leather and woollen goods – which is why locals crossing the border are often subject to lengthy checks.

Tri-Border Region

Tourists however, are free to move around in the triangle where the three countries meet. From the Brazilian side, in the daytime buses leave every hour to Puerto Iguazú and Ciudad del Este (Paraguay). Crossing the border at night is also nothing unusual, as the roulette and blackjack tables of the Iguazú casino bring a fair few Brazilians to Argentina.

Ciudad del Este

The route to Ciudad del Este in Paraguay is via the **Ponte da Amizade** (Friendship Bridge), spanning 8km/5 miles from Foz do Iguaçu across the Rio Paraná. Every day, thousands of visitors flock there to buy Paraguayan crafts and other goods. The Acaray casino on the riverbank lends a touch of Las Vegas to the proceedings.

Iguaçu Overview

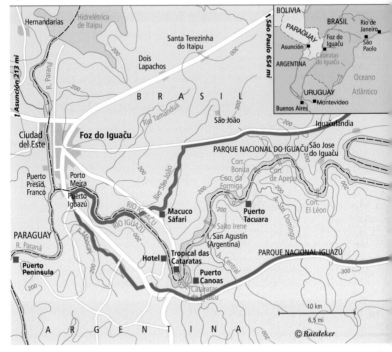

✱ Usina Hidrelétrica da Itaipu Binacional

The huge Itaipu hydroelectric power plant, about 10km/6.2 miles north of Foz do Iguaçu, is one of the large-scale prestige projects from the time of the Brazilian military dictatorship. The dam, 196m/643ft high and 7,760m/8,486yd long, and the power plant – a Brazilian-Paraguayan joint venture – were built between 1975 and 1984 in reaction to the worldwide hike in oil-prices.

The Usina Hidrelétrica da Itaipu Binacional is fed by the **Paraná res-** **Guided tours** **ervoir** extending northwards; its 18 turbines produce a quarter of the Brazilian and some 80 % of the Paraguayan energy requirements. Itaipu is the **largest hydroelectric power station in South America**, and indeed one of the most enormous plants of its kind in the world. Monday to Saturday there are guided tours (by bus) and the visitor centre (Centro de Visitantes) illustrates all the stages of its construction with audiovisual material. Both the dam and power station are situated at the end of Avenida Tancredo Neves.

✳ Goiás

Rk 53

State: Goiás (GO)　　　　　　**Population:** 22,000
Altitude: 496m/1,627ft

The town of Goiás, a UNESCO World Heritage Site since 2001, developed during the gold rush, starting life as the settlement of Arraial de Santana, founded by Bartolomeu Bueno in 1727.

He was the son of Bartolomeu Bueno da Silvas, a bandeirante from São Paulo who was given the nickname of Anhanguera and who in 1682 penetrated deep into the wilderness of Goiás. In 1739, the name of the settlement on the Rio Vermelho river, where rich gold deposits had been found, was changed to Vila Boa de Goiás.

What to see in and around Goiás

✳
São Francisco
de Paula

The Igreja Nossa Senhora do Carmo (1756) and the churches of São Francisco de Paula (1761) and Santa Barbara (1780), are amongst the oldest buildings in the town. The belltower of São Francisco de Paula is clad in wood and the ceiling of the choir chapel is decorated with paintings by **André Antônio de Conceição**. Still within the choir

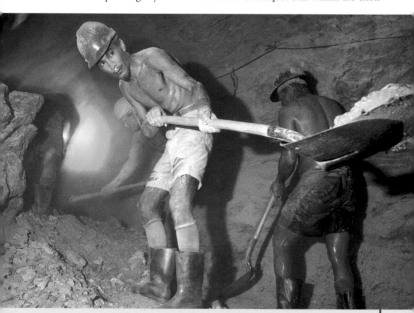

Today, instead of gold, precious stones are mined in Goiás.

▶ VISITING GOIÁS

INFORMATION
www.cidadeshistoricas.art.br/goias

GETTING THERE
Bus station
Avenida Dario de Paiva
Tel. (062) 33 71-15 10

EVENTS
Taking place two weeks before Holy Week, the procession of the »Meeting of the Images of the Mater Dolorosa and the Passion of Christ« opens the pre-Easter ceremonies in Goiás. One week before Holy Week, the procession of the Mater Dolorosa is held, and on the Sunday before that, the Palm Sunday procession. One of the most important events of Holy Week is the Procissão do Fogaréu on the Wednesday night, when all lights in the town go out. To the strains of drums and trumpets, hooded figures carry blazing torches through the streets; these are the farricocos, a representation of the Praetorian Guards who arrested Jesus. Over the following days, the processions of the Descent from the Cross and the Entombment of Christ are held; on Easter Saturday, Judas the Traitor is symbolically burned at the stake. Pentecost, 40 days after Easter, concludes the religious festivities.

SHOPPING
Associação dos Artesãos de Goiás
Largo do Rosário
Opening times: daily 8am – 5pm
Regional crafts

WHERE TO EAT
▶ **Inexpensive**
Goiás Ponto Com
Praça Coreto 19
Tel. (062) 33 71-16 9
Regional cuisine, good-value quick lunch options

WHERE TO STAY
▶ **Mid-range**
Fazenda Manduzanzan
Cachoeira dos Andorinhas
(8km/5 miles outside Goiás)
Tel. (062) 99 82-33 73
www.manduzanzan.com.br
Best hotel in town, often fully booked at weekends.

▶ **Budget**
Pousada do Ipê
Rua do Fórum 22
Tel. (062) 33 71-20 65
Simple rooms

---

chapel, the sculpture of the patron saint was created in the baroque style by the 19th-century sculptor Veiga Vale, who was from Goiás. Although harking back to the style of the 18th century, the ceiling of the nave was painted in 1869.

The church of Nossa Senhora da Boa Morte on Praça Castelo Branco was built in 1779 on the foundations of an earlier chapel. Today it houses the **Museum of Sacred Art**, showing 36 of the 200 sculptures in total that are believed to have been executed by Veiga Vale. **NS da Boa Morte**

Museu das Bandeiras The Museu das Bandeiras is situated in the former Câmara e Cadeia Pública (seat of the municipal authorities and prison) on Praça Brasil Caiado, built in 1766 under Dom José I. The stone walls, one metre/3.3ft thick, have been well preserved to this day. Amongst the museum's exhibits are **instruments of torture** from the time of slavery, as well as church furnishings, paintings, silver crockery, documents and handicrafts made by Carajá Indians. Opening times: Tue – Fri 9am to 5pm, Sat noon – 5pm, Sun 9am – 1pm.

Casa de Cora Coralina This house at 20 Rua D Cândido, built in 1784, was the residence of the Goiás-born poet Cora Coralina. Photos and furniture are on display, as well as videos on her life and work. Opening times: Tue – Sat 9am – 5pm, Sun 9am – 4pm.

Palácio do Conde dos Arcos Goiás has several other preserved 18th-century buildings, including the Palácio do Conde dos Arcos, dating from 1756 and with period furnishings, but now converted into an arts centre, and the Quartel do 20, an infantry barracks from 1747.

Balneário Santo Antônio Eleven kilometres/just under seven miles north of Goiás await the tempting bathing spots and campsites of the popular Balneário Santo Antônio. Reached by the GO-070 country road, these natural swimming pools are particularly popular at weekends.

Guarujá

Sb 57/58

State: São Paulo (SP)
Altitude: 5m/16ft

Population: 265,000

Guarujá, on the island of Santo Amaro, is the most chic and popular seaside resort in São Paulo state. Ferries for Guarujá leave from the town of Santos, 13km/8 miles away.

What to see in Guarujá

City beaches The biggest attraction of this town is its plethora of beaches, numbering 19 in total. Guarujá and Pitangueiras, the two most popular, are very close to the larger shopping streets. From there, boats leave for the islands of Pombeva and Cabras.

★ Beaches north of Guarujá The extensive Enseada beach, which is mainly used by watersports enthusiasts, lies 3km/1.8 miles north of Praia Pitangueiras. The Morro do Maluf, a hill right at the start of the beach, offers up fine views across the town and the nearby islands. The **Praias de Pernambuco** and Perequê beaches, 5km/3 miles and 10km/6.2 miles from Enseada Beach, are Guarujá's most luxurious swimming beaches. On the road

► VISITING GUARUJÁ

INFORMATION

Avenida Marechal Deodoro
da Fonseca 723
Tel. (013) 33 87-719 and
33 55-65 27
www.guiaguaruja.com.br

GETTING THERE

Bus station
Tel. (013) 33 86-23 25

WHERE TO EAT

► Expensive
Thai
Avenida Miguel Stéfano 1001
Praia da Enseada
Tel. (013) 33 89-40 00
Specialities from Thailand

► Moderate
Dalmo Bárbaro
Avenida Miguel Stéfano 4710
Praia da Enseada
Tel. (013) 33 51-92 98
Fish and seafood. This is a branch
of the restaurant of the same name
on the country road to Bertioga.

WHERE TO STAY

► Luxury
*Casa Grande Hotel
Resort & Spa*
Avenida Miguel Stéfano 1001
Praia da Enseada
Tel. (013) 33 89-40 00
www.casagrandehotel.com.br
A good quarter of the Praia da
Enseada is taken up by the colonial
façade of this holiday and conference
hotel (their banquet hall has seating
for up to 1,450 guests). 265 perfectly
appointed rooms plus 3 chalets (each
sleeping up to 6 people). Several
swimming pools, beach service, sauna
and gym, as well as a bar, restaurants
and internet access are available for
guests.

► Budget
Canto da Enseada
Rua São Paulo 132
Praia da Enseada
Tel (013) 33 51-48 19
16 air-conditioned apartments,
restaurant, bar, pool and beach
service

to Bertioga, right at the beginning of Praia de Pernambuco, rises a further vantage point, the **Morro do Sorocutuba**. On Perequê Beach, visit the former Capela dos Escravos (Slave Chapel) dating from the 18th century. Further on stretch the beaches of São Pedro, Iporanga and the Praia do Pinheiro, which is fairly difficult to reach but may be accessed by boat. Immediately before the bridge to Bertioga, look for the beaches of Praia Branca and Praia Preta.

To the south of town, three beaches deserve a special mention: Astúrias (1km/0.6 miles away) with its quiet waters, Praia do Tombo (2km/1.2 miles) with very rough waters and preferred by surfers, and Praia do Guaiúba (3km/1.8 miles), covered in dense vegetation with weak surf. Near the offshore islands (Ilhas do Mato), divers have a choice of rewarding diving spots.

Beaches south of Guarujá

Barra Grande, Forte Velho

Built in 1580, the fort of Barra Grande, 7km/4.3 miles from Guarujá and once the most important defensive structure on this stretch of coast, is located on the road to Santa Cruz dos Navegantes, but is also accessible by boat from the Ponta da Praia in Santos. From there, other boat services run to Forte Velho, 3km/1.8 miles from the centre of Guarujá town; this fort was built to protect Santos harbour.

✴ Igarassu

Sh 49

State: Pernambuco (PE) **Population:** 82,500
Altitude: 19m/62ft

Igarassu is one of the oldest settlements in all of Brazil. The town has its origin in a trading post that was established as early as 1530.

In Igarassu, several churches from the 16th and 17th centuries, as well as sugar cane mills and distilleries from colonial times are preserved. Igarassu (also spelled Igaraçu) lies 39km/24 miles north of ▶ Recife, the capital of Pernambuco.

What to see in Igarassu

Convento de Santo Antônio

✴ Built in 1588, the baroque Franciscan monastery Convento de Santo Antônio (Rua Barbosa Lima) dates back to 1588 and houses the **Igarassu art museum**. Particularly worth seeing are four paintings by unknown masters that used to be kept in the main church and which show the following episodes: the arrival of the Portuguese, the building of the main church, the miracle that stopped the Dutch from taking the roof off the church, as well as the plague epidemic of 1685 that raged in Recife, Olinda, Goiana and Itamaracá, but spared Igarassu, which was protected by the saints Cosmos and Damian. Opening times: daily 7am – 6pm.

São Cosme e São Damião

✴ Erected in 1535, the parish church of São Cosme e São Damião is the oldest surviving church in Brazil. It consists of just one nave and a façade with a triangular gable, both typical characteristics of 16th-century colonial church architecture. The church interior has been redesigned several times over the years, and only a few paintings remain from the original period.

Convento do Sagrado Coração de Jesus

At the Largo de São Cosme e São Damião, near the parish church, stands the Convento do Sagrado Coração de Jesus, dating from 1758. The former convent supposedly housed the first orphanage in Brazil.

Fisherman on the coast of Pernambuco

Itamaracá

The holiday resort of Itamaracá (pop 16,000) on the island of the same name, 20km/12.5 miles northeast of Igarassu and connected by bridge to the mainland, still has some buildings dating back to the 16th century. The small town, which was idyllic until a few years ago, is today a favourite weekend destination for the inhabitants of Recife, who particularly appreciate the beaches of Pilar at the centre, São Paulo, Rio Amba, Forno de Cal and Barra Verde in the south, and Jaguaribe, Lance dos Cações and Praia do Fortinho in the north.

Just under 7km/4.3 miles outside the town rises Forte Orange, origi-   **Forte Orange**
nally a Dutch fort dating from 1631, which was rebuilt 23 years later
by the Portuguese and renamed **Forte de Santa Cruz**. The idea was
to protect Igarassu from attack by sea. Opening times: Mon – Sat   ⊙
9am – 5pm, Sun 8am – 5pm.

✱ Ilhabela

State: São Paulo (SP)　　　　　　**Population:** 21,000
Altitude: 4m/13ft

With a surface area of just under 340 sq km/131 sq miles, the Ilha de São Sebastião, commonly known as Ilhabela (Beautiful Island) is the largest Brazilian maritime island. The range of mountains in the island's interior, often shrouded in mist – with the 1,379m/ 4,524-ft Morro de São Sebastião as the highest peak – is evidence of the volcanic origin of this tropical, densely-forested island.

▶ VISITING ILHABELA

INFORMATION

Ilhabela
Tel. (012) 38 96-67 37
www.ilhabela.sp.gov.br

São Sebastião
Tel. (012) 38 92-18 08
www.saosebastiao.com.br

GETTING THERE

Bus station
Vila Ilhabela
Rua Dr Carvalho 136
Tel. (012) 38 95-87 09

EVENTS

Semana International da Vela
The 10-day sailing regatta in July has
been held annually since 1973; today,
it has turned into a large-scale event
with live shows and lectures.

SPORTS • LEISURE

Colonial Diver
Tel. (012) 38 94-94 59
Diving off the protected Ilha das
Cabras

Lokal Adventure
Tel. (012) 38 96-57 77
Trekking up the Pico do Baepi

Companhia Adventura
Tel. (012) 38 96-35 57
Abseiling down the 30m/98-ft Três
Tombos Waterfall

WHERE TO EAT

▶ Expensive
Viana
Avenida Leonardo Reale 1560
Viana
Tel. (012) 38 96-10 89
Freshly-caught saltwater fish and
crustaceans. At weekends, forget
about securing a table without a
reservation.

▶ Inexpensive
A Redonda
Avenida Riauelo 6853
Praia do Curral, tel. (012) 38 94-91 54
Simple pizzeria

WHERE TO STAY

▶ Budget
Pousada Tamara
Rua Jacob Eduardo Toedli 163
Itaquanduba
Tel. (012) 38 96-25 43
www.pousada-tamara.com.br
17 air-conditioned apartments, pool
and beach service

Practically the entire island, which was used in the 17th and 18th
centuries as a pirates' lair, is protected as the **Parque Estadual de Ilhabela**. Thanks to its impressive waterfalls and many beautiful
beaches, Ilha de São Sebastião rose to become one of the most popular tourist destinations in the whole of São Paulo state.

What to see on Ilhabela

Ilhabela (place) Founded in 1532 on Ilha de São Sebastião, the village of Ilhabela can
be reached by ferry from the mainland town of São Sebastião, 7km/
4.3 miles away. Still remaining from colonial times are the church of

Ilhabela *Map*

Praia das
Palmeiras

5 km
3 mi
© Baedeker

Pta.
das Canas
Praia
Pacuiba
Praia
Jabaquara
Praia da Fome

Praia
Armação
Cachoeira
da Friagem

Praia das
Cigarras

**Pedras
do Sino** ●

Praia do
Poço

S
ã
o
S
e
b
a
s
t
i
ã
o

Praia do
Viana

Cachoeira
do Couro do Boi

Praia da
Serraria

Saco do
Indaia

Pico do Baepí
▲ 1025 m

Ilha da
Serraria

● **Ilhabela**

Praia
Perequê

Praia da
Caveira

Praia
Guanxuma

Engenho
d'Água

Saco de Eustáquio

São Sebastião ●

Pta. da
Cabeçuda

ⓘ

Cachoeira
da Toca

Baía de
Castelhanos

Praia dos
Castelhanos

Cachoeira dos
Três Tombos

Ilha das
Calhetas

C
a
n
a
l
d
e

Praia
Feiticeira

Saco do
Sombrio

Figueira

Praia
Grande

Pico de
São Sebastião
▲
1379 m

Saco
Grande

Pta. do
Veloso

Cachoeira
do Veloso

Cachoeira
do Areado

Praia das
Enchovas

Cachoeira
da Laje

Praia
Bonete

Pta. da
Pirabura

● **Borrifos**

Sepetiba
●

Pta. da
Sepetiba

Pta. do Boi

Nossa Senhora d'Ajuda, erected in 1532, parts of the town wall, cannons and the splendid sugar cane plantations, the first ever to have been set up on the northern coast of São Paulo.

In the eastern part of the island, Castelhanos Bay offers the beaches of Praia de Castelhanos, Saco de Sombrio, Saco de Eustáquio, Praia da Guanxuma, Praia da Caveira and Praia da Serraria, which can only be reached by untarmacked dirt roads or trails.

★
**Baía de
Castelhanos**

The beaches of Praia da Fome and Praia do Poço, situated on the northeastern coast of Ilhabela, can only be accessed by boat. Due to

**Beaches on
the northern
coast**

the light swell, the former trading centres for slaves are today a **haven for snorkellers and divers**. On the northwestern coast, look for the beaches of Pedras do Sino (with campsite, 4km/2.5 miles from Ilhabela town) and Armação (7km/4.3 miles). At the cape of Ponta das Canas, a sugar cane mill, a lighthouse and a ruined colonial fort are all worth a visit.

Beaches in the west and south

On the western side of Ilha de São Sebastião, the beaches of Engenho d'Água (2km/1.2 miles south of Ilhabela town), Perequê (4km/2.5 miles) and Feiticeira are of interest, as are Bonete and das Enchovas on the south coast. The Praia da Feiticeira (11km/6.8 miles) is considered the most exclusive beach on the island. On the hill rising opposite the beach, various **waterfalls** are asking to be admired. The overland route to the beautiful Bonete Beach is fairly hard going, and by boat it takes over an hour.

Engenho d'Água, Baepi peak

The Fazenda Engenho d'Água with its sugar cane mill and distillery dating back to the early 18th century, is situated south of Vila Ilhabela, near the beach of the same name, and once belonged to the largest plantations on the island. The Engenho d'Água, which united the administrative building and manor house under a single roof, is a two-storey building with old water pipes and a creaking water wheel. Starting from the sugar mill, hiking trails lead up to the 1,025m/3,363-ft Baepi Peak.

Islands

Around the Ilha de São Sebastião, several smaller islets such as the Búzios islands (a 1.5-hr crossing), Vitória, and Serraria Island (a two hour crossing) are the preferred destinations for scuba divers.

São Sebastião

Popular beach resort

Founded in 1636 and today very popular, the seaside resort of São Sebastião (pop 58,000) is distinguished most of all by its exemplarily strict environmental laws, designed to protect the slopes of the Serra do Mar from land speculation and pollution. **São Sebastião parish church** on Praça Major João Fernandes, a relic from colonial times, is worth seeing. The chapel of São Gonçalo, also dating back to the 17th century, houses a small museum of sacred art.

** Beaches

Between São Sebastião and Bertioga, a number of beautiful beaches follow one after the other: Baraqueçaba (6km/3.5 miles from town), Guaecá, Toque-Toque Grande (with waterfall), Toque-Toque Pequeno, Paúba, Maresias (27km/16.5 miles), Boiçucanga (42km/26 miles), Camburo (43km/26.5 miles), Baleia (45km/28 miles) and Barra do Saí (47km/29 miles). On the last five, yachts anchor alongside fishing boats, and exclusive apartment houses stand between simple fishing huts. From Praia de Boiçucanga it is not far to the last unspoilt beaches on this part of the coast, such as Praia Brava de Boiçucanga.

Ilhéus

Sf 53

State: Bahia (BA)   **Population:** 222,000
Altitude: 52m/170ft

The port town of Ilhéus, founded in 1534 as Vila Velha de São Jorge dos Ilhéus, lies in the south of Bahia. The town owes its former wealth to cocoa, the cultivation of which in the 18th century was promoted by the Jesuits, rising in the 19th century to the country's second-most important export.

The cocoa boom of the 1920s is also the background to the passionate love story between the mulatto woman Gabriele and the Arab Nacib in Jorge Amado's world-famous novel ***Gabriela, Clove and Cinnamon***, which is set in Ilhéus. Amado (► Famous People p. 69), the town's most famous son, was born on a cocoa plantation near Ilhéus. The Bahian coastal town is also the setting for other works of Amado, amongst them the novel *The Golden Harvest*.

▶ VISITING ILHÉUS

INFORMATION
Avenida Soares Lopes 1741
Tel. (073) 36 34-35 10
www.ilheus.com.br

GETTING THERE
Airport
Aeroporto de Ilhéus
Rua Brig E Gomes
Tel. (073) 32 31-76 29

Bus station
Estação Rodoviária
Tel. (073) 32 31-76 29

WHERE TO EAT
▶ Inexpensive
Armação
Rodovia Ilhéus-Canavieiras
km 4.5
Praia dos Milionários
Tel. (073) 36 32-18 17
Freshly-caught fish on Praia dos Milionários

WHERE TO STAY
▶ Mid-range
Ecoresort Tororomba
Rodovia Ilhéus-Canavieiras
km 24.5
Praia de Canabrava
Tel. (073) 32 69-12 00
www.tororomba.com.br
Beach hotel with 86 rooms and 4 chalets (for up to 4 people each). Resort in beautiful location in small forest, with some animal enclosures, walkways, children's playground and iron-rich spring.

▶ Budget
Village Enseada do Mamoan
Rodovia Ilhéus-Itacaré, km 2
Praia do Norte
Tel. (073) 36 57-60 50
www.hotelmamoan.com.br
48 air-conditioned rooms and 5 chalets, pool, bar, restaurant and children's playground

What to see in and around Ilhéus

Beaches

Behind Praia da Avenida stretches the centre of Ilhéus; the beaches of Malhado, Marciano and Norte lie further north. South of Ilhéus the beaches of Praia da Concha, with a view of the lighthouse and the Baía do Pontal, Praia do Sul (5km/3 miles from the city centre), Praia dos Milionários and Praia Cururupe (10km/6 miles), in the delta of the river of the same name, are all recommended. On **Praia Cururupe**, the Portuguese routed the Tupiniquin Indians in the terrible Batalha dos Nadadores battle in 1559. According to legend, when the bodies of the slain Indians washed ashore they covered the beach for two kilometres/over a mile.

Olivença

Worth a visit in Olivença, 19km/12 miles south of Ilhéus, are the 17th-century church of Nossa Senhora da Escada and the Tororomba spring, whose water has a blackish hue due to its high content of iron, magnesium and iodine. Just before Olivença the heavy surf draws numerous surfers to the beaches of Back Door, Cai n'Água and Batuba.

Ecoparque de Una

In the rural community of Una, some 60km/37 miles south of Ilhéus, the 11,400ha/28,170-acre Una Biological Reserve was established in 1980. This is one of the last surviving forest islands, and the

Lots of choice in the »Land of the Golden Fruit«

coastal rainforest (Mata Atlântica) here shelters the last remaining **micos leões dourados** (golden-headed lion tamarins) in Brazil, as well as other animal species whose survival in the wild is threatened. The Ecoparque can be explored on hiking trails that lead past, among other things, India rubber trees tapped by seringueiros (rubber collectors). Guided tours are available for visitors who book in advance by phoning tel: (073) 36 34-21 79.

Easily accessible, the 12km/7.5-mile beach of Comandatuba belongs to a seaside resort 70km/44 miles south of Ilhéus. There is a first-rate hotel and good tourist infrastructure here; the trips in sailing and fishing boats on the 500m/545-yd canal separating Comandatuba Island from the mainland are particularly attractive.

✱ **Ilha da Comandatuba**

✱ Itatiaia

Sc 57

State: Rio de Janeiro (RJ) and Minas Gerais (MG)

Brazil's oldest national park was established in 1937 in the extreme west of Rio de Janeiro state. The very popular nature reserve in the Serra da Mantiqueira extends into neighbouring Minas Gerais.

Gateway to the park is the town of Itatiaia on the Via Dutra trunk road (BR-116), just under 160km/100 miles from Rio de Janeiro. From Itatiaia, a 8.5km/5.3-mile cul-de-sac leads to the entrance of the reserve. Until 1908, the area today occupied by the national park belonged to the **Visconde de Mauá**, who sold it to the Brazilian state. After several agricultural projects failed, a forest reserve was established in 1914, followed in 1927 by a biological research station of Rio de Janeiro's Botanical Gardens. In the early 1930s, the president of the time, **Getúlio Vargas**, made this region, situated in a favourable position between São Paulo, Rio and Minas Gerais, his favourite sanctuary. It was at his instigation that on 14 June 1937 the area was officially declared the first national park in Brazil.

What to see in the Parque Nacional do Itatiaia

The park has a small visitor centre, as well as the **Museu Regional da Fauna e Flora** and an orchid garden, plus tarmacked paths. There is also a refuge that small groups can use; for more information, contact the IBAMA environmental protection agency at the park entrance, tel. (024) 33 52-14 61. The dry season (June – August) is the best time to visit the higher reaches of the national park, whilst in the low-lying parts, the period between October and February is good for a flying visit.

► VISITING ITATIAIA

INFORMATION

Posto Turístico
Praça Mariana Rocha 20
Tel. (024) 33 52-16 60, junction
(Ramal) 206

WHERE TO EAT

Only in the pousadas

WHERE TO STAY

► Mid-range
Donati
Parque Nacional, km 14
Tel. (024) 33 52-11 10
www.hoteldonati.com.br

Opened in 1931, this hotel has a good
restaurant, pool and natural lake. The
25 chalets are in varying states of
repair – be sure to check them first!

► Budget
Pousada Quatro Estações
Estrada do Parque Nacional 1390
(access road to the national park)
Tel. (024) 33 52-69 79
www.netlistas.com/
pousadaquatroestacoes
bike hire, swimming pool, sauna, 10
rooms (some adapted for wheelchair
users) and snack bar

✳
Landscape
Extending up to an altitude of around 750m/2,460ft, the diversity of
the Atlantic rainforest includes cedars, pines, Ipê and ironwood trees.
Above that the rocky mountainous region begins, reaching a height
of 2,787m/9,144ft around the **Pico das Agulhas Negras**. The splendid
landscape, seemingly alpine in parts, makes the Parque Nacional de
Itatiaia a popular destination for trekking.

Flora and Fauna
The diversity of scenery and plants – lush Mata Atlântica and high
mountain vegetation – is matched by the animal world: no fewer
than 67 species of mammal, amongst them monkeys, pakas and
sloths, as well as 360 species of bird, call the Parque Nacional do Itatiaia home.

Around the Parque Nacional do Itatiaia

✳
**Visconde
de Mauá**
The rural community of Visconde de Mauá is located 42km/26 miles
northwest of Itatiaia town, on the border with Minas Gerais. Its position at an altitude of 1,200m/3,937ft and the numerous surrounding forests with their roaring rivers and waterfalls make Visconde de
Mauá one of the most pleasant places in the **Serra da Mantiqueira**.
Mauá, Maromba (in Itatiaia district) and the town of Maringá in
Minas Gerais state, form the boundary of a mountainous region
well-known for its valleys – Vale das Flores, Vale do Pavão, etc.

Waterfalls
At the foot of the small **Véu da Noiva** (Bride's Veil) waterfall, around
11km/6.8 miles from Visconde de Mauá, a natural swimming pool
has formed. On the 30m/98-ft Escorrega Waterfall, 12km/7.5 miles

from Visconde de Mauá, it is possible to use the largest rock to slide down into the basin at its foot. The Santa Clara waterfall is a bit more difficult to reach, lying 12km/7.5 miles outside the town on the Maringá – Santa Clara road leading to Minas Gerais.

João Pessoa

Sh 49

State: Paraíba (PB)
Altitude: 47m/154ft

Population: 550,000

João Pessoa, the capital of Paraíba state, is the third-oldest city in the country and seems a lot quieter than most other large cities in northeast Brazil; despite the swimming beach reaching right up to the city, tourism in João Pessoa does not play the same part as in Natal or Recife.

Quality of life and environmental awareness are very important in Paraíba's friendly capital: modern buildings in João Pessoa are not allowed to exceed a certain height, and between 5 and 8am daily, the Avenida Cabo Branco promenade is reserved for cyclists and inline skaters. In addition, Paraíba's capital is competing with Curitiba for the title of the city with most greenery per inhabitant.

What to see in João Pessoa

On Praça São Francisco, north of today's city centre, the church of São Francisco and the convent of Santo Antônio count amongst the architectural highlights created by the master builders of the Franciscan order in Brazil. Whilst the convent was designed as early as 1589 by the monk Francisco dos Santos, work only started in 1701 with the building of the **Capela da Ordem Terceira**. The cloisters were completed around 1730, and it was to take another 49 years for the whole complex to be finished. The art historian Germain Bazin has called the façade of the convent of Santo Antônio »one of the most magnificent architectural compositions in all Latin America«. The monumental square is bordered on the sides by walls lavishly decorated with azulejos and sculptures, while the fine cross outside the entrance is typical for Franciscan churches. The sumptuous carvings on the pulpit were probably influenced by Indian art, and the ceiling of the nave is decorated with paintings in perspective. The convent of Santo Antônio also houses Paraíba's museum of religious and folk art. The convent's Chapel of the Third Order, entirely covered in gilded carvings and paintings, is known as **Capela Dourada** (Golden Chapel). On the pillars of the main altar look for sirens and other mythological figures. The side altars show off equally lavish decorations.

✱
São Francisco,
Santo Antônio

Casa da Pólvora	The Casa da Pólvora, a stone building from 1710, sits at the level of the Catedral Metropolitana, erected in 1586 to the west of the Franciscan ensemble on Ladeira de São Francisco. »Gunpowder House« houses the Museu Fotográfico Walfredo Rodrigues with photographs showing João Pessoa's history.
Jesuit college and convent	The Rua Duque de Caxias, with the Misericórdia church (1612), connects Praça São Francisco with Praça João Pessoa further south, where another significant complex of ecclesiastical architecture rises up: the Jesuit college (1586) and convent. The first houses the university's faculty of law, while the latter is today the seat of the state government under the name of Palácio da Redenção.
Parque Sólon de Lucena	East of Praça João Pessoa, look for the extensive Parque Sólon de Lucena city gardens, with an oval lake and magnificent royal palms. A little further north, in Rua Gouveia Nóbrega, visitors encounter the Parque Arruda Câmara, also called Bica Park, with a fountain dating back to the 18th century.
Espaço Cultural José Lins do Rego	The house at 800 Rua Abdias Gomes de Almeida (Tambauzinho district), where the writer **José Lins do Rego** (1901 – 1957) wrote his books, has been converted into an arts centre, with a library, conference hall, theatre, cinema, art gallery and planetarium.
✳ **Beaches**	Around 7km/4.3 miles east of João Pessoa stretches Tambaú Beach, known for the Hotel Tambaú which is reminiscent of a rocket launch pad. To the north, the swimming beaches of Praia de Manaíra (8km/ 5 miles), Praia do Bessa (11km/6.5 miles) and Praia do Poço (10km/ 6.2 miles) await; 14km/8.5 miles south of the town, Cabo Branco (White Cape), with the promontory of **Ponta do Seixas** marks the easternmost tip of the American continent. Even further south (18km/11 miles), Penha Beach has a church dating from 1854. This

 VISITING JOÃO PESSOA

INFORMATION

Av Almirante Tamandaré 100
Tel. (0 83) 2 26 – 70 78

GETTING THERE

Airport
Presidente Castro Pinto
Tel. (083) 32 32-12 00

Bus station
Rua Francisco Londres
Tel. (083) 32 21-96 11

WHERE TO STAY

► **Mid-range**
Tropical Tambaú
Av Almirante Tamandaré 229
Tel. (083) 32 47-36 60
Fax (083) 32 47-10 70
www.tropicalhotel.com.br
Beach hotel with 175 apartments, restaurant, bar, cinema, reading room, casino, nightclub, swimming pool. Medical care and car hire available in-house.

Sugar cane cultivation near João Pessoa

is where in the second half of November, the Festa da Nossa Senhora da Penha is celebrated – a popular festival with performances by dance groups and singers.

Joinville

State: Santa Catarina (SC)
Altitude: 3m/10ft

Population: 430,000

Whilst Joinville, north of Santa Catarina, is the most important industrial centre of the state, it also attracts tourists coming to admire its pretty timber-framed houses from the time of the German colonists.

Joinville developed from the Colônia Dona Francisca, founded in 1851 on a territory that the Prince of Joinville had been given as a present for his marriage to Dona Francisca Carolina, the sister of Dom Pedro II. The colony was established on the instigation of the Hamburg-based Colonization Society and welcomed German, Swiss and Norwegian immigrants.

▶ VISITING JOINVILLE

INFORMATION

Pórtico, Rua Quinze de Novembro/
BR-101
Tel. (047) 34 53-01 77
www.promotur.com.br

GETTING THERE

Airport
Aeroporto Regional
Av Santos-Dumont
Tel. (047) 34 67-10 00

Bus station
Rua Paraíba
Tel. (047) 34 33-29 91

EVENTS

Festival Internacional de Dança
Taking place in the Cau Hansen
conference centre, this 11-day dance
event in the second half of July is
considered one of the biggest dance
festivals in Latin America. Numerous
shows, live performances and lectures
in the shopping centres and in several
Joinville businesses accompany the
event.

WHERE TO EAT

▶ Moderate

Milano
Rua Anita Garibaldi 79
Anita Garibaldi district
Tel. (047) 34 55-43 55
This trattoria shares the Piazza Itália
with two other Italian restaurants.

WHERE TO STAY

▶ Mid-range

Blue Tree Towers
Avenida Juscelino Kubitschek 300
Tel. (047) 34 61-80 00
www.bluetree.com.br
84 rooms and excellent restaurant;
everything you could need.

▶ Budget

Pousada Vale Verde
BR-101 in the direction of Curitiba,
km 20
Estrada Bonita, Tel. (047) 34 64-13 77
www.pvaleverde.com.br
Four chalets (sleeping up to 6 guests
each) near a lake and waterfall. Broad
choice of sports.

What to see in Joinville

Museu Arqueológico do Sambaqui

One of the main attractions of Joinville is the Sambaqui Archeological Museum, situated east of the city centre at 600 Rua Dona Francisca; its 12,000 exhibits make it the most extensive in the whole country. Guided tours explain to visitors the way of life of the people who
were probably the first inhabitants of the coast of Santa Catarina –
the sambaquianos; »sambaquis« being shell middens.

Museu Nacional da Colonização e Imigração

The collection of the National Museum of Colonization and Immigration contains clothes, furniture, means of transport and items of
everyday life used by immigrants. The museum is housed in the **Palácio dos Príncipes**, which was built in 1870 for the Prince of Joinville
and his wife. The splendid avenue leading to the palace is lined by
palms over 100 years old.

Juazeiro do Norte

Sf 49

State: Ceará (CE)   **Population:** 212,000
Altitude: 377m/1,237ft

Juazeiro do Norte, in the far south of Ceará state, is one of the most important places of pilgrimage in Brazil. This is where Padre Cícero Romão Batista lived and worked; the priest is venerated as a saint by a large part of the population in the northeast to this day.

Up to the mid-19th century, neighbouring Crato was the most important urban centre in the Cariri valley – one of the most fertile regions in the rural state of Ceará. Towards the end of that century, however, Juazeiro do Norte increasingly began to challenge Crato's position, largely thanks to the works of Padre Cícero Romão Batista, a priest who opposed the Roman church and was suspended by it. However, the simple people saw him as a saint who could work miracles, and Padre Cícero and his followers called the tunes in local politics. Today the memory of this man of the church can still be felt all over the city.

Padre Cicero and his identical twins: a personality cult surrounds this man of the church.

VISITING JUAZEIRO DO NORTE

GETTING THERE

Airport
Aeroporto Regional Cariri
Av Virgílio Tàvora
Tel. (088) 35 72-21 18

Bus station
Avenida Castelo Branco
Tel. (088) 35 71-40 20

EVENTS

During the 4-day Dia do Romeiro pilgrimage celebration in early November, the city of Juazeiro do Norte is bursting at the seams in order to accommodate up to 500,000 worshippers of the popular saint Padre Cícero. Almost as many pilgrims flock to the city for the Dia da Nossa Senhora dos Dores on 15 September, for Padre Cícero's birthday on 20 July and the anniversary of his death on 24 March.

WHERE TO EAT

▶ **Inexpensive**
Restô Jardim
Avenida Leão Sampaio 5460
Lagoa Seca
(at the Barbalha exit)
Tel. (074) 35 71-77 68
Regional cuisine, catering for the many pilgrims.

WHERE TO STAY

▶ **Mid-range**
Verdes Vales
Avenida Plácido Aderaldo Castelo
Lagoa Seca
(6km/3.5 miles outside the city centre)
Tel. (074) 35 66-25 44
Good hotel with 98 air-conditioned apartments, bar, restaurant, pool, playing fields and gym. Hotel guests have free access to the Aquapark (open at weekends) next door.

What to see in Juazeiro do Norte

Memorial Padre Cícero
The memorial site on Praça do Cinquentenário keeps alive the memory of Padre Cícero; here religious objects, documents and photos provide evidence of the huge influence that this man of the church had in Juazeiro do Norte right up to his death. The **Museu Cívico Religioso Padre Cícero**, established at the final residence of Padre Cícero, keeps his personal belongings.

✷ **NS do Perpétuo Socorro**
The grave of Padre Cícero is situated at the chapel of Nossa Senhora do Perpétuo Socorro (1908), on Praça do Socorro opposite the memorial site. The Casa dos Milagres (House of Miracles) next to the chapel houses the votive offerings of the people that Padre Cícero is said to have helped.

Estátua de Padre Cícero
In **Colina do Horto**, a park above the city, look for the Stations of the Cross, with its 14 stations comprising 56 concrete figures in total. There is also a 27m/88ft statue of Padre Cícero. Many pilgrims visit the chapel dedicated to him.

REMEMBERING RAIMUNDO JACÓ

The Missa dos Vaqueiros (mass of the cattle herders) has been celebrated since 1971 in Serrita in the barren and drought-stricken sertão region, in memory of the cattle herder, and cousin of the musician Luis Gonzaga, Raimundo Jacó, who was murdered here in 1954.

Raimundo Jacó's murder has never been solved; the spot where he was found, struck dead by a stone, is today marked by a statue of him – a **concrete monument of a figure on horseback**. The will to bringing the perpetrators to justice was limited – not surprisingly in a rough region where an excess of curiosity can bring about eternal silence.

Protest against violence

The vaqueiros mass is, however, not only dedicated to the memory of Jacó, but is celebrated as a protest against all kinds of violence. It takes place every year on the third weekend of July, in open air and with the participation of hundreds of **vaqueiros** on horseback, wearing their traditional

Too much curiosity can lead to eternal silence.

leather clothing. The secular part of the event, lasting several days, consists of a fair, musical performances, rivers of firewater, and rodeos where the sertão cowboys prove their skills at roping young bulls. Simple accommodation can be had in the neighbouring town of Salgueiro.

Laguna

Sa 60

State: Santa Catarina (SC)
Altitude: 3m/10ft

Population: 48,000

Laguna is situated south of Florianópolis on the Atlantic coast, near the edge of an extensive lagoon area. Tourism is the most important economic factor in this small town. The carnival of Laguna is considered the best in Santa Catarina state.

Founded by bandeirantes from São Paulo, Laguna is a historic town, which became the centre of the Revolução Farroupilha. The rebellious gaúchos, who had entered Laguna under the command of the Italian revolutionary **Giuseppe Garibaldi** (1807 – 1882), declared the town in 1839 the capital of the República Juliana. Laguna is also the setting for one of the most famous love stories in Brazil: this is where Garibaldi met Ana de Jesus Ribeiro, alias Anita Garibaldi, who was to become his wife and remain loyally at her husband's side during his liberation wars in South America and later in Europe.

 VISITING LAGUNA

INFORMATION
Avenida Calistrato Muller Salles
 Portinho
Tel. (048) 36 44-24 41

GETTING THERE
Bus station
Rua Arcângelo Bianchini
Tel. (048) 36 44-02 08

EVENTS
Tombada de Laguna
The Tombada de Laguna is a festival which takes place in the second week of July. It commemorates the taking of the town by Giuseppe Garibaldi's Farroupilha marines in 1839.

WHERE TO EAT
▶ **Inexpensive**
Geraldo
Ponta do Barra
(10-min trip by ferry boat)
Tel. (048) 99 86-15 99

The house specialities are exquisitely prepared dishes based on freshly-caught saltwater fish, crustaceans and seafood.

WHERE TO STAY
▶ **Mid-range**
Laguna Tourist
Avenida Castelo Branco 1850
Praia do Gi
Tel. (048) 36 47-00 22
and (08 00) 704-60 22
www.lagunatourist.com.br
Close to the beach, this hotel has 96 air-conditioned apartments, a bar and restaurant, a swimming pool with children's slide, sauna and gym, tennis courts and a playground for the little ones.

What to see in and around Laguna

The Anita Garibaldi Museum on Praça República Juliana is housed in the city's former courthouse and administration building, constructed in 1747 in the Portuguese style. In the former residence of Anita Garibaldi on Praça Vidal Ramos, some of her personal possessions, as well as paintings with scenes from her life are on display.

Museu Anita Garibaldi

The church of Santo Antônio dos Anjos on Praça Victor Meirelles was built in 1696. Some parts are gilded and the church houses the painting ***Nossa Senhora da Conceição*** by the master painter from Santa Catarina, Victor Meirelles.

Santo Antônio dos Anjos

The coastal town of Imbituba lies 40km/25 miles north of Laguna. In this little port town, look out for the church of Vila Nova (1720), a prime example of Azorean architecture in Santa Catarina. From Imbituba, visitors can book trips to the islands of Santana de Dentro, Santana de Fora, Araras and Itacolomi. Another popular destination is Mirim Lake, 6km/3.5 miles to the south and accessible via the BR-101. The best beaches are Praia do Rosa, ideal for surfers, as well as the beaches of Luz, da Vila, Barra de Ibiraquera (18km/11 miles away and sharing its name with a lake), and, close to the town, Praia de Imbituba.

Imbituba

Museu Anita Garibaldi

Garopaba Garopaba, a fishing village a further 30km/18.5 miles north of Imbi-tuba, today has only 12,000 inhabitants and in low season offers nearly deserted beaches. In peak season (Dec – Feb) however, it is aroused from its slumber as up to 100,000 holidaymakers invade the place. The beaches of Silveira and Ferrugem are used every year for professional surfing contests.

Cabo Santa Marta Just under 20km/12.5 miles from Laguna – by ferry this takes only ten minutes – lies the coastal town of Cabo Santa Marta with the dune-fringed beaches do Cardoso and da Ligana and the lighthouse, erected in 1891. One of the main attractions is the nocturnal crab fishing that is also practised in the Lago de Santo Antônio and other parts of the Laguna coast.

Tubarão In the town of Tubarão (pop 8,500), 35km/22 miles west of Laguna, the Jorge Lacerda thermal power station, with its coal deposits, is open to visitors. There are a few hot springs in the area: the Guarda thermal springs (11km/6.5 miles away), the Rio do Pouso thermal springs (15km/9.5 miles) and the Termas do Gravatal (23km/14 miles).

! **Baedeker** TIP

Tunnel trip into Mina Modelo

Criciúma, 60km/37 miles southwest of Tubarão, boasts Brazil's only coal mine open to the public: the Mina Modelo. Visitors can enter one gallery by pit train. The entrance to the pit, shut down in 1955, is in Rua Paulino Bussulo. Opening times: daily 8 – 11.30am and 1 – 6pm.

Beaches, massive dunes and caves make the landscape around **Araranguá** – some 95km/59 miles south of Laguna or 5km/3 miles from Tubarão – one of the most charming stretches of coast in the Brazilian south. The main attraction is the **Praia do Morro dos Conventos**, 14km/8.5 miles from the town centre, near the estuary of the Rio Araranguá.

Macapá

Rk 45

State: Amapá (AP)
Altitude: 16m/52ft

Population: 284,000

Macapá lies at the northernmost and largest tributary of the Amazon delta, opposite the Marajó group of islands. Access to the town, sitting directly on the Equator, is from Belém by plane, boat or ferry.

In the late 17th century, Macapá was the scene of battles between the French settling in Guyana and the Portuguese emigrating to Brazil, who founded mission stations in the area and, in 1688, built the For-

▶ VISITING MACAPÁ

INFORMATION
Rua Independência 29
Tel. (096) 3212-5335
www.macapa-ap.com.br

GETTING THERE
Airport
Aeroporto Int. de Macapá
Rua H Maia, tel. (096) 32 12-53 35

Bus station
Praça Veiga Cabral
Tel. (096) 32 42-20 09

WHERE TO EAT
▶ Inexpensive
Chalé
Avenida Presidente Vargas 499
Tel. (096) 32 22-19 70
Fish and seafood

Cantinho Baiano
Avenida Beira-Rio 328

Tel: (096) 32 23-41 53
Fish dishes

WHERE TO STAY
▶ Mid-range
Ceta Ecotel
Rua do Matadouro 640
Fazendinha district
Tel. (096) 32 27-33 96
www.ecotel.com.br
The best-appointed hotel in Macapá
opened in 2000 with 65 apartments, a
bar and an outstanding restaurant,
swimming pool, sauna, football
pitches, volleyball court and gym.
Secure parking.

▶ Budget
Frota
Rua Tiradentes 1104
Tel (096) 3223-3999
33 acceptable rooms

taleza de São José de Macapá (now a regional museum) to secure the
border. It was only in 1713, under the terms of the Peace of Utrecht
treaty, that France officially recognized the Rio Oiapoque as the border between its possessions and those owned by Portugal. In 1758,
the settlement growing up around the fort received its town charter
under King Dom José I, as Vila São José de Macapá.

What to see in and around Macapá

The São José de Macapá fort in Avenida Cândido Mendes, built between 1764 and 1782 on a promontory extending into the Amazon,
today lies very close to the city centre. The blocks of stone used to
built the fort came as ship ballast from Portugal.

★
Forte São José
de Macapá

The Marco Zero de Equador on the Rodovia Juscelino Kubitschek,
only 5km/3 miles south of the city centre of Macapá, marks the line
of the Equator. In the O Zerão football stadium nearby, the players
have the rare opportunity to pass the ball to a teammate in the other
hemisphere, as the Equator runs right through the pitch.

Marco Zero

Mazagão Velho Just under 50km/31 miles southwest of Macapá, the village of Mazagão Velho was founded in the 17th century and still preserves a few houses from colonial times, as well as the odd custom, such as the **Festa de São Gonçalo** (6 – 10 January) and the **Festa de São Tiago** in July, with a procession, equestrian games and a masked ball.

Porto da Santana From Porto da Santana, 28km/17 miles south of Macapá, visitors can join boat trips, for instance to the Amazon islands (including the Ilha de Marajó) and the Igaparés, the narrow watercourses winding their way between these islands. To the north, trips lead to the Oiapoque region on the border with French Guiana.

There's a smile hidden in there …: man on the beach at Macapá

The nature reserve of **Lago Piratuba** covers a surface of 395,000ha/976,000 acres on the east coast of Amapá. Its boundary is marked by the Rio Araguari which at this level empties into the Atlantic. The nature reserve, with its mangrove swamps and tropical rainforests that provide an ideal habitat for alligators, manatees, turtles and many other animals, some of them rare, is only accessible by boat via the Araguari river. Travellers planning to visit the nature reserve have to apply for a permit issued by IBAMA: tel. (096) 32 16-11 16.

Pororoca – a natural spectacle in the Amazon delta

The name pororoca is of Indian origin and is an onomatopoeic description of the clash – particularly violent at spring tide – between the water of the sea and that of the Amazon emptying into the ocean at a rate of 240,000 sq km/93,000 square miles per second. In the first phase, the mass of water of the Amazon river penetrates the sea for hundreds of kilometres. Then the tide forces the river to retreat from the »conquered« area, and it rolls towards dry land, flooding beaches and lower-lying islands. This results in the river effectively being dammed; it cannot empty its waters into the sea, whilst the immense pressure of the river water prevents a further advance of the tide. But suddenly this fragile balance of forces collapses and the floods rise further, bursting upon the Amazon estuary. The waves grow into 4m/13-ft breakers roaring so loudly that the sound can be heard for miles around.

The phenomenon of the pororoca may be best observed at new and full moon between February and May (i.e. in the rainy season), in large parts of the Amazon estuary, in the Canal Perigoso between Ilha de Marajó and Ilha Caviana, as well as the estuary of the rivers Araguari and Capim.

At new moon and full moon

✳ Maceió

Sh 50

State: Alagoas (AL)
Altitude: 17m/56ft

Population: 780,000

Spreading along the strip of coast between Lagoa Mandaú and the Atlantic, the city of Maceió grew out of a sugar boiling plant founded in the 18th century on what is today Praça Dom Pedro II. In 1839, Maceió was declared the capital of Alagoas.

Sugar has remained the biggest export of Alagoas – the port of Maceió owes most of its wealth to the sugar export business. Thanks to the excellent beaches in the area, Maceió also gradually became a popular seaside resort.

What to see in Maceió

In the city centre, west of the cathedral of Nossa Senhora dos Prazeres (1840), look for the Deodoro Theatre, built in 1910 (Praça Deodoro). The Mercado Municipal in the Parque Rio Branco is a good place to buy local crafts.

Teatro Deodoro, Mercado Municipal

The Palácio Floriano Peixoto at 44 Praça Marechal Floriano Peixoto is the seat of the government of Alagoas, whilst the Museu Pierre Chalita shows images of saints, paintings from the 17th and 18th centuries, sculptures and liturgical objects, as well as ornate baroque altars.Opening times: Mon – Fri 8am – noon and 2 – 5.30pm.

✳
Museu Pierre Chalita

🕐

Near Maceió, some of the most tempting beaches of the northeast await. Often, at low tide around 2km/1.2 miles off the coast, closed water basins form that can be reached by jangada. Elsewhere, the sea water mixes with the water of the **Mandaú Lagoon** to the west of the city or with the water of the **Manguaba Lagoon** further south. Numerous navigable canals, where shellfish and crustaceans live, criss-cross the banks of the lagoons, surrounded by many fishing villages.

✳
Beaches and lagoons

Marechal Deodoro

Marechal Deodoro (pop 28,000) – the former capital of Alagoas and birthplace of Marshal **Manuel Deodoro da Fonseca** (1827 – 1892),

who proclaimed the Republic in 1889 and became Brazil's first president – lies 25km/15.5 miles southwest of Maceió on Manguaba Lagoon and is a protected site. The town preserves many colonial buildings from the 17th and 18th centuries.

★

Convento São Francisco

The convent of São Francisco, erected between 1684 and 1689 on Praça João XXII houses the **Museum of Sacred Art** of Alagoas, which includes golden liturgical objects, fine wood carvings and sculptures amongst its exhibits. The façade, only completed in the late 18th century, has limestone ornaments. Particularly worth seeing is the choir chapel with carvings on the main altar and ceiling paintings by **José Elói**, a notable artist of colonial Brazil. Elói also created a representation of Saint Clare of Assisi for the church of the São Francisco convent.

Museu Deodoro

This colonial-style house at 92 Rua Marechal Deodoro, where Deodoro da Fonseca was born, has been converted into a museum. Family photographs and copies of the marshal's furniture are on display; the originals are kept at the military museum in Rio de Janeiro. The museum's completely **uncritical presentation** of the life and deeds of Fonseca remains silent on his incompetent, arrogant style of leadership as president of Brazil, his intention to get rid of democratic institutions, as well as his military ethos which, in 1891, nearly led to a duel with a member of his cabinet. The increasingly grotesque political conduct of the former war hero could not prevent a city being named after him.

Coast south of Maceió

Beaches

South of Praia da Avenida extends Praia Sobral, but due to the effluent from a large chemical factory, neither of these two beaches are suitable for swimming.
The next beaches along are Praia do Trapiche, Praia do Pontal da Barra and stuning **Praia do Francês** with a fishing village that is part of Marechal Deodoro. In the 16th century, French sailing boats involved in dyewood smuggling docked here, hence the name of the beach.

★

Barra de São Miguel

Barra de São Miguel, situated 36km/22 miles southwest of Maceió on the northern bank of the Rio São Miguel, has just under 6,100 inhabitants. Outside the village lie the most beautiful beaches south of Maceió, including the rock-strewn Barra Beach which comes right up to the settlement; visitors wanting to get to the superb **Praia da Gunga** (3km/1.8 miles away) have to cross the Rio São Miguel by boat only.

← *Brazil at it's best:*
taking a break under the blue sky of Alagoas

▶ VISITING MACEIÓ

INFORMATION

Informações Turísticas
Praça Dois Leves 29
Tel. (082) 33 36-44 09
www.turismomaceio.com.br

GETTING THERE

Airport
Campo dos Palmares, BR-101 Norte
Tel. (082) 32 14-40 00

Bus station
Avenida Leste-Oeste (Freitosa)
Tel. (082) 32 21-46 15

EVENTS

Festas Juninas
Between 12 and 30 June there is a succession of quadrilles, firework displays and other regional festivities.

Maceió Festival
In November – a kind of carnival outside the silly season

WHERE TO EAT

▶ Expensive
Wanchako
Rua São Francisco de Assis 93

Jatiúca district
Tel. (082) 32 24-82 44
One of the rare Peruvian restaurants in Brazil. Spicy salsas and numerous culinary nods to Japan.

▶ Moderate
Canto da Beca
Avenida Dr Júlio Marques Luz 654
Jatiúca district
Tel. (082) 33 25-73 46
Regional cuisine from northeastern Brazil. One of the house specialities is shrimps prepared in coconut milk with cashew nuts.

WHERE TO STAY

▶ Mid-range
Jatiúca Resort
Lagoa da Anta
Praia da Jatiúca
Tel. (082) 33 55-20 20
www.hoteljatiuca.com.br
Situated between a freshwater lagoon and the open sea, with 96 air-conditioned rooms, partly suitable for wheelchair users. Various sports facilities, beach service, natural lake, pool and an excellent restaurant into the bargain.

Coast north of Maceió

Praia Pajucara The very popular Pajucara Beach is 3km/1.8 miles outside Maceió. Flat fishing boats, called **jangadas**, bring tourists to the swimming pools formed by the coral reefs and sandbanks at low tide. Some jangadas, converted into floating bars, serve drinks and snacks – it is not unusual for leftovers and litter to just be thrown into the sea, a practice that has quite evidently already damaged the coral reefs. Following on from Pajucara Beach, the Praia dos Sete Coqueiros and the Praia da Ponta Verde are 4km/2.5 miles and 5km/3 miles respectively from Maceió. The waters off Praia dos Sete Coqueiros are said to be polluted however.

Some 6km/3.5 miles from Maceió and very popular with surfers, Jatiúca Beach is lined with jangadas – with their reefed sails– and numerous fish traps. The swimming beaches of Cruz das Almas (7km/4.5 miles), Jacarecica (9km/5.5 miles) and Guaxuma (12 km/7.5 miles) further north are well worth visiting.

Praia Jatiúca

The yellow sand beach of Garça Torta, 14km/8.5 miles outside Maceió, lies near a fishing village. Nearby can be found the partially palm-fringed swimming bays of Riacho Doce (16km/10 miles) and Pratagi (17km/10.5 miles), a relatively recent tourist centre. Parts of this area, with the **Rio Cabocó** running through it, have mangrove vegetation, the aquatic plants of which serve as food for the sea cows. The manatee – an aquatic mammal that can reach up to 4.5m/14.5ft in length and weigh up to 600kg/105 stone – is threatened with extinction; this region however offers the chance – with a bit of luck – to admire a few specimens. Both beaches are protected from big waves by offshore coral reefs.

✶ Praia da Garça Torta, Praia Pratagi

North of Pratagi stretch the Praia de Ipióca (23km/14.5 miles from Maceió), with the house of Marshal **Floriano Peixoto**, the fishing village of Paripueira (33km/20.5 miles) and Sonho Verde Beach (38km/23.5 miles).

Praia de Ipióca

In Barra de Santo Antônio, 45km/28 miles from Maceió, visitors can find miles of beaches: Barra de Santo Antônio, Carro Quebrado and the remote bay of Pedra da Cebola. Another option is a boat trip to Croa Island, leaving from town.

✶ Barra de Santo Antônio

◄ ✶ Manaus

Re 47

State: Amazonas (AM)   **Population:** 1.4 million
Altitude: 93m/305ft

Lying in the heart of the tropical rainforest, Manaus is the capital of the state of Amazonas, as well as the legendary centre of the India rubber industry on the Rio Negro, which not far downriver joins with the Rio Solimões to form the Amazon proper.

The origins of the city go back to the small fort of São José, which was erected on the mouth of the Rio Negro. Around it grew the settlement of Barra do Rio Negro, later to become Manaus, and in 1755 it was made the capital of the newly created **Capitania São José do Rio Negro**. Its inhabitants dedicated themselves mainly to the gathering and cultivation of »sertão drugs«: cloves, cinnamon, indigo and cocoa. In the second half of the 19th century and the early 20th, Manaus experienced a period of extraordinary wealth thanks to the

▶ **VISITING MANAUS**

INFORMATION

Avenida Sete de Setembro 157
Tel. (092) 36 22-49 86
www.manausur.gov.br

GETTING THERE

Airport
Aeroporto Int. E Gomes
Av Santos-Dumont
Tel. (092) 36 52-12 12

Bus station
Rua Recife
Tel. (092) 36 42-58 05

BOAT TRIPS

This intricate network of rivers and igarapés (narrow watercourses) is ideal for an exploration of the tropical rainforest by boat. From Manaus, boat trips can be booked lasting anywhere between one day and two weeks. The longer the trip, i. e. the farther away from Manaus you go, the more intensive the experience of unspoilt nature.

The following Manaus-based agency rents out charter boats equipped for 10 to 25 people (with crew):

Viverde
Rua das Guariúbas 47
Tel. (092) 32 48-99 88
Fax (092) 36 39-54 04
www.viverde.com.br

WHERE TO EAT

▶ **Moderate**

① *Choupana*
Rua Recife 790
Adrianópolis district
Tel. (092) 36 35-38 78
Simple restaurant with good regional cuisine

WHERE TO STAY

▶ **Mid-range**

① *Taj Mahal*
Avenida Getúlio Vargas 741
Tel. (092) 36 27-37 37
High-rise hotel within sight of the Teatro Amazonas; 170 rooms, some of them suitable for wheelchair users. There have been several changes of name and management, but the panoramic views from the restaurant slowly revolving on top of the roof has always been one of the highlights of Manaus.

② *Best Western Lord Manaus*
Rua Marcílio Dias 217
Tel. (092) 36 22-28 44
www.bwlordmanaus.com.br
Well-established hotel with 102 air-conditioned rooms with TV, restaurant and bar, but in a noisy location. All credit cards accepted.

▶ **Budget**

③ *Ana Cássia*
Rua dos Andrades 14
Tel. (092) 36 22-36 37
There are 88 rooms, a simple restaurant, bar and sauna. Situated on a noisy street.

OVERNIGHTING IN JUNGLE LODGES

In the gallery forests along the Rio Negro upriver from Manaus there are numerous jungle lodges where visitors can spend a few days and get to know the Amazonian flora and fauna. All lodges have representatives in Manaus and ferry their guests by boat from Ponta Negra to their accommodation. Whilst the comfort level of the accommodation tends to be low, prices are fairly steep.

► Luxury
Amazon Ecopark Lodge
Igarapé do Tarumã Açu
(journey time:
approx. 40 min by boat from Manaus)
Tel. (092) 36 22-26 12
www.amazonecopark.com.br
60 wooden bungalows, with three air-conditioned apartments each. The guests have access to a restaurant and bar. Excursions by boat and jeep are on offer. Reservations required.

Amazon Riverside
(approx. 40 min by boat from Ceasa Port)
Tel. (092) 36 22-27 89
www.amazonriversidehotel.com
Accommodation entirely constructed from wood; 7 simple rooms with ceiling ventilator and tiny bathroom units. Warm water is only available at night. Rustic restaurant.

Flotel Piranha Lodge
Reserva de Desenvolvimento
Sustentável do Piranha
Município de Manacapuru
(driving time from Manaus: 90km/56 miles plus one hour by boat)
Tel. (092) 36 56-60 33
Floating hotel in a nature reserve at the confluence of Rio Solimões and Rio Manacaparu. Minimum stay three nights; reservations required.

Juma Lodge
Lago do Juma, Município de Careiro
(journey time from Manaus:
approx. 3.5hr by boat)
Tel. (092) 33 62-12 81
www.jumalodge.com.br
11 wooden apartments; only the wet rooms are built from stone. Boats available for hire. A generator provides electricity. Reservations required.

► Mid-range
Ariaú Jungle Tower
Lago Ariaú, Município de Iranduba
(journey time from Manaus:
approx. 2hr by boat)
Tel. (092) 21 21-50 00
www.ariau.tur.br
Now with 288 rooms, the largest jungle hotel near Manaus; amongst the facilities are viewing towers linked by 6.4km/4 miles of catwalk, an outstanding restaurant and a lecture hall. There is also a reintroduction station where animals confiscated from trappers are prepared for their return to the wild. Reservation required.

► Budget
Aldeia dos Lagos
Municípo de Silves
(journey time from Manaus:
3hr plus 1.5hr by boat)
Tel. (092) 35 28-21 24
Air-conditioned apartments on an island 365km/227 miles from Manaus. Rustic restaurant and bar.

high prices paid on international markets for India rubber from the Amazon. Most colonial buildings in the city date from this time, known as the rubber boom. Since 1967, the city has been a **free trade zone**. In the ensuing period, tax breaks attracted multinational companies to Manaus; they in turn brought industrial workers en masse, who settled in the inexorably spreading slums. The increasingly industrial character of the city has not been beneficial to the former charm of the Amazonian metropolis.

What to see in Manaus

★★
Teatro Amazonas

The Amazon Theatre (Praça São Sebastião), opened in 1896 and today a listed monument, is the most famous building in Manaus: an edifice in the style of the Italian Renaissance in the middle of the jungle. The theatre's 700 seats are covered in red velvet, the columns and statues were made using Italian marble and the stairs from English cast iron. Of the 198 chandeliers, 32 are made of Murano glass. The decoration of the stage curtain shows how the Rio Negro and the Rio Solimões come together to form the Amazon. **Domenico de Angelis** painted the ceiling frescoes. The dome is covered with coloured tiles, some of which form the national flag. These days, very few performances take place here. Opening times: Mon – Sat 9am to 4.30pm.

★
Alfândega, Cais Flutuantes

It was English engineers who built the Customs House (Alfândega) of Manaus in 1906. Their technical pièce-de-résistance however were the 300m/328yd-long docks (Cais Flutuantes); floating in the

The Teatro Amazonas is world-famous …

Rio Negro, they were designed to allow for the shifting water levels which can vary by up to 14m/46ft between rainy season and dry season. Today, both the customs house and the floating docks are listed monuments.

 Mercado Municipal

The covered market, erected in 1882, is situated between the Rua dos Barés and the Rio Negro, between the floating quays and the Igarapé de Educandos. With its cast-iron structure designed by **Gustave Eiffel** and manufactured in Paris, and colourful stained- glass windows, the market takes its inspiration from the former covered market of Les Halles in Paris. Today, the Mercado Municipal shelters a number of popular bars, informal eating places and restaurants.

Palácio Rio Negro

The Palácio Rio Negro in Rua Sete de Setembro, completed in 1910, used to be the residence of a German rubber trader; later, this splendid building served as the seat of the government of Amazonas state. Today, it houses an **arts centre** which occasionally has art exhibitions and concerts. Opening times: Tue – Fri 10am – 5pm, Sat/Sun 2 – 6pm.

… not least due to its location: in Manaus amidst the Amazonian jungle.

Museu do Indio The Museu do Indio (Indian Museum) displays over 3,000 exhibits on ethnic Indian groups that were or still are living on the upper reaches of the Rio Negro. Handicrafts made by them are for sale too. The museum is located in Rua Duque do Caixas 356. Opening times: Mon – Fri 8.30 – 11.30am and 2 – 4.30pm, Sat 8.30 – 11.30am.

Parque Ecológico do Janauary

Landscape A boat trip of approx. 45 minutes from Manaus takes visitors on the Rio Negro to the Janauary Ecological Park around the lake of the same name. The much-visited reserve of 9,000ha/22,250 acres brings

Manaus Map

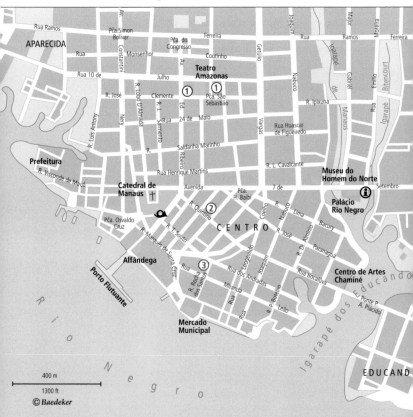

| Where to eat | Where to stay | ② Best Western Lord Manaus |
| ① Choupana | ① Taj Mahal | ③ Ana Cássia |

together the most diverse types of landscape, amongst them várzeas (alluvial plains) and igapós (swampy forests). Within the park, motor boats navigate the intricate network of narrow watercourses, the »igarapés«. The lush vegetation ranges from grasses such as the canarana to huge kapok trees.

One of the park's main attractions is a lagoon strewn with **Victoria amazonica**. The flower of the Victoria amazonica – a water lily only occurring in the Amazon region, with floating leaves that reach a diameter of up to 2m/6.5ft – has a very short life: it first blossoms in white, then turns purple and after three days, by which time it is dark red, it finally withers.

! *Baedeker* TIP

Encontro das Águas

Even on a short trip to Manaus, a day trip to Encontro das Águas, the confluence of the Rio Negro and Rio Solimões, is worth it. About 20km/12mi from Manaus the dark waters of the Rio Negro and the yellowish, light Rio Solimões flow alongside each other without mingling and present a fascinating natural spectacle. All of the travel agents in Manaus offer excursions to Encontro das Águas.

✱ ✱ Ilhas Anavilhanas · Parque Nacional do Jaú

Landscape

The Anavilhanas Islands lie between Manaus and Novo Airão in the Rio Negro, which at this point is as wide as 20km/12.5 miles. This cluster of islands forms the largest freshwater archipelago in the world, with 400 oblong river isles, as well as hundreds of lakes and watercourses, all intertwined across a distance of 90km/56 miles. With its surface area of around 350,000ha/865,000 acres, the Anavilhanas region illustrates a perfect cross-section of the Amazonian ecosystems.

Fauna

During the high-water period between December and April, nearly all the islands are submerged, with only 180 of them protruding from the floodwaters. Using local guides, the monkeys and sloths, parrots, toucans, woodpeckers and herons, as well as the snakes, caymans and turtles living on the narrow river islands are easier to spot at this time than when the water level is lower.

Parque Nacional do Jaú

In 1980, the adjacent tropical forest between the Rio Carabinani and the Rio Unini was declared the Parque Nacional do Jaú. This nature reserve bears the name of the **Rio Jaú**, the river that crosses its entire length. The second-largest national park in South America, it contains the world's largest blackwater reservoir. Experts consider the Parque Nacional do Jaú one of the most diverse biosphere reserves in the tropics. Half of all reptiles occurring in the central Amazon, and an almost incalculable wealth of fish and bird species can be found here. The park is also one of the last havens for now rare wildcats such as the puma and the ocelot.

Visitors wanting to explore the national park need a lot of time; the 250km/155-mile journey by boat from Manaus to Novo Airão alone takes around 18 hours, followed by another boat trip of six hours. Visitors to the national park must obtain the permission of the IBAMA environmental protection agency in Manaus, Rua Ministro João Gonçalves de Sousa: tel. (092) 32 37-51 77.

Parque Nacional do Pico da Neblina

Spreading on the northern banks of the Rio Negro a good 500km/ 310 miles further upstream, the Pico da Neblina National Park was established in 1979. On the national park's territory – in the Serra do Imeri, at the border between Brazil and Venezuela – rise the two mightiest mountains in the country: the 2,992m/9,816-ft **Pico 31 de Março** and the 3,014m/9,888-ft **Pico da Neblina**, Brazil's highest peak. Climbing the Picos requires – apart from the necessary time and physical fitness – the relevant equipment for an expedition like this: individual specialized operators offer packages. Makeshift accommodation can be had in São Gabriel da Cachoeira, 140km/87 miles from the national park.

Indian villages The Pico da Neblina National Park marks the southern border of the **Yanomami territory**, extending from Roraima in the northwest to the border with Venezuela. The main ethnic Indian group living in the region around the Pico da Neblina are the Tukano, whose villages lie near São Gabriel da Cachoeira.

Indian hunter on a tributary of the Amazon

In the extreme south of the park, the rock formations of São Gabriel **Rock formations**
da Cachoeira can be found, amongst which the **Bela Adormecida**
(Sleeping Beauty) is especially worth seeing. The river banks of São
Gabriel, with their glimmering beaches, are also well-known. This
area has the largest niobium deposits in the world; the exploitation
of this metal led to the last remaining Indians being driven out from
here.

★ ★ Natal

Sh 48

State: Rio Grande do Norte (RN)   **Population:** 713,000
Altitude: 30m/98ft

**Natal, the capital of Rio Grande do Norte state, was founded at
Christmas 1599 in the Rio Potengi estuary. The city owes its charming name – Natal, translated into English, means Christmas – to
the day when it was founded.**

Also called Cidade do Sol (City of the Sun) and Cidade das Dunas
(City of the Dunes), the coastal city is worthy of these grand names:
Natal is blessed with a sunny climate and there are endless duned
beaches in the area. Thus, the city, which might not look very Christ-
massy to Europeans, has over time become a popular tourist destination.

What to see in Natal

Rising on the Praia do Forte, 4km/2.5 north of the city centre, the   ★
Forte dos Reis Magos (Fortress of the Three Wise Kings), was de-   **Forte dos**
signed by the Spanish Jesuit **Gaspar de Santeres** and erected by the   **Reis Magos**
Portuguese between 6 January (hence the name) and 24 June 1598,
about 750m/820 yards before the mouth of the Rio Potengi, as a base
to guard against the French. The settlement that was later to become
Natal grew up around a mile from the fort. Due to the building materials used – taipa (clay with plant fibres) and sand – the original
fort did not withstand the onslaught of the sea. The fort owes its current aspect to the well-known Portuguese military architect **Francisco
de Frias da Mesquita**, creator of numerous fortifications from Maranhão to Cabo Frio, and of ecclesiastical buildings such as the convent of São Bento in Rio de Janeiro, who rebuilt it from 1614 onwards. In 1628, work finished on this seemingly impregnable stronghold that was meant to secure the Portuguese a lasting presence in
the northeast of Brazil; five years later however, the fort was attacked
and captured by the Dutch. Only in 1654 did the fort fall back into
the hands of those who had it built. Laid out on a star-shaped
ground plan, the fort has a circumference of 240m/262 yards and

VISITING NATAL

INFORMATION

Centro de Turismo
Rua Aderbal de Figueiredo 980
Petrópolis district
Tel. (084) 32 11-61 49

Secretaria de Estado do Turismo
Rua Mossoró 359
One of its branches is
at the bus station
Tel. (084) 32 05-10 00
www.natal.rn.gov.br

GETTING THERE

Airport
Aeroporto Int. Augusto Severo
Parnamirim
Tel. (084) 36 43-18 11

Bus station
Avenida Capitão-Mor Gouveia 1237
Tel. (084) 32 32-73-10

WHERE TO EAT
► Moderate
① *Buonustaio*
Avenida Afonso Pena 444
Petrópolis district
Tel. (084) 32 02-11 43
Italian restaurant with a well-chosen
drinks list

② *Raro Sabor*
Rua Seridó 722
Petrópolis district
Tel. (084) 32 02-18 57
Local and international cuisine. All
credit cards accepted.

► Inexpensive
③ *Hua Da Li*
Avenida Campos Sales 454
Petrópolis district
Tel. (084) 32 11-29 69
Chinese restaurant

WHERE TO STAY
► Mid-range
① *Residence Praia*
Avenida 25 de Dezembro 868
Praia do Meio
Tel. (084) 32 02-44 66
www.residencepraia.com.br
Beach hotel near the city centre with
118 air-conditioned rooms

Baedeker recommendation

► Mid-range
② *Pousada Villa do Sol*
Praia de Genipabú, Natal
Tel. (084) 32 25-21 32, fax (084) 32 25-20 37
www.villadosol.com.br
At 20km/12.5 miles from Natal, this ecotourism resort has 24 air-conditioned
apartments (standard or luxury), all with
TV, minibar, sea views and hammocks on
individual verandas. This is a great base for
hikes through the Águas das Dunas park
and snorkelling around the Corais de
Maracajaú, camel or horse-back rides
through the dunes, buggy drives, jangada
boat trips or windsurf lessons at the nearby
windsurfing school. Swimming pool and
panoramic terrace.

► Budget
③ *Marina Badaué*
Avenida Presidente Café Filho 750
Praia das Artistas
Tel. (084) 32 02-48 48
www.marinabadauehotel.com.br
46 rooms in a central location

④ *Yak Plaza*
Avenida Presidente Café Filho
Praia do Meio
Tel. (084) 32 02-42 24
www.yakplaza.com.br
78 rooms, restaurant, bar and pool

has five defensive bastions. The high building rising up at the centre of the inner courtyard once housed the gunpowder magazine and the chapel.Opening times: daily 8am – 4.30pm.   ⏱

Located south of the harbour in the Ribeira district, on the Rio Potengi, the **Cidade Alta** (Upper Town) is the centre of Natal and has the most historic buildings. On Praça André de Albuquerque, the Câmara Cascudo Memorial houses a library, an art museum and an art gallery, with a collection of documents on the historian Cascudo.   **Memorial Câmara Cascudo**

A few steps further south, in Rua Santo Antônio, the baroque church of Santo Antônio (do Galo), built in 1799, has a carved wooden altar as well as a **Museum of Sacred Art**, exhibiting religious objects from the 18th century.Opening times: Tue – Sun 1 – 5pm.   **Santo Antônio**   ⏱

The Museu Câmara Cascudo, east of the Cidade Alta in the Tirol district at 1398 Av Hermes da Fonseca, shows anthropological and folkloric exhibits, tools used by the Amazon Indians, fossils, skeletons, reconstructed sambaquis, Christian and Candomblé ritual objects, as well as regional handicrafts. Opening times: Tue – Fri 8 – 10.30am and 2 – 4.30pm, Sat/Sun 1–5pm.   **Museu Câmara Cascudo**   ⏱

Spot the horseman in the dunes of Genipabu near Natal.

Natal Map

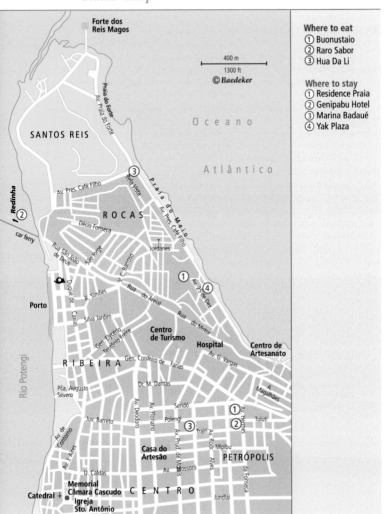

Forte dos
Reis Magos

400 m
1300 ft
© Baedeker

Where to eat
① Buonustaio
② Raro Sabor
③ Hua Da Li

Where to stay
① Residence Praia
② Genipabu Hotel
③ Marina Badaué
④ Yak Plaza

SANTOS REIS

O c e a n o

A t l â n t i c o

Redinha

car ferry

ROCAS

Av. Pres. Café Filho

Décio Fonseca

Rua São João de Deus

Jordanes

Porto

R. Simões

Rua do Areial

Silva Jardim

Centro de Turismo

Hospital

Centro de Artesanato

RIBEIRA

Gen. Cordeiro de Farias

Pça. Augusto Severo

Dr. M. Dantas

Seridó

Polengi

Trairi

Casa do Artesão

PETRÓPOLIS

U. Caldas

Memorial
Câmara Cascudo

C E N T R O

Catedral
Igreja
Sto. Antônio

Jundiaí

Rio Potengi

Centro de Turismo The former city jail of Natal, the **Casa da Detenção** situated at 980 Rua Aderbal de Figueiredo (in the Petrópolis district), houses local tourist attractions, including a museum, art gallery, craft shops, restaurant and disco. On Thursday nights, there are regular forró dance shows for tourists. Opening times: Mon–Fri 8am–5pm, Sat 8am–noon.

Beaches in the east and north of Natal

Along the eastern part of the Atlantic coast, close to the city, lie the beaches of Meio and Artistas (3km/1.8 miles from the centre Natal), Areia Preta and Pinto (5km/3.1 miles), and Barreira d'Agua (12km/7.4 miles). By day, the Praia dos Artistas is a popular meeting point for surfers, after nightfall it belongs to revellers; there are numerous nightclubs, restaurants and bars in the immediate vicinity of the city beaches.

City beaches

A beach buggy drive over the sand dunes of the beaches north of Natal toward the cape of São Roque – or the »elbow« of Brazil, as this South American headland that juts out furthest towards Africa is called – is an unforgettable experience. The first beach reached going north is the **Praia do Forte**, the core from which Natal grew, so to speak. Further along – on the opposite bank of the Rio Potengi – is Redinha Beach.

Buggy drive

Genipabu lies 30km/18.5 miles north of Natal, cut off from the former fishing village by the Rio Potengi. Ferries connect the two via the Praia da Redina. Along with the beaches, huge **shifting sand dunes** are the main attraction of Genipabu. The biggest dune lies directly behind the popular Praia de Genipabu and measures a good 60m/197ft – its sand is so fine that it is possible to slide down it on improvised skis or surfboards. Another way to explore the broad sandy sweeps of the Parque das Dunas is on a guided buggy drive. These little vehicles zooming along the beach are as ubiquitous in Genipabu as in Natal – each hotel will put guests in touch with reliable drivers.

★ ★
Genipabu, Parque das Dunas

A few kilometres north of Genipabu stretches the 6km/3.7-mile fine sand beach of Pitangui. This beach can be reached by buggy, after crossing the estuary of the Rio Ceará Mirim. Here holiday cottages lie in the shade of coconut palms, with the fishing village of Pitangui laid out around a clear-water lagoon. The offshore reefs block the onslaught of the waves, making this a good beach for safe swimming.

★ ★
Pitangui

The delta of the Rio Maxaranguape, 63km/39 miles north of Natal, has to be crossed by ferry. The swimming beach of Praia da Barra de Maxaranguape has a lovely setting, its fine sands framed by dunes, reefs and blue lagoons. Around 2km/1.2 miles further along comes the Cape São Roque.

Maxaranguape

Just over 80km/50 miles north of Natal, far beyond the towns of Pititinga and Rio de Fogo lies the fishing village of Touros. From here, visitors can get a fishing boat to the Parracho, a 5,000 sq m/53,800-sq ft seawater basin formed by corals.

★
Touros

Coast south of Natal

Ponta Negra ✳

The stretch of coast between Natal and the border with Paraíba has some of the most attractive beaches of the state. Some 14km/9 miles south of Natal, the Praia da Ponta Negra features »Bald Head Hill«, the **Morro do Careca** – a fixed dune over 100m/328ft in height, whose slope – with a 50 degree gradient to the beach – is so steep that visitors can ski on its fine sand. In terms of beach tourism, the holiday resort of Ponta Negra has superseded Natal; numerous hotels, pousadas and beach bars have sprung up here over the past few years. Prices are higher than in Natal, even though in December the Praia da Ponta Negra regularly falls victim to pollution by algae. As with the beaches north of Natal, a buggy drive is also a good option for exploring the beaches south of the »City of the Dunes«.

Búzios, Tibau do Sul, Praia da Pipa ✳

It might be better to bypass Ponta Negra by buggy and head for the coast behind the Barreira do Inferno, a good 20km/12.5 miles south of Natal at Praia do Cotovelo. From there follow the beaches of Pirangi do Norte (24km/15 miles from Natal), with its famous huge cashew tree, Pirangi do Sul (30km/18.5 miles) and Búzios, where freshwater sources rise directly on the beach in the shape of **Olhos de Água**, »water eyes«. The following vast stretch of beach, mostly running straight-as-a-die, is broken only at Guaraíra by the estuary of the Guaraíra Lagoon. Ferries, specifically designed to take buggies, ply their trade between Guaraíra and Tibau do Sul, on the other side of Lagoa Guaraíra, while separating the fishing village of Tibau do Sul, a good 80km/50 miles from Natal, and the difficult-to-access Sagi Beach lie such popular swimming bays as the Praia do Madeiro, Praia da Pipa, and the Praia do Amor.

Niterói

Sd 57

State: Rio de Janeiro (RJ)   **Population:** 450,000
Altitude: 5m/16ft

Niterói, in the east of Guanabara Bay, is connected with Rio de Janeiro on the opposite side by the Ponte Presidente Costa e Silva, which is just under 14km/8.5 miles long and 60m/197 feet high.

What to see in Niterói

Ponta de Gragoatá

The most interesting beaches and sights of Niterói are located south of the city centre and are accessible via the coastal road of Guanabara Bay. One of these is the Ponta de Gragoatá, a promontory extending into the Baía de Guanabara. At the southern tip of this headland, the Ponte Benjamin Sondré connects to the offshore **Ilha da Boa Viagem**

(Good Journey Island), where the church of Nossa Senhora da Boa Viagem, erected in 1683, as well as a fort from the same century may be visited. The 17th-century Forte do Gragoatá at the western tip of the promontory is not open to the public.

This futuristic, UFO-like building in an exposed position in the southeast of the Ponta de Gragoatá was designed by no less a figure than Brazil's star architect **Oscar Niemeyer**. The building's modern architectural concept corresponds very well with the Museum for Contemporary Art housed here, which shows changing exhibitions. The museum offers a superb view over Guanabara Bay.

✸ Museu de Arte Contemporânea

A few blocks from Praia de Icaraí, southeast of Ponta de Gragoatá, between Icaraí and Santa Rosa, stretches the Campo de São Bento, an extensive park with a lake, fountain and the Pascoal Carlos Magno arts centre. At weekends a craft market is held in the park.

Campo de São Bento

Behind Praia de Icaraí, the Fróis road leads above the bay along Cavalão Hill to the Saco (bay) de São Francisco (accessed also by a tun-

Saco de São Francisco

Looking across to Rio de Janeiro from the Museu de Arte Contemporânea

nel). At the end of Praia de São Francisco, a turning into the Estrada da Cachoeira provides one of the ways to get to the beaches at the inlet of the bay. At the boundary between Praia de São Francisco and Praia de Charitas rises the church of **São Francisco Xavier**, built in 1572. Nearby Viração Hill has the municipal park, which offers good views.

Jurujuba Beach, Forte Rio Branco

Avenida Quintino Bocaiuva leads past the Praias de São Francisco and Charitas, beyond which lie the beaches of Preventório, Várzea, Cais and Jurujuba. Not far from here, look for the 18th-century Forte Barão do Rio Branco.

Fortaleza de Santa Cruz

Avenida Carlos Emiliano, the extension of Quintina Bocaiuva, is the way to Jurujuba Beach. At the end of the street, the Estrada General Eurico Gaspar Dutra turns off to Pico Hill, upon which rises the **Forte do Pico**. At the foot of Pico Hill, the Fortaleza de Santa Cruz, built in 1632, has retained its aura of impregnability to this day. Some parts of the building were added later: the chapel, the prison and the Cova das Onças (torture chamber) date from the 17th century, the cistern from the 18th, and the artillery casemates from the 19th century. Together with the Forte São João on Morro Cara de Cão opposite, the fortress keeps guard over the narrowest part of Guanabara Bay.

★ ★ Olinda

Sh 49

State: Pernambuco (PE)   **Population:** 350,000
Altitude: 16m/53ft

Olinda, founded in 1537 on a hill north of the Rio Beberibe by the Portuguese Duarte de Coelho, was the first capital of Pernambuco. Today, the ensemble of colonial monuments from Olinda's heyday justifies the fetching name of the city – Olinda, »the Beautiful«. In 1982, the historic core of Olinda was added to the list of UNESCO World Heritage sites.

After its foundation, Olinda rapidly grew to be the centre of colonization, missionary work and sugar cane cultivation, but was soon overtaken by ► Recife, the more dynamic port 14km/8.5 miles further south , as it did not have its own deep-sea port. In 1710, after the elevation of Recife to the position of vila, the rivalry between the two towns culminated in the **Guerra dos Mascates**: the sugar barons of Olinda fought against the political rise of the mascates, the traders of Recife – but without success. From then on, Olinda lost, little by little, its political and economic importance.

▶ VISITING OLINDA

INFORMATION

Secretaria de Turismo
Rua do Bonsucesso 183
Amparo district
Tel. (081) 34 39-94 34
www.olindavirtual.net

Box de Turismo
Praça do Carmo 100
Carmo district
Tel. (081) 33 05-10 48

EVENTS

Olinda holds its carnival at the same time as the European carnival – 40 days before Easter. The attractions of the silly season in Olinda are: bonecos gigantes (giant costumed puppets made from papier-mâché), maracatú (theatrical, musical performances from traditional African groups), frevo (a lively blend of marching polka and acrobatic dance) and infectious good cheer.

WHERE TO EAT

▶ Moderate
① *Oficina do Sabor*
Rua do Amporo 335
Tel. (081) 34 29-33 31
Gourmet restaurant, decorated with crafts from the northeast. Regional

Drum rolls at the carnival of Olinda

ingredients in unusual combinations, e.g. lobster with mango. Unrivalled house speciality: shrimps with pitanga fruit and pumpkin. Views of Recife from the veranda.

② *Goya*
Rua do Amparo 157
Amparo
district Tel. (081) 34 39-48 75
The creative chefs of this culinary treasure trove steam freshly-caught fish in banana leaves or garnish shrimps with regional tropical fruit, buttery cheese and coconut. And as if that was not enough, they exhibit their own artistic efforts near the entrance and dining room of the restaurant.

③ *Kwetú*
Avenida Manuel Borba 338
Praça do Jacaré
Tel. (081) 34 39-88 67
Prepare to have your tastebuds tickled at a high culinary level by Belgian, French and northeastern Brazilian specialities.

WHERE TO STAY

► **Luxury**
① *Pousada do Amparo*
Rua do Ampara 199
Amparo district
Tel. (081) 34 39-17 49
www.pousadadoamparo.com.br

This pousada consists of two spacious converted 18th-century town houses. Inside, looking like they are just awaiting the photographer for an interior design magazine shoot, there are eleven air-conditioned rooms, as well as a bar and sauna. Guests also have the use of a swimming pool.

► **Mid-range**
② *Pousada Peter*
Rua do Amparo 215
Amparo district
Tel. (081) 34 39-21 71
www.pousadapeter.com.br
Here, the hotelier is an artist – or should that be the other way round? In any case, the foyer of this pousada seems like a small art gallery: there is hardly an inch of wall not decorated with a painting or sculpture. Behind the high entrance area, ranging down over five terraced levels are the breakfast room, the swimming pool, a garden with splendid view, and 13 very individual rooms. In 1988 this hotel in Olinda's Amparo district became the realization of the German owner's long-held dream.

What to see in Olinda

✳
NS do Carmo

On the Praça do Carmo, the ideal starting point for a stroll around the city, look for the church of Nossa Senhora do Carmo (1581), which was burned down by the Dutch in 1631 – as were all the churches in the city with the exception of the Igreja São João Batista dos Militares. This church is considered **Brazil's oldest Carmelite church**, even though of the original building only the 16th-century altar and the Renaissance façade of the entrance remain.

North of Praça do Carmo, following Rua São Francisco uphill to the upper part of town, the Largo de São Francisco boasts the oldest collection of Franciscan ecclesiastical buildings in Brazil, including the convent of São Francisco with the chapel of Sant'Ana and the church of **Nossa Senhora das Neves**, built in the late 16th century. The walls of both buildings are lined with azulejos and the ceilings decorated with paintings. A large colonial chest with magnificent carvings is kept in the sacristy of the church, and in the chapel of the lay order, look out for the crossing arch with its gilded carvings. Opening times: Mon – Fri 7am–noon and 2 – 5pm, Sat 7am – noon.

★★
Convento de São Francisco

🕐

Above the Largo São Francisco and dating from 1537, the cathedral (Sé) has beautiful paintings by unknown artists, some of them from the 17th century. The **Alto da Sé** (Cathedral Hill) offers superb views of Olinda and Recife. The various buildings surrounding the cathedral include the Seminário de Olinda (1549) with the Igreja Nossa Senhora da Graça, designed by the Jesuit priest Francisco Dias. To the west, the former bishops' palace (Palácio Episcopal) dating from 1676 houses the **Museum of Sacred Art of Pernambuco** (Rua Bispo Coutinho 726); continuing west on Rua Bispo Coutinho, take a right to the Imaculada Conceição (Immaculate Conception) church built

★
Igreja da Sé and around

Olinda Map

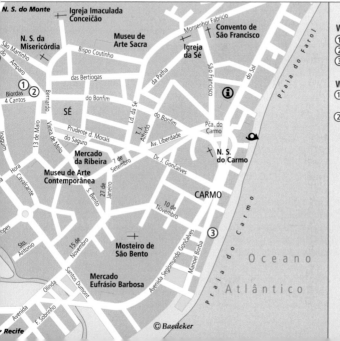

N. S. do Monte
Igreja Imaculada Conceição
N. S. da Misericórdia
Museu de Arte Sacra
Convento de São Francisco
Monsenhor Fabrício
Bispo Coutinho
Igreja da Sé
São Martinho
do Amparo
São Francisco
do Sol
Praia do Farol
das Bertiogas
Biordas 4 Cantos
Bernardo
Vieira de Melo
do Bonfim
Ld. da Sé
T. I. Altedo
do Bonfim
13 de Maio
SÉ
Prudente d. Morais
do Saguro
Av. Liberdade
Pça. do Carmo
ℹ
Hora
Cavalcante
Mercado da Ribeira
7 de Setembro
Dr. J. Gonçalves
N. S. do Carmo
Museu de Arte Contemporânea
S. Bento
27 de Janeiro
CARMO
Sto. Antonio
15 de Novembro
10 de Novembro
Avenida Segismundo Gonçalves
Manuel Borba
③
do Carmo
Mosteiro de São Bento
Olinda
Santos Dumont
Mercado Eufrásio Barbosa
Praia do Carmo
Oceano
Atlântico
F. Sobrinho
• Recife
© Baedeker

Where to eat
① Oficina do Sabor
② Goya
③ Kwetú

Where to stay
① Pousada do Amparo
② Pousada Peter

Brazil's oldest Carmelite church: Nossa Senhora do Carmo

in 1569. Before the Rua Bispo Coutinho becomes the Rua Bernardo Vieira de Melo leading downhill, it is worth visiting the Igreja da Misericórdia (1540) for its gilded wood carvings and paintings.

NS do Monte North of the churches of Imaculada Conceição and Misericórdia, the Igreja Nossa Senhora do Monte (1586) rises above the town. In the church, Gregorian chants can be heard around 5.30pm; on the square in front of the church, the Largo NS do Monte, cookies and liqueurs are for sale.

Museu de Arte Contemporânea South of the Igreja da Misericórdia, the former Inquisition jail (Cadeia Eclesiástica e Pública) and the 18th-century São Pedro Advíncula chapel (Rua Treze de Maio) house the Museu de Arte Contemporânea (Museum for Contemporary Art).

★ ★
Mosteiro de São Bento Both the Rua Treze de Maio and the Rua Bernardo Vieira de Melo join the Rua São Bento leading south towards the Benedictine monastery, built in 1582 and pillaged in 1631 by the Dutch. The subsequent years of reconstruction have given the group of convent buildings its current aspect. Its choir chapel is considered one of the most beautiful in all Brazil. The façade decoration of the São Bento convent church (1761) displays late baroque forms, while the ceiling of the sacristy shows scenes from the life of St Benedict. José Eloi, a noted painter in colonial times, created the painting, probably in 1785. Eloi is also credited with the large altarpiece ***Nossa Senhora da***

Piedade (*Our Lady of Pity*) in the sacristy. Amongst the sculptures exhibited in the convent, the ones most worth seeing are the *Menino Jesus de Olinda* (*Infant Jesus of Olinda*) by the monk Agostinho da Piedade (around 1640) and two masterpieces by the monk Domingo da Conceição, a Benedictine carver and sculptor: *O Senhor Morto* (*Dead Christ*), executed in 1679, and *O Senhor Crucificado* (*Christ on the Cross*), executed in 1688.

Baedeker TIP

Small-scale art

Along Rua do Amparo, artists both local and from elsewhere have settled in surprisingly high numbers. Today, their mostly tiny studios and sometimes very colourful galleries characterise the atmosphere of the neighbourhood. Some of the workshops are open to visitors, e. g. the studio Iza do Amparo (clothing, paintings) at house number 159, Amparo das Artes (changing exhibitions) at no. 164, Sérgio Vilanova (naive art) at 224 and Jairo Arcoverde (painting) at 252.

Rua Treze de Maio leads to Rua dos Quatro Cantos, the traditional meeting place of the carnival associations of Olinda and where visitors will find the sculpture *Senhor Atado* (*Jesus Bound*), created in 1773. This is one of the **Stations of the Cross**; the others are *Senhor Carregando a Cruz* (*Christ Bearing the Cross*) in Rua Bernardo Vieira de Melo, *Senhor Apresentado ao Povo do Castelhano* (*Christ Introduced to the Castilians*) in Rua 27 de Janeiro and *Nossa Senhora com Jesus* (*Our Lady with Jesus*) on the Largo do Amparo, all dating from 1773. In 1809, another sculpture was added to the cycle: *Senhor dos Montes das Oliveiras* (*Christ on the Mount of Olives*), on the Alto da Sé.

Around Olinda

A drive north along the coast is an opportunity to discover the beaches of Praia dos Milagres (near the centre of Olinda), Carmo, São Francisco, Bairro Novo, Casa Caiada and Rio Doce (6km/3.5 miles away). On Praia de São Francisco, look for the Fortim São Francisco coastal fort, dating back to the 16th century.
   Beaches near Olinda

Olinda's neighbouring community of Paulista has very good beaches, even if they are often overrun with people: Janga (8km/5 miles from Olinda), Nossa Senhora do Ó (13km/8 miles), Pau Amarelo (14km/8.5 miles) and Maria Farinha (22km/13.5 miles). At Praia do Pau Amarelo, look for the coastal bulwark of **Forte do Pau** Amarelo; it was erected, in 1719, at the site where in 1630 the Dutch first came ashore on the Brazilian mainland. Thanks to offshore reefs, the palm-lined beach has only light swell; there are also numerous stalls selling food. The picturesque palm beach of **Maria Farinha** reaches close to mangrove areas that are still unspoilt, and a line of sandbanks broken by navigable canals. Protected by offshore reefs, the surf is again very light, and in many places the water is quite shallow.
   Paulista

★★ Ouro Preto

`Sd 56`

State: Minas Gerais (MG) **Population:** 66,500
Altitude: 1,179m/3,868ft

Ouro Preto (Black Gold), declared a UNESCO World Heritage Site in 1980, is famous for having the biggest concentration of baroque architecture in the whole of Brazil. At a time when the baroque style was already history in Europe, the master builders of Ouro Preto held on to it for a long time, making it their own, a style of art manifested here in ornate churches, palaces and noble residences.

The town rose to be the centre of Tropical Baroque and received acclaim as an important centre of artistic activity, as the honourable title **»cradle of Brazilian art«** suggests. Originally, Ouro Preto was only a small village of gold prospectors and bounty hunters, quickly expanding after 1699 thanks to numerous gold finds. The town owes

The Praça Tiradentes in the heart of Ouro Preto

its name to the gold which was tinged black by iron ore. In 1711, the gold prospector settlement was raised to the status of a town, under the name of Vila Rica de Ouro Preto and was even the capital of the Gerais Mines province between 1721 and 1897. This jewel of 18th-century architecture, still mostly intact, nestles in the hilly landscape southeast of Belo Horizonte and thanks to the density of its historical buildings is considered the picture-perfect Minas Baroque town.

What to see in Ouro Preto

One of the very first buildings to go up in Ouro Preto, between 1701 and 1704, was the Father Faria chapel in Rua Padre Faria in the eastern neighbourhood of Alto da Cruz. Also known as **Nossa Senhora do Rosário dos Brancos**, the church boasts an opulent interior with gilded wood carvings and paintings. Also worthy of note are the ceiling frescoes and the sculpture of the Rosary Madonna attributed to Francisco Xavier de Brito. In the same street, look out for Padre Faria's fountain, the first work in soapstone by Antônio Francisco Lisboa, called Aleijadinho (Little Cripple), in 1761. Opening times: Tue – Sat 8.30 – 11.45am and 1.30 to 5pm, Sun noon – 5pm.

★ ★
Capela do Padre Faria

Leaving the Father Faria chapel in the direction of the town centre leads to Largo Santa Efigênia with the parish church of Santa Efigênia dos Pretos, built between 1733 and 1745. The wood carvings were executed by Francisco Xavier de Brito – who taught Aleijadinho – and other Minas Baroque artists.

★
Matriz Santa Efigênia dos Pretos

Erected between 1727 and 1746 by Manuel Francisco Lisboa, Aleijadinho's father, the parish church of Nossa Senhora da Conceição stands on Praça Antônio Dias, between the Largo of Santa Efigênia and the town centre. The square and the district it is in were named after the bandeirante from São Paulo who discovered the first grains of gold here in 1698, on the banks of the Tripuí river. The church shelters the **tombs of Aleijadinho and Maria Dorotéia Joaquina de Seixas**, the famous Marília de Dirceu, muse of the poet and Inconfidente conspirator Thomaz Antônio Gonzaga (1744 – 1810). Right next to the church, the **Aleijadinho Museum** has furniture from the colonial era, sculptures and liturgical garments. Opening times (museum): Tue – Sat 8.30 to 11.45am and 1.30 – 5pm, Sun noon to 5pm.

★ ★
Matriz NS da Conceição

Opened for business in 1702, the Chico Rei goldmine is 1,500m/1,640yd long. Chico Rei is at the centre of numerous legends: what seems to be certain is that he was an enslaved African tribal prince who managed to buy freedom for himself and the companions taken prisoner with him. The entrance to the Mina do Chico Rei mine, closed down in 1888, is at 108 Rua Dom Silvério; however, only a short section of the pit is open to the public. Opening times: daily 8am – 5pm.

Mina do Chico Rei

▶ VISITING OURO PRETO

INFORMATION
Praça Tiradentes 41
Tel. (031) 35 59-32 69
www.ouropretoturismo.com.br

GETTING THERE
Bus station
Rua Padre Rolim 661
Tel. (031) 35 59-32 52

EVENTS
»Carnaval« is celebrated at the same
time as in Europe, 40 days before
Easter. The street carnival of Ouro
Preto is considered the biggest and
best carnival event away from the
Brazilian coast.

WHERE TO EAT
▶ **Expensive**
① *Le Coq d'Or*
Rua Getúlio Vargas 270
(in the Solar NS do Rosário hotel)
Tel. (031) 35 51-52 00
Regional and French cuisine in classy
ambience

▶ **Moderate**
② *Casa do Ouvidor*
Rua Conde de Bobadela 42
Tel. (031) 35 51-21 41
Traditional specialities from Minas
Gerais

WHERE TO STAY
▶ **Luxury**
① *Estalagem das Minas Gerais*
Rodovia dos Inconfidentes
km 90
(8km/5 miles outside Ouro Preto,
on the road to Belo Horizonte)
Tel. (031) 35 51-21 22
and (031) 32 79-14 34
www.sescmg.com.br
Wheelchair and child-friendly complex with 112 rooms and 30 chalets in
its own park, with restaurant (cuisine
from Minas Gerais and international
dishes), Scotch bar, swimming pool,
sauna, sports facilities and helipad.
This exclusivity comes with a price tag
to match.

② *Solar Nossa Senhora
do Rosário*
Rua Getúlio Vargas 270
Largo do Rosário
Tel. (031) 35 51-52 00
www.hotelsolardorosario.com.br
37 air-conditioned rooms and nine
generously-sized suites in a 19th-
century town house and a more
recent annexe. A high-class restaurant
(Le Coq d'Or, see above), bar,
swimming pool, sauna and
dedicated car parking round off the
package.

▶ **Mid-range**
③ *Pousada do Mondego*
Largo de Coimbra 38
Tel. (031) 35 51-20 40
www.mondego.com.br
Beautifully restored town house,
originally built in 1747, with 24
rooms, bar, restaurant and parking
spaces. 18th-century works of art and
furniture decorate the interior. Not
suitable for small children.

▶ **Budget**
④ *Pouso do Chico Rey*
Rua Brigadeiro Musqueira 90
Tel. (031) 35 51-12 74
The Pouso do Chico Rey guesthouse,
opened as far back as 1957, is one of
Ouro Preto's oldest pousadas. Six
rooms with TV, with three sharing a
shower/WC.

Ouro Preto Map

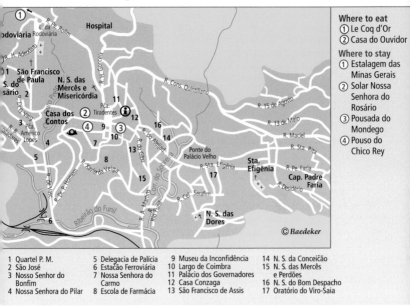

© Baedeker

★ ★
São Francisco de Assis

São Francisco de Assis, the baroque church of the Franciscan lay order, rises up in the centre of town, on Largo de Coimbra. For the French art historian Germain Bazin, this is »one of the most perfect monuments of art in the Western world, one of those works that, created entirely by a single person, show the original idea in a completely pure way«. It was **Aleijadinho** who was responsible for the design of the church itself, in the form of an irregular octagon, the sculptures on the intricately carved entrance and the lavabo (baptismal font) of the sacristy. Furthermore, Aleijadinho created all the wooden carvings in the choir chapel and on the other six altars. The perspective painting on the ceiling of the nave is considered the masterpiece of **Manuel da Costa Athayde**, the most important painter of the colonial era. Carried out between 1800 and 1809, it shows the classical motif of Maria's Ascension to Heaven in vibrant, vivid tropical colours; the Virgin Mary dominating the centre of the painting is a mulatto woman. Opening times: Tue–Sun 8.30–11.45am and 1.30–5pm.

⊙

★
NS das Mercês e Perdões

The church of Nossa Senhora das Mercês e Perdões, situated just south of Largo de Coimbra and the Igreja São Francisco church in Rua das Mercês, was built between 1743 and 1773. It contains two paintings by Antônio Martins da Silveira, dating from 1760/61.

★★
Praça
Tiradentes

Praça Tiradentes, situated in the centre of Ouro Preto and sur-rounded by colonial-era buildings, is a place where tragic fates were sealed. For countless slaves forcibly brought from West Africa, the former site of the slave market was a place of transition on a long journey of suffering that was to continue in the gold mines of Minas Gerais. It was also on this square that **Joaquim José da Silva Xavier** – called Tiradentes (Teethpuller) and inspired by the ideals of the French Revolution – experienced his last humiliation: in 1792 the severed head of the leader of the Inconfidência Mineira, a republican, anti-colonial movement that started in Ouro Preto, was publicly dis-played. The square would later be given his name and a monument erected here, in the heart of Ouro Preto, in honour of the martyr of the independence movement, while his murderers are long forgot-ten.

★
Museu da
Inconfidência

⏲

Between 1784 and 1846, the classical Casa de Câmara e Cadeia was erected on Praça Tiradentes; today, it houses the Inconfidência Mu-seum. Its collections comprise ecclesiastical treasures, sculptures by Aleijadinho – amongst them the image of St George that in the 18th century used to be carried on horseback through the town during Corpus Christi processions – as well as paintings by Athayde and documents relating to the Inconfidência Mineira. Opening times: Tue – Sun noon – 5.30pm.

Palácio dos
Governadores

⏲

The governors palace, opposite the Museu da Inconfidência, was de-signed in 1741 by the military architect José Fernandes Pinto de Al-poim, who had already worked on the São Bento convent of Rio de Janeiro. **Manuel Francisco Lisboa**, father of Aleijadinho, was one of the people involved in the construction of the governors palace. Within the building, the minerals museum of the mining school is worth a visit, exhibiting many precious gemstones from all around the world. Opening times: Tue – Fri noon – 5pm, Sat/Sun 9am – 1pm.

★★
NS do Carmo

⏲

The Carmelite church of Nossa Senhora do Carmo, a few paces west of the Inconfidência Museum in Rua Brigadeiro Musqueira, was built between 1766 and 1776 as probably the second building project of Manuel Francisco Lisboa. However, in 1770 Aleijadinho made sub-stantial changes to his father's designs; it is probable that the coat of arms above the entrance and the baptismal font in the sacristy were sculpted by him. The side altars (1807), with images of Saint John and the Virgin Mary Full of Grace, count among Aleijadinho's last works. The tabernacle in the sacristy was painted in 1812 by Manuel da Costa Athayde. Opening times: Tue – Sun 9.30 – 11am and 1 to 4.45pm.

Museu de
Arte Sacra,
Teatro Municipal

Next to the church of Nossa Senhora do Carmo, the 18th-century **Casa do Noviciado** in Rua Brigadeiro Musqueira houses the Museum of Sacred Art with various sculptures by Francisco Xavier de Brito.

The heart of tropical Baroque: Ouro Preto, with the church of Nossa Senhora do Carmo

In the same street stands the Municipal Theatre, opened in 1770, which is considered the oldest opera house in Brazil. Opening times: museum: Tue – Sun 9 –10.45am and noon – 4.45pm, Teatro Municipal: daily noon – 6pm.

⏱

Erected in 1782, the Casa dos Contos, situated west of Praça Tiradentes in Rua São José, has been called the finest secular building in Ouro Preto. At one time it was the residence of the intendant (administrative official) João Rodrigues de Macedo. Its main use, however, was as the place where under his supervision the gold found by prospectors was weighed and melted down. Temporarily, the building was also used as a jail, e. g. for Cláudio Manuel da Costa, who was found dead two days after being taken prisoner, and a few other fellow Inconfidênica conspirators. Visitors can still see the smelting ovens and 18th-century furniture, as well as the ceiling of the Salão Nobre, decorated with frescoes.

★
Casa dos Contos

Close by, the Chafariz dos Contos, a fountain dating from 1745, stands on Praça Reinaldo Alves de Brito. In colonial times, with only very few houses having their own water supply, the public fountains were an important part of daily life, not least as community meeting places.

Chafariz dos Contos

Rua São José and Rua Getúlio Vargas lead to Largo do Rosário with the church of Nossa Senhora do Rosário dos Pretos (Rosary Madonna of the Black People), dating back to 1785. The church's layout consists of two overlapping ellipses for the nave and the choir – a form that is extremely rare in Minas Gerais baroque; the interior of the church houses a sculpture of Saint Helena attributed to Aleijadinho. Opening times: Tue – Sun noon – 4.40pm.

★ ★
NS do Rosário dos Pretos

⏱

★★
Matriz
NS do Pilar

From the Igreja NS do Rosário church, Rua Antônio de Albuquerque leads southeast to Praça Monsenhor Castilho with the church of Nossa Senhora do Pilar, built between 1711 and 1733. Modest taipa clay walls hide opulent interior decoration, for which around 800kg/16 hundredweight of gold and silver were used. In 1736, Aleijadinho's uncle **Francisco Antônio Pombal** redesigned the nave into an irregular wooden decagon that was more suited to the stylistic forms of baroque architecture. The wooden carvings in the splendid choir chapel were executed, from 1747 onwards, by **Francisco Xavier de Brito**. Also worthy of note are the three paintings by Athayde, representing the way to Golgotha. Opening times: Tue – Sun 9 to 10.45am and noon – 4.45pm.

Bom Jesus de
Matosinhos

Rua Benedito Valadares, as well as Rua Cláudio de Lima and Rua Alvarenga, connect Largo da Matriz do Pilar with Cabeças, the northwestern part of town, where the church of Bom Jesus de Matosinhos (1785), also called São Miguel e Almas, stands. A niche in the façade shelters the soapstone statue of Saint Michael sculpted by Aleijadinho in 1778. Also look out for the paintings by Athayde showing the Last Supper and the Crucifixion. The church square holds the Chafariz do Alto das Cabeças fountain (1763).

Colonial houses,
Marília Bridge

Amongst the many preserved 18th-century buildings, don't miss the Casa da Baronesa (today's headquarters of the SPHAN state organization responsible for the preservation of historic monuments) and the Casa de Dom Manuel de Portugal e Castro (in private hands) on Praça Tiradentes, as well as the Casa dos Inconfidentes in Rua dos Inconfidentes. Marília Fountain and Marília Bridge on Largo de Dirceu, both built in 1758, are also worth seeing.

★ ✳ Mariana

A few kilometres east of Ouro Preto, Mariana, founded in 1696 as Arraial do Ribeirão de Nossa Senhora do Carmo and elevated to the status of a vila in 1711, still preserves a large number of 18th-century chapels and churches, with interiors mainly designed by the two most important artists of Minas Baroque: Antônio Francisco Lisboa (or Aleijadinho), and Mariana-born Manuel da Costa Athayde.

★★
Catedral
de NS da
Assunção

Erected between 1709 and 1760, the famous cathedral on Praça da Sé, also known as **Basílica da Sé** is dedicated to the Assumption of Mary. The three naves are separated from each other by arcades; the portico was furnished with sculptures by **Aleijadinho**. Athayde gilded the retable on the main altar and painted the canvas representing the Baptism of Christ. Also worth looking out for is the organ, made in Germany in 1701 and decorated with Chinese motifs, which was given to the church by Dom João V of Portugal in 1751. The frescoes on the ceiling of the chancel were painted by Manuel Rebelo e Sousa.

The Museu Arquidiocesano, housed in the former Casa Capitular (1770) a few steps from the cathedral, exhibits liturgical objects, furniture and vestments from the 18th and 19th centuries, as well as artworks by **Athayde** and other painters from Minas Gerais. One gallery is dedicated to Aleijadinho. The museum is situated at 49 Rua Frei Durão; in the same street, look for the Casa da Intendência, once the seat of the governing authority for gold and diamond finds. Opening times: Tue – Sun 8.30am – noon, 1.30 – 5pm.

★ ★
Museu Arquidiocesano

A splendid group of buildings stands proudly on Praça Minas Gerais, including the churches of São Francisco de Assis and Nossa Senhora do Carmo, as well as the Casa da Câmara e Cadeia (city hall). The soapstone portal relief of São Francisco (Saint Francis; 1763/94) was sculpted by Aleijadinho. Athayde, whose mortal remains are kept in the church, produced the two paintings representing the *Suffering and Death of Saint Francis of Assisi* and the ceiling frescoes in the sacristy.

★ ★
São Francisco de Assis

The layout of the church of São Pedro dos Clérigos, built in 1752 on an elevation, consists of two interlocking ellipses forming the nave and the choir – a characteristic style element of High Baroque, but seldom found in Brazil. The main altar is decorated with images by Athayde; the sturdy towers were only added around 1920.

★
São Pedro dos Clérigos

Believers have been flocking to the beautifully located church of São Pedro dos Clérigos since 1752.

Casa da Câmara e Cadeia ✴ Built in 1782, the Casa da Câmara e Cadeia still serves as the town hall of Mariana and is considered one of the main examples of colonial secular architecture in Brazil. Erected in 1784, the church of **Jossa Senhora do Carmo** was one of the first places where Athayde worked.

Situated west of the town centre, **Seminário Menor**, with the Nossa Senhora da Boa Morte chapel (1750) keeps paintings by various artists from Minas Gerais. Carried out in 1782, the ceiling frescoes in the chancel of the church are considered the masterpiece of Antônio Martins da Silveira, who managed to create the illusion of space in a very confined area.

Nossa Senhora do Rosário dos Pretos The interior of the church of Nossa Senhora do Rosário dos Pretos in Rua do Rosário, built between 1752 and 1775, was decorated by Athayde in 1823.

Palmas · Ilha do Bananal

Sa 51

State: Tocantins (TO)	**Population:** 137,500
Altitude: 1,179m/3,868ft	

Like Brasília, the capital of Tocantins is a new city that has been growing fast since its inception in 1989, following a large-scale plan and divided into sectors. Modern buildings dominate the city centre.

The city streets crossing at right angles have numbers, , the only exceptions being the two main thoroughfares of Avenida Juscelino Kubitschek and Avenida Teotônio Segurado. The sheer fact that the city's population has risen exponentially from 2,000 in 1991 to nearly 140,000 inhabitants today raises substantial doubts about the implementation of the principle of controlled growth proclaimed by the urban planners.

✴ Ilha do Bananal · Parque Nacional do Araguaia

To be honest, there wouldn't be much to attract visitors to Palmas, if the city deep in the Brazilian hinterland wasn't the starting point for visits to the Ilha do Bananal and the Parque Nacional do Araguaia.

This is where the **Rio Araguaia** (350km/217 miles), forming the natural western border of Tocantins, divides in two to flow around the Ilha do Bananal, at 20,000 sq km/over 7,700 sq miles one of the largest river islands in the world. Situated over 300km/186 miles from the provincial capital, the islet can only be reached by air taxi (from Palmas airport) or via difficult roads. Lying in the transitional area between Amazonian rainforest and cerrado steppe, this region has many meandering watercourses and lagoons, and is home to a flora and fauna particularly rich in biodiversity. Alongside anteaters, emus, herons, snakes and river turtles, crocodiles and panthers find a safe haven here, which explains why the northeasterly third of the island, the Parque Nacional do Araguaia – is protected.

When to visit

The best time to visit is between June and September, as there is hardly any rain in this period and the falling water levels of the Rio Araguaia and its tributaries reveal beaches and sand banks.

Jalapão

Situated at 265km/165 miles from Palmas and characterized by cerrado savannah and smaller forest islands, the natural landscape in the southeastern part of Tocantins is traversed by several rivers, only sparsely populated and another safe haven for rare animals. The town of **Ponte Alta do Tocantins** is the place to find accommodation and local guides. Again, the ideal time to visit is the dry season between July and September.

► VISITING PALMAS

GETTING THERE
Airport
AERSO, Avenida Teotônio Segurado
Tel. (063) 32 19-37 00

Bus station
AERSO, Avenida Teotônio Segurado
Tel. (063) 32 28-56 88

EVENTS
Carnapalmas
Carnival in July – celebrated, as in Bahia, by booming trios elétricos.

WHERE TO EAT
► **Inexpensive**
Fratelli
104-S, Rua SE 07, Lote 24
Tel. (063) 32 15-50 10
Excellent pizzeria

WHERE TO STAY
► **Mid-range**
Pousada das Artes
103-S, Avenida LO 01, 78
Tel. (063) 32 19-15 00
www.pousadadasartes.com.br
38 air-conditioned apartments, car parking, sauna with bar, swimming pool. Only American Express and Visa cards are accepted.

► **Budget**
Casa Grande
Avenida Teotônio Segurado 201-S
Conjunto 1, Lote 1
Tel. (063) 32 15-18 13
Alongside its 37 air-conditioned rooms, this guesthouse offers car parking, a swimming pool and a simple restaurant.

★★ Pantanal

Rg 54/55

State: Mato Grosso (MT) and Mato Grosso do Sul (MS)

Spreading across the border area of Mato Grosso and Mato Grosso do Sul, east of Rio Paraguai, the swampy plain of the Pantanal is crisscrossed by several watercourses. In times of high water, large parts of this area become completely flooded.

At low water levels however, the area is transformed into valuable pasture. During the rainy season (October – March), the Pantanal turns into a huge labyrinth of rivers and lagoons stretching into neighbouring Bolivia and Paraguay.

▶ VISITING PANTANAL

INFORMATION

Sematur
Rua Richuelo 1
Cavalhada, Cáceres
Tel. (065) 32 23-59 18

IBAMA Poconé
Tel. (065) 33 45-11 87

GETTING THERE · WHEN TO VISIT

A visit to the Pantanal is most worthwhile at times of low water (roughly April to September), when visitors can expect to see a lot more wild animals than during the high water season. Also, when the waters are lower, the mosquitoes are less of a nuisance. The starting point for tours into the Pantanal are the towns of ▶ Cuiabá, ▶Campo Grande and ▶ Corumbá, where hotels and travel agencies offer excursions.

WHERE TO EAT

▶ Moderate

Kaskata Flutuante
Rua Colonel José Dulce, Cáceres
Tel. (065) 32 23-29 16
Restaurant situated on the riverbank. Exclusively regional dishes.

WHERE TO STAY

▶ Luxury

Refúgio Ecológico Caiman
On the Agachi road
73km/45 miles outside Miranda
Tel. (065) 32 42-14 50
www.caiman.com.br
Fazenda with four lodges in vast grounds, with the same number of pools and a good choice of excursions

▶ Mid-range

Porto Jofre Pantanal
Porto Jofre (situated at the end of the Transpantaneira trunk road)
tel. (065) 36 23-02 36 u. 36 37-15 93
www.portojofre.com.br
Air-conditioned rooms, restaurant, bar, landing strip and boat pier. Motor launches may be hired here for trips into the national park.

Pousada Araras Eco Lodge
On the Transpantaneira, km 65
Pixaim, Tel. (065) 96 03-05 29
www.araraslodge.com.br
A wide array of outings on offer

This one's for real!
Cayman in the Pantanal →

✱ ✱
**Fauna
and flora**

What makes a visit to the expansive, primitive landscape of the lush green Pantanal particularly worthwhile – during the dry season (April – September) at least – is the incredible wealth of animals. The Pantanal's swamps, savannahs and lakes play host to the highest number of crocodiles in the world – according to expert estimates, about 32 million of them.

Alongside the caymans, the Pantanal is home to 50 different types of reptile, 80 types of mammal and over 650 bird species, as well as vast numbers of insects. To safeguard this biodiversity, an area covering 135,000ha/over 52,000 acres in the far south of Mato Grosso state has been designated as the protected **Parque Nacional do Pantanal Mato Grossense**. Despite this, the entire ecosystem is more threatened than ever, on the one hand by the toxic sewage generated by the gold mines (containing mercury, among other things), on the other by poachers and illegal trappers.

✱ Paranaguá

Sa 58

State: Paraná (PR)	**Population:** 116,500
Altitude: 3m/10ft	

Founded in 1648 in the bay of the same name, Paranaguá is the oldest town in Paraná state and, to this day, its principal port of export.

Several preserved historic buildings lend Paranaguá a certain colonial charm, but in terms of tourism, it is most attractive as the gateway for trips to the Ilha do Mel, as well as the start and terminus of the famous Paranaguá – Curitiba (▶Tours p. 147) railway line.

What to see in Paranaguá

✱
**Colonial
buildings**

In the Old Town, don't miss the colonial buildings in Rua da Praia: the 18th-century Casa de Monsenhor Celso and the Palácio do Visconde de Nácar (1856), today the city hall. In Rua da Praia, which runs alongside the beach, look for one of the oldest monuments of Paranaguá, the **Fonte Velha de Beber Água**, also called Bica dos Padres, a fountain erected in 1656.

Also worth seeing are the cathedral of Nossa Senhora do Rosário on Largo Monsenhor Celso, dating from 1578, as well as the churches of São Benedito (1710) and São Francisco das Chagas – all three are listed buildings.

✱
**Colégio
dos Jesuítas**

Construction of the Jesuit college was already well underway when the religious order was driven out of Brazil in 1760. Despite the abrupt ending of the works, the college still counts as one of the most precious buildings in southern Brazil. Its side wings frame the cloisters erected level with the Rio Itiberê river bed. On the building's ground floor, an opening still visible today once led into the cellar vaults connecting the college with the Porto dos Padres (Port of the Padres), 3km/1.8 miles away. Presumably, the Jesuits used these underground escape routes when the decree issued by the Portuguese prime minister Marquês de Pombal forced them to flee the country. Today, the Jesuit college houses the **Museum of Archaeology and Ethnology**, exhibiting fossils and objects used by African cultures, Indian peoples and the coastal dwellers, some of whom immigrated from the Azores (Rua General Carneiro 66).

✳ Ilha do Mel

From the town beach of Pontal do Sul, 48km/30 miles east of Paranaguá, boats cross over to the Ilha do Mel (Honey Island), a beautiful and still unspoilt nature reserve. The trip lasts around 30 minutes. There are a few pousadas in the village of **Nova Brasília**, but most local tourists prefer to rent a fishermen's cottage or camp on the pristine beaches. On the island, look for the listed Fortaleza Nossa Senhora dos Prazeres (or Forte Barra), dating from 1767, and the Farol das Conchas, a 60m/197-ft lighthouse erected in 1872. Another point of interest is the Gruta das Encantadas (Enchanted Cave). The most famous beaches of Cassual, Ponta do Bicho and Fortaleza lie to the north, while to the south unfold the Praias do Farol, Grande, do Miguel, de Fora, das Encantadas, Nova Brasília and do Limeiro.

> ▶ **PARANAGUÁ**
>
> ### INFORMATION
> Rua Des Hugo Simas 373
> Tel. (041) 34 23-21 55
> www.paranagua.pr.gov.br
>
> ### GETTING THERE
> *Bus station*
> Rua João Estevão
> Tel. (041) 34 23-33 61

Parque Nacional do Superagüi

North of Ilha do Mel, the Ilha das Peças and the Ilha do Superagüi form the Superagüi National Park. There are two ways to reach the park: from Paranaguá by boat, or from Antonina by car, driving along the bay plus another 80km/50 miles on an untarmacked road to Guaraqueçaba, a fishing village not far from the border with the neighbouring state of São Paulo.

Guaraqueçaba, separated from the nature reserve by an estuary, has a few simple hotels and restaurants. Visitors to the Superagüi National Park can hire boats with a skipper here – a handful of agencies offer excursions. Within the park proper there is no tourist infrastructure. All visits require permission from the IBAMA environmental protection agency; for more information, contact the IBAMA office in Guaraqueçaba, 3 Rua Dr Ramos Figueira, tel. (041) 34 82-12 62.

★★ Parati

State: Rio de Janeiro (RJ)   **Population:** 30,000
Altitude: 5m/16ft

Founded in the 17th century, the port town of Parati experienced a veritable boom thanks to the gold prospected in the first half of the 18th century in Minas Gerais. At its peak, the town counted 1,700 houses, as well as 150 sugar cane mills and distilleries.

The gold prospected in Minas Gerais was shipped to Rio de Janeiro from here; today's SP-171 road from Guaratinguetá via Cunha to Parati represents a section of the old gold trail used by the bandeirantes to cross the rough **Serra do Mar**. It is thought that over a million kilos of gold were transported by this route to the port on the Rio Perequê Açu, in order to be shipped onwards by ship to Portugal. After the opening of the Camino de Garcia Pais direct route between Minas Gerais and Rio de Janeiro, Parati rapidly fell into oblivion. Maybe this is the very reason though that it was able to preserve the majority of its colonial buildings, which, together with a wonderful location against a backdrop of mountains covered with Atlantic

Colonial architecture in splendid surroundings: Parati

VISITING PARATI

GETTING THERE

Bus station
Rua Jango Pádua
Tel. (024) 33 71-12 24

EVENTS

Alongside the 10-day Festa do Divino (May/June) and other religious festivals, Parati is an all-year-round venue for music festivals, whether it be classical music and jazz or Brazilian folk music. August sees an exhibition of folk art, a street theatre festival and the Festival de Pinga e Produtos de Parati, where the local sugar cane firewater (pinga) and other produce typical of the area are available for sale and sampling.

WHERE TO EAT

► Expensive

Le Grite d'Indaiatiba
BR-101 in the direction of
Angra dos Reis
Sertão de Indaiatiba
Tel. (024) 33 71-71 74
Unusual restaurant (diners can wait for their meal at a waterfall) with dishes prepared to French recipes. Worth a detour!

► Moderate

Punto Divino
Rua Marechal Deodoro 129
In the historic centre of Parati
Tel. (024) 33 71-13 48
Pizzeria

► Inexpensive

Armazém do Antum
Praça da Matriz 3
In the historic centre of Parati
Tel. (024) 33 71-62 66
Arabic dishes

WHERE TO STAY

► Luxury

Santa Clara
BR-101 in the direction of Angra dos Reis, km 567
Ponta da Navalha
Tel. (024) 33 71-89 00
www.santaclarahotel.com.br
Opened in 1999, with 34 air-conditioned apartments, bar, restaurant, swimming pool, sauna and boat pier. The restaurant and most rooms have sea views.

► Mid-range

Coxixo
Rua do Comércio 362
Tel. (024) 33 71-14 60
Fax (024) 33 71-15 68
www.hotel-coxixo.com.br
Guesthouse located in the historic centre, with 33 apartments, restaurant, bar, car parking, sauna and swimming pool

► Budget

Pousada do Ouro
Rua Dr Pereira 145
Tel. (024) 33 71-13 78
Fax (024) 33 71-13 11
www.pousadaouro.com.br
This guesthouse lies right in the centre of Parati and comprises 26 rooms, restaurant, bar, swimming pool, sauna and a gym.

Pousada das Acácias
Ponte Branca
Tel. (024) 33 71-15 61
Alongside 21 air-conditioned rooms, the guesthouse offers its residents a swimming pool, a volleyball court and a play area for children.

rainforest, lend the town its extraordinary charm. Today, now tourism has awakened the town from its temporary lethargy, the streets and lanes, with their countless bars, restaurants, souvenir shops and boutiques, are full of life. At the same time, the picturesque little town has managed to hang onto its romantic, slightly museum-like atmosphere.

What to see in Parati

✹ ✹
Colonial buildings

In the centre of Parati, the cobbled streets from the colonial era are lined by fine buildings with lattice windows. Further landmarks in the city are the Câmara Municipal (town hall) in Rua Dr Samuel Costa, near the Rua do Comércio, and the Chafariz de Mármore (Marble Fountain, 1850) on Praça Macedo Soares.

✹
NS dos Remédios

Rua Nova da Praia and Rua da Matriz border the spacious Praça da Matriz, with the parish church of Nossa Senhora dos Remédios, built between 1789 and 1873 but never finished. The art collection of the church includes paintings by Anita Malfati. The annual Festa de Nossa Senhora dos Remédios on 8 September is celebrated enthusiastically by the entire population of Parati.

Santa Rita

Rua da Matriz leads to Largo de Santa Rita with the church of Santa Rita (1722), which is often used for choir concerts. Next to the church is the Museu de Arte Sacra (Museum of Sacred Art).

NS do Rosário

Built in 1725, the church of Nossa Senhora do Rosário lies on Largo do Rosário, near the Rua do Rosário, the intersecting Rua da Praia and Rua do Comércio. The church with its gilded wooden altars was constructed and used by slaves.

Forte Defensor Perpétuo

Erected in 1703 and restored in 1822, the Forte Defensor Perpétuo, the »Fortress of Eternal Defence«, rises 1km/0.6 miles outside the city centre in Vila Velha. The building still houses artillery from the time of the first settlers and a gunpowder store. Today, the **Museu de Arte e Tradições Populares** (Museum of Art and Folklore) shows its exhibits here.

✹
Beaches

The beaches of Parati – and there are over 60 of them – form an arc around the central **Praia do Pontal**. In the north, the following beaches are particularly worth exploring: Corumbé (7km/4.3 miles from Parati), Grande (10km/6.2 miles), Graúna (15km/9.3 miles), Barra Grande (19km/12 miles), São Roque (22km/13.5 miles), Taquari (26km/16 miles) and Tarituba (25km/15.5 miles), which is in the vicinity of the nuclear power stations of Angra dos Reis. To the south stretch the beaches of Parati Mirim (27km/16.5 miles), Laranjeiras (40km/25 miles), Sono and Ponta Negra (the latter accessible by boat from Praia de Laranjeiras). The beaches of Baré, Conceição,

Lula, Mamanguá, Rosa, Vermelha, Cajaíba and Deserta are also only accessible by boat. The promontories of Ponta do Leste and Ponta da Trindade form the boundary with the coastal zone of Rio de Janeiro.

Over 40 islands adorn the coast of Parati, many of them blessed with beaches that are still completely unspoilt. This island world can be explored by hired saveiros (schooners) or other water crafts. The islands of Araújo (near Corumbé) and Cedro (north of town), as well as the more southerly **Ilha do Algodão** (Cotton Island), not far from the beaches of Parati Mirim and Mamanguá, deserve a special mention.

✳
Islands
off Parati

✳ Serra da Bocaina

Parati lies on the southeastern edge of the Serra da Bocaina. Recognized in 1971 as a national park, the Serra da Bocaina shelters the largest remaining patch of Mata Atlântica forest; visitors can explore many rivers, waterfalls, lakes, caves, fish ponds and viewpoints. Amongst the hundreds of animal species here, expect to see monkeys, deer, tapirs, toucans and capybaras.

The old mule route, used in the 18th century to transport gold from Minas Gerais to Parati, the Trilha do Ouro, runs 70km/44 miles right through the national park, from São José do Barreiro in the north to

Trilha do Ouro

Swampy landscape in the Serra da Bocaina

Parati and Mambucaba. The trail can be walked on foot or explored on horseback – horses are available for hire. Keen hikers might want to consider the sweat-inducing ascent to the 2,200m/7,218-ft Pico da Boa Vista. Tours along the Trilha do Ouro are offered by various trekking agencies in São José do Barreiro.

São José do Barreiro São José do Barreiro is one of the gateways to the Parque Nacional da Serra da Bocaina. Several country estates from the time of the coffee boom are dotted around the town, e.g. the Fazenda Pau d'Alho 3km/1.8 miles from the edge of town. The country estate nestling between forests, rivers and waterfalls includes the manor house as well as former slave quarters.

Parintins

Rg 47

State: Amazonas (AM)　　**Population:** 90,000
Altitude: 27m/88ft

Parintins lies on the Amazonian island of Tupinambarana, between Manaus and Santarém. The town lives off cattle rearing and the export of tropical hardwood. Parintins' claim to fame is the Boi Bumbá festival, which developed from a local custom into a mass event.

What to see in Parintins

✴ **Boi Bumbá** In the second half of June, Parantins hosts a very popular folklore festival, a mighty show based around two papier-mâché bulls called Garantido and Caprichoso. Boi Bumbá is the Amazonian version of the **Bumba Meu Boi** from Maranhão, where figures of local folklore such as boto tucuxi join the traditional figures. Since the inauguration of the purpose-built Bumbódromo stadium in 1988, each year this show has been attracting an ever-increasing number of spectators. These days the festival has up to 80,000 guests and, as the town cannot fit them all in, many overnight in hammocks on the Amazon boats on which they came to Parintins: sleep, however, is of minor importance during this carnivalesque festival.

▶ **PARINTINS**

INFORMATION
EMAMTUR
Tel. (092) 35 33-18 26
www.parintins.com

GETTING THERE
Passenger ships connect the small town with Manaus (taking 26 hours), Óbidos (12hr), Santarém (20hr) and Belém (60hr). The small airport of Parintins receives flights from Manaus, Óbidos and Santarém.

When the waters of the Amazon recede in the Parintins area, the Ilha dos Papagaios (Parrot Island) emerges from the floods. Every evening at around 5pm, hundreds of parrots descend onto the island; this colourful spectacle of nature reaches its peak in November.

Ilha dos Papagaios

✶ Petrópolis

Sd 57

State: Rio de Janeiro (RJ)
Altitude: 809m/2,654ft

Population: 287,000

Petrópolis, the former summer residence of the imperial court and subsequent official summer retreat of the president of the Republic, is one of the most pleasant health resorts in the mountainous highlands of Rio de Janeiro; average temperatures here hover around 17 °C/63 F all year round.

Towering over the numerous parks and a good selection of hotels, mighty peaks rise nearby, including the Pico do Meu Castelo (1,400m/4,593ft) and the Pico do Açu (2,232m/7,323ft). A part of the area belongs to the Parque Nacional da Serra dos Órgãos. The Austrian writer **Stefan Zweig** emigrated to Petrópolis and took his own life here in 1942 in his house at 34 Rua Gonçalves Dias in the suburb of Valparaiso. Between 1894 and 1902, Petrópolis served as a temporary seat for the government of Rio de Janeiro.

What to see in Petrópolis

The Gothic forms of the cathedral of São Pedro de Alcântara in Rua da Imperatriz may be misleading as to the period in which the church was built: begun in the 19th century, the building was only completed in 1925. It shelters the remains of Dom Pedro II, the Empress Dona Teresa Cristina, of Princess Isabel and her spouse, the Conde d'Eu.

✶ **São Pedro de Alcântara**

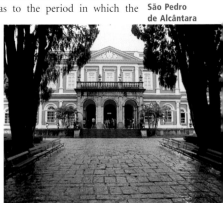

On the same road, further southeast, the Bosque do Imperador (Emperor's Forest) with the classical **Palácio Imperial** (Imperial Palace) today houses the Museu Imperial. Of particular interest amongst the exhibits are the sceptre and crown of Dom Pedro

The imperial palace of Petrópolis

► VISITING PETRÓPOLIS

INFORMATION
Informações Turísticas
Casa do Barão de Mauá
Praça da Confluência 3
Tel. (024) 22 43-35 61
www.petropolis.rj.gov.br

IBAMA Teresópolis
Avenida Rotariana
Tel. (021) 36 42-10 70
Information on the Serra dos Órgãos
National Park

GETTING THERE
Bus station
Rua Dr Porciúncula 75
Tel. (024) 22 37-01 01

WHERE TO EAT
► Expensive
Locanda della Mimosa
Alameda das Mimosas 30
(in the hotel of the same name)
Vale Florido (access via BR-040)
Tel. (024) 22 33-54 05
Italian-inspired gourmet temple in a
salon decorated in romantic style.
Trout, duck and cassoulet dishes,
accompanied by selected wines. Children under eight are not allowed.

► Moderate
Alameda 914
Alameda Paranhos de Oliveira 914
Tel. (024) 22 25-16 37
Excellent snail, mushroom and cod-based dishes. Further house special-

ities are: polenta, cassoulet and fillet
in Madeira sauce. Recommended.

► Inexpensive
Fiammetta
Estrada União Indústria 9153
Condomínio Granja Basil
Itaipava district
Tel. (024) 22 22-88 88
Pizzas from the charcoal-fired oven

WHERE TO STAY
► Luxury
Pousada Tankamana
Estrada Júlio Cápua
Vale do Cuiabá
Tel. (024) 22 22-91 81
www.tankamana.com.br
Complex with four apartments and
eleven chalets, partly rustic, partly
more comfortably equipped. Restaurant, bar, sauna, swimming pools,
archery facilities and horses for hire.
A popular place for honeymooners.

► Mid-range
Pousada Mata Atlântica
Rua João Xavier 344 B
Bingen district
Tel. (024) 22 42-14 73
www.matatlantica.net
Nicely-sized complex with four rooms
and three (slightly more expensive)
chalets, a swimming pool, sports
facilities and car parking, as well as a
bar and restaurant.

II, the crown jewels, artworks and various objects from the imperial
family's estate, as well as documents and furniture from the 19th
century. Adjacent to the museum, the **Palácio Grão Pará**, dating
from 1860, is the residence of the descendants of Dom Pedro II.
Opening times (Museu Imperial): Tue – Sun 11am – 5.30pm.

Following Rua da Imperatriz and Rua 13 de Maio in a northwesterly direction brings visitors to Praça da Confluência with the Palácio de Cristal (Crystal Palace) that the Conde d'Eu had purpose-built for a flower show between 1879 and 1884. Opening times: Tue – Sun 9am – 5.30pm.

✴

Palácio de Cristal

⏲

On Avenida Koeler, connecting Praça Princesa Isabel with Praça Rui Barbosa, stand the palace of Princess Isabel (1853) – today a cultural centre – and the Palácio Rio Negro (1890), the former seat of the government of Rio state.

Casa da Princesa Isabel

Widely called **Casa Encantada** (Enchanted House), the house of the famous inventor and aviation pioneer Alberto Santos-Dumont (1873 – 1932), with astronomical observatory and viewing terrace, lies in Rua do Encanto, west of Praça Rui Barbosa. The building was erected in 1918 and served Santos-Dumont, who also gave his name to the city airport of Rio de Janeiro, as a residence and inventor's workshop up to his suicide in 1932. Opening times: Tue – Sun 9.30am – 5pm.

✴

Casa de Santos-Dumont

⏲

Teresópolis

Alongside Petrópolis, the climatic and thermal spa resort of Teresópolis (pop 125,000) is one of the most important tourist centres in the mountains inland from Rio de Janeiro. Situated northeast of Petrópolis, the city is surrounded by – and forms the gateway to – the waterfalls, mountain springs and brooks of the Serra dos Órgãos. In the city, look for the mineral springs of **Fonte Amélia** (in Ponta do Ingá) and the (radioactive) **Fonte Judite** (in the Bairro do Alto). The Cascata dos Amores (Lovers' Waterfall) is also worth a visit. The Cascata do Imbuí, a waterfall on the Rio Paquequer, lies 6km/3.7 miles off the road to Petrópolis.

Spreading upwards from the valley floor, the city of Teresópolis boasts several viewpoints from which the whole region can be surveyed. Especially interesting are the 1,054m/3,458-ft Colina dos Mirantes, accessible via Rua Jaguaribe, and the Mirante do Soberbo on the BR-116 federal road, from where, on clear days, splendid views of the rock needle of Dedo de Deus (Finger of God) may be enjoyed.

✴

Colina dos Mirantes, Mirante do Soberbo

✴ Serra dos Órgãos

The Parque Nacional da Serra dos Órgãos stretches some 70km/44 miles north of Rio de Janeiro between Teresópolis, Petrópolis and Cascatinha. The reserve is popular with mountain climbers because of its rock crenellations and peaks, including the 1,692m/5,551-ft **Dedo de Deus** (Finger of God), the 1,320m/4,331-ft Dedo de Nossa Senhora (Our Lady's Finger), the towering Nariz do Frade (Monk's

Nose), 1,980m/6,496ft high, the 2,050m/6,726-ft Agulha do Diabo (Devil's Needle) and the Pedra do Sino (Bell Rock), at 2,263m/ 7,424ft the highest peak in the national park. The Rio Soberbo flows through the park, forming various lakes and ponds, amongst them the rock-framed Poço Verde (Green Pond). Just below this, a small natural history museum exhibits books, stuffed birds and some landscape paintings by the German naturalist Karl Friedrich Philipp von Martius (1794 – 1868), who visited Brazil in the 19th century.

Fauna and flora   Various paths lead into the interior of the national park, which supports orchids and all kinds of low-growing plants, but also jequitibas, cedars, perobas and other endemic trees. The animal world is mainly represented by pakas, armadillos, coatis and – though visitors are lucky to see them – small anteaters and deer. Parrots and various kinds of venomous snake, such as the jararaca (lance-head viper), also call this area home.

Rainforest in bloom in the Serra dos Órgãos

Those who have come equipped with camping gear may stay overnight in one of the five campsites of the national park. Otherwise,
the towns of Teresópolis and Petrópolis offer accommodation. Hikes
in the park should only be undertaken accompanied by a local guide.
The best times for visiting the reserve are May to October (for hill-
walkers) and November – February for visitors keen to swim in the
natural pools and lakes.

**Tourist
infrastructure**

Pirenópolis

Sa 53

State: Goiás (GO)
Altitude: 770m/2,526ft

Population: 21,500

Today a national cultural monument, Pirenópolis was founded in
1731, after the discovery of the Meia Ponte gold deposits by the
bandeirante Bartolomeu Bueno Filho. The picturesque little town
on the Rio das Almas river is a popular destination for weekend
excursions from Brasília and Goiânia. However, Pirenópolis is also
one of the mystic sites of the Central High Plateau, where many
cults and alternative communities live.

What to see in and around Pirenópolis

The listed parish church of Nossa Senhora do Rosário was built between 1728 and 1732 on Praça da Matriz; it is the oldest church in

**Matriz NS
do Rosário**

 VISITING PIRENÓPOLIS

INFORMATION
Rua do Bonfim 14
Tel. (062) 33 31-27 29
www.pirenopolis.tur.br

GETTING THERE
Bus station
Via Matutino
Tel. (062) 33 31-10 80

WHERE TO EAT
▶ **Moderate**
Le Bistrô
Rua do Rosário, tel. (062) 33 31-21 50
Regional and international dishes on
offer.

WHERE TO STAY
▶ **Mid-range**
Pousada dos Pireneus
Chácara Mata do Sobrado 80
Tel. (062) 33 31-10 28
www.pousadadospireneus.com.br
Pousada with 105 air-conditioned
apartments, bar, restaurant, pool,
water slide, sauna and bike hire

▶ **Budget**
Pousada do Abcateiro
Rua Pireneus 61, tel. (062) 33 31-14 01
www.abacateiro.com.br
Pool, car parking and nine rooms
with TV

Goiás, and at a metre/over 3 feet in thickness, its clay walls are arguably the sturdiest in the whole of Brazil.

★
NS do Bonfim

Also situated in the Old Town, the church of Nossa Senhora do Bonfim was built between 1750 and 1754 and possesses an image of Christ from Bahia painted onto two wooden panels.

Fazenda Babilônia

The listed Fazenda Babilônia, situated 25km/15.5 miles southwest of Pirenópolis, was set up between 1800 and 1805. The huge overhanging roof spanned the whole group of buildings: the manor house, the sugar mill, the firewater distillery, the workshops and slaves' huts.

★ Porto Alegre

Rk 61

State: Rio Grande do Sul (RS)   **Population:** 1.4 million
Altitude: 46m/151ft

Porto Alegre, situated on the lagoon-rich coast of Rio Grande do Sul, was founded by Azorean settlers on 26 March 1772 under the name of Porto dos Casais. The city lies on the left bank of the Rio Guaíba at the spot where five rivers converge to form the Lagoa dos Patos (Duck Lagoon).

Today, the commercial hub of Porto Alegre forms the centre of a catchment area including the nearby stretch of coast and the municipalities of the Serra Gaúcha, predominantly settled by the descendants of German and Italian immigrants.

What to see in Porto Alegre

Parque Farroupilha

Farroupilha Park unfolds near the old city centre. The triangular arrangement – lined by the Avenidas Osvaldo Aranha, João Pessoa and José Bonifácio (with the church of Santa Terezinha, inspired by Gothic models) – possesses ancient trees, a lake and a small zoo. This is also the place to find the Auditório Araújo Viana, a kind of open-air stage, and the **Museu da Força Expedicionária Brasileira** (FEB) with weapons, uniforms and photos documenting the deployment of Brazilian armed forces in the Second World War in northern Italy. A further attraction of the Farroupilha Park is the Brique da Redenção, a flea market held every Sunday morning.

Museu Júlio de Castilhos

While the Museu Júlio de Castilhos (Historical Museum) at 1205 Avenida Duque de Caxias shows fossils and Indian handicrafts, it is predominantly concerned with the life and works of Júlio de Castil-

hos and Borges de Medeiros, two statesmen from Rio Grande do Sul. ⏱
Opening times: Tue – Fri 10am – 7pm, Sat/Sun 2 – 6pm.

The Praça Marechal Deodoro stands at the centre of a cluster of historically significant buildings dating from the 18th to the 20th centuries. The origins of the **Catedral Metropolitana** go back to 1772, the
year when the building of the church was first begun. The forms visible today, inspired by the Renaissance, only started to appear from
the 1920s onwards. Work was interrupted time and again, so that the
church was only able to be completed in 1986. Particularly eyecatch-
ing is the marble dome, guarded on either side by two towers, each
50m/164ft high.

Praça Marechal Deodoro

Built in 1896 and decorated in the style of Louis XVI, Palácio Piratini
is the seat of the government of Rio Grande do Sul. The wall paintings of the listed palace on Praça Marechal Deodoro were created by
the Italian artist Aldo Locatelli who emigrated to Rio Grande do Sul. ⏱
Opening times: Mon – Fri 9 – 11am and 2 – 5pm.

Palácio Piratini

Porto Alegre dockside in evening light

VISITING PORTO ALEGRE

INFORMATION

Informações Turísticas
Mercado Público
Praça Quinze de Novembro
Tel. (051) 32 25-06 77

GETTING THERE

Airport
Aeroporto Int. Salgado Filho
Tel. (051) 33 58-20 00

Bus station
Largo Vespasiano Júlio Veppo
Tel. (051) 32 10-01 01

EVENTS

Semana da Farroupilha
A boozy week, every year around 20
September, with gaúcho dress, dishes
and drinks from Rio Grande do Sul,
sometimes accompanied by a programme of events

Feira do Livro
In the first half of November, in the
open air on Praça da Alfândega, right
next to the Museu de Arte, the
traditional annual book fair attracts
many visitors.

WHERE TO EAT

► Expensive
① *Chez Phillippe*
Avenida Independência 1005
Tel. (051) 33 12-53 33
French-inspired cuisine. Diners,
Mastercard and Visa are accepted, but
not American Express.

► Moderate
② *Na Brasa*
Rua Ramiro Barcelos 389
Floresta district
Tel. (051) 30 19-51 45
Speedy waiters serving grill dishes.

③ *Atelier de Massas*
Rua Riachuelo 1482
Tel. (051) 32 25-11 25
Pasta dominates here. All credit cards
accepted.

WHERE TO STAY

► Luxury
① *Plaza São Rafael*
Avenida Alberto Bins 514
Tel. (051) 32 20-70 00
www.plazahoteis.com.br
Traditional establishment with 283
air-conditioned rooms, some reserved
for non-smokers, partly suitable for
wheelchair users. Restaurant, bar,
swimming pool, sauna and gym.

► Mid-range
② *Hotel Everest*
Rua Duque de Caxias 1357
Tel. (051) 32 15-95 00
www.everest.com.br
Central location, offering residents
153 air-conditioned apartments as
well as a good restaurant with bar.

③ *Grande Hotel Express*
Rua Riachuelo 1070
Tel. (051) 32 87-44 11
www.master-hoteis.com.br
Built in 1992, this hotel (92 rooms) is
next to a shopping centre, where
residents are served breakfast and
lunch.

► Budget
④ *Master Express*
Rua Sarmento Leite 865
Cidade Baixa
Tel. (051) 32 11-36 36
www.master-hoteis.com.br
City hotel with 96 air-conditioned
apartments. No restaurant and rather
spartan decor.

On the western side of Praça Marechal Deodoro, the Palácio Farroupilha completes the centre of political powers. The parliamentary
building (Assembléia Legislativa) has its architectural roots in the late
18th century, but has suffered several changes over the years.

**Palácio
Farroupilha**

A few paces north of the square, the São Pedro Theatre, built in the
classical style in 1858, is one of the most beautiful buildings in Porto
Alegre. The restoration of the listed building was funded by wealthy
citizens, safeguarding the theatre's
original forms but at the same time
integrating functional elements of
contemporary theatre buildings.
Guided tours by appointment: tel.
(051) 32 27-51 00.

✱
**Teatro
São Pedro**

! **Baedeker TIP**

Porto Alegre from above

Fancy seeing Porto Alegre from a height of
450m/nearly 1,500ft aboard a DC 3? No
problem, if you can get 18 to 26 people together
on a Saturday. The crew wear historic uniforms
and serve champagne. Reservations at Aeroclube
do Rio Grande do Sul, Avenida Juca Batista
8101, tel. (051) 32 45-16 78.

Shortly before reaching the Rio
Guaíba, Av Duque de Caxias joins
Rua dos Andradas, better known
under its older name of Rua da
Praia, the true centre of the capital.
This is where to find the church of
Nossa Senhora das Dores, erected
between 1883 and 1891 and housing Portuguese paintings, and the
Museu de Comunicação Social in the former publishing house of the
A Federação newspaper, which documents the development of Brazil-
ian newspaper journalism since 1920.

At 736 Rua dos Andradas, at the junction with Rua Araújo Ribeira,
lies the Mário Quintana cultural centre. Housed in what used to be
the Majestic – once the most famous Grand Hotel in town – it consists of theatre halls, a video club, library, plus exhibition and
conference rooms. The ground floor shows films on the poet **Mário
Quintana**, who lived in the former hotel until 1980. His books are
for sale here too. The glass domes on the terrace offer views of the
Rio Guaíba. Opening times: Tue – Fri 9am – 9pm.

✱
**Casa da
Cultura Mário
Quintana**

🕐

Between Rua da Praia and Avenida Mauá stand several notable buildings. The public market, built in 1869 on Praça XV de Novembro offers food, imported goods, many varieties of the mate tea so typical
of the area and crafts from gaucho country. Opening times: Mon to
Fri 7.30am to 7.30pm, Sat 7.30am – 6.30pm.

Mercado Público

🕐

Porto Alegre boasts numerous museums and art collections; of particular interest is the Museu de Arte do Rio Grande do Sul (MARGS)
near Praça da Alfândega (Rua Sete de Setembro 1010). Under its
roof, visitors can find a specialized library and an art gallery, as well
as a collection of sculpture, tapestry and ceramics. The art gallery
has works by Portinari, Di Cavalcanti, Debret, Manabu Mabe and ar-

✱
**Museu de
Arte do Rio
Grande do Sul**

Porto Alegre *Map*

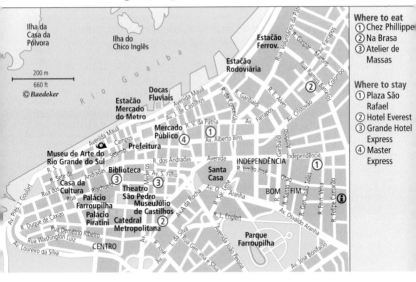

Where to eat
① Chez Phillippe
② Na Brasa
③ Atelier de Massas

Where to stay
① Plaza São Rafael
② Hotel Everest
③ Grande Hotel Express
④ Master Express

tists from southern Brazil such as Carlos Scliar, Vasco Prado, Francisco Stockinger, Frank Schaeffer, Marcelo Grassmann and many others. Opening times: Tue – Sun 10am – 7pm.

Museu de Ciências The Museum of Natural History and Technology at 6681 Avenida Ipiranga comprises some 10,000 mineralogical, zoological and archeological exhibits, effectively forming nearly an entire inventory of the natural treasures of Rio Grande do Sul state. The museum is situated on the campus of Porto Alegre University (PUC-RS) near the Jardim Botânico. Opening times: Tue – Sun 9am – 5pm.

Avenida Padre Cacique leads to the 131m/428-ft **Morro Santa Tereza** (Hill of Saint Teresa), which is still within the city limits and offers good views of the Rio Guaíba river.

No visit to Porto Alegre is complete without stopping by one of the centres of gaucho traditions. The **cultural centres**, with their

! *Baedeker* TIP

Boat trip to the Jacuí Delta

An unusual but convenient way to explore Porto Alegre and the surrounding area is a boat trip on the Rio Guaíba. There are two leisure boats to choose from: the *Cisne Branco* leaves from the entrance to the Portão Central do Porto (behind Praça da Alfândega), while the *Noiva do Caí* departs for the scenic Delta do Jacuí from the pier in front of the Usina do Gasómetro cultural centre (Avenida João Goulart). The boats stop at the Ilhas do Lage and dos Marinheiros, giving the opportunity in summer to take a dip at one of the small beaches.

proud names such as Os Maragatos (members of the federalist movement in Rio Grande do Sul), Tropeiros da Tradição (traditional mule-drivers) or Ponteiros do Rio Grande (cattle herders from Rio Grande), offer tourists typical dishes served with chimarrão (green tea), and entertain with music and dance. The Movimento Tradicionalista Gaúcho (Traditionalist Gaucho Movement, Rua Guilherme Schell 60) gives detailed information on the activities of individual centres.

Around Porto Alegre: the Serra Gaúcha

Rising north of Porto Alegre, the high plateau of the Serra Gaúcha has a range of hills exceeding 1,000m/3,280ft. This is ideal terrain for long hikes in an alpine setting, hence the area's popularity with German settlers, from 1824 onwards, and Italian settlers, from 1875 onwards – both groups felt at home here. The latter soon started to apply the vinicultural skills acquired in their faraway home country to the Brazilian south – with excellent results. Today, a large proportion of Brazil's vines ripen around the winegrowing communities north of Porto Alegre. The fact that the region is not only at the centre of wine production, but also of wine consumption, is good news for visitors, who can sample a nice drop in the numerous charming wine cellars of the winegrowing towns.

Hiking paradise and centre of wine-growing

A little over 30km/18.5 miles north of Porto Alegre lies the city of São Leopoldo (pop 194,000), which was founded in 1824 by the first group of German settlers in Rio Grande do Sul. The colonists that settled on the left-hand bank of the Rio dos Sinos dedicated themselves to agriculture, small industry and crafts, laying the foundations for the future industrial development of the city. In Avenida Feitoria, the Casa do Imigrante is the house that took in the first German settlers in the region. The collections of the São Leopoldo museums are a reminder of this formative period.
Also worth seeing are the Museu do Trem (Railway Museum) in the former railway station, built in 1875 by the English, and the Parque de Recreação do Trabalhador, 6km/3.5 miles out of town (access via the BR-116 federal road).

São Leopoldo

Gramado (pop 26,000) lies in the Quilombo valley, 115km/71 miles northeast of Porto Alegre, and is the venue for the annual **Brazilian Film Festival** in August. The small town, famed for its rough climate as much as its blooming hydrangeas in summer, has several houses that cannot hide their Alpine heritage. The town is also much vaunted for its exquisite home-made chocolate and its sumptuous Italian and German cuisine. Be sure to pay a visit to a Café Colonial; the opulence of their menus is overwhelming. Only 2km/1.2 miles outside Gramado, the Cascata dos Narcisos and Véu da Noiva plunge down 20m/65ft.

Gramado

IGNOMINIOUS PAST

Rio Grande do Sul likes to play up the European look of its population. Pointing to an autonomous culture nearly exclusively born out of Portuguese, Spanish, Italian and German elements, the southernmost Brazilian state vies for tourists and investments. However, the image of Rio Grande is deceptive; what the advertising strategists usually fail to mention is the reason why there are hardly any Indian and African influences in the country of the gaúchos.

Rio Grande do Sul is rightly considered the most individualistic Brazilian state. Geographically and culturally, the »country of the gaúchos« has more in common with the bordering countries to the west and south, Argentina and Uruguay, than with the tropical regions of Brazil further north. The strong influence of the La Plata states on the area has a long-standing tradition: the first Europeans, settling in what is today Rio Grande do Sul, were Spanish missionaries.

The Jesuits establish missions

From 1626 onwards, Jesuit fathers, coming from Argentina and crossing what is today Brazil's western border, the Rio Uruguai, founded the first of 32 »reductions« (missions) in São Nicolau, in the area populated by Guaraní Indians. At that time, Rio Grande do Sul lay outside the Portuguese sphere of influence as set out in the **Treaty of Tordesillas** as early as 1494; Portugal itself had for 46 years been dominated by force by the Spanish crown. Over the following

The state of Rio Grande do Sul is also known as the »country of the gaúchos«.

100 years, nobody hindered the Jesuits in their pursuit of the Christianization of the Guaraní. 150,000 baptized Indios in total were to settle around their mission churches, erected at intervals of 45 kilometres/28 miles. Some of the reservations founded by the Jesuits quickly attained a population of 20,000, some four times more than the population of Buenos Aires in Argentina at that time.

Daily life in the Guaraní republic

In the area controlled by the missions, not only corn, manioc, maté tea and sweet potatoes were grown, but also cotton, barley, rice, tobacco, fruit, wine, wheat and sugar cane. In **São João Batista** one of the first iron foundries in South America was established; the Jesuits also taught the Guaraní about animal husbandry. The self-governing communes of the Guaraní republic knew neither money nor private property. Daily working hours were restricted to six to eight hours; all tools, means of transport and produce were collectively owned and allocated to members of the community according to need. It is worth stopping for a few moments to think about what the political map of South America would look like if the Portuguese bandeirantes had not gradually pushed the boundaries of their influence across the demarcation line of the Tordesillas treaty, destroyed the revolutionary Jesuit state and, by 1835, all but wiped out the Guaraní Indians, bringing their number, originally an estimated two million, down to 130 survivors.

»Hostile takeover«

Over time, members of the bandeirantes raids seized the large **estancias**, as the cattle farms established by the Jesuits were called. The clans in the widely dispersed cattle ranches on the borders with Argentina and Uruguay form the base of the gaúcho population. Here, in the vast pampas steppes of the campanha, the weather-beaten cowboys – wearing their typical hats with chin strap, wide bombacha trousers, red neckties and riding boots that are most associated with Rio Grande do Sul – remain in the saddle to this day. The Portuguese crown initially supported the rough clans, in order to secure the territory of its Brazilian territory against Spanish Castile. Particularly deserving defenders of the new borders, drawn up in the Treaty of Madrid of 1750, were even rewarded with illustrious titles of nobility of the Brazilian empire.

Revolution

When the Brazilian central administration lowered import tariffs on foreign meat products in 1835, sharply increasing competition for south Brazilian cattle farmers, Rio Grande do Sul saw the outbreak of a massive uprising. As in other Brazilian provinces, the seeds of revolution had already been sown, with the central government the previous year rescinding the right to regional legislation. Practically the entire Guarda Nacional in Rio Grande do Sul deserted, forming the basis of the feared cavalry of the **Farroupilha separatists**, who for ten years fought bloody battles with the troops of the Brazilian central government. The longer the war went on, the more the revolutionary armies recruited African slaves, promising them freedom once victory had been secured over the forces loyal to the government. The extraordinary bravery shown by the »lanceiros negros« is mentioned, amongst others, in the somewhat embellished memoirs of the Italian professional revolutionary Giuseppe Garibaldi. After joining other Italian captains in a luckless fight on the side of the Farrapo's naval forces, Garibaldi retreated to his native country.

Betrayal

Towards the end of the war, the courageous **Lanceiros Negros** were betrayed by their own general, David Canabarro. Painstakingly separated from the general's white contingents, the two divisions were attacked by government troops – despite capitulation negotiations already underway – and virtually wiped out. A substantial proportion of the soldiers killed in action during the Farroupilha Revolution were black. The victors deported the surviving black soldiers to Rio, where their trail goes cold; the most likely scenario is that they were used as slaves on the plantations.

A recommended drive into the rural surroundings of Gramado follows the Linha Bonita 6km/3.7 miles out of town, on a hairpin-bend road leading down the serra to Gramado Rural with 15 typical farmhouses, a water mill and a small church. A little further on, an old firewater distillery is open to visitors. The private museum of the Fioreze family exhibits 700 copper and iron tools and other equipment used by the Italian immigrants.

✱ Gramado Rural

The next stop is the , a 15m/49-ft waterfall that plunges down into a basin which is 10m/11yd wide. On the way back, following the Linha Furna, 20km/12.5 miles before Gramado, drivers will come across the Ponte do Raposo, an iron bridge spanning the Rio Santa Cruz river.

◄ Cascata do Panelão

Canela

Canela (pop 34,000), a well-known holiday resort in the Serra Gaúcha, lies in the Quilombo valley, 119km/74 miles northeast of Porto Alegre. A small proportion of the population is of German descent, while the architecture of the houses – and the chalets too, with their windows framed by flowers – is strongly reminiscent of towns in the Swiss Alps. In winter, temperatures can drop below freezing, and sometimes even a few snowflakes make an appearance.

Alpine atmosphere

Lying just under 10km/6.2 from town, among the attractions of the **Parque Caracol** are an impressive waterfall (Cascata do Caracol), which plunges 131m/430ft, tropical and subtropical forests, numerous animal species and the Rio Caracol, forming further waterfalls and small beaches. A waymarked trail leads through the park to the foot of the highest cascade, which displays its full glory in the early morning light. Opening times: daily 8am – 6pm.

> **!** *Baedeker* TIP
>
> ### Rota Romântica
>
> The highlights of the Serra Gaúcha may be comfortably explored by hire car along the »Romantic Road«. The drive, a good 170km/105 miles long, starts in Porto Alegre and leads initially to São Leopoldo, Novo Hamburgo and Novo Petrópolis, then on to Gramado, Canela and finally to São Francisco de Paula.

Castelinho Caracol, situated on the road leading to the park (Estrada do Parque do Caracol), was erected in 1913. The oldest timber-framed building in town, it houses the Franzen family museum, showing furniture, household goods and tools brought over from Germany by the family in the early 20th century.

Castelinho Caracol

The Ferradura Valley, a canyon 420m/1,378ft deep, also lies on the Estrada do Parque do Caracol, 16km/10 miles outside Canela, and was cut into the Serra Gaúcha mountains by the Rio Santa Cruz river. Here, the river forms a waterfall, the **Cascata Arroio Caçador**.

Vale Ferradura

Caxias do Sul

Caxias do Sul (pop 360,500), 120km/75 miles north of Porto Alegre, was founded by Italian immigrants who formed, from 1871 onwards, the colony of Conde d'Eu. Don't miss out on a visit to the small and large wineries in the area to sample the local wines. The city's most important culinary attraction however is the famous Italian cantinas, preparing the regional speciality of galeto (formerly songbirds, but today chicks no older than 30 days) and of course spaghetti, tagliatelle and tortellini to perfection.

Rincão da Lealdade Rincão da Lealdade, the centre of the gaúcho tradition, is situated on the way into the city, near the BR-116 state road. There are regional grill specialities here, plus musical and dance performances and an exhibition showing tools used by the early gaúchos and the region's first settlers.

✳ São Pelegrino Built in the neo-Gothic style, the church of São Pelegrino (Avenida Itália 54), dating from 1953, is decorated with wall frescoes by **Aldo**

Maize field in Serra Gaúcha

Locatelli – the Italian artist based in Rio Grande do Sul – that represent the Stations of the Cross. The church also has a copy of Michelangelo's famous *Pietá*. The high reliefs on the large bronze doors show scenes from the colonization by Italian immigrants.

The Museu Municipal at 586 Rua Visconde de Pelotas, which mainly documents the Italian settlement, also has some sculptures worthy of note, for example the painted wooden likeness of the *Virgin Mary with Child* (1885) by Pietro Stangherlin.

Museu Municipal

Rua Matteo Gianela preserves a typical two-storey house from the colonial era (1875). Initially this was the residence of the Luchesi family, later serving as a forge, and later still a warehouse. The museum installed here today shows, among other things, tools used by the Italian colonizers.

Casa de Pedra

In the Parque de Exposições Centenário, 4km/2.5 miles out of town on Rua Ludovico Cavinato, stands a miniature replica of Caxias do Sul from 1885. The history of the area's settlement is illustrated by a multimedia show.

Parque de Exposições Centenário

Bento Gonçalves

Bento Gonçalves (pop 91,500), one of the most important winemaking communities in the southernmost Brazilian state, lies 128km/80 miles north of the provincial capital Porto Alegre. Originally growing out of the Colônia Dona Isabel, founded in 1870 by the Italian government and settled by Italian immigrants, today the town bears the name of one of the leaders of the Farroupilha Revolution (► Baedeker Special p. 330).

Anyone wanting to see all the different stages of wine production should visit the small – mostly family-run – wineries in the districts of Faria Lemos, São Pedro, Monte Belo and Pinto Bandeira during the time of the grape harvest (January to March). The big wine-producing companies (Casa Cordelier, Casa Valduga, etc.) usually organize guided tours complemented by audiovisual material and ending with a chance to sample a drop of the local vintage.

Wineries

The Museu do Imigrante (Immigrants' Museum) at 127 Rua Erny Hugo Dreher, exhibits tools and personal effects of this region's pioneers. The first settlers hailed from the Veneto and Trento areas. Opening times: Tue – Fri 8 – 11.15am and 1.30 – 5.15pm, Sat 1 to 5pm, Sun 9am – noon.

Museu do Imigrante

⊙

In the southeast of Bento Gonçalves, the Igreja de São Bento church, completed in 1982, is a somewhat unusual church building, with a shape – deliberately secular – inspired by a wine barrel.

Igreja de São Bento

Garibaldi

With its 28,500 inhabitants, the small mountain town of Garibaldi is the secret capital of the Brazilian wine industry. Around 60% of home-grown wines and 80% of Brazilian sparkling wine production come from here. The small town lies 13km/8 miles south of Bento Gonçalves. It takes its name from the Italian freedom fighter **Giuseppe Garibaldi**, who spent time in South America between 1834 and 1848, and as the commander of a warship played a significant role in the Farroupilha War from 1835 to 1845, before returning to Italy.

In and around Garibaldi, a multitude of vineyards and sparkling wineries organize guided tours and wine tastings. Some of the best-known are: Georges Aubert, Avenida Rio Branco 1276, tel. (054) 34 62-11 55, Cooperativa Garibaldi, Avenida Rio Branco 833, tel. (054) 34 62-11 00 and Peterlongo, Rua Manuel Peterlongo 216, tel. (054) 34 62-13 55.

✶
Cantinas

Porto Seguro

Sf 54

State: Bahia (BA)   **Population:** 96,000
Altitude: 49m/161ft

It was near the port town of Porto Seguro, in the extreme south of Bahia, that in the year 1500 the caravels of Pedro Álvares Cabral first anchored off the Brazilian mainland. Cabral, emissary of the Portuguese crown, called the patch of ground on which he was the first European to stand, Ilha da Vera Cruz.

Today, the very beach where once Tupiniquin Indians, expecting a show of mutual respect, committed the fatal error of coming out peacefully to meet Cabral and his companions – the Tupiniquin were exterminated very quickly – is thronged with masses of holiday-makers, making the town, with sweeping beaches in its immediate vicinity, one of the most popular holiday resorts in Brazil. Clubs, bars and the famous beach parties of Porto Seguro, attracting crowds of students from as far as Rio de Janeiro and São Paulo, make the Bahian nights go on till daybreak. Completely geared towards tourism, Porto Seguro can also boast one of the oldest cultural monuments in Brazil, conferring to the town the status of a Monumento Nacional.

← *A hanging workstation:*
  gaúchos do their day's work in the saddle

What to see in Porto Seguro

Igreja da Misericórdia

Porto Seguro is divided up between the busy Lower Town (Cidade Baixa) and the historic core in the Upper Town (Cidade Histórica, Cidade Alta). Erected between 1526 and 1530, the Igreja da Misericórdia in the Upper Town is one of the oldest surviving churches on Brazilian soil. Its interior is decorated with the paintings *Merciful Christ* from 1526 and *Our Lady of Sorrows* from 1582.

The church of **Nossa Senhora da Pena**, dedicated to the patron saint of the town, dates from 1535 and contains a **representation of St Francis of Assisi**, brought here from Portugal by Gonçalo Coelho on his 1503 expedition; this is the oldest religious icon in Brazil. Close by the church stands a memorial stone (Marco do Descobrimento), erected by Gonçalo Coelho to commemorate the discovery of this area.

> ! **Baedeker TIP**
>
> **More carnival, anyone?**
>
> As soon as the rousing street carnival of Salvador has come to an end, the carnivalesque atmosphere takes over Porto Seguro. Some of the best bands take the next plane and continue on the trios elétricos (trucks converted into movable stages for musicians and instruments) in Porto Seguro at exactly the point where they left off the previous day in Salvador. Caught up in the relentless pounding of the axé or samba-reggae rhythms, the whole town dances for a good week.

Around Porto Seguro

★ ★ Beaches

North of the town extend the beaches of Curuípe (3km/1.8 miles out of town), Mundaí (6km/3.7 miles), Itaperapuã (7km/4.3 miles), Rio dos Mangues (9km/5.5 miles) and Ponta Grande (12km/7.5 miles). The latter is situated close to the coast road leading to Santa Cruz Cabrália (25km/15.5 miles).

Santa Cruz Cabrália

The Old Town of Santa Cruz Cabrália, situated 25km/15.5 miles north of Porto Seguro, still preserves the ruins of some Jesuit buildings, with the church of **Nossa Senhora da Conceição** and other buildings from colonial times standing out nearby. Amongst the beaches, Praia da Ponta do Mutá (16km/10 miles from Porto Seguro) and the one of Coroa Vermelha (17km/10.5 miles) are worth mentioning; at the latter, a brazilwood cross marks the place where the first mass on Brazilian soil was celebrated. In the north, fine beaches stretch towards Belmonte, but are only accessible by boat, e. g. Santo Antônio (a 1-hr drive), Guaiú (75min) and Mugiquiçaba (1.5hr).

★ Arraial d'Ajuda, Trancoso

Reaching Arraial d'Ajuda, 4km/2.5 miles south of Porto Seguro, involves catching a ferry across the estuary of the Rio Buranhém. The main sight in the village is the church of **Nossa Senhora d'Ajuda**, erected between 1549 and 1551, but it is predominantly the fairly pristine beaches that attract visitors. The Praia de Mucugê is not far from Arraial, whilst the even more famous beaches of Pitinga and Taípe are situated between the village and Trancoso, an idyllic settlement 25km/15 miles south of Porto Seguro. The magnificent Pitinga Beach is (occasionally) a nudists' paradise, and, together with Taípe Beach, lined by high rocky cliffs, counts among the most beautiful on this stretch of coast. The latter may be explored by a charming hike lasting around three hours, from Arraial d'Ajuda to Trancoso.

✳ Parque Nacional do Monte Pascoal

Established in 1961 across an area of 22,500ha/60,000 acres, the Monte Pascoal National Park boasts extremely varied flora and fauna, as well as diverse landscapes. Alongside forest areas, with plants such as jequitibás, maçarandubas, palisander trees, jatobás, perobas and brazilwood, there are picturesque beaches, reefs, dunes, lakes and restingas (sand/clay soil with low-growing shrub vegetation). The landscape changes from sand banks, mangrove and tropical forest to swamps, lagoons and salt and freshwater lakes, and several threatened animal species live here, including the preguiças de coleira (a type of sloth), various monkeys, huge otters, giant armadillos

On Trancoso beach

► VISITING PORTO SEGURO

INFORMATION
Praça Manuel Ribeiro Coelho
Tel. (073) 32 68-13 90
www.portosegurotur.com.br

GETTING THERE
Airport
Estrada do Aeroporto
Tel. (073) 32 88-18 80

Bus station
On the BR-367 federal road
Tel. (073) 32 88-10 39

GOING OUT
There are beach parties practically
every night at different beach bars –
just follow the racket emanating from
the loudspeaker towers.

WHERE TO EAT
► Inexpensive
Recanto do Sossego
Praia da Mutá
Tel. (073) 36 72-12 66

Friendly beach bar with an appealing
menu

WHERE TO STAY
► Mid-range
Villaggio Arcobaleno
Rodovia BR-367
Praia de Taperapuã
Tel. (073) 36 79-20 00 and
(08 00) 284-52 22
www.hotelarcobaleno.com.br
Hotel close to the beach with 160 air-
conditioned apartments. Good selection of sports and leisure activities, a
very good restaurant, children's play
area, pool and beach bar.

► Budget
Pousada Nascente
Estrada do Aeroporto 437
Tel. (073) 32 88-29 00
www.pousadanascente.com.br
19 rooms, bar, swimming pool and
car parking. Pets are welcome.

and pampas deer. Other animals to look out for include macucos or
macucas (an endangered, tropical, tree-roosting bird), king vultures
and other bird species.

Monte Pascoal One of the main attractions of the national park is the 536m/1,558-ft
Monte Pascoal, the very mountain that was first spotted on the hori-
zon – at Easter 1500 – as the first sighting of Brazil from on board
Cabral's caravels. For climbing to the summit, allow at least 2.5
hours walking time.

Getting there The park lies 160km/100 miles south of Porto Seguro and is accessible via the BR-101 state road, and then by following a road that
branches off towards the national park at Itamaraju. A good 30km/
18 miles from here is the entrance to the park. The Parque Nacional
do Monte Pascoal is open daily and has a visitor centre. Its proximity
to the Atlantic and the resulting climate makes the park a suitable
all-year-round destination.

Porto Velho

State: Rondônia (RO)   **Population:** 335,000
Altitude: 85m/279ft

Porto Velho, capital of Rondônia state, lies on Rio Madeira, the longest tributary of the Amazon. The colonization of Rondônia started with the construction of the infamous Madeira–Mamoré 'Devil's Railway' (between Porto Velho and Guajará Mirim on Rio Mamoré), sealed in the Treaty of Petrópolis in 1903.

This connection was intended to enable the transport of produce from Bolivia and to compensate La Paz for the loss of Acre, annexed by Brazil. Driven through the jungle, the railway line cost thousands of lives, but made a lasting contribution to the development of Porto Velho and other urban centres in Rondônia, where many workers involved in the construction of the railway settled.

What to see in and around Porto Velho

The station of Ferroviário Madeira–Mamoré, now shut down, lies at the beginning of Avenida Sete de Setembro, very close to the Cai'   **Railway museum**

In the Amazonian hinterland, the prospects for education are few: school in the rainforest of northern Brazil

▶ VISITING PORTO VELHO

INFORMATION
www.portovelho.ro.gov.br

GETTING THERE
Airport
Aeroporto Nacional Belmont
Avenida L Sodré
Tel. (069) 30 25-74 50

Bus station
Avenida Governador Jorge Teixeira
Tel. (069) 32 22-22 33

WHERE TO EAT
▶ **Inexpensive**
Massa Leve
Avenida Guanabara 2753
SJ Bosco district
Tel. (069) 32 21-34 41
Italian restaurant with an extensive
drinks list

WHERE TO STAY
▶ **Mid-range**
Vila Rica
Avenida Carlos Gomes 1616
São Cristovão
Tel. (069) 32 24-34 33
and (08 00) 11-01 44
www.hotelvilarica.com.br
The best hotel in Porto Velho offers
115 air-conditioned rooms with TV,
minibar and telephone. Other facilities include a good restaurant, internet access, swimming pool, tennis
courts and a football pitch.

▶ **Budget**
Samaúma
Rua Dom Pedro Segundo 1038
Tel. (069) 32 24-53 00
Spartan and simple, 33 rooms with air
conditioning, telephone and TV

Água port. Today the station houses the railway museum, showing memorabilia from the Madeira–Mamoré railway line, including a steam engine from 1878 called **Maria Fumaça** (Smoking Maria). One-hour trips on a 7km/4.3-mile stretch of the railway track only run on Sundays at 9am, as long as there are at least 15 passengers. The terminus of the special service is Cachoeira de Santo Antônio at Rio Madeira; around 4.30pm, the train is back in Porto Velho.

Teotônio The fishing village of Teotônio, also situated on Rio Madeira, can be reached by a 1.5-hour boat trip from Porto Velho (overland, it is a 45km/28-mile drive on the BR-364 federal road). In September, look out for the piracema – the migration upriver of shoals of fish.

Parque Nacional de Pacaás Novos Established in 1979, the Pacaás Novos National Park, covering a total area of nearly 765,000ha/1,890,000 acres in total across the municipal districts of Porto Velho, Guajará Mirim, Ariquemes and Ji Paraná. It lies on an extensive high plateau covered in sparse **cerrado vegetation**, the Chapada dos Pacaás Novos, in the western central part of Rondônia, some 400km/250 miles from Porto Velho. Access to the region is via the BR-364 federal road (in the direction of Cuiabá), leading through Ariquemes and Ji Paraná, which each have an airport; in both cities, minor roads branch off towards the park. This remote national park in the Brazilian middle of nowhere has no infrastructure whatsoever. For more information, contact IBAMA, Av Governador Jorge Teixeira 3559, Porto Velho, tel. (069) 32 24-65 68.

★ ★ Recife

Sh 50

State: Pernambuco (PE)   **Population:** 1.4 million
Altitude: 4m/13ft

Until the 17th century, Recife (= reef) only really served as the port for Olinda further up the coast, being no more than a settlement founded on the confluence of Rio Capibaribe and Rio Beberibe. Its expansion began in 1630 with the Dutch occupation.

Within ten years, the village of fewer than 200 houses mushroomed into a town of over 2,000 residences. The Dutch drained the island of Antônio Vaz (today the Santo Antônio neighbourhood, with some of the city's finest buildings) and connected it by bridge with the mainland. They were also responsible for introducing the sobrados magros, multi-storey houses with stepped gables. Even the expulsion of the Dutch from Brazil in 1654 could not stop the rise of Recife accompanying the economic and political decline of the neighbouring – and originally more important – town of Olinda.

Time moves at different speeds: Recife seen from Olinda

▶ VISITING RECIFE

INFORMATION

Informações Turísticas
Aeroporto Internacional
Tel. (081) 34 27-81 83

Recife Antigo district
Praça do Arsenal da Marinha
Tel. (081) 32 24-23 61
www.recife.pe.gov.br
www.pernambuco.com/turismo

GETTING THERE

Airport
Aeroporto Int. dos Guararapes
Praça S Filho
Tel. (081) 34 64-41 88

Bus station
Terminal Integrado de Passageiros
Tel. (081) 34 52-19 99

EVENTS

Carnaval
Takes place at the same time as the
European carnival, forty days before
Easter. Amongst the carnival hotspots
are all public places in Recife Antigo
and the bridges leading into the city,
the Pátio de São Pedro, the Pátio de
Santa Cruz, the Pátio do Terço and
the Avenida Guararapes.

Recifolia
October: one of the carnivalesque
events outside the official carnival
season that have become popular all
over Brazil

WHERE TO EAT

▶ Moderate

① *Dão João*
Rua do Apolo 134
Recife Antigo district
Tel. (081) 32 24-26 61
International and Pernambucan cuisine; few other tourists.

② *Leite*
Praça Joaquim Nabuco 147
Santo Antônio district
Tel. (081) 32 24-79 77
Opened in 1882, one of the most
traditional restaurants in Pernambuco. Lunch only, good drinks list.

▶ Inexpensive

③ *Recife Antigo*
Praça Comunidade Luso-Brasileira
Forte do Brum, Recife Antigo district
Tel. (081) 32 24-17 81
Regional and international dishes.
Mainly locals eat here.

WHERE TO STAY

▶ Luxury

Atlante Plaza
Avenida Boa Viagem 5426
Boa Viagem district
Tel. (081) 33 02-33 33
and (08 00) 814-433
www.atlanteplaza.com.br
Modern hotel with 231 well-appointed rooms, a good restaurant, bar
and beach service. Spacious lobby
area, three lifts with panoramic views
stretching to the Atlantic, swimming
pool, sauna and fitness centre.

▶ Mid-range

Holiday Inn
Avenida Engenheiro Domingos
Ferreira 3067, Boa Viagem district
Tel. (081) 21 22-39 39
and (08 00) 118-778

www.modesto.com.br
Opened in 1998, this hotel has over 130 generously appointed rooms, car parking, a restaurant, bar, pool, sauna and gym. All credit cards are accepted here, but no cheques.

► Budget

① *Recife Plaza*
Rua da Aurora 225
Boa Vista district
Tel. (081) 32 31-12 00
www.recifeplazahotel.com.br
Traditional establishment, with 80

air-conditioned rooms with telephone and TV, a good restaurant, bar, swimming pool, sauna and gym.

Savaroni
Avenida Boa Viagem 3772
Boa Viagem district
Tel. (081) 34 65-42 99
www.hotelsavaroni.com.br
The Hotel Savaroni with 64 air-conditioned apartments has been around for a while, but has a good restaurant, a bar and swimming pool.

Recife, the capital of Pernambuco, is today the cultural, entertainment and service hub of the Brazilian northeast, with a modern appearance creating an interesting contrast with the monuments of the past. Several rivers and canals, spanned by a multitude of bridges, criss-cross the metropolis. Recife owes its fancy nickname of the »Venice of Brazil« to the numerous watercourses and bridges characterizing the urban landscape, a comparison that – with all due respect – raises false expectations and may lead to disappointment. The carnival of Recife, however, does not have to shy away from comparisons; with its Galo da Madrugada (Dawn Cockerel), the town can lay claim to organizing one of the biggest carnival processions in the world.

A city of contrasts

Santo Antônio district

The Palácio das Princesas, situated in the north of Santo Antônio district, at the confluence of the Capibaribe and Beberibe rivers and also known as Palácio do Governo, was built in 1841 and is the seat of the Pernambuco government. In 1850, the Teatro Santa Isabel was built in the classical style a bit further southwest, on the banks of the Capibaribe river.

Palácio das Princesas

The church and Franciscan monastery of Santo Antônio on Rua do Imperador date from 1606. The lay order's Capela Dourada (Golden Chapel), a part of the monastery, was completed in 1695, although work on the interior continued into the 18th century. Its gilded **carvings from palisander (rosewood) and cedar wood** are some of the finest in the country. The chapel's ceiling and walls display paintings with religious and secular subjects. Next door is the Museu de Arte Sacra (Museum of Sacred Art, Rua do Imperador 206). Opening times: Mon – Fri 8 to 11.30am and 2 – 5pm, Sat 8 – 11.30am.

✶ ✶
Convento Santo Antônio, Capela Dourada

🕐

Recife Map

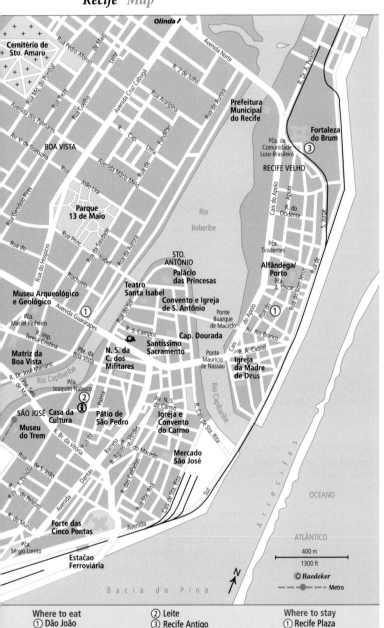

Cemitério de Sto. Amaro

Rua Pedro Afonso

Leite

Av. de Maio

R. 2 de Julho

Rua Araripina

Rua da Aurora

Avenida Norte

Prefeitura Municipal do Recife

R. Dr. A. Peixoto

Fortaleza do Brum

③

Pça. de Comunidade Luso-Brasileira

RECIFE VELHO

Avenida Cruz Cabugá

Rua Coelho

Rua Trindade

Avenida dos Palmares

Av. V. de Suassuna

Rua Mq. do Pombal

BOA VISTA

Rua João Lira

Avenida Maria Melo

R. Cap. Lima

R. da Fundição

Cais do Apolo

R. do Ocidente

R. S. Jorge

Parque 13 de Maio

Rua Gervasio Pires

Rua Princ

Rua do Hospício

Rua do

Riachuelo

Rua da Saudade

Rua da Isabel

Rua da Aurora

Rio Beberibe

Pça. Tiradentes

STO. ANTÔNIO

Palácio das Princesas

Alfândega/ Porto

Pça. A. Oscar

Museu Arqueológico e Geológico

Avenida Guararapes

①

Teatro Santa Isabel

Convento e Igreja de S. Antônio

Rua do Sol

Ponte Buarque de Macedo

Rua do Bom Jesus

Rua de

①

Pça. Maciel Pinheiro

R. Imp. Teresa Cristina

Pte. da Boa Vista

R. S. Campos

Cap. Dourada

Cais do Apolo

Av. Rio Branco

R. A. Cabral

Matriz de Boa Vista

R. Dr. José Mariano

Rua Seb. de Maio

Rio Capibaribe

N. S. da C. dos Militares

Santíssimo Sacramento

Ponte Maurício de Nassau

Igreja da Madre de Deus

Pça. Joaquim Nabuco

②

①

Palma

Av. N. S. do Carmo

Rio Capibaribe

SÃO JOSÉ

Casa da Cultura

Pátio de São Pedro

Igreja e Convento do Carmo

Museu do Trem

Rua Br. da Vitória

Barreto

R. Águas Verdes

R. Tr. do Macedo

Cais de Sta. Rita

Rua de S. João

Dantas

R. das Calçadas

Mercado São José

A r r e c i f e s

OCEANO

R. F. Peixoto

R. do Peixoto

Avenida

Rua Sta. Rita

Cais de Sta. Rita

Sul

ATLÂNTICO

R. do Muniz

Forte das Cinco Pontas

Avenida

400 m

1300 ft

Pça. Sérgio Loreto

Estação Ferroviária

N

© *Baedeker*

Metro

B a c i a   d o   P i n a

Where to eat
① Dão João

② Leite
③ Recife Antigo

Where to stay
① Recife Plaza

Standing on Praça da Independência, a few steps further south, the
Igreja do Santíssimo Sacramento, the parish church of the Santo
Antônio district, was erected between 1753 and 1791. Its altars show
elements of both baroque and classical style.

★
Santíssimo
Sacramento

Rising on Rua Nova, west of Igreja do Santíssimo Sacramento, the
baroque church of Nossa Senhora da Conceição dos Militares was
completed at the beginning of the 18th century. Work on the interior
decoration however, consisting of paintings and gilded carvings, only
finished in 1771. On the ceiling of the nave, opulent carvings frame
an image of the Virgin Mary, created in 1781 by an anonymous artist. The magnificent fresco on the chancel ceiling represents the first
battle of Guararapes. It is credited to **João de Deus Sepúlveda**, the
most important painter in 18th-century Pernambuco.

★
NS da
Conceição dos
Militares

On Avenida Dantas Barreto, the façade of the church and friary of
Nossa Senhora do Carmo is testimony to the dominance of the baroque style. The church of the Carmelite order, torched by the Dutch,
was restored from 1663 onwards; work however dragged on for
nearly a century – as shown by the stylistic differences in the individual altarpieces. The Renaissance entrance of the chancel chapel was
executed following the original designs.

★
NS do Carmo

São José district

East of the group of Carmelite buildings, visitors should not miss the
Pátio de São Pedro in the district of São José, lined by several colonial buildings. Here, crafts made from wood, straw and leather are
for sale, and in May the courtyard becomes the stage for the Festival
de Cirandas.

★
Pátio de
São Pedro

Designed by **Manuel Ferreira Jácome**, the cathedral of São Pedro dos
Clérigos, the most important monument on the Pátio de São Pedro,
was built between 1728 and 1782. The gound plan consists of an
elongated rectangle, its shorter side incorporating the octagonal nave.
The façade is characterized by a Gothic-style verticality, while the entrance is baroque. The pulpit, altars and galleries are carved from
stone, the doors from palisander wood. The fresco adorning the
church ceiling, *St Peter Blessing the Catholic Congregation*, is the main
work of João de Deus Sepúlveda.

★ ★
Catedral São
Pedro dos
Clérigos

The market of São José, east of the cathedral, is the biggest in Recife.
The parts for the metal construction (1875) came over from Europe.

Mercado de
São José

Below the market, on Largo das Cinco Pontas, near Rio Pina, stands
the Forte das Cinco Pontas, which originally was a Dutch fortress
erected in 1630 and today is housing the municipal museum of Recife. It was here that in 1825 the monk Caneca, fighting for the

★
Forte das
Cinco Pontas

Confederação do Equador (The Confederation of the Equator) movement, was executed by firing squad and other republican leaders strung up. The memory of the martyr has been kept alive to this day; in the first half of January, the **»Martyrdom of Frei Caneca«** is ⏱ staged in the streets of the city. Opening times: Tue–Fri 9am to 6pm, Sat/Sun 1 to 5pm.

Museu do Trem On Praça Visconde de Mauá, the Railway Museum – small but worth seeing – informs visitors, amongst other things, about the importance of the railway in the opening up of the Brazilian northeast.

✳ Recife Antigo district

Vibrant neighbourhood The bridges of Ponte Doze de Setembro, Ponte Maurício de Nassau (Moritz of Nassau) and Ponte Buarque de Macedo form the most important connections between Santo Antônio and the Recife Antigo district, which is surrounded by the Rio Beberibe and the Pina Basin. Extensive redevelopment has not only saved the old dock area around **Praça Tiradentes** from dereliction, but even given it a new lease of life. Today, Praça do Arsenal da Marinha, Rua do Bom Jesus and Rua Apolo in particular, are lined by scores of rustic restaurants and popular music bars jostling for space. During carnival time, the Recife Antigo district and the bridges leading into the area form one of the epicentres of events.

Forte do Brum The customs house and the port administration are located on the coastal road (Avenida Alfredo Lisboa). Further inland to the north stands the Forte do Brum (Praça Comunidade Luso-Brasileira), a Dutch construction dating from 1629 that today houses a military ⏱ museum. Opening times: Mon–Fri 9am–4pm.

Boa Vista district

Matriz da Boa Vista The Boa Vista district extends on the left bank of the Rio Capibaribe. Here, on Rua da Imperatriz, rises the main church of Boa Vista, constructed between 1788 and 1813. The Archaeological and Geological Museum of Pernambuco (Museu Arqueológico e Geológico de Pernambuco) displays its exhibits in Rua do Hospício.

NS da Conceição The church of Nossa Senhora da Conceição, also known as Jaqueira Chapel, was built in 1766 on a country estate that today forms part of the city. The chapel proper, together with the tower and the sacristy, form a single structure, making it look like a miniature baroque church. The façade, resembling in its architectural design the monastery church of São Bento in Olinda, is ascribed to **Francisco Nunes Soares**, the architect of this Benedictine complex. The main altar is colourfully painted and covered in gold leaf, while Portuguese azulejo tiles were used for the interior decoration of the church.

What to see in the other districts

The city beaches of Praia do Pina and Praia da Boa Viagem lie just 4km/2.5 miles (and 5km/3 miles) south of the city centre. Part of the carnival of Recife – with trios elétricos, frevo dances and axé music – takes place here on the promenade Avenida Boa Viagem. In October, outside the main carnival season, the area close to the beach is given over to the »Recifolia« carnival.

Boa Viagem

With the Museu do Homem do Nordeste, Recife's Casa Forte district offers a particularly interesting attraction: the exhibits of this anthropological museum reflect the unique diversity of the traditional **folk art of the northeast**. Alongside work by local craftspeople, such as caxixis clay figurines, ex-votos and wooden dolls, works of the so-called »literatura de cordel« (string literature, so called because of the string used to hang up the booklets for sale), Afro-Brazilian ritual objects and tools from the time of slavery are on display (Avenida 17 de Agosto 2187). Opening times: Tue, Wed, Fri 11am – 5pm, Thu 8am – 5pm, Sat/Sun 1 – 5pm.

✴
Museu do Homem do Nordeste

☉

The Praia da Boa Viagem is not exactly top secret.

Oficina de Cerâmica F Brennand

Numerous erotic clay sculptures made by **Francisco Brennand**, an artist influenced by Picasso and Gaudí and whose fame extends far beyond Recife, may be admired in his workshop in Avenida Caxangá in the Várzea district. Some of the sculptures are shown in the open, amidst a tropical garden, others in a former slate and tile factory. Opening times: Mon – Fri 8am – 5pm, Sat/Sun 1 – 4pm.

Around Recife

Guararapes

In grateful remembrance of the two Luso-Brazilian victories at Guararapes, the church of **Nossa Senhora dos Prazeres** was built from 1656 onwards on the battle site. The church, its walls adorned with azulejos, lies in the Guararapes Historical Park, 15km/9 miles south of Recife. Immediately after Easter, the Festa da Pitomba, one of the biggest popular festivals of Recife, is celebrated here. In September, hundreds of participants re-enact the battle of Guararapes.

Porto de Galinhas

The sandy beaches of Porto de Galinhas, 72km/45 miles from Recife, are among the most beautiful swimming beaches in all of Pernambuco. At low tide, jangada fishing boats take tourists out to the natural pools forming in the offshore reefs, where they can swim or dive. Only 5km/3 miles from Porto de Galinhas, surfers also find ideal conditions: **Praia Maracaípe** is even the site of a Brazilian surfing championship. Cacimbas Beach (50km/31 miles from Recife) attracts visitors with a rock formation lapped by the waves, featuring small basins and caves.

Caruaru

Thanks to its clay figures, called **figurinhas de barro**, Caruaru (130km/80 miles west of Recife) was classified by UNESCO as one of the most important centres of craft production in South America. Whilst the ceramic works of art are sold in many coastal towns as popular souvenirs, the museums and markets of Caruaru give a deeper insight into the tradition of local crafts, which characterize the town to his day.

Museu do Barro

The Museu do Barro (Espaço Cultural Tancredo Neves) at 100 Praça da Criança shows the clay figures made by Mestre Vitalino, who died in 1977, and the town's other important craftsmen. The tools used by the famous master are kept in the Museu Mestre Vitalino in the

Alto do Moura part of town, 7km/4.3 miles from the town centre, near the Vila dos Ceramistas.

★
Feira Livre

The town's foremost tourist attraction, the Feira Livre, takes place on Wednesdays and Saturdays in the town centre. The market sells ceramics, ornately decorated leatherware and braided goods. Alongside the many stalls, musicians, poets, performers and all kinds of artists lend the market a colourful vibrant flair. The **Feira de Artesanato**, another craft market, is held daily in Parque 18 de Maio.

Nova Jerusalém

Around 50km/31 miles northwest from Caruaru, Easter time sees the annual **Passion play of Nova Jerusalém**, the Paixão de Cristo. On an open-air stage between the towns of Fazenda Nova and Brejo da Madre de Deus, up to 500 performers stage the Crucifixion of Christ. The stage is an exact stone replica of the biblical city as it is supposed to have looked at the time of Christ. The performances now attract 70,000 spectators every year. It is said that in 1951, a brochure of the famous Obergammergau Passion play fell into the hands of its founder, Plínio Pacheco ...

Fishermen in Porto de Galinhas pushing a jangada boat ashore

Rio Branco

Rb 50

State: Acre (AC)   **Population:** 253,000
Altitude: 153m/502ft

The original core of the capital of Acre state, built on the Rio Acre, took shape in 1882 during the rubber boom in Amazonia, under the name Empresa (Company).

Twenty years later, Empresa became the headquarters for those Brazilians revolting against Bolivia's rule of the region. After Acre's integration into the Brazilian state under the Treaty of Petrópolis in 1903, the settlement was elevated to the status of a vila. The place was given its current name in 1912, in honour of Baron Rio Branco, the man behind the Treaty of Petrópolis, murdered in 1903 in the Bolivian-Brazilian border country.

What to see in and around Rio Branco

Casa do Seringueiro North of the government palace (Palácio do Governo) in the city centre, at the junction of Avenida Getúlio Vargas and Avenida Brasil, stands the Casa do Seringueiro (House of the Rubber Tapper) shows an exibition telling visitors about the life of the rubber tappers, using photos, diagrams and the replica of a seringueiro house.

Chico Mendes also fought for the preservation of the Brazilian rainforest.

► VISITING RIO BRANCO

INFORMATION
Praça Povos da Floresta
Tel. (068) 32 32-39 98
www.pmrb.ac.gov.br

GETTING THERE
Airport
Aeroporto Int. Presidente Médici
AC-040
Tel. (068) 32 11-10 00

Bus station
Avenida Uirapuru
Cidade Nova
Tel. (068) 32 21-41 95

WHERE TO EAT
► Moderate
Restaurante do Aeroporto
In the airport building
BR-364, in the direction of Sena
Madureira
(20km/12.5 miles outside the city
centre)
Tel. (068) 32 11-10 67
The best restaurant in Rio Branco,
with Brazilian and international
dishes and an extensive drinks list.
All credit cards are accepted.

WHERE TO STAY
► Mid-range
Imperador Galvez
Rua Santa Inês 401
Aviário
Tel. (068) 32 23-70 27
Acceptable hotel with 42 air-condi-
tioned apartments with TV, a good
restaurant, internet access, swimming
pool, car parking and gym. Diners,
Mastercard and Visa are accepted;
American Express, amongst others, is
not.

► Budget
Guapindaia Centro
Rua Floriano Peixoto 394
Tel. (068) 32 23-23 99
Centrally located, 20 simple air-con-
ditioned rooms with TV, plus car
parking

In the city centre, near Praça Rodrigues Alves, the Museu da Borracha (Rubber Museum) shows historical and and ethnographic material (Avenida Ceará 1177). Opening times: Tue – Sun 7am – 5pm.

Museu da Borracha
⏱

Named after the murdered union leader, rubber tapper and environ-
mentalist Chico Mendes (►Famous People p. 70), the city park has
cycle paths and hiking trails.

**Parque Ambien-
tal Chico Mendes**

Xapuri, situated some 200km/125 miles south of Rio Branco at the
confluence of the Rio Acre and the Rio Xapuri, is famous worldwide
for the environmental campaign of Chico Mendes, the seringueiro
leader assassinated in December 1988. Visitors can see the **Chico
Mendes Foundation and Chico Mendes Museum**, housed in his former residence, and the ecological tree nurseries in the jungle, set up
by the syndicate of the Xapuri rural workers, headed by Chico
Mendes himself up to his violent death.

Xapuri

Rio de Janeiro

State: Rio de Janeiro (RJ)   **Population:** 5.9 million
Altitude: 2m/6ft

Founded on 1 March 1565 on the western edge of Guanabara Bay, the Sugarloaf metropolis is heralded as the most beautiful of cities, as Cidade Maravilhosa – the Wonderful City.

However, the former capital of Brazil does not merely keep its promises; contemplation of the work of art that is Rio de Janeiro, with its unique composition of conical mountains, endless beaches, bays, high-rise silhouettes and tropical vegetation, exceeds expectations with its cornucopia of impressions. It is a special feeling to be standing atop the famous Sugarloaf, the city of millions at one's feet, to receive the blessing of the Saviour on the Corcovado or – in much more secular style – to watch a future Pelé on Copacabana showing his ball skills with typical Brazilian flair and style.

»In six days, God created the world, on the seventh day, Rio de Janeiro«, claim the cariocas, the inhabitants of Rio de Janeiro. That might be so, but not everything here is beautiful and glamorous; the people living in the **favelas**, the slum quarters, have to live day by day with the fact that the city's beauty won't fill any bellies. Social necessity leads to crime, and a lot of social necessity in one place leads to a lot of crime in one place. This plagues Rio de Janeiro to this day, even though the strong presence of the police has done a lot to reduce attacks on tourists. Even so, visitors to the metropolis should take care not to display their Rolex or gold jewellery everywhere, as one person's adornment is capable of making another's livelihood.

Spreading favelas

History

The origins of the city go back to the period between 1555 and 1567, during which time the Portuguese and the French fought with their Indian allies for supremacy of Guanabara Bay. Portugal was striving for a complete annexation of the area, as the only way to finally crush **França Antârtica**, the Calvinist colony founded by Nicolas Durand de Villegaignon in the Baía da Guanabara. After the victory of the Portuguese, the settlement was transferred onto Morro do Castelo, which was more easily defended but no longer exists.

In the 18th century, the city grew considerably, expanding with its role as the port of exit for the gold coming from Minas Gerais. The precious commodity had been transported by pack animals to Parati,

Rio becomes the capital

← *Rio de Janeiro, the Cidade Maravilhosa or »Wonderful City« at sunrise*

Rio de Janeiro Overview

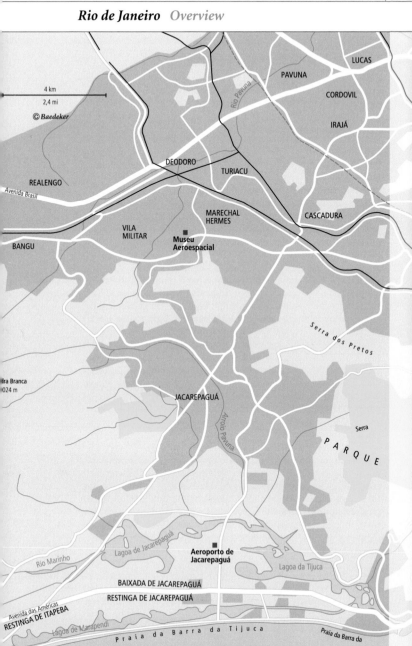

LUCAS

PAVUNA

CORDOVIL

IRAJÁ

Rio Pavuna

4 km
2,4 mi

© Baedeker

DEODORO

TURIACU

CASCADURA

REALENGO

Avenida Brasil

MARECHAL
HERMES

VILA
MILITAR

■ Museu
Aeroespacial

BANGU

Serra dos Pretos

dra Branca
024 m

JACAREPAGUÁ

Arroio Pavuna

Serra

P A R Q U E

Rio Marinho

Lagoa de Jacarepaguá

■ Aeroporto de
Jacarepaguá

Lagoa da Tijuca

BAIXADA DE JACAREPAGUÁ

RESTINGA DE JACAREPAGUÁ

Avenida das Américas
RESTINGA DE ITAPEBA

Lagoa de Marapendi

P r a i a   d a   B a r r a   d a   T i j u c a

Praia da Barra da

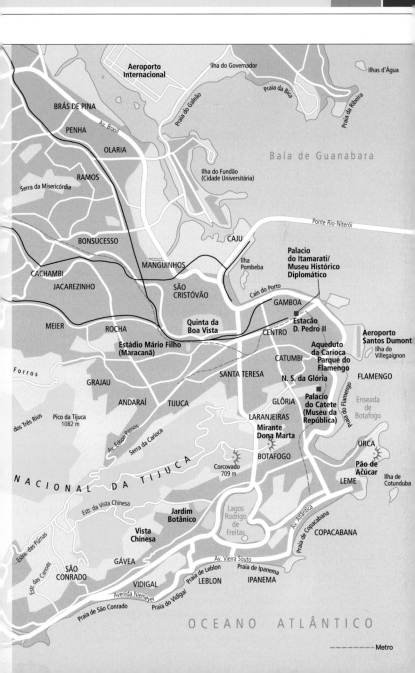

Ilhas d'Água

Aeroporto Internacional

Ilha do Governador

BRÁS DE PINA

Praia da Bica

Praia da Ribeira

PENHA

Av. Brasil

OLARIA

Praia do Galeão

RAMOS

Serra da Misericórdia

Baía de Guanabara

Ilha do Fundão
(Cidade Universitária)

BONSUCESSO

Ponte Rio-Niterói

CACHAMBI

MANGUINHOS

CAJU

Palacio
do Itamarati/
Museu Histórico
Diplomático

JACAREZINHO

SÃO
CRISTÓVÃO

Ilha
Pombeba

Cais do Porto

MEIER

ROCHA

Quinta da
Boa Vista

GAMBOA

Estacão
D. Pedro II

Aeroporto
Santos Dumont

Estádio Mário Filho
(Maracanã)

CENTRO

Ilha do
Villegaignon

Forros

GRAJAU

CATUMBI

Aqueduto
da Carioca
Parque do
Flamengo

SANTA TERESA

N. S. da Glória

FLAMENGO

ANDARAÍ

TIJUCA

Serra da Carioca

GLÓRIA

Pico da Tijuca
1082 m

LARANJEIRAS

dos Três Rios

Av. Edson Passos

Palacio
do Catete
(Museu da
República)

Enseada
de
Botafogo

Mirante
Dona Marta

NACIONAL DA TIJUCA

BOTAFOGO

URCA

Corcovado
709 m

Pão de
Açúcar

Estr. da Vista Chinesa

LEME

Ilha de
Cotunduba

Jardim
Botânico

Lagos
Rodrigo
de
Freitas

Vista
Chinesa

Av. Atlântica

Estr. das Fúrnas

GÁVEA

COPACABANA

Estr. das Canoas

Av. Vieira Souto

Praia de Copacabana

SÃO
CONRADO

VIDIGAL

Praia de Leblon

Praia de Ipanema

LEBLON

IPANEMA

Avenida Niemeyer

Praia do Vidigal

Praia de São Conrado

OCEANO ATLÂNTICO

----- Metro

Angra dos Reis and other small ports up to this point; now, it began to be shipped from Rio. In addition, the fact that the viceroys transferred their seat of government in 1763 from Salvador to Rio de Janeiro is evidence of the city's new socio-economic role.

1 January 1502	Americo Vespucci anchors in »January Bay«.
1555	The French found a base on Ilha de Villegaignon.
1 March 1565	Estácio de Sá founds what was later to become Rio de Janeiro, near Sugarloaf, and drives the French out of Guanabara Bay.
1763	Rio de Janeiro becomes the capital of Brazil.
1807/08	The entire court of Portugal relocates to Rio de Janeiro.
1960	Brasília takes the relay from Rio as the capital of Brazil.

Brilliant rise

When in 1807/08 Napoleon's France, together with Spain, its ally at the time, threatened to occupy Portugal, the Portuguese court fled Lisbon for Rio de Janeiro. This started an economic and cultural boom for the city, going hand in hand with a dramatic rise in the population. After the proclamation of the Republic in 1889, Rio remained the capital of Brazil, but lost this status in 1960 to Brasília.

Centro

Praça Quinze de Novembro

It makes sense to start a visit to Rio in the city centre, which up to the early 20th century was the hub of public life, for instance at Praça Quinze de Novembro, in front of which the ferries for Niterói and Ilha de Paquetá depart from the Estação das Barcas. Since the bulk of the traffic was banished underground, the occasional antiquities and arts markets have been held in and around the square. On the square stands the **Chafariz da Pirâmide** (1789), a fountain designed by the sculptor Valentim da Fonseca e Silva from Minas Gerais, also called Mestre (Master) Valentim. Mestre Valentim ranks alongside Aleijadinho as one of the most important artists of colonial Brazil. The fountain created by him once served as the water supply for ships anchoring at the quays in front of the Paço Imperial.

Paço Imperial

At Largo do Paço, opposite Praça Quinze de Novembro, rises the Paço Imperial, built in 1743 in the colonial style. The best-preserved public edifice in Old Rio, it was the seat of government of the viceroys and the imperial palace. The side facing the bay shows a portal made from Pedra de Lioz, a marble-like stone. The building was designed by the military architect **José Fernandes Pinto Alpoim**, in the 18th century the most important master builder of Rio de Janeiro. Completely restored, today it serves as a cultural centre.

▶ VISITING RIO DE JANEIRO *map p. 368/369*

INFORMATION

RIOTUR
Aeroporto Internacional
 International arrivals office:
Tel. (021) 33 98-40 77
Inland arrivals
office:
Tel. (021) 33 98-22 46

Centro de Atendimento ao Turista
Avenida Princesa Isabel
Copacabana district
Tel. (021) 25 41-75 22
www.rio.rj.gov.br

GETTING THERE

Airports
Aeroporto Int. do Rio de Janeiro
(Galeão – Tom Jobim)
Avenida Vinte de Janeiro
Tel. (021) 33 98-50 50

Aeroporto Nacional S Dumont
Praça S Salgado Filho
Tel. (021) 38 14-70 70

Bus stations
Américo Fontenelle
Rua B de São Félix
Tel. (021) 22 33-78 19

Mariano Procópio
Praça Mauá 5 (centre)
Tel. (021) 25 16-48 02

Menezes Cortes
Rua São José 35
Tel. (021) 25 33-88 19

Novo Rio
Av Francisco Bicalho 1
São Cristovão
Tel. (021) 32 13-18 18

CARNIVAL
▶Baedeker Special p. 90

WHERE TO EAT

▶ Expensive

① Da Brambini
Avenida Atlântica 514 B
Leme district
Tel. (021) 22 75-43 46
Small Italian restaurant. House speciality is seafood, mouth-wateringly prepared.

② Marius
Avenida Atlântica 290 B
Leme district
Tel. (021) 25 42-23 93
For many years Rio's best churrascaria with a broad selection of grilled rodízio meat and mixed salads.

③ Porcão II
Avenida Infante Dom Henrique
Aterro do Flamengo
Tel. (021) 25 54-88 62
Churrascaria with rodízio system. The choicest beef fresh from the roasting spit; the best seats in the restaurant throw in free views of Sugarloaf.

④ Porcão I
Rua Barão da Torre 218
 Ipanema district
Tel. (021) 25 22-09 99
Headquarters of the Porcão chain, today represented in
many towns in Brazil. Many locals still swear by this tried and tested original location.

⑤ Gibo
Rua Jangadeiros 28 A
Ipanema district
Tel. (021) 25 21-96 10
Excellent Italian gourmet restaurant. Few tourists, all credit cards accepted.

⑥ *Le Saint Honoré*
On the 3rd floor of the Le
Méridien hotel
Avenida Atlântica 1020
Leme district
Tel. (021) 38 73-88 80
Top French restaurant under star chef
Dominique Oudin

⑦ *Sol e Mar*
Avenida Repórter Nestor Moreira 11
Tel. (021) 22 95-18 96
Sol e Mar on Botafoto Bay is one of
the few restaurants with a terrace
right on the sea. In the evenings,
reservations are a good idea, as this is
a prime location to admire Sugarloaf
at dusk, accompanied by unobtrusive
live music.

▶ **Moderate**
⑧ *Yemanjá*
Rua Visconde de Pirajá 128 A
Ipanema district
Tel. (021) 22 47-70 04
For years now one of the best places
to sample Afro-Brazilian specialities
in the Sugarloaf metropolis

WHERE TO STAY
▶ **Luxury**
① *Sheraton Rio Hotel & Towers*
Avenida Niemeyer 121
Praia do Vidigal
Tel. (021) 22 74-11 22
and (08 00) 116-000
www.starwood.com
Business hotel with direct access to
the (serviced) beach and a banqueting
hall for up to 1,000 guests. 559 rooms
and suites.

② *InterContinental Rio*
Avenida Pref Mendes de Morais 222
Praia de São Conrado
Tel. (021) 33 23-22 00
and (08 00) 210-07 22
www.ichotelsgroup.com

A dream beach right outside the door
and 414 generously laid out rooms
with veranda; partly suitable for
wheelchair users. Generously sized
swimming pool.

③ *Caesar Park*
Avenida Viera Souto 460
Ipanema district
Tel. (021) 25 25-25 25
and (08 00) 210-789
www.caesarpark-rio.com
Beach service and a restaurant on the
roof terrace are the highlights.

④ *Sol Ipanema*
Avenida Viera Souto 320
Ipanema district
Tel. (021) 25 25-20 20
and (08 00) 761-50 01
www.solipanema.com.br
Hotel with 90 comfortable rooms in a
perfect location. Small pool and bar
on the roof terrace.

⑤ *Rio Othon Palace*
Avenida Atlântica 3264
Praia da Copacabana
Tel. (021) 25 25-15 00
www.othon.com.br
With 585 rooms, built in 1976 for
large groups of tourists. Central
location on the Copacabana. Beach
service, swimming pool, fitness centre
and sauna.

⑥ *Copacabana Palace*
Avenida Atlântica 1702
Praia da Copacabana
Tel. (021) 25 48-70 70
and (08 00) 211-533
www.copacabanapalace.
orient-express.com
Opened in 1923 and extended in
1950, the Copacabana Palace has long
been a national monument.

► Mid-range

⑦ *Debret*

Avenida Atlântica 3564
Praia da Copacabana
Tel. (021) 25 21-08 99
www.debret.com
In a perfect location, but opened in 1972 and now showing its age. Some of the 94 rooms and all 13 suites (with room safe) have views of the Atlantic. The 12th floor is occupied by a terrace restaurant.

⑧ *Acapulco Copacabana*

Rua Gustavo Sampaio 854
Leme district
Tel. (021) 22 75-00 22
www.acapulcocopacabanahotel.com.br
City hotel with 115 rooms. Showing its age slightly, but has been refurbished. No restaurant.

⑨ *Argentina*

Rua Cruz Lima 30
Flamengo district
Tel. (021) 25 58-72 33
www.argentinahotel.com.br
Built in 1933, 80 air-conditioned twin and four-bed rooms, restaurant, bar and car parking

⑩ *Novo Mundo*

Praia do Flamengo 20
Tel. (021) 21 05-00 00
www.hotelnovomundo-rio.com.br
Opened in 1950 for the World Cup. 231 spacious rooms. These days at least partially suitable for wheelchair users.

► Budget

⑪ *APA Hotel*

Rua República do Peru 305
Tel. (021) 25 48-81 12
www.apahotel.com.br
Simply appointed budget hotel; 52 small rooms, two blocks from the beach

⑫ *Santa Clara*

Rua Décio Vilares 316
Copacabana district
Tel. (021) 22 56-26 50
www.hotelsantaclara.com.br
Simple budget hotel; three blocks from Copacabana Beach

The classical Copacabana Palace

Highlights Rio de Janeiro

Mosteiro de São Bento
One of the most important baroque buildings in Brazil
► page 367

São Francisco da Penitência
Church with opulent interior decoration
► page 371

Pão de Açúcar (Sugarloaf)
The symbol of Rio de Janeiro
► page 378 and 380

Corcovado
As famous as Sugarloaf, thanks to the statue of Christ the Redeemer
► page 388

Palácio Tiradentes ✷

Opposite the imperial palace rises the parliamentary building housing the state government of Rio de Janeiro, the Assembleia Legislativa, dramatically framed by a sweeping drive. The neo-classical Chamber of Deputies was inaugurated in 1926 on Avenida Presidente Antônio Carlos at the exact spot where the jail used to stand. In honour of probably its most famous prisoner, freedom fighter **Tiradentes**, who did time here in 1792, the parliament is also often called Palácio Tiradentes. Opening times: Mon – Sat 10am – 5pm, Sun noon – 5pm.

Arco do Teles

The houses of the Teles de Menezes family, designed by Alpoim, once stood just a few paces from Praça Quinze de Novembro. The archway leading into the Travessa do Comércio is all that is left from this group of buildings, originally consisting of three residences, that burned down in 1790. Today still, the narrow cobblestoned lanes of this neighbourhood witness cultural open-air events, whilst the multi-storeyed houses with their thick walls shelter traditional bars and fancy restaurants.

NS da Lapa dos Mercadores ✷

The Travessa do Comércio crosses Rua do Ouvidor, which in the later imperial reign was the centre of the newspaper industry and the luxury goods trade. This is where the church of Nossa Senhora da Lapa dos Mercadores rises up, a splendid baroque edifice built in 1747. The pride and joy of this church is a carillon with twelve bells, first used in 1872.

Rua Primeiro de Março

In Rua Primeiro de Março, running crossways with Rua do Ouvidor, look for the church of Santa Cruz dos Militares (1780 – 1811), the church of the Carmelite lay order Monte do Carmo and the parish church of Nossa Senhora do Carmo da Antiga Sé, which between 1808 and 1889 served as the Capela Real (Royal Chapel). The two Carmelite churches are only separated by a passageway. The **Igreja da Ordem Terceira do Monte do Carmo**, built from the year 1755 onwards, shows a baroque façade and a limestone portal imported from Lisbon. The tops of the towers are clad in azulejos in the Moorish style. Also worth a look are the carvings in white and gold leaf by Mestre Valentim in the chapel of the novitiate. In the former cathedral, **Nossa Senhora do Carmo da Antiga Sé**, also dating from the 18th century and boasting a wealth of wood carvings, the silver high altar and a painting by Antônio Parreiras showing the *Nossa Senhora do Carmo* (*Our Lady of Mount Carmel*) are the main points of interest. In the church of **Santa Cruz dos Militares**, Mestre Valentim created all the carvings; however, practically all of them perished in a fire, as well as the wooden statues of Saints Matthew and John. The museum next door keeps religious and military exhibits.

Rua Primeiro de Março, Rua da Quitanda and other roads crossing Rua do Ouvidor lead to Largo da Candelária (Praça Pio X), which turns into the large Avenida Presidente Vargas. Construction work on Rio's largest church, Nossa Senhora da Candelária, on the Largo, dragged on from 1775 into the late 19th century. The church, built in the classical style, displays strong Italian influences; its ground plan is in the shape of a Latin cross, and the customary wooden de-

✱
NS da
Candelária

The church of Nossa Senhora da Canelária is the largest in Rio.

Rio Centro Map

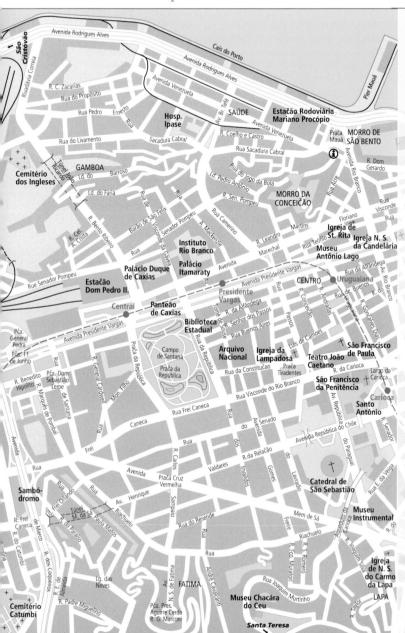

400 m
1300 ft
© Baedeker

Ponte Alm.
Arnaldo Luz

ILHA DAS COBRAS

Ilha Fiscal

Igreja e Mosteiro
de São Bento

1 Igreja e Museu Sacro
  da Santa Cruz dos
  Militares
2 Igreja N. S. da Lapa
  dos Mercadores
3 Igreja da Ordem Terceira
  do Monte do Carmo
4 Igreja N. S. do Carmo da
  Antiga Sé
5 Paço Imperial
6 Palácio Tiradentes

Inhaúma

Otoni

Rua 1. de

Aires
Rosário

R. do Ouvidor

R. 7. de
Setembro

Avenida Presidente Kubitschek

Março

Pça. 15 de
Novembro

1
2
3
4

5
6

Rua Dom Manuel

Museu Naval e
Oceanográfico

B a í a   d e   G u a n a b a r a

R. da Assembléia

Av.
Erasmo
Braga

Av. Nilo

Rua

Av. Graça

Péçanha

Almirante Barroso

Av. Pres. Antônio Carlos

Museu da Imagem
e do Som

Museu
Histórico Nacional

R. Mal. Aguinaldo

N. S. do
Bonsucesso

Avenida

Museu
Nacional
Belas Artes

Rua Porto Alegre

Santa Casa da
Misericórdia

CASTELO

Aeroporto
Santos
Dumont

Theatro
Municipal

Arariboia

R. Santa Luzia

Avenida General Justo

Avenida Marechal Câmara

Biblioteca
Nacional

Santa Luzia

Palácio da
Cultura

Pça.
Ana
Amélia

Av.
F. Roosevelt

Pça.
Virgílio de
Melo Franco

Cinelândia

México

Teatro
Mesbla

Rua

Avenida Rio Branco

Igreja de
Santa Luzia

Passeio

Damas

Trevo dos Estudantes

Pça.
Senador
Salgado
Filho

Estação
Central

Passeio
Público

R. Teixeira
de Freitas

Avenida Presidente Wilson

Ave. Infante Dom Henrique

Rua Jardel Jerculis

Museu de
Arte Moderna

Ilha de
Villegaignon

Museu do
Instituto
Histórico e
Geográfico
Brasileiro

Ave. Aug.
Severo

Parque
do
Flamengo

Monumento aos Mortos
da II Guerra Mundial

B a í a   d e   G u a n a b a r a

Metro

The ugly side of Rio: the inexorable spread of the slums

cor was replaced by multi-coloured marble. Its interior blends baroque and Renaissance elements, the ceiling of the church nave is adorned with six paintings by **João Zeferino da Costa**, the high altar features pillars of Carrara marble, and the heavy doors are wrought from bronze. The Candelária church made worldwide headlines in 1993, when military police shot dead street children camping in front of the church.

★★
Ilha Fiscal A bridge connects the quays of Rio's Old Town with the Ilha das Cobras (Snake Island), which was fortified in colonial times by the Portuguese and today is an important base for the Brazilian navy. Only the much smaller island of Ilha Fiscal (Fiscal Island), which rose from earthworks in the Baía de Guanabara and is connected with the Ilha das Cobras by a drivable harbour wall, is open to civilian visitors. This island, under 7,000 sq m/75,000 sq ft in surface, is adorned by a pale green castle built in the neo-Gothic style. The playfully designed palace was completed in 1880 following designs by **Adolpho José Del Vecchio** and, nine years later, served as the ballroom hosting the last glittering party of the Brazilian Empire, just before the downfall of Dom Pedro II. The emperor, with his full beard, and Princess Isabel are portrayed on glass windows of the palace. All visits to Ilha Fiscal and the small castle start at the quays of Espaço Cultural da Marinha, in Avenida Alfred Agache, aboard the restored tug

Laurindo Pitta. On the quays of the Espaço Cultural da Marinha, two warships, the *Riachuelo* (1973) submarine and the *Bauru* torpedo fighter from the Second World War, are anchored as »floating museums«. Departure times for Ilha Fiscal: Wed, Fri and Sun at 1, 2.30 and 4pm.

Rio's ferry terminal is also the point of departure for visits to Ilha de Paquetá, one of the prettiest parts of Rio, with just over 3,000 inhabitants. Situated in the middle of Guanabara Bay, an hour by boat from Praça Quinze de Novembro, the island, which only allows transport on foot, by bike or by horse-drawn carriage, preserves many historic buildings. Particularly worth a look are the **Solar Del Rey**, a palace where the Portuguese king Dom João VI would often spend time, the São Roque chapel (1698), the residences of José Bonifácio de Andrada e Silva – the father of Brazilian indepencence – and the writer Joaquim Manuel de Macedo, as well as the beaches of José Bonifácio and Comprida (or Moreninha).

Ilha de Paquetá

Rio's port is dwarfed by the Morro de São Bento. Sitting proudly on top of this hill, occupying a strategically advantageous position, are the church and monastery of the Benedictine order (Mosteiro de São Bento) – these are amongst the most important baroque buildings in Brazil. The first stage of the monastery's construction lasted from 1633 to 1641; its design, developed by the military architect **Francisco Frias de Mesquita**, was subjected to several changes in the second half of the 17th century: the towers, for example, were only erected in the following 50 years, one after the other. The church of São Bento, which originally only had one nave, was gradually expanded by a total of eight side chapels. Its interior decoration involved the best artists of the order. Most of the supremely lavish carvings were executed by the monk **Domingos da Conceição** (1643 – 1718), who also created the images of St Benedict and St Scholastica on the high altar. The chancel chapel exhibits silver work by Mestre Valentim and –

✶ ✶ Mosteiro de São Bento

> **!** *Baedeker* TIP
>
> **Rio on the Net**
> The lavishly illustrated website of the RIOTUR company promoting tourism in the city of Rio de Janeiro (www.rio.rj.gov.br/riotur) has attractively presented information on the sights of Rio, including opening times, history, architecture, shopping and much more, in English and Portuguese.

if visitors start the interior lighting by dropping a coin into the slot – 14 paintings by Cologne-born monk Ricardo do Pilar (1630 – 1700), the foremost Benedictine painter in colonial Brazil. His masterpiece, the painting *Senhor dos Martírios* (*The Martyrdom of Christ*), adorns the sacristy of the convent.

The modernized annexe of the seminary today houses an elite boys' high school, with an excellent reputation in Brazil. Some of the Benedictine monks teach various subjects here on a daily basis. Along-

Rio • Copacabana Map

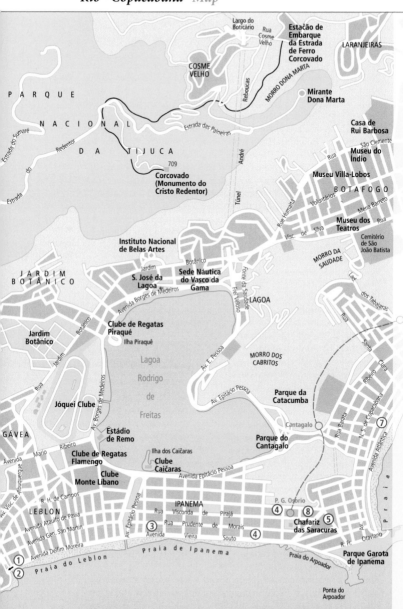

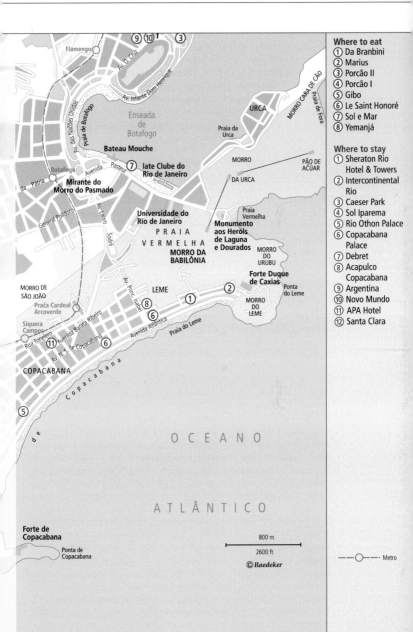

Where to eat
① Da Branbini
② Marius
③ Porcão II
④ Porcão I
⑤ Gibo
⑥ Le Saint Honoré
⑦ Sol e Mar
⑧ Yemanjá

Where to stay
① Sheraton Rio
  Hotel & Towers
② Intercontinental
  Rio
③ Caeser Park
④ Sol Iparema
⑤ Rio Othon Palace
⑥ Copacabana
  Palace
⑦ Debret
⑧ Acapulco
  Copacabana
⑨ Argentina
⑩ Novo Mundo
⑪ APA Hotel
⑫ Santa Clara

Flamengo

Av. O. Cruz

Av. Infante Dom Henrique

MORRO CARA DE CÃO

Praia de Fora

Enseada
de
Botafogo

URCA

Praia da
Urca

Praia de Botafogo

Av. das Nações Unidas

Bateau Mouche

Botafogo

da Pátria

Pasteur

⑦ **Iate Clube do
Rio de Janeiro**

MORRO
DE URCA

PÃO DE
AÇÚAR

Avenida

**Mirante do
Morro do Pasmado**

General Polidoro

Av. Lauro Sodré

**Universidade do
Rio de Janeiro**

P R A I A

V E R M E L H A

**MORRO DA
BABILÔNIA**

Praia
Vermelha

**Monumento
aos Heróis
de Laguna
e Dourados**

MORRO
DO
URUBU

MORRO DE
SÃO JOÃO

**Praça Cardeal
Arcoverde**

Siqueira
Campos

Rua Tonelero

Av. Princ. Isabel

⑧

① **LEME**

②

**Forte Duque
de Caxias**

Ponta
do Leme

MORRO
DO
LEME

⑪ Avenida Barata Ribeiro

⑥

⑥

Av. N. S. de Copacabana

Avenida Atlântica

Praia do Leme

COPACABANA

C o p a c a b a n a

d e

C o p a c a b a n a

⑤

O C E A N O

A T L Â N T I C O

**Forte de
Copacabana**

Ponta de
Copacabana

800 m

2600 ft

©*Baedeker*

—— O —— Metro

side the church, (male) visitors also have access to the outer area of the monastery of São Bento. The sacristy, chapter house, cloisters, reading room and monks' cells lie in the enclosed area, which is why they can only be visited as part of the processions at Palm Sunday, Corpus Christi and All Souls. **Mass with Gregorian chants** can be heard in the Mosteiro São Bento on Sundays from 10am. The steep access road to the monastery hill lies at 68 Rua Dom Gerardo; there is also a lift for pedestrians to use. Guests are expected to wear long trousers and closed shoes and sport a groomed appearance. Opening times: daily 8 – 11am and 2.30 to 6pm.

Museu Histórico Nacional

On Praça Marechal Âncora, the group of buildings making up the National Historical Museum – the former Casa de Trem (1762) and the former armoury (1764) – comprise a library, a historical archive, important collections of coins and weapons, as well as sacred works of art. Look out for the oval paintings by **Leandro Joaquim**, which depict events in the city's history and have high artistic and documentary value. Opening times: Tue – Fri 10am – 5.30pm, Sat/Sun 2 – 6pm.

São Cristóvão district

Praça Mauá

West of the São Bento hill, in front of the Mauá pier, Praça Mauá is the busy hub of Rio's port area. Running west from this square, Avenida Rodrigues Alves hugs the harbour and leads to the São Cristóvão district, with its imperial gardens and palaces today used as parks and museums.

Quinta da Boa Vista, Museu Nacional

One of the most interesting destinations in São Cristóvão is the 115x200m/125x220-yd Quinta da Boa Vista park, with lakes, grottoes and small forests, as well as botanical and zoological gardens. Surrounded by the park, the palace of Quinta da Boa Vista served as the residence of the imperial and royal families between 1808 and 1889, before being redesigned, in several stages, to become the Palácio de São Cristóvão. Today, the palace houses the National Museum, with the most comprehensive zoological, ethnological and archaeological collection in the country, totalling over a million exhibits. Opening times: Tue – Sun 10am – 4pm.

Maracanã Stadium

The Estádio do Maracanã, also called the Estádio Jornalista Mário Filho, is situated south of Quinta da Boa Vista, with access via Av Maracanã or Av Pres Castelo Branco. Built in 1950 for the fourth football World Cup, with a capacity of 170,000 people, this is the largest football stadium in the world. Guided tours start from Portão 16: Mon – Fri 9am to 5pm, Sat/Sun 10am – 4pm.
Next to Maracanã are the tracks of the Célio de Barros stadium and the Gilberto Cardoso indoor arena, which holds up to 20,000 spectators.

Largo da Carioca

Avenida Rio Branco starts on Praça Mauá, west of Morro de São Bento, and runs straight as a die across a large part of the city centre. Following Avenida Rio Branco – starting from Praça Mauá – in a southerly direction, visitors arrive at the Largo da Carioca, a popular meeting point for artists and crafts people.

Avenida Rio Branco

Enthroned on a hill above Largo da Carioca are the Franciscan church and convent of Santo Antônio, as well as the Igreja da Terceira Ordem de São Francisco da Penitência, the church of the Franciscan lay community. Erected between 1608 and 1620, the convent church is the oldest in town; the convent itself dates from 1780.

★
Santo Antônio

Built from 1657 onwards, the church of São Francisco da Penitência stands next to the abbey of Santo Antônio. Working on its interior decoration, only completed in 1773, were **Manuel and Francisco Xavier de Brito**, two renowned Portuguese sculptors and carvers. Both used a similar style, the so-called Brito style, with decorative forms that also influenced Aleijadinho and other masters of Brazilian High

★ ★
São Francisco da Penitência

Once part of the water supply: the Arcos da Lapa Aqueduct

Baroque. Adorning the ceiling of the chancel is Brazil's first illusionistic painting, executed between 1732 and 1736 by **Caetano da Costa Coelho**, who later went on to decorate the ceiling of the nave in the same manner. The church is considered the foremost example of the fully-fledged baroque style in Rio de Janeiro. Guided tours: Wed – Fri 9am – noon and 1 – 4pm.

✳ ✳
Confeitaria Colombo

Largo da Carioca is the starting point for the narrow Rua Gonçalves Dias, lined on both sides by the façades of two to three-storey buildings from the colonial era. In this street, look out for the art-nouveau Confeitaria Colombo café. The furniture, Belgian crystal mirrors and dark wood panelling of this elegant café, dating from 1894, have remained mostly unchanged to this day. On the first floor there is a 1922 tea salon decorated with a lot of stucco and chandeliers, with the seating arranged around a large oval opening in the ground floor ceiling. Light enters the magnificent space through a large art-nouveau-style skylight, decorated with colourful glass, lending the café a special ambience. Opening times: Mon – Fri 9.30am – 8pm, Sat 9am – 5pm.

✳
Nova Catedral (Catedral de São Sebastião)

Largo da Carioca is the starting point for Avenida República do Chile, where between 1964 and 1976 the São Sebastião Cathedral emerged, 80m/262ft high and holding up to 20,000 people. The striking church, inspired by a Mexican pyramid, has the shape of the lower section of a cone and a diameter of 106m/116yd. Right across the street, on the other side of Avenida República do Chile, soars the no less conspicuous and sturdy administration building of the state-owned petrol company Petrobras.

✳
Arcos da Lapa

The line of arcades of the Arcos da Lapa (Aqueduto da Carioca) aqueduct, built from natural stone and running for 220m/240yd, rises south of the cathedral. The row of arches, up to 64m/210ft high, were constructed in the colonial era to channel the water of the Rio Carioca to the **Largo da Carioca**: the first major civil engineering project realized in Rio de Janeiro. The aqueduct is one of the landmarks of the city and the district of Lapa, which, in the first half of the 20th century, was the heartland of Rio's bohemians. Today, Rio's last tram – its little yellow carriages affectionately called bondinhos by the locals – clatters over the former aqueduct up to the district of Santa Teresa. The old-fashioned tramway's railhead and turning loop lie at 75 Rua Professor Lélio Gama, also housing the tiny **Museu do Bonde** (Tram Museum). Opening times: Tue – Sat 9am – 4pm.

Santa Teresa district

✳
Santa Teresa, Museu Chácara do Céu

Since 1896, the trams have run a shuttle service to Santa Teresa, giving a ride to scores of ticketless travellers clinging onto the running boards. Santa Teresa district borders several favelas and has quaint, steeply rising streets and old houses, today mainly inhabited by artists and intellectuals. Worthy of note are the church and convent of Santa Teresa, a group of buildings dating from 1750 that is attributed to Alpoim, as well as the Museu Chácara do Céu, erected in 1957 on Morro do Curvelo. The museum houses the fine Raymundo Ottoni de Castro Mayas art collection and lies amidst a park laid out following designs by landscape gardener **Roberto Burle Marx**. Amongst the approximately 8,000 works of art on display are Chinese sculptures from the 17th to 19th centuries, as well as works by Matisse, Picasso, Dalí and Degas. Opening times: Tue – Sun noon–5pm.

> **!** *Baedeker* TIP
>
> **Parque das Ruínas**
>
> Right next to the Chácara do Céu, and connected to it by a footbridge, stretches the Parque das Ruínas (Ruins Park), a modern event location erected around the remains of the Palais Murtinho Nobre – the centre of cultural life in early 20th-century Rio. At weekends, the open spaces, affording splendid views of Rio, the Baía de Guanabara and Sugarloaf, are used for concerts or events for children. Entry is free.

Praça Tiradentes and Campo de Santana

Up until the first half of the 20th century, Praça Tiradentes on Rua Visconde do Rio Branco was the hub of Rio's theatrical scene. This was where in 1813 the Teatro São João, today Teatro João Caetano, was built, the most important stage in imperial Brazil.

Teatro João Caetano

A bit farther east stands the 18th-century church of São Francisco de Paula. The carvings on the main altar and in the Nossa Senhora das Vitórias chapel were created by **Mestre Valentim**. The church also contains paintings by Victor Mereilles and other 19th-century artists.

São Francisco de Paula

Rua Frei Caneca leads out of the city centre to the Campo de Santana (Praça da República) and the Sambódromo. Campo de Santana, a leafy park with a lake and several fountains, was the stage for the triumphal procession of Dom Pedro I after he was crowned Emperor, but in 1889 witnessed the proclamation of the Republic, and with it the end of the monarchy in Brazil. Opposite the park, a statue of the Duque de Caxias on horseback, created in 1899 by Rodolfo Bernardelli, crowns the **National Pantheon**, which houses the remains of the army leader.

Campo de Santana

The Sambódromo in Avenida Marquês de Sapucaí, where the carnival parades of Rio's best samba schools have taken place since 1984, was designed by star architect **Oscar Niemeyer** and can hold up to 50,000 spectators. The adjoining carnival museum shows trophies won by the samba schools. Here, visitors in town outside the carnival season can get an idea of Rio's spectacular carnival parade and the magnificent sequinned costumes.

★
Sambódromo

Praça Cristiano Ottoni (Avenida Presidente Vargas, opposite Campo de Santana) holds the railway station built in 1937 and named after Dom Pedro II. Very close by, at 196 Rua Marechal Floriano, the **Palácio do Itamarati** houses the Museum of History and Diplomacy. This building, inspired by Italian classicism and completed in 1854, was until 1897 the official residence of the presidents of the Republic. Today, the documents exhibited here illuminate the work of Brazilian diplomats since the colonial era. Guided tours: Tue, Wed, Fri 2, 3 and 4pm.

Cinelândia district

From Largo da Carioca, Avenida Rio Branco leads to Cinelândia, one of the **political and cultural centres** of the city. The splendid public buildings date from the first decade of the 20th century, when Rio was also the economic and political centre of the Republic of Brazil.

The **National Library**, housed in a classical building dating from 1910 at 219 Avenida Rio Branco, is the largest and most important in the country. Amongst the highly valuable volumes, in part brought over to Brazil by the Portuguese royal family in 1808, there are, for instance, two bibles dating back to 1642 and a **first edition of the Lusiades** (Os Lusíadas), Luis de Camões' Portuguese national epic published in 1572. Opening times: Mon to Fri 9am–8pm and Sat 9am–3pm.

Extravaganza at the Sambódromo

★★
Museu Nacional de Belas Artes

The Museu Nacional de Belas Artes (National Museum of Fine Arts), dating from 1908, is located only a few metres from the National Library at 199 Avenida Rio Branco. Particularly worth seeing are the Eliseu Visconti Gallery, with Brazilian paintings from the 19th and

20th centuries, and the Frans Post Gallery, holding paintings by North and South American artists, plus others representing the Portuguese, French, Dutch, Flemish, Belgian, German and Spanish schools. Opening times: Tue – Fri 10am – 6pm and Sat – Sun 2 – 6pm.

Teatro Municipal, Praça Floriano

Inaugurated in 1909, the Municipal Theatre was inspired by the Parisian Opera. The lobby is adorned with crystal glass doors and staircases made from Carrara marble. The paintings on the proscenium curtain and the foyer ceiling on the first-floor gallery are by **Eliseu Visconti**, while elsewhere there are others by Rodolfo Amoedo. The Assírio Hall on the basement floor, clad with ceramics and today holding a restaurant, is also not to be missed. The entrance to the theatre gives out onto Praça Floriano, where the statue of Floriano Peixoto rises over 15m/nearly 50ft high. Opening times: Mon – Fri 9am – 5pm, Sat noon – 4pm, all with prior booking: tel. (021) 22 99-17 11.

Academia Brasileira de Letras, Palácio Gustavo Capanema

The Academia Brasileira de Letras (Academy of Humanities) and the Palácio Gustavo Capanema (formerly Palácio da Cultura) lie near Cinelândia. The building of the academy in Avenida Presidente Wilson, a replica of the Petit Trianon in Paris, dates from 1922. The Palácio Gustavo Capanema, named after the culture minister of Brazil at the time, was designed between 1937 and 1945 by a group of architects working under **Le Corbusier** and including collaborators of the calibre of Lúcio Costa and Oscar Niemeyer. Cândido Portinari was commissioned for the wall paintings, while Roberto Burle Marx laid out the adjacent gardens. The Palácio Gustavo Capanema, at 16 Rua da Imprensa, which crosses Avenida Rio Branco, houses a permanent exhibition showing models of Niemeyer's most famous buildings.

Passeio Público

Extending between Cinelândia and Lapa on Avenida Beira Mar, the city park, called Passeio Público, impresses with its beautifully laid out green spaces. The design of the layout stems from 1783, and is the work of **Mestre Valentim**, who was supported by the painter Leandro Joaquim and other artists. The pavilions are noteworthy for their paintings by Joaquim and sculptures by Mestre Valentim, including the baroque entrance portal, the stone steps, the pyramid fountain and the bronze statues of Apollo, Mercury, Diana and Jupiter. In 1861, the garden was redesigned by the landscape architect Auguste Glaziou. The Passeio Público is also now home to a monument honouring the memory of the first president of Brazil, Deodoro da Fonseca.

Flamengo and Glória districts

Parque do Flamengo

Running southeast of the city park, the Avenidas Beira Mar and Infante Dom Henrique line the bays of Glória and Flamengo, which were largely artificially created when it was decided to establish the large Flamengo Park (Parque Brigadeiro Eduardo Gomes). Also known as Aterro (earth embankment) do Flamengo, the area is criss-crossed by wide avenues connecting the centre with the southern part of the city, and has children's play areas, sports facilities, roller skate tracks and runways for model aeroplanes – not forgetting the Marina da Glória which is Rio's yacht harbour and equipped with a floating quay. The green spaces of the Parque do Flamengo were laid out by Brazil's most famous landscape architect, Roberto Burle Marx.

Museu de Arte Moderna

Avenida Infante Dom Henrique also gives access to the Museum of Modern Art (MAM) in the Parque do Flamengo, which fell victim to a fire in 1978 and was rebuilt over the following years. Its collection, comprising works by Tarsila do Amaral, Emiliano Di Cavalcanti, Anna Malfatti, Cândido Portinari and Lasar Segall, ranks among the most important in the whole of Brazil. Opening times: Tue – Fri noon – 5.30pm, Sat/Sun noon – 7pm.

The Corcovado forms the backdrop to the church of Nossa Senhora da Glória.

A conspicuous monument in the Aterro do Flamengo is the memorial for the victims of the Second World War, resting on a granite and concrete plinth and also sheltering a Tomb of the Unknown Soldier. The lower level of the Monumento aos Mortos da Segunda Guerra Mundial houses the Mausoleum of the Fallen. Every first Sunday of the month, at 9am, the changing of the guard is performed here with military pomp.

Monumento aos Mortos da Segunda Guerra Mundial

Rio's Glória district, framed by the neighbourhoods of Lapa, Santa Teresa, Laranjeiras and Flamengo, spreads above Avenida Beira Mar and Aterro do Flamengo. Rising on an octagonal floor plan, the Nossa Senhora da Glória do Outeiro church of the Imperial Brotherhood was the first church in Brazil to deviate from the single-nave model. Built between 1714 and 1739 on Ladeira da Glória, it is decorated with azulejos. Part of the church, the **Museu Imperial** keeps 2,000 exhibits, amongst them precious silver, jewels belonging to Empress Teresa Cristina and valuable liturgical objects. Opening times: Mon to Fri 8am – 5pm, Sat/Sun 8am to noon.

✶ NS da Glória do Outeiro

⏲

Catete and Laranjeiras districts

Since the capital was transferred to Brasília, the Palácio do Catete in Catete district, which was the seat of the Presidency between 1897 and 1960, has housed the Museum of the Republic. The classical edifice was built between 1858 and 1866 on the orders of the Baron of Nova Friburgo. Most visitors want to see the room in which **President Getúlio Vargas** committed suicide in 1954. The palace is situated at 153 Rua do Catete, in the immediate vicinity of Catete Metro station. Opening times: Wed 2 – 5pm, Sat/Sun 2 to 6pm.

✶ Museu da República

⏲

Also in Rua do Catete (no. 181), the Edison Carneiro Museum for Ethnic Art shows exhibits from all parts of the country: ex-votos, Afro-Brazilian ritual objects, practical ceramic wares and craftwork techniques. Opening times: Tue – Fri 11am – 6pm, Sat/Sun 3 – 6pm.

Museu de Folclore Edison Carneiro

⏲

Built between 1909 and 1914, Palácio Laranjeiras lies in the district of the same name at 407 Rua Paulo César de Andrade. Serving in the past as residence of the Conde d'Eu and Princess Isabel, as well as the Presidents of the Republic (from da Fonseca to Vargas), it is still used as the seat of the governor of Rio de Janeiro state.

Palácio Laranjeiras

Botafogo, Urca and Leme districts

Extending in the deeply cut bay between the beaches of Flamengo and Urca lies Praia do Botafogo, 800m/875yd long, with its yacht and rowing clubs steeped in tradition. Flamengo Beach is on the way to the viewpoint on Morro do Passado (Botafogo district), a green space promising picturesque views of the bay and Sugarloaf.

✶ Mirante do Passado

Museu do Índio

Between Rua São Clemente and the São João Batista cemetery, the Indian Museum at 55 Rua das Palmeiras gives public access to around 14,000 exhibits: baskets, handicrafts made from bird feathers, ceramics, musical instruments and weapons. The museum also comprises a specialized library, with photographs and material on microfiche.

Indian crafts are for sale here, too. In the park of the museum, Guaraní Indians have constructed a house on stilts with a roof made from bamboo and straw, and a garden with traditional produce, to give the visitor an idea of the Indians' daily life. Opening times: Tue – Fri 9am – 5.30pm, Sat/Sun 1 – 5pm.

Morro da Urca, Morro Cara de Cão

Behind Botafogo Beach, the hills of Urca and Cara de Cão (Dog Face), as well as Sugarloaf jut out into Guanabara Bay, thus narrowing the entrance to the bay. Praia da Urca, 100m/110yd long, stretches at the foot of the Urca and Cara de Cão hills, not far from the place where the original core of Rio de Janeiro was, namely between Morro Cara de Cão and Sugarloaf. Atop Morro Cara de Cão rise the forts of São João, São José and São Teodósio.

★ ★ Pão de Açúcar (Sugarloaf)

Symbol of Rio de Janeiro

On the seventh day, God created Rio de Janeiro, at least this is the firm belief of the cariocas. How many hours He took to form the Sugarloaf is not known even to the proud inhabitants of Rio. Without a doubt, a thing of such beauty is not created in a hurry. Indeed it took several million years until this quintessential picture postcard icon emerged, as, induced by the climate, the outer layers of rock peeled away, leaving the form we see today.

Train to the summit

The easy way to climb Sugarloaf – a so-called »inselberg« consisting of coarse gneiss that is over 500 million years old – is via the cable car, which has been running since 1913 and was overhauled in the early 1970s. The first car takes visitors initially from Praça General Tibúrcio in the Praia Vermelha district up to the top of **Morro da Urca** (215m/705ft), where visitors get out and take a second car to the 394m/1,293-ft summit of Sugarloaf. The silver-coloured capsules of the Sugarloaf cable car transport up to 75 passengers at any one time and run daily between 8am and 10pm. The summit of the Pão de Açúcar allows visitors an impressive view of Rio de Janeiro and Guanabara Bay. Even the Dedo de Deus (Finger of God), pointing towards the sky in the Serra dos

Copacabana Palace * Built in the 1920s on Av Atlântica, the Copacabana Palace Hotel, today a listed building, conjures up the power, wealth and refined lifestyle of the period when Rio was the capital of the country. It was at the Copacabana Palace that, in 1933, Ginger Rogers and Fred Astaire glided across the dancefloor together for the first time, in the film *Flying Down to Rio*.

Forte de Copacabana * Inaugurated in 1914, the fort of Copacabana rises at the end of the beach at Praça Coronel Eugênio Franco and houses the **Artillery Museum**, which, together with the Casa de Deodoro (Praça da República) and the Casa de Osório (Rua Riachuelo, in the centre) belongs to the Army Museum. There are towers with large-calibre cannons from the early 20th century here, as well as modern armoured cars and rocket-launchers on exhibit. Also worth looking out for are two scraps of the Brazilian flag, borne by rebellious soldiers holding the fort as they set out to fight the government troops in 1922; 18 of them were slaughtered at the beach. In commemoration of their uprising, a monument was erected on Avenida Atlântica. Opening times: Tue – Sun 10am – 8pm.

Forte Duque de Caxias The coastal battery on Praça Júlio Noronha at the other end of Copacabana at Morro do Leme (Leme Hill) was built between 1776 and 1779. In 1895, it was rebuilt amidst fear of an Argentinian invasion and given eight more cannons, becoming known as **Forte do Leme** in 1935, a name it has kept ever since. Thirty years later, the fort was turned into a study centre for army staff, the Centro de Estudos de Pessoal do Exército. Opening times: Sat to Sun 9am to 5pm.

Praia do Diabo, Praia do Arpoador This small beach spreading between the promontories of Copacabana and Arpoador often has stormy waves, and bears the name of Praia do Diabo (Devil's Beach). The next beach along, beyond Ponta do Arpoador, is Praia do Arpoador (Beach of the Harpoonist), bordering Praia de Ipanema. The bays surround the **Pedra do Arpoador**, a viewpoint for the southern city beaches of Rio and the Sugarloaf.

Ipanema and Leblon districts

Praia de Ipanema ** Lined by Avenidas Vieira Souto and Delfim Moreira, the Praias de Ipanema and Leblon, originally a single beach, are separated by the Jardim de Alá Canal. Along the spacious beach promenades, hotels, street cafés and restaurants abound. Ipanema Beach owes its worldwide fame to the bossa nova song *The Girl from Ipanema*.

Praça General Osório Praça General Osório in Ipanema is adorned by the Saracuras Fountain, created by Mestre Valentim in 1795. This is where the Feirarte takes place, a fair where antiquities, crafts, paintings and

© Baedeker

On the way to the summit: the cable car up Sugarloaf Mountain is the highlight of any visit to Rio.

75 people fit into the silver cable car going up the Pão de Açucar.

CABLE CAR UP TO SUGARLOAF

**This is an absolute must: the cable car ride up to Sugarloaf Mountain.
If you haven't stood up here and gazed across the Cidade Maravilhosa
and Guanabara Bay, then you haven't really been to Rio de Janeiro.**

Operating hours:
Daily 8am–10pm

① **Base station**
The trip starts at Praça General Tibúrcio in Praia Vermelha district. The Sugarloaf cable car can take up to 75 passengers.

② **Morro da Urca**
Change at 215m/705ft altitude, at Morro da Urca, to start the last and most exciting stage of the ascent of Sugarloaf.

③ **Peak of Sugarloaf**
At an altitude of 394m/1,293ft, there are sensational views of Rio de Janeiro and Guanabara Bay. Beyond Botafogo Bay, the huge statue of Christ spreads out his arms.

*Spectacular ascent to
Sugarloaf Mountain*

④ **Praia Vermelha**
After returning from Sugarloaf, the beach of the district of the same name is a good place for a dip into the balmy waters of the Atlantic.

⑤ **Morro do Leme**
Sugarloaf's far less attractive neighbour. The Forte Duque de Caxias was erected at the foot of the hill in the late 18th century to guard against a feared Argentine invasion.

⑥ **Praia de Copacabana**
The beautiful people of Rio de Janeiro parade along this »catwalk of the vanities«, which extends along Copacabana district's 4km/2.5 miles of beach.

Sugarloaf Mountain at dusk

Órgãos near Teresópolis, can be seen in the distance. A particular feast for the eye is the spectacular view bathed in the red glow of sunset.

Copacabana district

Stretching over 4km/2.5 miles behind the hills of Urubu and Leme, the world-famous Praia de Copacabana is far more than a beach; it is a place to see and be seen, a **catwalk of the vanities**, with a circus of bodies on display, some fitter than others, but usually barely hidden by the most up-to-date swimwear. This is the meeting place not only for sun worshippers, but also for sports fans, traders, idlers, the curious, locals and tourists, the poor and the rich – in short, the entire kaleidoscope of Rio's society.

It might only just be a century old, but today, the district of Copacabana is the most famous in all Rio de Janeiro. Near the beaches – on Avenida Atlântica, Avenida Nossa Senhora de Copacabana running parallel to it, and in the roads crossing it – there are the most and some of the best hotels, restaurants and nightclubs in Rio. Street cafés with their tables jostling for space on the wide sidewalks are an image of daily life in this southern part of Rio.

★
Praia de
Copacabana

Ideal spot
for nightlife

Golden rule in Rio: don't ever let your wife go swimming on her own!

similar goods are traded. On Sundays, there is an antiquities market on the Praça de Quental in the Leblon district.

✱ ✱ Lagoa Rodrigo de Freitas

The Rodrigo de Freitas lagoon stretches between the blocks of the Ipanema, Leblon and Lagoa districts and the Jardim Botânico. Several roads and avenues lead from this area of town to the surrounding Avenidas Borges de Medeiros and Epitácio Pessoa and to the parks and clubs lining the over 9.5km/6 miles of lake shoreline.

Access to the Cantagalo Park on the lagoon's eastern bank is via Avenida Epitácio Pessoa. The park comprises skating lanes, a boat hire outfit and many other sports facilities. Next to it extends Catacumba Park (Marcos Tamoyo Park), strewn with fruit trees and offering five viewing points as well as many picnic spots. Only pedestrians are allowed in, and occasional open-air events take place here.

Parque do Cantagalo, Parque da Catacumba

Situated on the western side of the lagoon, in the immediate vicinity of the leisure facilities of the Flamengo Club and the racecourse of Rio's Jockey Club, the **Brigadeiro Faria Lima** park (access via Rua Borges de Medeiros) has an amusement park and a helipad. Northwest of the jockey club unfold the Botanical Gardens with 5,000

✱ Jardim Botânico

types of plant from all over the world. Here, visitors can find ponds with rare fish, Victoria Amazonica waterlilies and other plants from the Amazon region. Half of the area still preserves its original vegetation. **Prince Regent Dom João** had the gardens laid out in the early 19th century, specifically for the acclimatization of tropical plants collected by him from all corners of what was then the Portuguese empire, e. g. avocado trees, clove bushes, royal palms and a plethora of other exotic plants. Rio's Botanical Gardens also have a specialized library and two museums: the Botanical Museum and the Herbarium (Museu de Plantas Secas), used for research purposes. Opening times: daily 8am – 5pm.

Vidigal and Barra da Tijuca districts

Praia do Vidigal

Access to the beach of Praia do Vidigal, 600m/over 650yd long, next to the Morro Dois Irmãos hill is via the Dois Irmãos tunnel and Avenida Niemeyer. Its luxury hotels stand in stark contrast to the nearby Favela do Vidigal, one of the largest slums in Rio.

✳ São Conrado

The beach of São Conrado, 1km/0.6 miles long, runs from the end of Avenida Niemeyer to the São Conrado tunnel; access is via the Estrada da Gávea and the Avenida Prefeito Mendes de Morais coastal road. Its strong waves attract many surfers.

✳ Praia da Barra da Tijuca

The beach of Barra da Tijuca extends across 18km/11 miles from the Ponta do Joá to the Recreio dos Bandeirantes, comprising also the large **Lagoa de Marapendi** lagoon as well as the coastal, tropical forests of the Restingas de Itabeba and Jacarepaguá. Further inland lie the Lagoas de Jacarepaguá and da Tijuca, where stretches of beach with bars and restaurants alternate with nearly completely unspoilt sections, patronized by surfers.

Recreio dos Bandeirantes

Praia Recreio dos Bandeirantes beach, pounded by forceful waves, ends at the Pontal de Sernambetiba; access is via the Avenida Sernambetiba coastal road and the Avenida das Américas, running along the Restinga de Jacarepaguá.

✳ ✳ Museu Casa do Pontal

Arguably the most beautiful, and definitely the largest **collection of folk art** from the Brazilian northeast can actually be found in the south of the country, just outside Rio. Between the swimming beach of Recreio dos Bandeirantes and the Serra de Grumari nature reserve, a narrow road turns off inland to the Museu Casa do Pontal at 3295 Estrada do Pontal. The collection, amassed here by the French patron of the arts Jacques Van de Beugue over the course of his life, shows over **5,000 selected exhibits** from northeastern Brazil. Hundreds of painted clay figurines – so-called caxixis – are arranged in groups to form beautiful scenes from a circus, traditional equestrian tournaments or famous popular festivals. The figures, made by the best craftspeople – more often than not commissioned by Van de Beugue himself – show doctors during consultations, mother and newborn child together, processions, repentista balladeers, farmers producing manioc flour, and at-

! **Baedeker** TIP

A child-friendly splash

As attractive as Rio is for adults, this city of millions has very little to offer families with children. At least the two spacious new leisure pools with theme parks southwest of the city centre go a little way towards redressing this: Rio Water Planet, Estrada dos Bandeirantes, Vargem Grande, opening times: daily 10am to 5pm, www.riowaterplanet.com.br, and Wet 'n Wild, Avenidas das Américas, Recreio dos Bandeirantes, www.wetnwildrio.com.br.

tacks by lawless cangaceiro bandits. Even the colourful procession of the famous samba schools in Rio's carnival arena may be admired in miniature – at the pressing of a button, they start marching, powered by amazingly simple mechanisms. Opening times: daily 9am to 5.30pm.

✴ ✴ Parque Nacional da Tijuca

Covering over 3,200ha/over 7,900 acres, the Parque Nacional da Tijuca, established in the early 1960s and today the green lung of Rio, was originally covered in lush Atlantic rainforest, all of which, however, by the mid-19th century, had made way for the spreading coffee plantations. In 1861, Emperor Pedro II had the area of today's national park, its soil entirely depleted by the extensive coffee cultivation, bought up from the plantation owners and replanted with flora from the Serra do Mar – with overwhelming success. The dead soil metamorphosed into a rampant forest landscape, which, with its hills, brooks and waterfalls, represents an idyllic counterpoint to hectic urban life. Strictly speaking, the park consists of several parts: the Serra da Carioca, the peaks of Pedra Bonita (656m/2,152ft) and Pedra da Gávea (828m/2,716ft) and Tijuca Forest with the Morro do Corcovado (704m/2,310ft) and the statue of Christ the Redeemer (see below), as well as its highest elevation, the Pico da Tijuca, at 1,022m/3,353ft.

To get into the national park, take the Estrada das Canoas (which becomes Estrada da Pedra) from the São Conrado district, and then

✴
Vista Chinesa

the Estrada da Gávea Pequena, which forks into the Estrada da Boa Vista and the Estrada da Vista Chinesa. The former leads to Alto da Boa Vista, with the main entrance to the Tijuca Forest, the latter to the Vista Chinesa viewpoint, at a height of 380m/1,257ft yielding fantastic views of the **Lagoa Rodrigo de Freitas** with the adjacent Botanical Gardens, as well as of part of the Atlantic coast off the Ipanema and Leblon districts.

✷ ✷
Tijuca Forest

Tijuca Forest is one of the largest urban forest areas on earth. As early as 1870, nine years after planting was started, it was already home to over 62,000 newly planted trees – mainly indigenous types. The main access to Tijuca Forest is on Praça Afonso Viseu (Alto da Boa Vista), which also has a fountain by Grandjean de Montigny (1846). The Estrada do Imperador leads immediately away from the main entrance to the **Cascatinha Taunay**, a waterfall plunging to a depth of 30m/nearly 100ft. A bit further on, the interior of the Mayrink Chapel, built in 1860, shelters paintings by Cândido Portinari (1903 – 1962). From here, several paths lead to the numerous attractions of Tijuca Forest: in the north, the peaks of Pedra do Conde (821m/2,693ft), Excelsior (688m/2,257ft) and Caveira; to the west, the grottoes of Saudade, Paulo and Virginia, the waterfalls of Diamantina and Gabriela, the caves of Belmiro and Luís Fernando, as well as the peaks of Bico de Papagaio (989m/3,245ft) and Pico da Tijuca (1,022m/3,353ft), the mightiest elevation of the park.

✷
Museu
do Açude

The Museu do Açude, located near Tijuca forest on Estrada do Açude (Alto da Boa Vista), has valuable porcelain collections from the West India Company, paintings by Brazilian and foreign artists showing the old Rio de Janeiro, and azulejos from the 17th to 19th centuries. Like the Chácara do Céu, the Museu do Açude owes its existence to Raymundo Castro Maya's passion for collecting, with the museum taking shape in his former summer residence. Opening times: Thu – Sun 11am – 5pm.

Cosme Velho district and the Corcovado

✷
Mirante
Dona Marta

From Cosme Velho, the Estrada das Paineras (closed to cars at weekends) leads to Tijuca Park. The winding country road is inordinately popular with cariocas for day trips – every weekend sees thousands of people jogging, on their bikes or just strolling, all appreciating the shade of the Estrada das Paineras as much as the four waterfalls lining it. About halfway, the access road to the Mirante Dona Marta viewpoint branches off from the Estrada das Paineras. The 362m/1,188-ft rocky ledge offers view across the Favela Dona Marta slum and Botafogo Bay out to Sugarloaf.

Alongside Sugarloaf Mountain, this is the second symbol of Rio: →
the statue of Christ the Redeemer on the Corcovado.

★ ★
Corcovado

Cosme Velho (Rua Cosme Velho 513) is also the location of the base station of the rack railway, constructed in 1931, that plies the 35km/21.5-mile route to the 704m/2,304-ft granite peak of the Corcovado (the Hunchback). Operating hours: daily 8.30am – 6.30pm. At the very top rises the statue of **Christ the Redeemer** (Cristo Redentor), the symbol of Rio and famous all over the world. Counting the eight metres/26 feet of the plinth, with a chapel next to it, the statue soars to a height of 38m/125ft and weighs 1,145 tons/1,262 short tons. The head and hands were chiselled following designs by French sculptor Paul Landowsky. The arms of Cristo Redentor, extending in a north-south axis, span 28m/30yd and seem to be blessing the city of millions lying below. After dark, the statue is illuminated by hundreds of spotlights. In early 2008, the statue was struck by lightning, to dramatic effect, but no damage was incurred. In terms of views, the Corcovado bears comparison with Sugarloaf.

★
Largo do Boticário

Opening up on Rua do Cosme Velho, near the stop of the Corcovado railway, Largo do Boticário is one of the most picturesque squares in town. Its houses were built in 1946 in the colonial style, using parts of buildings destroyed during work on Avenida Presidente Vargas.

★
Museu Internacional de Arte Naïf do Brasil

Also in Rua Cosme Velho, only 50 metres/55 yards from the base station of the rack railway leading up to the Corcovado, the International Museum of Naive Art of Brazil (MIAN) shows works from over 130 countries.

The oldest paintings date back to the 15th century, but the main attraction is a painting, 7m/23ft wide and 4m/13ft high, featuring a highly original representation of the city of the Sugarloaf, which can claim to be the biggest artwork of its kind in the world. Opening times: Tue – Fri 10am – 6pm, Sat/Sun noon – 6pm.

Zona Norte

Samba neighbourhoods

In the district of Tijuca, north of Tijuca Forest, the public rehearsals of this district's samba schools, the Acadêmicos do Salgueiro and the Unidos da Tijuca, attract many spectators. In neighbouring Vila Isabel, one of the hot samba centres, the Unidos de Vila Isabel rules. Above Vila Isabel, the Mangueira favela is the birth place of the **Estação Primeira de Mangueira**, the most popular samba schoool in town. The rehearsals of the Escolas start as early as mid-September, taking place mostly on Friday and Saturday nights. However, these can in no way be compared to the parade of the samba schools in the Sambódromo carnival arena; they represent more an inexpensive and fairly loud dance entertainment of Rio's middle and lower classes.

NS da Penha de França

The way up to the church of Nossa Senhora da Penha de França, built in 1871 on a 69m/226-ft rock, is on steps hewn into the rock.

In October, for the Festa da Penha, many pilgrims make their way to the church, near the Ilha do Governador in the northern suburb of Penha.

The Aerospace Museum (Museu Aeroespacial) is located not far from Avenida Brasil at Campo dos Afonsos. Its hangars keep replicas of the *14 Bis* and the *Demoiselle*, built by aviation pioneer **Alberto Santos-Dumont**, as well as replicas of other aircraft, motors used in Brazilian aviation, plus photos and documents on Santos-Dumont, the national airmail service and Brazilian participation in the war in Italy. The entrance to the Museu Aeroespacial is at 2000 Avenida Marechal Fontenele. Opening times: Tue–Fri 9am–3pm, Sat/Sun 9.30am–4pm.

✷✷
Museu
Aeroespacial

⊙

✶ Sabará

Sd 55

State: Minas Gerais (MG)
Altitude: 724m/2,375ft

Population: 115,500

Sabará, situated only 25km/15.5 miles east of Belo Horizonte in the Rio das Velhas valley, developed out of a settlement founded by the bandeirante Borba Gato from São Paulo, who first discovered the gold reserves in the Rio das Velhas.

In 1711, under the name Vila Real de Nossa Senhora da Conceição de Sabará, the town was declared the administrative seat of the Rio das Velhas area. The 18th-century wealth based on the region's gold riches can still be seen today in the churches and manor houses of this heyday.

What to see in Sabará

Rising on Praça Getúlio Vargas, the church of Nossa Senhora da Conceição, built between 1701 and 1710, is a typical edifice of early Minas Baroque; the façade of clay and wood, appearing slightly clumsy, hides a surprisingly rich interior decoration with a golden altar and Chinese-influenced paintings in the chancel. On the church square, Praça Getúlio Vargas, look for the bubbling 18th-century **Chafariz da Confraria** village fountain.

✶
Matriz NS
da Conceição

The church of Nossa Senhora do Carmo was built of stone from 1763 onwards. In 1771, **Aleijadinho** (▶Baedeker Special p. 58) created the façade and the emblem of the Carmelite order, carved from soapstone, on the main entrance. The images of the saints on the side altars, the pulpits and the figures supporting the choir stalls

✶
NS do Carmo

were also made by him. The ceiling frescoes in the nave, executed in 1813 by Joaquim Gonçalves da Rocha, show the prophet Elias borne heavenwards in his fiery chariot.

★
NS do Ó

It is easy to miss the small and somewhat unusually formed church of Nossa Senhora do Ó in Sabará. The plain façade of the church, built between 1717 and 1720 on the Largo NS do Ó, contrasts with the ornate decoration inside. The wall panelling shows golden motifs on a red or blue background, and their similarity to Chinese lacquer work is no coincidence: the Portuguese employed craftspeople here who would have been at least familiar with the techniques and motifs – pagodas and birds in flight – of the East Asian colonies. More remarkably however, the small church of Our Blessed Lady of Ó stands for a popular name given to the pregnant Virgin Mary, and once a year – on 25 March, the calculated date of the Immaculate Conception, nine months before Christmas – becomes the centre of a ritual typical of Brazilian folk Catholicism. Pregnant women all over Brazil pray to Nossa Senhora do Ó, despite the official church's displeasure at this cult – after all, it is said that these prayers reduce the risks at birth.

Minero with bike

VISITING SABARÁ

INFORMATION

Rua Dom Pedro II no. 223
Tel. (031) 36 72-76 90
www.sabara.mg.gov.br

GETTING THERE

Bus station
Avenida Prefeitio Victor Fratini
Tel. (031) 36 72-12 55

WHERE TO STAY

Most tourists visit Sabará as part of a
day trip from ► Belo Horizonte,
where they can find a wide range of
hotels and pousadas.

As building work on the church of Nossa Senhora do Rosário dos Pretos stopped in 1768 and was never completed, it looks like ruins today, with the finished chancel wall abutting the old chapel made from taipa (clay). The unfinished church juts out on Praça Melo Viana and houses the small **Museu de Arte Sacra** (Museum of Sacred Art). Its collection includes works by Aleijadinho. Opening times: Tue – Sun 9 – 11am and 1 – 5pm.

NS do Rosário dos Pretos

The Museu do Ouro (Gold Museum) in Rua da Intendência was established in the **Casa de Fundição e Intendência**, the former Intendancy, which was the agency responsible for gold found in the area (founded 1720). This is the only royal gold foundry that has remained nearly unchanged in Brazil; gold dust was weighed here and cast into ingots, with a quinto (fifth) having to be paid over to the Portuguese crown.

★ Museu do Ouro

The town hall is housed in the Solar do Padre Correia town house dating from 1773. The rococo altar in its private chapel, covered with gold leaf, is attributed to Aleijadinho. The building is part of the architectural ensemble of Rua Dom Pedro II, where the Casa Azul (Blue House), built in 1773, also attracts the attention of visitors. Opening times: Mon – Fri noon – 5pm.

★ Solar do Padre Correia

Sabará's municipal theatre, erected in 1819 in the English style on Rua Dom Pedro II, ranks among Brazil's oldest repertory theatres and is famous to this day for its good acoustics. Opening times: daily 8am – noon and 1 – 5pm.

Teatro Municipal

Preserving objects from the time of the bandeirantes and the gold prospectors, the house of Manuel de Borba Gato (born 1649) at 71 Rua Borba Gato honours the memory of the man who in the year 1700 discovered the first gold deposits in Sabará and died 18 years later in this town.

Casa Borba Gato

✶ ✶ Salvador

State: Bahia (BA)   **Population:** 2.4 million
Altitude: 8m/26ft

Situated on Baía de Todos os Santos (All Saints Bay), Salvador – the capital of Bahia state and, up to 1763, capital of the whole of Brazil – is the political, economic and cultural hub of the northeast. The baroque city is also a gem of colonial architecture, rich in art treasures, palaces, churches and convents.

Since the Old Town of Salvador was declared a UNESCO World Heritage Site in 1985, giving rise over the following decade to an extensive restoration of the old architectural fabric, thousands of tourists flock here every year. However, it is not only the architecture that draws visitors, but also the African influence that lends Salvador its unique attractive flair.

The sound of Afro-Brazilian music calling dance lovers every evening, capoeira performances on the streets, religions such as the Candomblé and the aromas of the informal restaurants on street corners run by Baianas dressed all in white, are evidence of the three hundred years that Salvador spent being the most important trading hub for slaves in Brazil. Today still, dark skin hues make up the majority of the inhabitants here, in probably the most African city outside the continent of Africa.

Cidade Baixa (Lower Town)

The church of Nossa Senhora da Conceição da Praia was built between 1739 and 1773 in the downtown area – today mainly a commercial, business and services centre – on the square of the same name, southwest of the Elevador Lacerda. The towers, connected diagonally to the façade, and the bevelled corners of the interior show the influence of baroque architecture. The ceiling frescoes in the nave, carried out by **José Joaquim da Rocha** in 1773, are considered a masterpiece of perspective painting.

✶
NS da
Conceição
da Praia

The Mercado São Joaquim in Água de Meninos and the Mercado Modelo have local crafts, Afro-Brazilian ritual objects and many curios for sale. The Mercado Modelo, housed in the former customs house (Alfândega) on Praça Visconde de Cairu, was faithfully reconstructed in 1984 following a fire. There are often capoeira performances in front of the Mercado Modelo.

Mercado
São Joaquim,
Mercado Modelo

← *The Old Town of Salvador da Bahia is a gem of colonial architecture and has been listed as a UNESCO World Heritage site.*

▶ VISITING SALVADOR

INFORMATION

Bahiatursa
Pelourino office
Rua das Laranjeiras 12
Tel. (071) 33 21-24 63

Mercado Modelo office
Praça Visconde de Cairu
Tel. (071) 32 41-02 42
www.bahia.com.br

GETTING THERE

Airport
Aeroporto Deputado Luís Eduardo
Magalhães
Estrada do Côco
Tel. (071) 32 04-10 10

Bus station
Avenida Antônio Carlos Magalhães
Tel. (071) 34 60-83 00

EVENTS

Lavagem do Bonfim
The most important religious festival
in Salvador begins every year on the
second Sunday in January: led by
Candomblé priestesses in bright white
festive costume, a huge crowd makes
the pilgrimage from the church of
Nossa Senhora da Conceição da Praia
in Salvador's Lower Town, to the
church of Bonfim. Once there, the
priestesses, called mães de santo, and
their helpers »wash« the flight of steps
leading up to the pilgrimage church
with scent and scatter flowers on
them. This rite mixes Catholicism and
Candomblé in the syncretism that is
typical of Bahia: officially, it is the
Senhor de Bonfim (Jesus) that is
worshipped, but unofficially the picturesque festival is celebrated for
Oxalá, the father of all Orixá deities.
The Lavagem do Bonfim is followed
by a popular festival lasting several
days and lubricated by rivers of beer
and firewater.

WHERE TO EAT

▶ Expensive

Boi Preto
Avenida Otávio Mangabeira / corner
of Avenida Yemanjá
Boca do Rio district
Tel. (071) 33 62-88 44
One of Salvador's best churrascarias
(steakhouses) with a rodízio revolving
buffet. All credit cards accepted.

▶ Moderate

Yemanjá
Avenida Otávio Mangabeira 4655
Jardim Armação district Tel. (071)
34 61-90 10
For years now Salvador's top
restaurant for Afro-Brazilian cuisine.
Speciality: fish and seafood. At weekends, even diners with a table booked
have to be prepared for a lengthy wait.

▶ Inexpensive

Bistro Portosol
Rua César Zama 51
Porto da Barra district
Tel. (071) 32 64-73 39
House specialities are Austrian and
Hungarian dishes.

WHERE TO STAY

▶ Luxury

Sofitel
Rua Passárgada
Farol da Itapoã district
Tel. (071) 33 74-85 00
www.accorhotels.com.br
28km/17.5 miles from the city centre.
Complex surrounded by parklands
boasting 206 air-conditioned rooms
and a broad range of sports facilities,
including a 9-hole golf course.

Pestana Bahia
Rua Fonte do Boi 216
Rio Vermelho district
Tel. (071) 21 03-80 00
and (08 00) 266-332
www.pestana.com
The hotel was opened in 2001 and has
430 apartments with superb views.
Good restaurant, pool, sauna and
gym.

► **Mid-range**
① *Pousada Solar dos Deuses*
Largo do Cruzeiro do São Francisco
12
Pelourinho district
Tel. (071) 33 21-17 89
www.solardosdeuses.com.br

Small but beautifully formed. Opened
in 2005 in a central location in the
Old Town. Seven rooms decorated in
the colonial style but with modern
comforts, overseen by attentive Swiss
management.

Baedeker recommendation

► **Mid-range**
Praia do Forte Eco Resort
Avenida do Farol
Tel. (071) 36 76-40 00
www.ecoresort.com.br
One hour north of Salvador: with palm
beach, spa, and pools. Young children are
looked after in the »Clube Infantil«.

The central Praça Visconde de Cairu is a good starting point for a ✳
boat trip to the harbour fortress of Forte São Marcelo (or Forte do **Forte São**
Mar), which was designed in 1623 by **Francisco de Frias da Mesqui-** **Marcelo**
ta. This master builder also created the Forte São Diogo (1609 to
1612) in Salvador and the impressive fortress of Reis Magos (1614)
in Natal. Construction work on the São Marcelo fort, rising up
abruptly from the sea, was completed by the Dutch, who occupied
the city between 1624 and 1625.

Following Avenida Lafaiete Coutinho in a southwesterly direction ✳
along the coast, leads to the Avenida do Contorno, with the Solar do **Solar do Unhão**
Unhão group of colonial buildings, housing a restaurant with regular
Afro-Brazilian shows as well as an important collection of sculptures.

Some 500m/550yd further on, at Praia da Gamboa, look out for the **Forte Gamboa,**
ruined 18th century fort of São Paulo da Gamboa. A litte bit further **Forte São Pedro**
inland, on the southern side of the Rua Gamboa de Cima rises the
imposing São Pedro fort, also dating from the 18th century.

On Largo da Campo Grande, one of the city's major junctions, a **Largo da**
monument honours the victorious Brazilian troops who, after de- **Campo Grande**
feating the Portuguese in November 1822 near Pirajá and subsequently liberating Salvador from the siege of the imperial army, entered the city on 2 July 1823.

✳
At 2340 Avenida Sete de Setembro, which crosses the district of Vitó- **Museu de Arte**
ria and leads to the beaches of Porto da Barra and Farol da Barra in **da Bahia**

Salvador Map

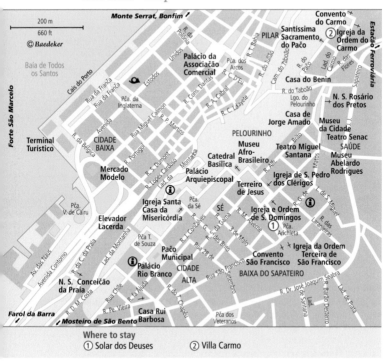

200 m
660 ft
© Baedeker

Monte Serrat, Bonfim

Baía de Todos os Santos

Forte São Marcelo

Cais do Porto

Rua da França
Rua da França

Pça. da Inglaterra

Terminal Turístico

CIDADE BAIXA

R. da Bélgica

Avenida

Rua Miguel Calmon

R. Portugal

R. S. Dumont

Mercado Modelo

R. Lopes Cardoso

Lad. da Montanha

R. P. Martins

Montanha

Palácio Arquiepiscopal

Pça. V. de Cairú

Elevador Lacerda

Pça. T. de Souza

Igreja Santa Casa da Misericórdia

Pça. da Sé

Paço Municipal

Palácio Rio Branco

CIDADE ALTA

N. S. Conceição da Praia

Av. das Naus

Avenida Contorno

R. da Praia

R. D. M. Costa

Rua Chile

R. da Ajuda

R. Pe. Vieira

Casa Rui Barbosa

Mosteiro de São Bento

Farol da Barra

R. Cons. Dantas

R. C. D'Eu

R. A. Cabral

R. C. Lafayete

Estodos

Unidos

R. da Polônia

R. do Julião

Cam. do Tabolão

R. do Paço

Cam. do Tabolão

Lgo. do Pelourinho

R. do Tabolão

PILAR

Santíssima Sacramento do Paço

Palácio da Associação Comercial

Pça. dos Arcos

Casa do Benin

PELOURINHO

Museu Afro-Brasileiro

Catedral Basílica

Terreiro de Jesus

SÉ

R. J. Conceição

Rua 28 de

G. de Brito

3 de Maio

R. da Gama

Rua São Francisco

Rua do Tijolo

BAIXA DO SAPATEIRO

Convento São Francisco

Rua do Chapel

Pça dos Veteranos

Convento do Carmo

Santíssima Sacramento do Paço

Igreja da Ordem do Carmo ②

Estação Ferroviária

R. da Tabolão

R. do Paço

Sapateiro

R. das Flores

N. S. Rosário dos Pretos

Casa de Jorge Amado

Museu da Cidade

Teatro Senac

SAÚDE

Teatro Miguel Santana

Museu Abelardo Rodrigues

Igreja de S. Pedro dos Clérigos

Igreja e Ordem de S. Domingos

Pça. Arichieta

Igreja da Ordem Terceira de São Francisco

R. do M. Viuva

R. de S. Miguel

R. das Laranjeiras

R. Dr. José Joaquim Seabra

R. Barão Destero

Lad. de Santana

Lad. de Praia

Where to stay
① Solar dos Deuses
② Villa Carmo

the east of All Saints Bay, the art museum of Bahia has been housed in the former residence of the Goes Calmon family since 1943. On display are furniture, silverware and azulejos from colonial Bahia, Chinese porcelain and paintings by modern Bahian artists. Opening times: Tue–Fri 2–7pm, Sat/Sun 2.30–6.30pm.

Museu Geológico do Estado, Museu de Carlos Costa Pinto

Also on Avenida Sete de Setembro, the State Geology Museum shows valuable gemstones from all over Bahia, whilst the Museum Carlos Costa Pinto houses silverware and furniture from the 17th to the 19th centuries, gold jewellery, paintings, china and the country's largest collection of balangandãs (decorative clasps worn by the women of Bahia).

Barra

Avenida Sete de Setembro leads into the district of Barra, with its countless bars, restaurants and hotels; Barra has a reputation as the second-most important nightlife district after Pelourinho (see below). From the city beach of Porto da Barra – polluted, though still very popular – the promenade runs south towards the mighty citadel of **Forte Santo Antônio da Barra** (1598), which in the 18th century was equipped with a lighthouse (Farol) and today plays host to the Museu Náutico da Bahia, with a collection containing items salvaged from the large Portuguese sailing vessel *Sacramento*, which sank in 1668. Opening times: Tue – Sun 8.30am – 7pm.

Monte Serrat and Bonfim

The Forte de Monte Serrat, a 16th-century coastal stronghold on the Ponte de Humaitá on Rua Santa Rita Durão, has a significant collection of firearms.

Forte de
Monte Serrat

North of the fortress, the Igreja do Senhor do Bonfim, built between 1745 and 1754 on the Largo do Bonfim, is Bahia's most famous and popular pilgrimage church. The Sala de Ex-Votos, a room filled to the brim with votive gifts, is evidence of the local population's deep faith in the miracles of its patron saint.

★
Igreja do
Senhor do
Bonfim

Cidade Alta (Upper Town)

The Upper Town and Lower Town are connected by steeply inclined streets and several elevators, amongst them the Plano Inclinado do Gonçalves (funicular) and the Elevador Lacerda (elevator). The Plano Inclinado runs from the downtown Rua de Francisco Gonçalves to Praça Ramos de Queiroz. Built in 1930, the tower-like structure of the Lacerda elevator, a 72m/236-ft Salvador landmark and a favourite hunting ground for pickpockets, connects the Praça Visconde de Cairu (in the port area) with the Praça Tomé de Souza in the historic Upper Town. From here, enjoy the superb views of downtown, with the harbour, the Baía de Todos os Santos and the offshore Itaparica Island.

Plano Inclinado,
Elevador Lacerda

Amongst the 17th-century buildings on Praça Tomé de Souza, the Palácio Tomé de Souza (Paço Municipal) and the Palácio Rio Branco, the former government palace, originally builtin 1549, but reconstructed in 1919, are particularly eye-catching. The only one that is open to visitors is the Palácio Rio Branco, with its magnificent hall of mirrors. Opening times: Mon 2 – 6pm, Tue – Fri 10am – noon and 2 – 6pm.

Paço Municipal,
Palácio Rio
Branco

The 18th-century Palácio Arquiepiscopal (Archbishop's Palace) at the southwestern end of the Praça da Sé square, was connected with the old cathedral by a passageway. The Praça da Sé has lost its role as elegant promenade, marketplace and church square to the tree-shaded Terreiro de Jesus next door. Here, live concerts several times a week help to make the square a favourite meeting point for locals and tourists, who particularly appreciate the now legendary Cantina da Lua.

Palácio
Arquiepiscopal,
Terreiro de Jesus

★ ★
Catedral
Basílica

Here on the Terreiro de Jesus, the Catedral Basílica, the church once attached to the former Jesuit college, shows its splendour to the full. The current cathedral is the fourth building on this spot and was only completed in 1656. The façade's panelling with Portuguese stone dates from the late 17th century, the **opulent interior decoration** however, was only tackled in the 18th century, reflecting various styles – from baroque to neoclassical. The high nave has a magnificent coffered ceiling. A passage behind the chancel leads to the sacristy, replete with impressive ornamental ceiling frescoes, and splendid cabinets made from the finest wood, ivory and tortoiseshell. The walls of the sacristy are lined with Portuguese azulejos. In the 18th century, the **Jesuit college** next door was the largest of its kind outside Rome. Since the expulsion of the Jesuits, this rambling building has only been used for secular purposes: in the 19th century, a part of the former convent took in the university's medical faculty. Today, three museums are housed here, focussing on Afro-Brazilian culture, archaeology and ethnology as well as the history of medicine. However, by far the largest part of the convent, along Rua Alfredo Brito, remains empty today and is increasingly taken over by tropical plants. Another part of the abbey – including the inner chapel – burned down in 1905. Opening times of the church and sacristy: Mon – Sat 8 – 11.30am and 2 – 5pm, Sun 10.30am – noon. The museums are open all day from 9am – 5pm.

★ ★
Convento
e Igreja São
Francisco

The southern corner of Terreiro de Jesus leads into the pedestrianized area of Praça de Padre Anchieta, bordered by Rua São Francisco and the main entrances of the church and the convent of São Francisco. Dating from 1587, the **Franciscan convent** was destroyed during the conflict with the Dutch and only rebuilt in 1686. Since 1752, the walls of the cloisters surrounding an interior courtyard have been tiled with beautiful Portuguese azulejo tiles – the largest collection of its kind in South America. Stylistically a mix of mannerism and baroque, the church was built between 1708 and 1750. The pediment is completely baroque, while the interior is a perfect example of the Lisbon ideal of a lavishly decorated »**golden church**«. Contrary to the binding architectural rules of this mendicant order, the church was given not one but three naves, all of them furnished with magnificent carvings. Gilding the main altar alone took two years. The carvings in the chancel chapel (1738 – 1740) blend with the azulejo images to form a harmonious whole. Opening times: Mon – Sat 8am – 5.30pm, Sun 7am – noon.

★ ★
Igreja da
Ordem Terceira
de São Francisco

Right next to the Franciscan convent, also with its main entrance giving onto the Rua São Francisco, it's hard to miss the church of the lay order, built in 1703. Its richly decorated façade immediately catches the eye, having been designed in the Churrigueresque style – which takes its name from the Spanish architect José Benito de Churriguerra (1650 – 1723) and is popular in Mexico. Figures of

Museu Abelardo Rodrigues

Rua Gregório de Matos, leading to the Pelourinho square, boasts the **Teatro Miguel Santana** (staging performances combining folklore and elements of Candomblé), the Solar do Ferrão (1701) with the Abelardo Rodrigues Museum, showing the most important private collection of sacred art in Brazil, as well as the headquarters of the »**Filhos de Gandhy**«, the traditional Afro-Brazilian music and carnival group. Only a stone's throw away is the information centre for the dynamic »Olodum« bloco afro, whose percussionists became famous worldwide through musical collaborations with Paul Simon and Michael Jackson.

Igreja do Santíssimo Sacramento do Paço

Already in the Pilar district – often also called Carmo – on the Ladeira do Paço, above an imposing flight of steps rises the Igreja do Santíssimo Sacramento do Paço, built in 1737. Despite boasting five rococo altars worth seeing, the church has been closed to visitors for a while.

Baedeker TIP

In pole position for carnival

During carnival, Praça Castro Alves is the meeting place for the floats coming from Campo Grande with numerous trios elétricos – booming articulated lorries bearing musicians and dancers – and the thousands of members of the »Filhos de Gandhy« afoxé pouring in from the Pelourinho, becoming one big mass of humanity dancing to the surging samba-reggae rhythms.

The group of buildings belonging to the Carmelite order, erected north of the Pelourinho on Largo do Carmo and consisting of church and convent, dates back to the late 16th century. Set ablaze in 1788, it was reconstructed 40 years later. Today the **Convento do Carmo** houses a hotel. In the lay order's church (Igreja da Ordem Terceira do Carmo), built in 1636 in the classical style, look out for the baroque altar. The museum attached to the church shows a fine, life-size sculpture of *Dead Christ*, carved from cedarwood by Francisco Chagas in 1710 and studded with rubies, as well as an organ with pipes imported from France.

Praça Castro Alves

The Praça Castro Alves is an important link between the upper and lower parts of town. The spacious square bears a monument erected in memory of Castro Alves, the Bahian poet and champion of Brazilian independence.

Casa de Ruy Barbosa

Running northeast from Praça Castro Alves, Rua Ruy Barbosa leads to the Casa de Ruy Barbosa, the former residence of the lawyer and author from Bahia, now used as a museum. Amongst the exhibits are awards, documents, manuscripts, photos and personal effects belonging to Ruy Barbosa. Access to the museum is via 12 Rua dos Capitães, near Rua da Ajuda.

A German priest taking a break outside the church →

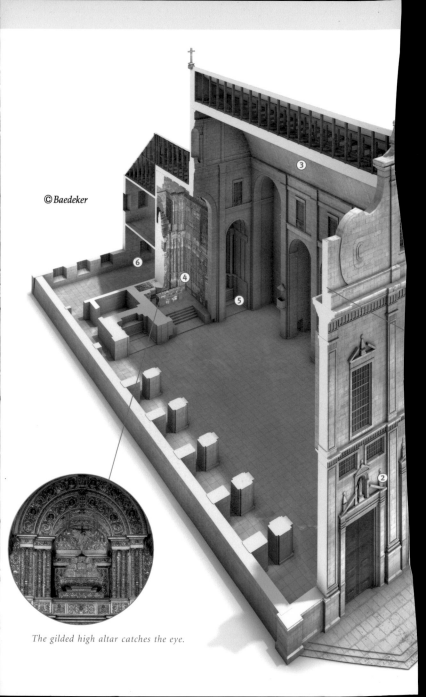

© Baedeker

The gilded high altar catches the eye.

Front view of Salvador's
Catedral Basílica

Bell towers on each side
frame the church front.

CATEDRAL BASÍLICA

✴ ✴ On Terreiro de Jesus, the reconstructed Catedral Basílica rises in all its splendour. Completed in 1656, its front is clad in Portuguese stone and the interior is lavishly decorated, with a gilded high altar, ceiling frescoes, precious wood, ivory and tortoiseshell.

Ⓧ Opening times:
Mon¬–Sat 8–11.30am and 2–5pm,
Sun 10.30am–12.30pm

① Façade
The church front was clad in stone brought from Portugal in the late 17th century.

② Statues of Jesuit saints
The statues of the three Jesuit saints Ignatius of Loyola, Francisco Xavier and Francisco Borja are carved from marble.

③ Coffered ceiling
A splendid baroque coffered ceiling adorns the nave.

④ High altar
Gilded and lavishly decorated: a visible symbol of the former wealth of the Jesuit order

⑤ Passage to the sacristy
To the right of the altar, a small corridor leads to the sacristy.

⑥ Sacristy
The ceiling is decorated with ornamental paintings and Portuguese azulejos adorn the walls.

From outside, the cathedral of Salvador seems fairly understated and inconspicuous.

saints and angels adorn the façade, whose richly ornate surfaces are veined with tendrils. Its interior was redecorated in the 19th century in the classical style and now includes a small **Museum of Sacred Art**. Opening times: Mon – Fri 8am – noon and 1 – 5pm.

✷ ✷ Pelourinho

Situated northwest of the Terreiro de Jesus, the part of the Old Town called Pelourinho (Pillory) is the baroque heart of Salvador's Upper Town. Although UNESCO, in 1985, declared this part of town to be Latin America's most important group of 17th and 18-th century colonial buildings and a **World Heritage Site**, this did nothing to stop its dilapidation. It took a massive urban regeneration effort from 1992 onwards to completely redevelop the old run-down part of town. In several stages, hundreds of old sobrado houses were cleared and renovated, roofs retiled and courtyards gutted. Today, the Pelourinho district is a promenade – policed until late at night – for tourists and locals. It boasts popular bars, good restaurants and open-air stages such as the Largo de Tereza Batista, the Berro D'Água or the Largo de Pelourinho – made famous by the public rehearsals of the musicians of the bloco afro »Olodum«.

The Pelourinho is just the place for a leisurely stroll.

The front end of the slanting Largo do Pelourinho is taken up by two spacious town houses, both accommodating museums: the Museu da Cidade, with exhibits on the Afro-Brazilian Orixá deities, and the Jorge Amado foundation, which tells in detail the story of the life and works of Bahia's most famous writer.

Museu da Cidade, Fundação Casa de Jorge Amado

The eastern flank of the Pelourinho square is lined by several two-storey sobrado houses, one of them occupied by the restaurant attached to the »Senac« catering college. Next to the gabled houses, with two to three storeys, follow the portal and belltowers of the blue-washed parish church of Nossa Senhora do Rosário dos Pretos. The church was built between 1704 and 1781 by slaves working countless night shifts. The figures of the saints in the interior of the »Our Lady of the Rosary of Black People« church have a dark skin colour.

✷ NS do Rosário dos Pretos

Igreja e Mosteiro de São Bento, Igreja e Convento de Santa Teresa

Southwest of Praça Castro Alves, Avenida Sete de Setembro is lined with an extensive group of buildings belonging to the Benedictine order, the Igreja e Mosteiro de São Bento. The 17th-century church, crowned by a dome, and parts of the convent (begun as early as 1581), can be accessed via the Largo de São Bento. Inside the convent, the **Museu de Arte Sacra** shows sculptures by the monk Agostinho and some fine pieces of goldsmith's work. The church was designed by the Benedictine monk Frei Macário de São João, who is also credited with the designs for the nearby Igreja e Convento de Santa Teresa group of buildings that have more architectural interest. The church and the former convent of the Discalceates (Shoeless Carmelites) mendicant order were built from 1670 onwards on Rua do Sodré; today, the convent houses another museum of sacred art worth seeing, with numerous baroque exhibits.

Islands in Baía de Todos os Santos

The Baía de Todos os Santos is dotted with numerous islands, amongst them the Ilha da Madre de Deus (Mother of God Island) off Candeias, with a church dating back to the 17th century. The Ilha dos Frades is blessed with beautiful waterfalls and coconut palms, while the inhabitants of Ilha da Maré, with its colonial church of Nossa Senhora das Neves, specialize in the manufacture of bone lace.

Itaparica

With its 240 sq km/93 sq miles, the Ilha de Itaparica is one of the largest marine islands in Brazil. Some 49,000 people live on the small island, which is graced by beautiful beaches and forms a huge breakwater, sealing off and protecting the interior of the Baía de Todos os Santos. The ferries going to the island depart from the Terminal Marítimo de São Joaquim (Água dos Meninos) at 1051 Avenida Oscar Pontes, in Salvador's Lower Town. The one-hour boat trip affords some attractive views of Salvador's urban skyline.

Around Salvador

São Francisco do Conde

Counting 25,000 inhabitants and situated 81km/50 miles northwest of Salvador, São Francisco do Conde is reached via the BR-324 federal road leading to Feira de Santana and the BA-522 rural road. The small town on the northern shore of All Saints' Bay boasts numerous buildings from the colonial era, such as the church of **Santo Antônio** and the **convent of São Francisco** – both dating from the 18th century and tiled with Portuguese azulejo picture tiles – on Praça Artur Sales, at the corner with Rua João Florêncio Gomes. The centre preserves the Paço Municipal (former municipal administration and prison) and various residential houses worth seeing. On the island of Cajaíba, ten minutes from town by boat, there are sugar cane mills and distilleries, as well as houses from the colonial era. An exclusive five-star resort is currently being developed on the island.

Beach in the Baía de Todos os Santos

Santo Amaro

São Francisco do Conde's neighbouring town, Santo Amaro, has some 56,500 inhabitants and is a centre of sugar cane cultivation in the northern Recôncavo Baiano, the name given to the area around the Baía de Todos os Santos. The town, situated 84km/52 miles from Salvador, has preserved some imposing buildings from the 17th and 18th centuries, amongst them the **Convento dos Humildes** convent, erected in 1793 on Praça Padre Inácio Terxeira do São Araújo. Amongst the buildings on Praça da Purificação, with its fountain (1856), look for the Paço Municipal (1727) and the parish church of Nossa Senhora da Purificação from 1668. The church is decorated with Portuguese paintings and azulejo tiles. As part of the Festa de Nossa Senhora da Purificação festival (Jan/Feb), the church is ritually »washed« by the followers of the Candomblé faith.

★
Cachoeira

Cachoeira, a historic town with a population of 30,500, was once the stronghold of the Brazilian troops that defeated the Portuguese army in 1822 and 1823. It is situated in the west of the Recôncavo region, 40km/25 miles west of Santo Amaro and 116km/72 miles from Salvador, where tobacco plantations mingle with the sugar cane planta-tions. Particularly worth seeing in the town is the **Casa da Câmara e Cadeia** (town hall and prison) built between 1698 and 1712. During the War of Independence it was the seat of the government of Bahia, today, it houses the Paço Municipal and Historical Archive. Also on

*In capoeira, good body
control is essential.*

MYSTICAL SUBCULTURE

**The martial art dance of capoeira shares its origin with the syncretistic
religions of the Candomblé and Umbanda, namely the two centuries of
oppression of black slaves in Brazil. In the northeastern state of Bahia, those
elements of Afro-Brazilian culture have remained in their purest form.**

The **capoeira** begins with a ladainha, a
solo litany praising one of the African
orixá deities or a capoeira master, or
mestre. The choir of dancers and
musicians responds to the call of the
capoeirista leading the song. This is
the moment when the typical percussion instruments come in: the berim-
bau, the pandeiro and the agogó, a
metal double bell. Their driving
rhythms provide the adrenalizing
musical setting for the capoeira.

The »fight«

Two capoeiristas step into the centre
and start their dancing duel, very
slowly, as if in slow-motion. At this
point, the performers still seem like
two rivals carefully gauging each
other, concentrated down to the tips
of their fingers. When the large
atabaque drum takes over the rhythm,
the movements become faster and
more purposeful, without actually
landing the feigned hits. Attacks,
feints, handsprings and counter attacks in fast sequence are under-
pinned, to dramatic effect, by the hard
beat of thin sticks relentlessly working

the hide of the small repinique drums,
and only finish with the surging
applause of the onlookers, quick to
gather around the performers.

Origin of the capoeira

Capoeira was developed by displaced
Bantus from West Africa, who were
forced into slave labour on the sugar
cane plantations of Bahia. Converting
their dances into a defence technique
allowed them to use their whole **body
as a weapon**, as slaves were prohibited
from bearing real arms. The name
capoeira is purely Brazilian; it is not
found in any African language. Initially musical accompaniment was only
added as a camouflage for the martial
arts training, as any suspicion of
organized resistance would inevitably
have resulted in harsh punishment by
the slave owners.

Escape to the cities

In the early 19th century, more and
more capoeristas left the plantations
for the cities, where they found refuge
in the terreiros, in return protecting
these **Candomblé** temples. The autho-

rities treated them as outlaws, ruffians and good-for-nothings, and Bahia's mounted police cracked down extremely hard both on capoeira groups and on Candomblé congregations. In spite of this, Afro-Brazilian orixá deities continue to be worshipped fervently, and the attraction exerted by this community of belief, initially formed as a replacement for the family ties torn apart by slavery, remains unbroken.

The gods of Candomblé

Since then, tens of thousands of **terreiros** have been dedicated to the African orixás – such as Oxalá, the Prince of Peace and creator of the world, Iansã, the goddess of the sea, commanding the winds and storms, or Xangô, the boisterous master of thunder and lightning - particularly in large cities outside Bahia with a high percentage of black inhabitants. The terreiros are inhabited by the Candomblé priests. Most congregations are headed by a priestess, by the name of Ialorixá or »mae de santo« (Mother of the Deity). During the protracted religious ceremonies, the mae de santo is supported by the ogãos, male council members, and a certain number of women, ekedes. The ekedes are charged with assisting the **»filhas do santo«** (Daughters of the Deity) when, caught in a state of trance and oblivious to their surroundings, they become mediums for the orixá deities summoned by sustained drumming.

Umbanda

The relatively recent Umbanda religion emerged around 1920, spreading

»*Any suspicion of organized resistance would inevitably have resulted in harsh punishment by the slave owners.*«

initially in the southeast of Brazil, and going on to increasingly gain followers in Bahia. Umbanda is mainly associated with the Brazilian middle classes and owes a lot more to Catholicism and Indian natural religions than Candomblé. Despite their African origin, Umbanda rituals are celebrated in Portuguese.

the Praça da Aclamação, the 18th-century church of the Carmelite Third Order (Ordem Terceira do Carmo) is furnished in the rococo style, with gilded altars and wooden carvings from Macau, as well as a baroque altar. The parish church of Nossa Senhora do Rosário, built between 1693 and 1754 on Rua Ana Nery has attractive ceiling frescoes and Portuguese azulejos. From the square of the 18th-century Nossa Senhora da Conceição do Monte church there are splendid views of Cachoeira and the neighbouring São Felix.

Valença

The town of Valença, with some 77,500 inhabitants and 248km/154 miles southwest of Salvador, has well-preserved colonial buildings such as the Paço Municipal and the Sagrado Coração de Jesus parish church, erected in 1759 on Largo da Matriz, as well as the Igreja Nossa Senhora do Amparo (Alto da Colina). With a little luck, visitors can watch saveiros (paragliders) being built on the Rio Una or explore the beaches of Guaibinzinho, Taquari and Ponta do Curral, 20km/12.5 miles from the town centre. The main attraction however, is the surrounding islands with their beautiful, unspoilt beaches and some of the oldest settlements in Brazil.

Ilha de Tinharé, Morro de São Paulo

On the Ilha de Tinharé, a good 1.5 hours from Valença by boat, the attractive car-free holiday town of Morro de São Paulo boasts swimming beaches totalling 20km/12.5 miles and lined by palm groves and coral reefs, which form pools at low tide. Standing on a hill is a fortress dating back to 1630, while the lighthouse (Farol) dates from 1835. The church, dedicated to the patron saint, **Nossa Senhora da Luz**, was built in 1855. Some 4km/2.5 miles from here, on the way to Gamboa, look out for the freshwater spring of Fonte do Céu (Heavenly Spring). In peak season, Morro de São Paulo gets very busy. Passenger ferries to Ilha de Tinharé depart from Salvador's Lower Town from the Terminal Turístico Marítimo, at 410 Avenida da França, opposite the Mercado Modelo. The crossing takes about two hours.

Ilha de Cairu

The Ilha de Cairu, 30km/18.5 miles from Valença, harbours one of the first urban settlements in the country. Today, Cairu is nearly completely abandoned, but still preserves a rich heritage of colonial buildings, such as the Nossa Senhora do Rosário church and the convent of Santo Antônio (1661). Boats running between Valença and the Ilha Boipeba regularly dock at Cairu.

Ilha de Boipeba

The estuary of the Rio do Inferno, only 400m/437 yd wide, separates Tinharé Island to the north from Boipeba Island. However, the crossing from Valença to the village, with only 300 inhabitants, takes around five hours. The main attractions of Boipeba, founded in 1565 on the mouth of the Rio do Inferno, are its magnificent beaches – Tassimirim, Cueira and Moreré – with the fishermen's saveiros gliding through the clear water, and, at low tide, the natural water pools, only 500m/545yd from the coastline. During rough seas, the ferry connections to the neighbouring Ilha de Tinharé are suspended.

Coast north of Salvador

The stretch of coast north of Salvador is accessed via the Estrada do Côco, as the BA-099 from Itapoã to the border of Sergipe is known for the extensive palm groves lining the road. Access roads branching off from the trunk road lead to the swimming beaches of Lauro de Freitas, Buraquinho, Busca Vida, Jauá, Interlagos, Arembepe, Foz do Jacuípe, Itacimirim, Praia do Forte, Ponta Acu da Torre, and Imbassaí, as well as to Porto Sauípe, 65km/40 miles from Salvador.

✳ Estrada do Côco

Seventy kilometres/43 miles from Salvador, the sandy beaches ahead of Praia do Forte, lined with slim coconut palms, have particular scenic appeal. On the beach before Praia do Forte, look for the largest Brazilian **centre of the Tamar project** for marine turtle conservation. Here the eye is drawn to the nearby ruins of the Casa da Torre de Garcia d'Avila, a magnificent 16th-century ranch, described by chronicler Fernão Cardim as »the most beautiful in all Brazil, completely made of stucco (...), with a hexagonal vault and three entrance gates, and lavish ornaments«. All that remains today are the mighty arcades, a few walls and the hexagonal chapel with alvenaria vault and pyramid roof, reminiscent of similar buildings in the Portuguese Alentejo region.

✳ Praia do Forte, Casa da Torre de Garcia d'Avila

Santarém

Rh 47

State: Pará (PA)
Altitude: 51m/167ft

Population: 263,000

Founded at the confluence of the Rio Tapajós and the Amazon, the city of Santarém is the second-largest in Pará state and one of the oldest settlements in the entire Amazon Basin.

What to see in and around Santarém

Outside the city, the Encontro das Águas marks the confluence of the Amazon with the crystal-clear, blueish-green waters of the Rio Tapajós. For the best views, head for the Mirante Tapajós on Rua Colonel Joaquim Braga, behind the Frei Ambrósio school.

Encontro das Águas

Situated some 15km/9 miles outside the city, in the area flooded by the Amazon, the Maicá Lagoon boasts the Pouso das Garças (Herons' Rest), where at sunset hundreds of white herons congregate.

Maicá Lagoon

▶ VISITING SANTARÉM

INFORMATION
Santarém Tur
Tel. (093) 35 22-48 47

GETTING THERE
Airport
Aeroporto Internacional
 Rodovia Fernando Guilhom
Tel. (092) 35 22-43 28

Bus station
Avenida Cuiabá
Tel. (091) 35 22-33 92

WHERE TO EAT
▶ **Inexpensive**
Peixaria Piracatu
Avenida Mendonça Furtado 174
Prainha district
Tel. (093) 35 23-51 10

Together with the market, this restaurant, specializing in the preparation of Amazon fish, is the most important meeting place in Santarém.

WHERE TO STAY
▶ **Mid-range**
Amazon Park
Avenida Mendonça Furtado 4120
Liberdade district
Tel. (093) 35 23-28 00
www.amazonparkhotel.com.br
Built in the 1970s, this hotel features lobbies and halls in cathedral-like dimensions. 60 air-conditioned rooms and a park-like garden with pool, the best restaurant in town and information stalls for all of the local tour agencies. This is the nerve centre of Santarém.

Alter do Chão

The fishing village of Alter do Chão on the Rio Tapajós can be reached by boat from Santarém in two hours, or overland after a 38km/24-mile drive southwest on a road following the river bank. Alter do Chão has the most beautiful river beach of Amazonia; also, the **Centro da Preservação do Arte Indígena** (Centre for the Preservation of Indian Art) in Rua Dom Macedo Costa is worth seeing.

Parque Nacional da Amazônia

Established in 1974, the Amazonia National Park, situated north of the Rio Tapajós on the territory of the municipalities of Itaituba (Pará) and Maués (Amazonas), stretches across an area of 994,000ha/nearly 2.5 million acres. At least a tenth of the park has been irretrievably destroyed by gold prospectors, the rest consists of dense, primary lowland rainforest boasting a great diversity of mammal species, but no tourist infrastructure whatsoever. Visits should only be undertaken with local guides. For information, contact the IBAMA office in the nearby small town of Itaituba, tel. (091) 35 18-15 30. To get to the national park from Santarém involves a 370km/230-mile drive southwest; access is via a relief road of the Transamazônica, leading via Belterra and Alter da Chão, from where there are boats to Itaituba.

The wild beauty of the Amazonian rainforest ➔

Santo Ângelo

Rh 60

State: Rio Grande do Sul (RS)   **Population:** 77,000
Altitude: 281m/922ft

Santo Ângelo is the most important town to have developed out of the 17th-century Jesuit missions in southern Brazil. To protect the Guaraní Indians from slave hunters, Jesuits founded the Guaraní Republic, consisting of 30 mission stations in what is today Paraguay, Argentina and Brazil.

Seven of them – known as Sete Povos das Missões (Seven Missions) – lie in southern Brazil: in addition to Santo Ângelo there is São Nicolão, São Lourenço, São Luís Gonzaga, São João Batista, São Miguel and São Borja. The expulsion of the Jesuits from the Portuguese-ruled territories from 1759 onwards spelt the end of the missions, which were left to go to ruin.

The remains of Jesuit missionary activity in São Miguel das Missões

What to see in and around Santo Ângelo

The most important sight in town is the cathedral, a 1929 replica of the church of São Miguel das Missões (see below). The cathedral holds a wooden statue depicting the *Dead Christ*, which was rescued from the redução (»reductions« was the name for the fortified villages where the Indians lived under the supervision of the Jesuits) of São Miguel.

Catedral

The Centro de Cultura Missioneira (Centre of Missionary Culture) in Rua da Universidade de Missões is a historical museum with exhibits from the Sete Povos das Missões, the Seven Missions of the Jesuits.

Centro de Cultura Missioneira

São Miguel das Missões (pop 7,700) can be reached from Santo Ângelo via the BR-285 (53km/33 miles along the São Borja road). The town, listed as a UNESCO World Heritage Site, still boasts the ruins of the church of São Miguel as the only reminder of mission architecture in Brazil. The church, erected between 1737 and 1744, was designed by the Italian Jesuit **Giovanni Batista Primoli**. As a model, Primoli used *Il Gesú*, the mother church of the order in Rome, the façade of which was to influence those of Jesuit churches all over the world for centuries. The Missions Museum, right next to the church on Praça de São Miguel, was designed by **Lúcio Costa** (1902–1998) and built using material from ruins, and stones from the quarry once exploited by the Jesuits. It shows fragments of sculptures and remains of buildings collected in the Sete Povos das Missões; an audiovisual presentation illustrates the history of the mission stations. Opening times: daily 9am–noon and 2–6pm.

✳ ✳ São Miguel das Missões

▶ SANTO ÂNGELO

INFORMATION
Praça Pinheiro Machado
Tel. (055) 33 12-01 00
www.santoangelo.rs.gov.br

GETTING THERE
Airport
Sepé Tiaraju
Tel. (055) 33 13-24 60

Bus station
Rua Sete de Setembro
Tel. (055) 33 13-26 18

Some 30km/18 miles southwest of Santo Ângelo, look for the remains of the São João Batista mission, with on one wall the relief image of Jesuit priest Father Anton Sepp.

São João Batista

Of the Redução São Lourenço, 65km/40 miles southwest of Santo Ângelo, only the ruins of the church, built in 1626, remain. It is a similar picture in, the first of the seven mission stations, situated 125km/77 miles west of Santo Ângelo.

Redução São Lourenço

São Luís Gonzaga The main attraction of São Luís Gonzaga (pop 70,000), a town situated 80km/50 miles west of Santo Ângelo, is the Santuário Caaró pilgrimage church, erected in 1626, where to this day pilgrims worship the blessed Jesuit brothers **Roque Gonzales and Afonso Rodrigues**, the founders of the Guaraní Republic.

Santos

Sb 57

State: São Paulo (SP) **Population:** 418,000
Altitude: 2m/6ft

The port town of Santos occupies the eastern part of São Vicente island. Spreading out around the port of Vila São Vicente, established in 1534, the town had to wait for its heyday until the mid-19th century, when the coffee boom started in São Paulo.

Santos quickly became the world's foremost point of export for coffee, and today still boasts the most significant port facilities in Brazil.

What to see in Santos

Largo Marquês de Monte Alegre — The access road to Santos (SP-150) passes close to the seafront by the Largo Marquês de Monte Alegre in the Valongo district, with the Rede Ferroviária Federal railway station of 1867, modelled on London's Victoria Station. Rising on the same square are the church (built between 1640 and 1691) the chapel and the convent of Santo Antônio do Valongo.

Mosteiro de São Bento — On the other side of the road leading into Santos rise the Morro São Bento and Monte Serrat. The former has the one-time convent of São Bento (1650), with a **Museum of Sacred Art**. The entrance to the museum is at 795 Rua Santa Joana d'Arc.

Monte Serrat — From Praça Correia de Melo in the centre of Santos, a cable car leads up to Monte Serrat. Its peak is occupied by a chapel, erected in 1609 and dedicated to the mountain's patron saint Nossa Senhora do Monte Serrat. From this height there are sweeping views across the city and the port. Operating hours: daily 8am – 8pm.

Convento do Carmo — Rua Quinze de Novembro leads into the Praça Barão do Rio Branco square, with the Carmelite convent (1589) and the Chapel of the Third Order (1760). The latter is most notable for the paintings by the monk **Jesuíno de Monte Carmelo** and those executed by **Benedito Calixto**. The funeral chapel of the Andrada family houses the remains of José Bonifácio de Andrada e Silva (1763 – 1838), the »father of Brazilian independence«, and his brothers.

VISITING SANTOS

INFORMATION

Disk Tur
Tel. (013) 32 22-41 66
www.santos.sp.gov.br

Informações Turísticas
Aquário Municipal office
Avenida Bartolomeu de Gusmão
Ponta da Praia
Tel. (013) 32 36-99 96

GETTING THERE

Bus station
Praça dos Andradas 45
Tel. (013) 32 19-21 94

WHERE TO EAT

▶ **Moderate**
Tertúlia
Avenida Bartolomeu de Gusmão 187
Ponta da Praia district

Tel. (013) 32 61-16 41
Rodízio-style meat, fresh from the
churrasco grill

WHERE TO STAY

▶ **Mid-range**
Mendes Panorama
Rua Euclides da Cunha 15
Gonzaga district
Tel. (013) 32 89-26 27
www.grupomendes.com.br
Beach hotel with 104 rooms (some
reserved for non-smokers) with air-
conditioning and TV. Internet access
and beach service. All credit cards
accepted.

Avenidas Presidente Wilson and Bartolomeu de Gusmão lead along **City beaches**
the coast to the various beaches of Santos, which total 7km/4.3 miles
in length. The best are Praias José
Menino, Gonzaga, Boqueirão, Em-
baré and Ponta da Praia. The Avenida Bartolomeu de Gusmão ends
in Ponta da Praia district. From
the Ponte dos Práticos, boats leave
for trips around Santos Bay.

On Avenida Bartolomeu de Gusmão, the **Museu de Pesca** (Fishing
Museum) shows an extensive col-
lection of model ships, stuffed fish and the massive bones of a
whale. Opening times: Wed – Sun 9am – 5pm.

> ! **Baedeker** TIP
>
> **Passeio de Bonde**
> In a 15-minute round trip, restored trams, dating
> back to 1910, pass the town's most important
> sights. The point of departure is Praça Mauá.
> Operating hours: Tue – Sun 11am – 5pm.

At the docking point for the Guarujá ferries on the **Ponte dos Práti-** **Museu do Mar**
cos, only a few blocks from the beach, the Sea Museum at 81 Rua
República do Equador exhibits stuffed marine animals, shells and
corals, as well as technical equipment used in oceanography. Opening
times: daily 9am – 6pm.

The port of Santos is an important factor in the economy of the region.

Around Santos

Baixada Santista Santos is a good base for trips to the coastal towns of the Baixada Santista. To the north lie the fashionable resorts of Guarujá and Bertioga, to the south São Vicente – once the starting point for the settlement of the entire surrounding area – Praia Grande and Mongaguá.

Bertioga Bertioga (pop 30,000), 67km/41 miles north of Santos, boasts swimming beaches with a total length of 44km/27 miles. The most interesting of these, Praia São Lourenço, 10km/6.2 miles long (21km/13 miles from the town centre), Praia Guaratuba (32km/20 miles) and Praia Boracéia (35km/22 miles), are situated northeast of the town and offer good water quality.

Forte São João Rising on Praia da Ensada near the port of Bertioga, the Forte São João, erected in 1547, is the oldest coastal fort in the whole of Brazil.

From here, ferries run to Guarujá. Amongst the events held in Bertioga, the Festa da Tainha (Mullet Festival), celebrated in July, is particularly popular.

Praia Grande

The origins of the coastal city of Praia Grande (pop 194,000), 16km/ 10 miles southwest of Santos, go back to the 16th century, when the first immigrants from São Vicente settled here. Today the city is overrun with holiday homes and apartment blocks, and in summer there are thousands of holiday-makers. The beaches of Canto do Forte (1km/0.6 miles north of the city centre), Boqueirão (centre) and Guilhermina (1km/0.6 miles south) are considered polluted. The situation is not much better on the beaches of Tupy, Cidad Ocian, Vila Mirim and Vila Caiçara – which doesn't stop the locals from flocking to the swimming bays in the Antarctic summer (Dec – Feb).

Mongaguá

The community of Mongaguá (pop 35,000), 41km/25 miles from Santos, owes its charm to its quiet beaches, totalling 12km/7.5 miles in length, and the rampant, lush vegetation of the Serras de Guaperuvi, do Barigui and de Mongaguá. The sea is polluted, at least in parts, off the beaches of São Paulo, Praia Grande (4km/2.5 miles from the centre), Vera Cruz (3km/1.8 miles), Agenor Campos (9km/ 5.5 miles) and occasionally in Flórida Mirim (12km/7.5 miles). For good swimming, head for the beach of Balneário América, 15km/9.5 miles away.

⋆ São João del Rei

Sc 56

State: Minas Gerais (MG)
Altitude: 910m/2,985ft

Population: 79,000

Founded in 1699, at the time of the gold rush in the south of Minas Gerais, São João del Rei was one of the main theatres of conflict in the War of the Emboabas (1708 – 1709).

At the time, the bandeirantes from São Paulo, who had discovered the veins of gold, were fighting for supremacy with the Portuguese and Brazilians flocking in droves from other regions to the Região das Minas (Mining Region). The town is dominated by the **Rio das Mortes** (River of the Dead), with its old stone bridges and merchants' houses from the colonial era. São João del Rei is the birthplace of José da Silva Xavier, known as Tiradentes (Teethpuller), the leader of the local independence movement, who was later executed. The first elected president of Brazil after the military dictatorship (1964 to 1985), Tancredo Neves, was also from here, although he died before taking office.

What to see in and around São João del Rei

NS do Pilar — Dedicated in 1721 to the town's patron saint Nossa Senhora do Pilar, the cathedral in Rua Getúlio Vargas boasts several gilded altars from the period around 1745. The nave and sacristy feature rococo ceilings, while the chancel has wall frescoes. The façade of the church was designed in the classical style.

▶ **SÃO JOÃO DEL REI**

INFORMATION
Praça Frei Orlando 90
Tel. (0 32) 33 79-29 51

GETTING THERE
Bus station
Rua Cristóvão Colombo 599
Tel. (032) 33 54-15 25

Near the cathedral of Nossa Senhora do Pilar, and also in Rua Getúlio Vargas, a little further along, the **Museu de Arte Sacra** (Museum of Sacred Art) displays exhibits from the town's churches, among them a figure of Christ mourned by Maria Magdalena, studded with rubies symbolizing drops of blood.

NS do Rosário — Southwest of the cathedral, the Largo do Rosário (Praça Gastão da Cunha) features the church of Nossa Senhora do Rosário, built in 1719 by slaves, and two merchants' houses, the Solar dos Lustosas and the Solar dos Neves, birthplace of Tancredo Neves.

NS do Carmo — Northeast of the cathedral of Nossa Senhora do Pilar, Rua Getúlio Vargas leads into the Praça Carlos Gomes square, with the church of Nossa Senhora do Carmo (1734). The church houses some works by the great artist **Aleijadinho**. Nearby stands the Chafariz do Largo do Carmo, a 19th-century fountain.

Museu Ferroviário — Avenida Presidente Tancredo Neves runs along Rio das Mortes towards the arterial road to Belo Horizonte and Rio de Janeiro. Railway enthusiasts will want to head for Avenida Hermílio Alves, running along the other riverbank, with the well-equipped Museu Ferroviário (Railway Museum), including the 19th-century railway station and rolling stock. Opening times: Tue – Sun 9am – 11am and 1 to 5pm.

São Francisco de Assis — Heading southwest from Praça dos Expedicionários leads to Praça Frei Orlando, graced with some of the town's most important buildings. The dominant feature is the splendid church of São Francisco de Assis, designed in 1774 by Aleijadinho and decorated with sculptures executed by the master sculptor. The façade of the baroque church, with slightly outward-curving side walls, shows relief ornaments of soapstone, with the coat of arms of the Third Order and of the Portuguese crown beneath. On Sundays, 9-o'clock mass is accompanied by baroque music.

✳ Tiradentes

Named after the hero of the independence movement, the town of Tiradentes, 14km/8.5 miles east of São João del Rei, grew up out of nowhere during the gold rush. Today however, it has only a little under 6,000 inhabitants, living in a nearly untouched colonial town whose authentic architecture is like a trip back in time. This explains why Tiradentes is used as a histori-cal backdrop in practically all tele-novelas (soap operas) set in the time of slavery. Most noteworthy amongst its ecclesiastical buildings, is the parish church of **Matriz de Santo Antônio** (1710), with its gilded altars and a colourful painted organ manufactured in 1779. The design for the façade, completed in 1810, was one of Aleijadinho's last works. The most eye-catching feature of the interior is the chancel, crowned by festoons and supported by carved pillars. The Padre Toledo Museum is housed in the former residence of the Inconfidente priest at 190 Rua Padre Toledo, where the conspirators gathered for the first time.

> ! **Baedeker** TIP
>
> **By steam train to Tiradentes**
> The trip from São João del Rei railway station to Tiradentes takes about 30 minutes – a nostalgic railway journey, with a hissing steam engine belching black smoke. The tourist train runs Fridays to Sundays – the departure from São João del Rei is at 10am and 3pm, with the return from Tiradentes at 1pm and 5pm.

✳ ✳ São Luís

Sc 47

State: Maranhão (MA)
Altitude: 24m/79ft

Population: 870,500

Today, the name is the only reminder of this city's French past: São Luís was the capital of France Equinoxiale, the colony set up by the French in 1612 in the north of Brazil on the island of São Luís in São Marcos Bay.

The architecture of São Luís is mainly Portuguese in style, its society marked by the descendants of African slaves. Much less touristy than Salvador, which is equally characterized by its African heritage, São Luís has managed to preserve an aura of tropical seclusion and ro-mantic contemplation. Strolling though the narrow lanes of the UNESCO-listed Old Town, its charms are hard to resist.

What to see in São Luís

Hardly anything in the townscape reminds the visitor of the French presence; the narrow streets and the multi-storeyed houses clad with

✳ ✳
Old Town

azulejos are typically Portuguese. In the historic centre of São Luís, entirely a listed UNESCO World Heritage Site, the close link to Portugal is even more evident: some houses have balconies with cast-iron balustrades, roof terraces and wraparound galleries with shutters designed to keep out the heat.

Cais da Sagração, Palácio dos Leões

A good walk through the Old Town might start on the Cais da Sagração, the harbour quay next to Largo do Palácio, where in former times boats and ships docked, carrying sugar and cotton for export. Only a few steps further along, in **Avenida Dom Pedro II**, the Palácio dos Leões (Lions' Palace) is open to visitors, today housing both the government and state art museum. A French fort once stood on this spot, which was used, up to 1615, to protect the capital of France Equinoxiale.

Painter in the Old Town of São Luís

The church on Praça Dom Pedro II, next to the Episcopal Palace, **Matriz da Sé**
was built between 1690 and 1699 by the Jesuits, but had to wait until
1763, the year that the Portuguese prime minister Marquês de Pombal expelled the Jesuits from the country, to become the seat of a
bishopric. In 1922, the church was
redesigned in the classical style.
Look out for the Matriz da Sé's
gilded high altar.

At 273 Rua Portugal in the Old
Town, look for the **Museu de Artes
Visuais** (Museum of Visual Arts),
showing works by artists from
Maranhão, as well as Portuguese
azulejos from the 19th and 20th
century. Opening times: Tue–Sun
9am–6pm.

A stone flight of stairs between Rua
Portugal and Djalma Dutra was
given the name of »**Beco da Catarina Mina**«, in memory of the emancipated slave Catarina Rosa de
Jesus, who knew how to capture
the hearts of the social elite and
rose to power over land and slaves
around São Luís.

The Casa do Maranhão museum
was established in the former customs house (Alfândega) in Rua do
Trapiche in the historic heart of

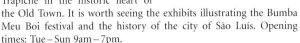

São Luís

the Old Town. It is worth seeing the exhibits illustrating the Bumba
Meu Boi festival and the history of the city of São Luís. Opening
times: Tue–Sun 9am–7pm.

**Casa do
Maranhão**

Built between 1815 and 1817, the Arthur Azevedo Theatre in Rua do   **Teatro Arthur
Sol** was one of the first to be built in a Brazilian provincial capital.   **Azevedo**
The **classical theatre**, completely renovated in 1993, is today considered one of the most modern stages in Brazil. Guided tours: Mon to
Fri 3pm.

The façade of the Fonte do Ribeirão, a public well built in 1796 in   **Fonte do
Rua dos Afogados** (Largo do Ribeirão), shows three latticed windows   **Ribeirão**
hiding subterranean passageways that serve as drains and to collect
ground water. The passages span the foundations of large parts of
the historic Old Town, stretching all the way to the Carmelite
church. Figures of Neptune grace the five spouts of the well.

▶ VISITING SÃO LUÍS

INFORMATION
Informações Turísticas
Aeroporto Marechal Cunha Machado
Avenida dos Libaneses
Tel. (098) 32 44-45 00

Avenida Ana Jansen office
Ponte d'Areia district
Tel. (098) 32 27-84 84
www.guiasaoluis.com.br

GETTING THERE
Airport
Marechal C Machado
Av Santos-Dumont
Tel. (098) 32 17-61 01

Bus station
Avenida dos Franceses
Santo Antônio
Tel. (098) 32 49-24 88

EVENTS
Several popular festivals are cele-
brated in São Luís, some of them of
African origin, e. g. the Tambor de
Crioula (June) and the Tambor de
Mina (July), dedicated to St Sebastian.

Bumba Meu Boi
The most important folklore performance however is the Bumba Meu
Boi, combining Indian, African and
Luso-Brazilian influences. On 22
June, two days before the feast of St
John, the protagonist of the song and
dance performance, the boi (ox), is
»born«, ready to be »baptized« the
following day at the group's ritual site.
This is the prelude to a party that lasts
until 30 July, or even into September,
when the boi – a structure made from
wood and buriti palm fibre, covered
in embroidered velvet, glass beads and
colourful sequins, all hiding a dancer
– finally »dies«. As the feast was
originally a parody of the slave-own-
ing society by the oppressed, it was
sporadically banned by the authorities.

WHERE TO EAT
▶ Inexpensive
A Varanda
Rua Genésio Rego 185
Monte Castelo district
Tel. (098) 32 32-84 28
Family restaurant with terrace, spe-
cializing in fish and seafood. A dining
experience to be savoured at a
leisurely pace, as the preparation of
the dishes takes time.

Cabana do Sol
Rua João Damasceno 24 A
Praia do Calhau
Tel. (098) 32 35-25 86
Regional fish and meat dishes, some
barbecued. Decidedly large portions.

WHERE TO STAY
▶ Mid-range
São Luís Park Hotel
Avenida Avicêna
Praia do Calhau
Tel. (098) 32 16-545
www.accorhotels.com.br
Best hotel in São Luís, 10km/6.2 miles
outside the city centre. A private park
surrounds 111 well-appointed rooms,
a restaurant, bar and pool.

▶ Budget
① *Portas da Amazônia*
Rua do Giz 129
Praia Grande
Tel. (098) 32 22-99 37
www.portasdaamazonia.com.br
Eleven generous rooms in a historic
townhouse

São Luís Map

South of Praia Grande, visitors can see more interesting buildings from the colonial era. At 43 Rua Jacinto Maia, the Cafua das Mercês, the former slave market, today houses a museum (Museu do Negro) which, among other items, shows a torture chair. Opening times: Tue Sat 2pm – 5.30pm.

Cafua das Mercês
⊙

Built in the first half of the 17th century, the Igreja do Desterro (Church of Banishment) gave its name to the square on which it stands. The oldest church in all of Maranhão, it was plundered and destroyed by the Dutch in 1641, but later rebuilt.

Igreja do Desterro

Beaches Unfolding near São Luís are several beaches, nestling between dunes. However, watch out for the breakers that can reach heights of up to 7m/23ft, and also the cars that speed across some of the coastal stretches. Amongst the most popular beaches are Praia do Calhau (8km/5 miles out of town), Ponte d'Areia in the north of the island, with the **ruined fort of Santo Antônio** (1691), the beach of São Marcos, unsuitable for swimming but boasting the remains of the late 18th-century Fort of São Marcos, and finally Praia de Araçaji, 19km/12 miles outside São Luís, one of the most enticing beaches on this whole stretch of coast.

A crumbling idyll: Alcântara

Alcântara

The town of Alcântara (pop 21,500), situated on the other side of São Marcos Bay, on the mainland, has been declared a national cultural monument. Situated some 20km/12.5 miles from São Luís, it can be reached by ferry (80min), air taxi (10min) or – making a detour – by bus (53km/33 miles). Typical of Alcântara are its churches and the houses tiled with colourful azulejos – testimony to a time when the town was a favourite refuge of the rural nobility of Maranhão. Sadly, of many buildings only ruins remain, often no more than hollow shells. However, high tech has also now made an entrance into Alcântara, in the shape of the nearby **Centro Aerospacial**, where the Brazilian aerospace sector is undertaking its space research.

Matriz de São Matias Most of the town's old buildings are grouped around Praça Gomes de Castro and along Rua Grande. On the square rises the ruined main church of São Matias, which was erected in 1648 not far from the »pelourinho« (pillory).

✱
Museu Histórico de Alcântara
🕐
The town hall is based in the former prison, the 18th-century Cadeia Pública, also located on Praça Gomes de Castro. The historical museum of Alcântara can also be found here, exhibiting a fine collection of sacred art and furniture from the 18th and 19th centuries. Opening times: daily 9am – 1.45pm.

In the church of Nossa Senhora do Carmo, dating from 1663, look for a fine baroque altar.

In the same street, the Museu do Folclore (Museum for Folk Art) exhibits effigies and standards used in the traditional Festa do Divino (Festival of the Divine Holy Ghost).

NS do Carmo, Museu do Folclore

✳ Parque Nacional dos Lençóis Maranhenses

The Lençóis Maranhenses National Park, with 155,000ha/380,000 acres, can be found 370km/230 miles east of São Luís. From Barreirinhas – at the southern edge of the national park – visitors can enter the park using a 4x4 vehicle, or take a boat to the fishing settlements of Mandacaru and Atins, and start exploring the park area from there – but only with a local guide! During the 5-hr boat trip on the Rio Preguiça, **mangrove forests and palm groves** alternate. Only towards the end will you start seeing creepers and huge dunes made of the finest sand.

Created in 1981, the national park has no tourist infrastructure; even the IBAMA (environmental protection agency) office is situated outside the reserve, in Barreirinhas, Rua Anacleto de Carvalho, tel. (098) 32 22-72 88.

Infrastructure

The national park is considered the only desert on Brazilian soil. The snow-white dunes immediately bring to mind bed sheets – an association which gave the area its name (Lençóis = sheets) – and they extend 50km/31 miles into the interior. The climate here is hot and semi-humid, with an annual precipitation of 1,500 to 1,700mm/59 to 67 inches on average. Plants only thrive near the rivers (Rio Preguiça and Rio Alegre), on sandbanks and in mangrove areas, where occasionally dippers or other species of water bird can be found nesting.

Snow-white desert

Visitors are fortunate if they see pakas (a South American rodent) or other mammals. The half-empty beaches are safe havens for marine turtles. All in all the area is really only inhabited in the winter, during the rainy season; with the onset of the dry period, the fishermen leave behind their thatched clay huts constructed on the water's edge, to look for work in the agricultural sector in the nearby towns.

Only inhabited in the winter

One of the foundations of life in this region are the lakes formed between December and May by the intense rainfalls. Their water, shimmering blue or green, yellow or brown, contributes to this area's wild beauty. In the remaining months most lakes dry up, returning to their aspect of »bed sheets«, part of the morraria (chain of dunes) that, relentlessly whipped by the wind, continually changes shape.

Wild beauty

✶ ✶ São Paulo

State: São Paulo (SP)   **Population:** 12 million
Altitude: 780m/2,559ft

Economically and culturally, São Paulo, capital of the state of the same name and the biggest metropolis in South America, is by far the most important city in Brazil.

São Paulo is also, however, the very incarnation of the urban behemoth – chaotic, hectic, oversized in its geographic dimensions, colossal in terms of the sheer size of its population and exhausting for anyone wanting to get around in this metropolis of millions, regardless of the means of transportation. The daily gridlock in São Paulo's street canyons – reminiscent of Manhattan – and the time lost in the labyrinth of the urban jungle, also represents the biggest productivity problem of this economic hub. Even so, over 50 % of Brazil's industrial production comes from São Paulo, and all large firms and service providers have branches here. This is where the beneficiaries of the city's economic expansion live their lives accordingly, while those at the other end of the scale eke out a living in the favelas on the margins of the city. São Paulo is the city with the most obvious social differences in a country generally characterized by enormous **disparities between poor and rich**. However, the city has always been and continues to be a magnet for European and Asian immigrants, lending it a determinedly multicultural flair, finding expression in countless international restaurants. It is easy to take a culinary world tour in Sao Paulo, but equally easy to spend the night in the pubs and bars, to spend lots of money in the shopping malls in the city centre, or to enjoy all the cultural and leisure activities on offer in one of the world's largest cities.

In São Paulo, there is no Sugarloaf or Corcovado to serve as oversized signpost to guide foreign visitors as there is in Rio de Janeiro. The city is confusing in its layout, chaotic, and due to its immense scale, impossible to explore in its entirety for the short-term visitor. Usually, a visit to São Paulo is limited to the centre and its extended surroundings, with the districts of Liberdade and Bela Vista, as well as the famous **Avenida Paulista**. The parts of town that are of interest to tourists can be easily and quickly reached by metro, in contrast with the confusing bus network,.While convenience speaks for the metro, there is certainly more to see and experience on the buses. The metro, which runs undergound, has three lines with a fourth one under construction and more in planning. There are also fast lane buses that connect metro stops.

Orientation and transport

← *São Paulo – the largest metropolis in South America*

► VISITING SÃO PAULO *map p. 438/439*

INFORMATION

Informações Turísticas
Aeroporto Guarulhos office
Tel. (011) 32 31-44 05

Praça da República
Tel. (011) 32 31-29 22
www.cidadesaopaulo.com

GETTING THERE

Airports
Aeroporto Int. de São Paulo/
Guarulhos
Tel. (011) 64 45-29 45

Aeroporto Nacional de Congonhas
Tel. (011) 50 90-90 00

Bus station
Terminal Bresser
Rua do Hipódromo
Tel. (011) 66 92-51 91

Terminal do Jabaquara
Rua dos Jequitibás
Tel. (011) 50 12-22 56

Terminal Barra Funda
Rua Mário de Andrade 644
Tel. (011) 36 66-46 82

Terminal Tietê
Avenida Cruzeiro do Sul 1800
Tel. (011) 32 35-03 22

GOING OUT/SHOPPING

The city districts grouped under the
name of Jardins (gardens) – Cerqueira César, Jardim Europa, Jardim
América, Jardim Paulistano, Itaim,
etc. – can boast fancy restaurants and
hotels, as well as exclusive designer
shops. Apart from this, they have
gradually become the centre of São
Paulo nightlife. These districts lie
southwest of Avenida Paulista, running through Cerqueira César, west of
Ibirapuera Park, south of the Pinheiro
neighbourhood and east of Rio Pinheiro; slowly but surely, the elegant
office blocks and residences of the
Jardims are outstripping these boundaries. Among the various access
roads, Rua Augusta is one of the most
famous streets in the metropolis of
São Paulo, and Rua Oscar Freire is the
popular shopping centre for luxury
goods.

WHERE TO EAT

► Expensive

① Baby-Beef Rubaiyat
Alameda Santos 86
Paraíso district
Tel. (011) 31 41-11 88
Grill restaurant, established for over
30 years, serving meat of excellent
quality (over 20 cuts) home-reared by
the proprietors. On Thursdays and
Saturdays try feijoada, a bean stew
with substantial side dishes from the
buffet, on Fridays fish and seafood.

Fasano
(in the hotel of the same name)
Rua Vitório Fasano 88
Cerqueira César district
Tel. (011) 38 96-40 00
For decades, this family-run affair has
been a byword for Italian cuisine.
These days, a new chef complements
the classic creations such as pasta with
mushrooms or veal cutlet à la Mila-
nesa with innovative dishes, such as
ravioli with a duck filling, in a sauce
rounded off with oranges.

Koyama
Rua Treze de Maio 1050
Bela Vista district
Tel. (011) 32 83-18 33
São Paulo's leading Japanese restau-

rant serves sushi, sashimi and shabu shabu soup following traditional recipes from the imperial city of Kyoto.

Massimo
Alameda Santos 1826
Cerqueira César district
Tel. (011) 32 84-03 11
Italian gourmet restaurant, excellent grill dishes, daily changing menu. Highlights include trout cooked slowly in a salt crust and kid goat oven-roasted with tomatoes, rosemary and white wine.

Rodeio
Rua Haddock Lobo 1498
Cerqueira César district
Tel. (011) 30 83-23 22
Churrascaria specializing in grill dishes such as palmito assado (whole palm hearts cooked slowly) or picanha a fatiha (a juicy rump cut, served slice by slice); patronized mainly by the local elite, with prices to match.

► Moderate

Z'Deli
Alameda G Monteiro da Silva 1350
Jardim Paulistano district
Tel. (011) 30 64-30 58
Kosher cuisine, complemented with a large selection of tarts, quiches, apple strudel and other desserts.

Hi Pin San
Rua Dr Ivo Define Frasca 99
Vila Olímpia district
Tel. (011) 38 49-11 91
Varied Chinese dishes, partly served in heated metal bowls.

There is no shortage of fine dining in São Paulo.

► **Inexpensive**
Baalbeck
Alameda Lorena 1330
Cerqueira César district
Tel. (011) 30 88-48 20
Simple restaurant with Lebanese cuisine

WHERE TO STAY
► **Luxury**
Emiliano
Rua Oscar Freire 384
Cerqueira César district
Tel. (011) 30 69-43 69
www.emiliano.com.br
Modern business hotel with all mod cons. 57 apartments, and the suites come with CD and DVD players. One room is equipped for video conferences. Also a pool, sauna and fitness centre.

InterContinental
Alameda Santos 1123
Jardim Paulista district
Tel. (011) 31 79-26 00
www.ichotelsgroup.com
Modern business hotel with 189 spacious and amply furnished rooms, excellent restaurant, bar, swimming pool and sauna

► **Mid-range**
① *Pergamon*
Rua Frei Caneca 80
Consolação district
Tel. (011) 31 23-20 21
www.pergamon.com.br
Modern designer hotel; opened in

1999, with 120 well fitted out rooms, car parking, restaurant, bar and fitness suite. All credit cards accepted.

Novotel São Paulo Morumbi
Rua Min Nélson Hungrai 450
Morumbi district
Tel. (011) 37 58-62 11
www.accor.com.br
191 rooms, some suitable for wheelchair users, car parking, restaurant, bar and swimming pool

► **Budget**
② *Eldorado Higienópolis*
Rua Marquês de Itu 836
   Higienópolis district
Tel. (011) 33 61-68 88
Well-preserved hotel of long-standing tradition in a residential area close to the city centre. 153 rooms, some with safe. Hotel guests can use restaurant, bar, car parking and a swimming pool.

Ibis Paulista
Avenida Paulista 2355
Cerqueira César district
Tel. (011) 35 23-30 00
www.accorhotels.com.br
Budget hotel, opened in 2003 in an excellent location. 235 rooms, some reserved for non-smokers, some also adapted for wheelchair users, car parking, restaurant and bar. All credit cards accepted.

Centro Antigo

Catedral Metropolitana The best starting point for an exploration of the metropolis is the Old Town, on the hill between the Tamanduateí and the Anhangabaú valley. This is where, on the central Praça da Sé, the neogothic cathedral rises, erected on the site of an older episcopal church. Construction work stretched over 42 years, and it was not until 1954, the 400th anniversary of the foundation of São Paulo, that the new main church was finally able to be consecrated. Its façade is decorated with statues of Old Testament prophets and the disciples of Christ.

Starting from Praça Clóvis Bevilácqua, an eastern extension of Praça da Sé, Avenida Rangel Pestana features the Igreja da Ordem Terceira do Carmo (Church of the Third Carmelite Order), built in 1632. Very typical style elements of the 17th century are displayed here, on the baroque high altar in particular. The crucifix in the sacristy was imported from Portugal in 1684.

Igreja do Carmo

The Pátio do Colégio, north of Praça da Sé, is the cradle of São Paulo. This is where the priests Manuel da Nóbrega and José de Anchieta founded the college of the Society of Jesus as a place of residence and study for the Jesuits, and it was here on 25 January 1554 that the first mass was held in the settlement. Today, the Pátio do Colégio houses a historical museum, the **Casa Anchieta**, and the Capela de Anchieta. Of the original 16th century building, only the doors and a clay wall are left. Opening times: daily 9am – 5pm.

✸
Pátio do Colégio

Both the church of **São Francisco de Assis**, dating from 1647, and the **Capela da Ordem Terceira de São Francisco**, the church of the Franciscan lay order, erected between 1676 and 1791, can be found on Largo de São Francisco, west of Praça da Sé and Pátio do Colégio. The third building in this group, the convent of São Francisco, has been the seat of the Academy of Law since an imperial decree of 1828. The academy has been incorporated into the University of São Paulo (USP) since 1932.

✸
Largo de São Francisco

Touching Praça do Patriarca, Rua São Bento runs along the Anhangabaú Valley to meet, further north, Avenida São João, which crosses the valley and carries on westwards. It was on this crossing that in the years between 1922 and 1930, the Martinelli Building was erected, the first skyscraper in all of South America. After its inauguration, the building housed a luxury hotel with casino, banqueting halls, a cinema and – at the very top – the grand residence of the owner, the successful Italian immigrant Giuseppe Martinelli. The stairs and floors were laid with Carrara marble, the doors and window frames imported from Riga, and the pinkish cement for the skyscraper was brought all the way from Sweden.

Edifício Martinelli

Rua São Bento leads to the square of the same name, with the Basílica (1910/1922) and the Benedictine convent, erected in the late 16th century. The church boasts an organ with 6,000 pipes manufactured in 1908 in Germany, alongside artworks by renowned Benedictine artists, amongst them the monk **Frei Agostinho de Jesus**, who between 1650 and 1652 executed the paintings of São Bento (Saint

✸✸
Basílica e Mosteiro de São Bento

São Paulo *Overview*

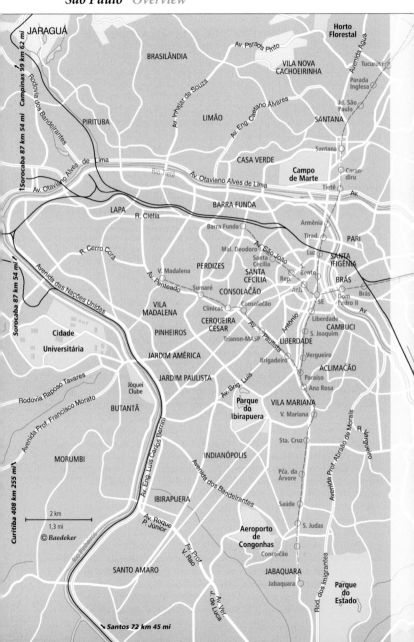

JARAGUÁ

HORTO FLORESTAL

BRASILÂNDIA

Av. Parada Pinto

VILA NOVA CACHOEIRINHA

Avenida Água

Tucuruvi

Parada Inglesa

Av. Imbiajar de Souza

LIMÃO

Av. Eng. Caetano Álvares

Jd. São Paulo

PIRITUBA

SANTANA

Rodovia dos Bandeirantes

Campinas 99 km 62 mi

Sorocaba 87 km 54 mi

CASA VERDE

Santana

Santana

Carandiru

Av. Otaviano Alves de Lima

Rio Tietê

Campo de Marte

Tietê

Av.

Av. Otaviano Alves de Lima

LAPA

R. Clélia

BARRA FUNDA

Barra Funda

Armênia

Mal. Deodoro

Tirad.

PARI

R. Cerro Corá

Av. São João

Luz

SANTA IFIGÊNIA

Santa Cecília

PERDIZES

SANTA CECÍLIA

S. Bento

V. Madalena

Rep.

BRÁS

Brás

Av. Penteado

Sumaré

CONSOLAÇÃO

Anh.

VILA MADALENA

Clínicas

Consolação

SÉ

Dom Pedro II

Av.

Avenida das Nações Unidas

Sorocaba 87 km 54 mi

CERQUEIRA CÉSAR

Av. Paulista

Antônio

Liberdade

S. Joaquim

CAMBUCI

PINHEIROS

Trianon-MASP

LIBERDADE

Cidade Universitária

JARDIM AMÉRICA

Brigadeiro

Vergueiro

JARDIM PAULISTA

Av. Brig. Luís

ACLIMAÇÃO

Paraíso

Rodovia Raposo Tavares

Jóquei Clube

Parque do Ibirapuera

Ana Rosa

Avenida Prof. Francisco Morato

BUTANTÃ

VILA MARIANA

V. Mariana

R. Vergueiro

Av. Eng. Luis Carlos Berrini

Sta. Cruz

Avenida Prof. Abraão de Morais

MORUMBI

Curitiba 408 km 255 mi

INDIANÓPOLIS

Pça. da Árvore

Avenida dos Bandeirantes

2 km

1,3 mi

© Baedeker

IBIRAPUERA

Saúde

Av. Roque P. Júnior

Aeroporto de Congonhas

S. Judas

Av. Prof. V. Rio

Rua Pinheiros

SANTO AMARO

Conceição

JABAQUARA

Rod. dos Imigrantes

Av. Ver. J. de Luca

Jabaquara

Parque do Estado

➤ Santos 72 km 45 mi

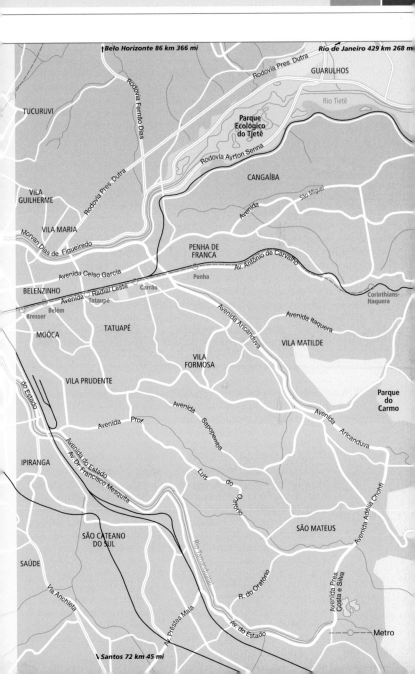

↑ *Belo Horizonte 86 km 366 mi*

Rio de Janeiro 429 km 268 mi

GUARULHOS

Rodovia Pres. Dutra

Rio Tietê

TUCURUVI

Parque
Ecológico
do Tjetê

Rodovia Fernão Dias

Rodovia Ayrton Senna

CANGAÍBA

São Miguel

VILA
GUILHERME

Rodovia Pres. Dutra

Avenida

VILA MARIA

Morvan Dias de Figueiredo

Avenida Celso Garcia

PENHA DE
FRANCA

Av. Antônio de Carvalho

BELENZINHO

Radial Leste

Penha

Avenida

Carrão

Corinthians-
Itaquera

Tatuapé

Avenida Itaquera

Belém

Avenida Aricanduva

Bresser

TATUAPÉ

VILA MATILDE

MOÓCA

VILA
FORMOSA

VILA PRUDENTE

Avenida

Sapopemba

Parque
do
Carmo

do Estado

Avenida

Prof.

Avenida

Aricanduva

IPIRANGA

Avenida do Estado

Luiz

do

Orório

Av. Dr. Francisco Mesquita

Avenida Adélia Chohfi

SÃO CATEANO
DO SUL

SÃO MATEUS

Rio Tamanduateí

SAÚDE

Avenida Pres.
Costa e Silva

Via Anchieta

R. do Oratório

Av. Presdes Maia

Av. do Estado

—◦— Metro

↙ *Santos 72 km 45 mi*

Benedict) and Santa Escolástica (Saint Scholastica) for the convent. Inside, look out for the stained-glass windows and a Russian icon studded with pearls, rubies and turquoises. The gable is graced with a golden rooster – a present from the English Queen Elizabeth II, given in honour of the inauguration of the São Paulo Museum of Art (MASP) in 1968. The church's clock tower dates from 1921. At weekends, the early morning masses are celebrated in front of the high altar, accompanied by Gregorian chants (Sat 6am, Sun 10am).

! **Baedeker** TIP

Sunday sightseeing by bus
The Praça da Sé square is the starting point for several bus tours taking visitors to see São Paulo's sights: the »São Paulo Verde« tour heads for some of the numerous parks that the megalopolis has to offer; the »Roteiro Cultural« stops at museums and cultural centres, and the »Roteiro Histórico« concentrates on historically significant neighbourhoods and buildings. The Largo de Bento is the starting point for the »Roteiro das Igrejas« bus tour, leading to some of the most beautiful churches in São Paulo.

Centro Novo

In 1872, São Paulo had only 31,000 inhabitants and still kept by and large to the boundaries of the original settlement. From 1880 onwards, the coffee plantations and the railway network saw a massive expansion. Many immigrants flocked to the city, too: a development that brought São Paulo unexpected wealth and vertiginous growth. The natural city limits of the rivers were crossed, and the historic core extended by new areas, the so-called Centro Novo.

★★
Teatro Municipal

The **Viaduto do Chá** (Tea Viaduct) crossing built in 1889 on Rua São Bento, vaulting over the Anhangabaú, connects the Old Town with Praça Ramos de Azevedo, dominated by the Teatro Municipal. Building work on the theatre, representing an eclectic mixture of Art Nouveau and Italian Renaissance, lasted from 1903 to 1911. Architect Ramos de Azevedo took inspiration from the Parisian Opera; his opulent interior décor is suffused in bronze, marble, crystal and sparkling mirrors. Tourists can only enter the theatre as part of a guided tour: Tue and Fri noon and 2pm. The associated **Museu do Teatro Municipal** (Theatre Museum) has photos and props as reminders of particularly memorable live performances: tenor Enrico Caruso sang here in 1917, and jazz greats such as Ella Fitzgerald and Duke Ellington performed in the 1950s. Guided tours: Tue and Thurs noon and 1pm.

NS da Consolação

Not far from here rises the tower (75m/246ft) of the Nossa Senhora da Consolação church, built between 1907 and 1914 in the neo-Romanesque style. The church's high altar came from Paris and was made from bronze, marble and oak wood; also worth seeing are the six paintings by Benedito Calixto.

Highlights São Paulo

Basílica e Mosteiro de São Bento
Renowned artists of the Benedictine order are immortalized here.
► page 431

Avenida Paulista
The hub of economic life – not only of São Paulo, but the whole of Brazil
► page 442

Museu de Arte de São Paulo (MASP)
Renoir, van Gogh, Matisse, but also Brazilian artists such as Portinari and Di Cavalcanti are shown here.
► page 442

Museu da Imagem e do Som
A fascinating museum of film, TV and radio
► page 443

On Avenida Ipiranga, at the corner with Avenida São Luís, the Itália Building, with its 42 storeys, soars 164m/538ft above the city. From the restaurant in the two top storeys, diners can enjoy – at night, in particular – magnificent views of the whole city. The vista reaches over Praça da República, the former Campos dos Curros – a rest stop for herds of pack animals and cattle in the early 19th century – and far out over the sea of houses that is São Paulo, seemingly growing unchecked beyond the horizon with no discernible urban planning. At weekends, a **craft market**, also selling stamps, coins and semi-precious stones, is held on the tree-lined Republic Square, which also has a pond.

★
Edifício Itália, Praça da República

In the urban development of São Paulo, the inauguration of the Santa Ifigênia Viaduct in 1910 and the laying out of the Parque Dom Pedro II formed two more milestones. The viaduct across the Anhangabaú valley secured the connection between Largo São Bento and Largo Santa Ifigênia in the north of the Old Town.
The park, extending east of Praça da Sé and Largo São Bento, once used to house the parliamentary building. Today, the park is no more than the green centre of a busy network of roads leading north in the direction of the Tietê river and east to the Brás and Moóca districts.

Viaduto Santa Ifigênia, Parque Dom Pedro II

The municipal market halls (Mercado Municipal), opened in 1933, were laid out following designs by architect **Ramos de Azevedo**. The building, featuring 72 pretty stained-glass windows in the Gothic style, lies north of Parque Dom Pedro II at 306 Rua da Cantareira, accessible via Avenida Mercúrio and Avenida do Estado. The long rows of arcades and mighty vaults of this magnificent building still impress today. It can fit in over 300 market stalls, as well as numerous restaurants and snack stalls. Opening times: Mon–Sat 7am to 6pm, Sun 7am–1pm.

Mercado Municipal

Running below the Santa Ifigénia Viaduct, Avenida Prestes Maia is one of the routes to the monumental Estação da Luz, opened in 1901 and modelled entirely on an English railway station, with all the building materials being imported. In front of the station extends the Parque da Luz, a green space laid out in 1825 with small lakes, a waterfall and exotic trees – Asian banyans and copals – where 40 different species of birds nest. The park lies in the Bom Retiro district, once the hub of São Paulo's Jewish colony and today one of the centres of Korean immigration. The entrance to the park is at 99 Rua Ribeiro da Lima.

! Baedeker TIP

Asian street festivals

A glimpse of the sense of tradition and community of the inhabitants of Liberdade – also called Little Tokyo – can be gained from the street festivals on Praça da Liberdade: Tanabata Matsuri (mid-July), Toyomatsuri (14 Dec) and Mochitsuki (31 Dec), celebrated with surprising dedication by old and young alike.

Outside the Teatro Municipal

The Convento da Luz, founded in 1774, as well as the convent church (Igreja da Imaculada Conceição da Luz), can be found adjacent to the Parque da Luz, at 76 Avenida Tiradentes. Neither the convent nor the cemetery are open to the public, but the church may be visited during mass times. A part of the convent houses the **Museu de Arte Sacra** (Museum of Sacred Art), which boasts a comprehensive and valuable collection of around 11,000 exhibits (16–19th centuries), including statues, paintings, reredos, crucifixes and colonial furniture. Opening times: daily 6.30–11am and 2 to 5pm.

Igreja e Convento da Luz

The Pinacoteca do Estado (State Museum of Art), opened in 1905 at 141 Avenida Tiradentes, is the oldest museum in São Paulo. Ten exhibition rooms showcase paintings, drawings and engravings, mainly by Brazilian artists of the 19th and 20th centuries. Opening times: Tue–Sun 10am–5.30pm.

★
Pinacoteca do Estado

Arterial roads crisscross the megalopolis.

São Paulo Map

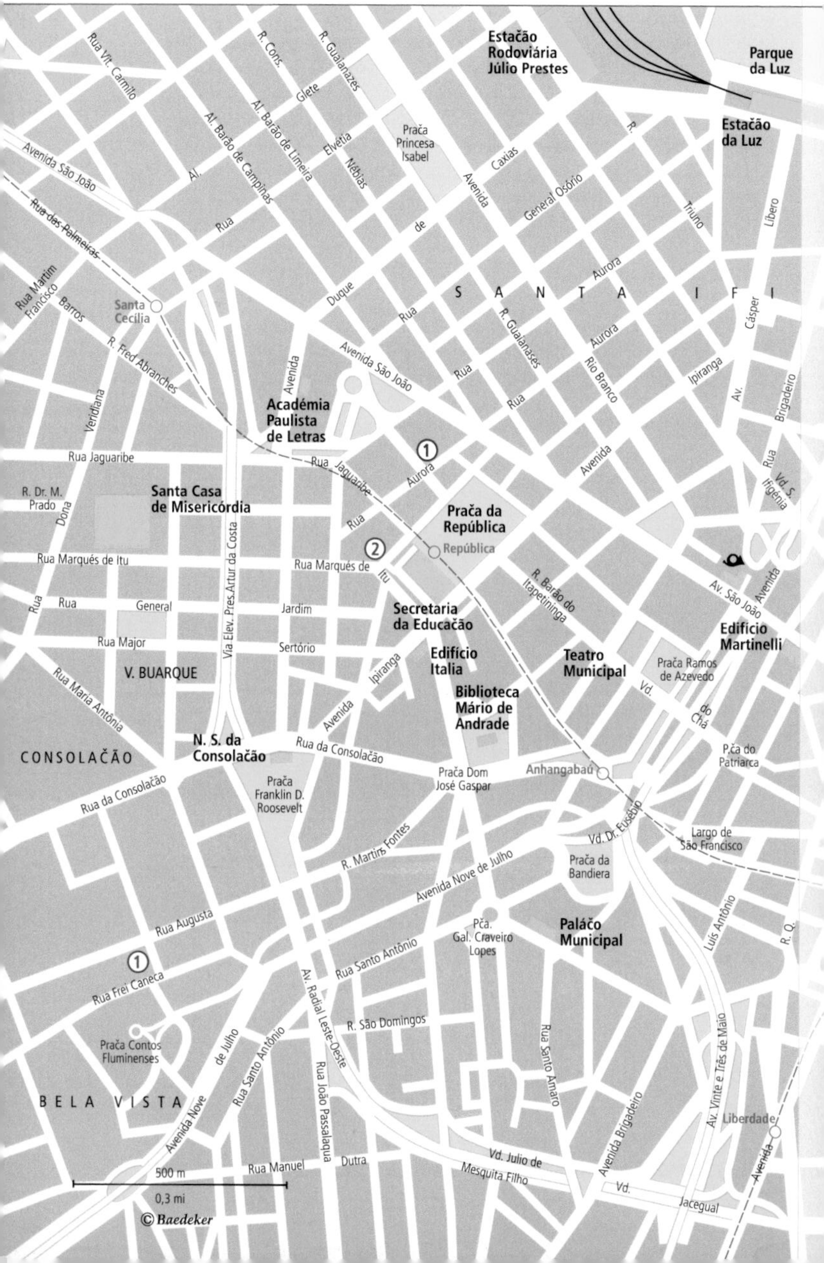

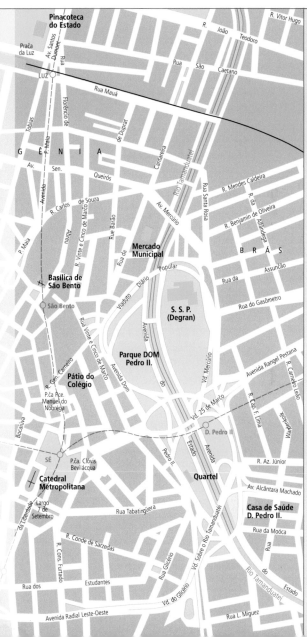

Pinacoteca
do Estado

Praça
da Luz

Av. Santos Dumont

LUZ

Rua Mauá

Rua João Teodoro

R. Vítor Hugo

Rua São Caetano

Florêncio de

Tobias

G   Ê   N   I   A

Av.   Sen.

Avenida

Queirós

R. Carlos de Souza

P. Maia

R. Vinte e Cinco de Março

Rua Barão

de Duprat

Cantareira

Rio Tamanduateí

Av. Mercúrio

R. Mendes Caldeira

R. da
Alfândega

R. Benjamin de Oliveira

R. Santa Rosa

Rua da

Mercado
Municipal

B   R   Á   S

Popular

Rua da   Assunção

Basílica de
São Bento

São Bento

Viaduto   Diário

Rua do Gasômetro

S. S. P.
(Degran)

Rua Vinte e Cinco de Março

Parque DOM
Pedro II.

Avenida   Dom

Avenida

do

Vd. Mercúrio

Avenida Rangel Pestana

R. Carneiro Leão

Pátio do
Colégio

P.ça Pce.
Manuel do
Nóbrega

Bocaiúva

R. Gen. Carneiro

Vd. 25 de Março

Pedro II.

Estado

Avenida

D. Pedro II

MaravelVuk

R. Cap. F. Lima

R. Az. Júnior

SÉ

P.ça Clóvis
Bevilácqua

Catedral
Metropolitana

da Liberdade

Largo
7 de
Setembro

Rua Tabatingüera

Quartel

Av. Alcântara Machado

Casa de Saúde
D. Pedro II.

Rua da Moóca

R. Conde de Sarzedas

Rua Glicério

Vd. Sobre o Rio Tamanduateí

Rua

do

Rio Tamanduateí

Estado

R. Cons. Furtado

Rua dos   Estudantes

Vd. do Glicério

Avenida Radial Leste-Oeste

Rua L. Miguez

 Metro

Liberdade district

Asian Quarter

Starting in 1908, an increasing number of Asian immigrants, Japanese, Chinese and Koreans in particular, moved into the district of Liberdade, south of Praça da Sé, around the Rua Glavão Bueno. Here, many streets are illuminated with Far East-style lanterns; visitors can dive into the culinary world of Asia and enjoy the colourful variety of Far Eastern specialities in the countless restaurants and snack bars.

Museu da Imigração Japonesa

The Museu da Imigração Japonesa (Museum of Japanese Immigration) at 381 Rua São Joaquim houses some 1,000 exhibits: objects of art and daily life, books, photos and replicas of the ships that brought the Japanese immigrants to Brazil. All these documents illustrate how the Japanese managed to adapt to changed living conditions and to integrate into the new world. Opening times: Tue to Sun 3.30 – 5.30pm.

! **Baedeker** TIP

Asian street festivals

The Asian street festivals on Praça da Liberdade give insight into the value of tradition and solidarity to the residents of Liberdade – also called Little Tokyo: Tanabata Matsuri (mid-July), Toyamatsuri (14 Dec.) and Mochitsuki (31 Dec.), which are celebrated with surprising vigour by young and old.

A good example of the degree to which the Japanese, Koreans and the comparatively small band of Chinese still hang on to their old traditions, is the Feira Oriental, the **Far-Eastern street market** that on a Sunday is held on Praça da Liberdade: the stalls sell Asian delicacies, plants and crafts.

Bela Vista district

Little Italy

The lively Bela Vista district, popularly known as Bixiga – crossed by Avenida Brigadeiro Luís Antônio, which connects the historic centre with Avenida Paulista, leading on then to Ibirapuera Park – has over time been swallowed up by the Centro Novíssimo. This neighbourhood, characterized by Italian immigrants, São Paulo's »**Piccola Italia**«, is rich in theatres, bars, typically Italian restaurants, cinemas and other cultural establishments. Nightlife concentrates around Rua Treze de Maio, where the rich musical tradition of various ethnic groups have all contributed to modern Brazilian music. In terms of sights, look for the Museu de Memórias do Bixiga, which retraces the history of this neighbourhood, and the Nossa Senhora de Aquiropita parish church at 478 Rua Treze de Maio. In front of this church, in August of every year, an exuberant festival has been taking place since 1910.

The Japanese community of Liberdade upholds its traditions. →

Avenida Paulista

Centre of economic life

Avenida Paulista, laid out in 1891 for the villas of the coffee and industrial barons, today seems a compact mass of concrete, consisting of high rises with roofs that serve as helipads. As the centre of the economy and high finance, it has also developed a vibrant cultural life of its own, and become one of the landmarks of São Paulo.

Casa das Rosas

Avenida Paulista begins on the edge of the Paraíso neighbourhood on Praça Oswaldo Cruz. Right next to it, at the very beginning of the street, look for the Casa das Rosas (House of Roses) with the **Galeria Estadual de Arte** (State Art Gallery). The Casa das Rosas was the last commission of the architect Ramos de Azevedo before his death in 1928; de Azevedo also designed the municipal theatre of São Paulo. Construction, however, only began seven years after his death. For the interior, sheets of glass, Belgian tiles and Portuguese marble were used. The building owes its name to the gardens, laid out in geometrical patterns in the French style. The gallery, opened in 1991, has some 300 works of art – engravings, paintings, sculptures and installations – by artists such as Oscar Pereira da Silva, Emiliano Di Cavalcanti, João Cándido Portinari and Arcângelo Ianelli.

> ## ! *Baedeker* TIP
>
> ### Milking snakes in Butantã
> Known all over the world for its studies in poisonous snakes, the Butantan Institute (Avenida Vital Brasil 1500) in Butantã district specializes in vaccines and serums. At the snake farm there, the venom is extracted from the reptiles – they are »milked«, so to speak – in order to develop anti-venoms. The museum of poisonous animals, exhibiting over 400 types of cobra and numerous other species of snake, serves as a salubrious reminder of the necessity of such studies. Opening times: Tue – Sun 8am – 5pm.

★ ★
Museu de Arte de São Paulo (MASP)

In terms of Western art, the Museu de Arte de São Paulo (Art Museum of São Paulo), or MASP for short, inaugurated in 1968 in the Cerqueira César district, is the most important in the whole of Latin America. Its collections comprise works by famous impressionists and modern masters such as Auguste Renoir, Vincent van Gogh, Henri Matisse, Pablo Picasso, Joan Miró, João Cándido Portinari, Emiliano Di Cavalcanti and Edgar Degas. Realized by the architect Lina Bo Bardi, one of the main features of the project is an open-air complex used for concerts. In 2007, MASP lost valuable paintings by Picasso and Portinari to an audacious robbery – unfortunately, both works were uninsured. Opening times: Tue – Sun 11am – 6pm, www.masp.art.br.

Trianon Park

On the other side of Avenida Paulista extends the Trianon Park (which also called Parque Tenente Siqueira Campos) with old trees and aviaries, a true island of calm, leisure and relaxation amidst the big city buzz.

A particularly interesting cultural establishment is the Museu da Imagem e do Som (Museum of Image and Sound), abbreviated to MIS, at 158 Avenida Europa. The MIS, in the Jardim Europa district, possesses valuable material on the history of Brazilian film, television and radio and is considered one of the most vibrant museums in town. Opening times: Tue – Sun 2 – 6pm. Entry is free!

✳
Museu da Imagem e do Som

🕐

Zona Sul (southern districts)

The responsibility for the design and landscaping of Ibirapuera Park, opened in 1954, was entrusted to **Oscar Niemeyer and Roberto Burle Marx**. The park is not only a leisure paradise for the Paulistas, with a lake (albeit polluted), fountains, play areas, fitness trails, roller skating rink and open-air stage for concerts; with its numerous monuments, museums and administrative buildings, it is also of great architectural and cultural interest, comprising the pavilions of the Biennale, a planetarium, the Monumento às Bandeiras and the Museu de Arte Moderna (MAM).

✳ ✳
Parque do Ibirapuera

With up to 200,000 visitors daily crowding in at weekends, it is also jokingly called Praia dos Paulistanos (Beach of the Inhabitants of São Paulo). The park extends along Avenida Pedro Álvares Cabral, which is accessible via the Avenidas Manuel da Nóbrega, Brasil, 23 de Maio, Ibirapuera, Brigadeiro Luís Antônio and some others (access: Portão 6).

At the beginning of Avenida Pedro Álvares Cabral rises the Monumento às Bandeiras in honour of the Brazilian pioneers, a magnificent work by **Victor Brecheret** with imposing heroic figures. A little farther, opposite the Palácio Nove de Julho parliamentary building look for the monument to Pedro Álvares Cabral, who discovered Brazil for the Portuguese.

Monumento às Bandeiras

The obelisk, 72m/236ft high, honours the memory of those who died in 1932 fighting for a new constitution. At its base, the Mausoleu do Soldado Constitucionalista is the tomb of the soldiers who defended constitutionalism.

Mausoleu do Soldado Constitucionalista

Housed in the Biennale pavilion, the Museu de Arte Contemporânea (Museum of Contemporary Art) has over 5,000 exhibits belonging to a wide selection of modern and contemporary art movements: from Picasso, Modigliani, Klee and Léger to Tarsila do Amaral, Portinari and Di Cavalcanti, to name just a few of the most important painters.

✳
Museu de Arte Contemporânea

Established in 1948, the Museu de Arte Moderna (Museum of Modern Art) is housed in the Grande Marquise do Ibirapuera and shows sculptures and paintings by artists such as Anita Malfatti, Tomie Ohtake and Tarsila do Amaral.

✳
Museu de Arte Moderna

Museu da Aeronáutica e do Folclore

Entrance no. 2 of the Ibirapuera Park leads to the Museu da Aeronáutica e do Folclore (Museum of Aviation and Folk Art). The ground floor shows model aeroplanes, while the remaining floors are given over to folk art, with nearly 20,000 exhibits from the whole of Brazil.

★
Museu Lasar Segal

In the Vila Mariana district, east of Ibirapuera Park and south of Paraíso, the Lasar Segal Museum keeps oil paintings, watercolours, drawings, engravings and utensils belonging to the Lithuanian artist. The former residence (Rua Berta 111) of Segal, who emigrated to Brazil and up to his death in 1957 was one of the driving forces of Brazilian modernism, also houses a library, a workshop for fine arts and a screening room. Opening times: Tue–Sat 2–7pm, Sun 2 to 6pm.

Parque da Independência

In Ipiranga district, which extends east of Vila Mariana, it is worth seeing the Parque da Independência (Independence Park) with the **Museu Paulista** (also called Museu do Ipiranga), the Independence Monument and the Imperial Chapel with the mortal remains of Dom Pedro I, as well as the Empress Dona Leopoldina. The Casa do Grito stands at the spot where Dom Pedro I uttered the »Grito do Ipiranga«, the legendary slogan »Independence or Death« (▶History p. 45). The Museu Paulista – which also contains a centre of historical documentation – houses objects, clothes and furniture from the imperial era. Its forms, inspired by Italian classicism, stand in sharp contrast to the simple Casa do Grito. Opening times: Tue–Sun 9am–4.45pm.

Jardim Zoológico

Founded in 1958, the zoo of São Paulo in the Água Funda district is one of the largest animal parks in the world, comprising not only animal enclosures, play areas and green spaces for rest and picnics, but also a patch of Atlantic Rainforest and the springs of the Ipiranga river. The entrance to the zoo is at 4241 Av Manuel Estéfano.

Zóo Safári

The Zóo Safári, also situated in Água Funda (Avenida do Cursino 6338), may be crossed by car to spot the lions, zebras, bears and other animals of the African continent that live here in »freedom«. Jardim Zoológico and Zóo Safári are connected by a 4km/2.5-mile path, where park transport takes tourists from one to the other. Opening times: Wed–Fri 10am–4.30pm, Sat/Sun 9am–4.30pm.

Morumbi

The elegant Morumbi neighbourhood extends south of Cidade Jardim. Just below, west of the jockey club at 480 Rua Engenheiro Oscar Americano, the Parque Alfredo Volpi (also called Parque do Morumbi) boasts a forest, a lake and a go-kart track.

★
Fundação Luísa e Oscar Americano

The Luísa and Oscar Americano foundation was established in a house built in the modernist style, with a pretty garden, at 3700 Avenida Morumbi, where the architect Oscar Americano lived with his wife. Here, furniture, silver and porcelain from the imperial period are on display, as well as eight oil paintings by Frans Post, the Dutch painter famous for his Brazilian scenes. The estate also comprises a forest criss-crossed by walking trails. Opening times: Tue–Fri 11am to 5pm, Sat/Sun 10am–5pm.

Avenida Giovanni Gronchi connects Praça Vinícius de Moraes with the Morumbi football stadium, the largest in the city, and leads on to the southern districts on the left-hand bank of the Pinheiros and Grande Rivers. Part of the football stadium is the **Memorial São Paulo Futebol Clube**, a mix between museum, merchandise shop and clubhouse, where the greatest and most important goals scored by Brazilian footballing artists are celebrated in a multimedia show.

Stadium of Morumbi

While the football fans will tend to be drawn to the Memorial São Paulo Futebol Clube, motorsports fans will want to make a pilgrimage to Morumbi cemetery and the grave of Ayrton Senna (►Famous People p. 75), the racing driver who died far too young.

Cemitério Morumbi

The view across the São Paulo skyline is reminiscent of Manhattan.

Autódromo de Interlagos Southeast of the Santo Amaro district lie the Interlagos Autodrome and the Billings reservoir. The Autodrome, where every year the only Formula One race in South America takes place, is situated directly below the Rio Grande Canal, between the Guarapiranga and Billings reservoirs. Access is via Avenida Interlagos.

Represa Billings Formed by the Rio Grande, the Billings reservoir extends over several outer districts of São Paulo. The huge lake is crossed by the Rodovias Anchieta and Imigrants in the direction of Santos, and there are three different ferries, all free to use. The lake's banks are lined with restaurants and water sports clubs, while swimmers and anglers are also catered for.

Zona Oeste (Western districts)

Pinheiros At 430 years of age the oldest district in São Paulo, Pinheiros draws level with the Cidade Universitária along the right-hand bank of the river of the same name. Until now a middle class residential area with a high percentage of students, Pinheiros is falling victim to the same invasion of nightclubs, fashionable boutiques and restaurants that already characterize the aspect of the Jardims districts just beyond Avenida Rebouças. This street, as well as Avenida Teodoro Sampaio and Rua Cardeal Arcoverde run straight through the district in the direction of Avenida Paulista. The riverbank road leads to the western and northern districts on the Tietê river (of which Pinheiros river is a tributary); Rua Henrique Schaumann, the extension of Avenida Brasil, and Avenida Sumaré cross the districts of Perdizes and Sumaré, also in the west of the city.

Museu da Faculdade de Medicina On the Avenida Dr Arnaldo, between Pinheiros and Cerqueira César, rise the buildings of the Medical Faculty of São Paulo University, and the most enormous hospital complex in Latin America, with the Hospital das Clínicas, the Emílio Ribas Hospital and the Instituto do Coração (Heart Institute). Amongst other things, the complex houses the Historical Museum of the Faculty of Medicine; its collection illustrates the history of the institute since its foundation in 1913.

Avenida Henrique Schaumann, Praça Benedito Calixto In the area bordered by Avenida Rebouças and Cardeal Arcoverde, Avenida Henrique Schaumann is flanked by numerous nightclubs, bars and restaurants, frequented mainly by students. Near Av Henrique Schaumann, the Mercado das Pulgas (Flea Market) takes place on Saturdays on Praça Benedito Calixto, a green space framed by the Avenidas Teodoro Sampaio and Cardeal Arcoverde.

Vila Madalena Directly north of Pinheiros lies Vila Madalena, a neighbourhood which is mainly home to students, artists and intellectuals, giving it the reputation of a centre of bohemian lifestyle. Here, the **Feira da**

Vila Madalena street festival (Rua Wisard, Rua Mourato Coelho and Rua Fradique Coutinho) is famous: on every first weekend of the month, mobile restaurants, market stands and stages for concerts are set up, attracting scores of visitors to the neighbourhood.

At the terminus of the Metro line to Barra Funda stands the Memorial da América Latina, a massive complex of monuments consisting of seven buldings and two squares connected by a pedestrian bridge. This mammoth architectural project, another creation by architect **Oscar Niemeyer** (► Famous People p. 71), is characterized by large empty spaces and sweeping concrete panels. Some roof constructions rest on cross beams up to 90m/98yd long. Next to the Metro station is the reception area, a restaurant, a library and the Salão de Atos, the Athos Hall, decorated by a **wall painting by Portinari** showing the Brazilian freedom fighter Tiradentes and 15m/49-ft bas-relief panels by Carybé and Poty. The square is graced by a Franz Weissmann sculpture and a monumental, 7m/23-ft concrete hand designed by Oscar Niemeyer. The palm of the hand features a chiselled map of the American continent.

Memorial da América Latina

In Pirituba, in the extreme west of São Paulo, rises the Pico do Jaraguá (1,135m/3,724ft), the city's highest elevation. At its foot spreads the Parque Estadual do Jaraguá, with a forest, waterfalls, sports facilities, hiking trails, play areas and kiosques. Access by car is via the Estrada Turística do Jaraguá, which branches off from Via Anhanguera at km marker 18. The entrance is at 311 Rua do Horto. Opening times: Tue – Sun 8am – 5pm.

✳
Parque Estadual do Jaraguá

From Jaraguá Park to Anhanguera Park, a green space with eucalyptus forests opened in 1979, it is another 7km/4.3 miles. Within the area live coatis (raccoon-like creatures with long snouts), armadillos, capybaras and other mammals, as well as numerous kinds of snakes. Access to the park is at 1000 Avenida Fortunata Tadelli Natuci.

Parque Anhanguera

Around São Paulo

In Embu (pop 208,000), just under 30km/18 miles from São Paulo, and reached from the city via the Régis Bittencourt (BR-116) trunk road, important colonial architecture blends with works by contemporary artists, who have helped to make this town a **Terra das Artes**, a place for the arts. The town has a grand total of 100 craft workshops, dozens of antique dealers and some 50 factories producing furniture in the colonial style. At weekends and on public holidays, Praça 21 de Abril hosts the Feira das Artes art market, where paintings, metalwork, basketware and goods made from rustic clay, wood, ceramics and leather are all for sale. Amongst Embu's modern artworks, the Cruzeiro da Paz on the Alto do Cruzeiro altar stands out: a cross, 18m/59ft high, with 14 panels executed by various artists,

✳
Embu

An artist's studio in Embu

showing the Passion of Christ and some legends that have grown up around this old Jesuit settlement. The chapel of São Lázaro, built in 1932, also contains sculptures by local artists. The church of **Nossa Senhora do Rosário do Embu** at 67 Largo dos Jesuítas, built in the 17th century and restored in 1940, takes pride of place amongst the colonial buildings. Its simple outer walls contrast with the interior of the nave, decorated with opulent talha carvings. The monastery next door to the church preserves frescoes executed in ox blood.

Museu de Arte Sacra dos Jesuítas

With the Museu de Arte Sacra dos Jesuítas (Museum for Religious Art of the Jesuits) the town can claim a colonial gem. Housed in the church of **Nossa Senhora do Rosário**, which was built by Indians, the collection is well worth seeing, comprising small statues created by the Indians living in the Jesuit settlement, under instruction of the padres. Opening times: Tue – Fri 1 – 5pm, Sat/Sun 10am – 5pm.

Itapecerica da Serra

The historic town of Itapecerica da Serra (pop 111,000), a little over 30km/18.5 miles from São Paulo via Régis Bittencourt (BR-116), has two churches of very different styles. **Nossa Senhora dos Prazeres** on Largo da Matriz, dating from 1562, and the **Kinkakuji Temple**, situated 4km/2.5 miles outside the town on the old road to São Lourenço, a replica of the fully gilded temple erected 690 years ago in Kyoto, in Japan. The only other replica can be found in Honolulu. The temple is surrounded by a Japanese garden with three carp ponds and various kinds of Asian plants, laid out by landscape architect Kato Matsumoto, creator of the gardens of Ibirapuera and Liberdade.

Paranapiacaba

Another attractive destination is Paranapiacaba (60km/37 miles southeast of São Paulo). This small mountain village looks like a little piece of England, founded as it was by English engineers and workers involved at the time in the construction of the Santos-Jandiaí railway line. From São Paulo, the best way to get here is either by car, via the SP-122, or on the tourist train from Estação da Luz to Paranapiacaba. Paranapiacaba preserves the wooden houses of the railway workers; the **Museu Ferroviário** (Railway Museum), near the station, exhibits old locomotives such as the *Dom Pedro II*, built in 1862. Another curiosity, needless to say, is the clock tower, built to resemble London's Big Ben. Some paths lead from the village down the slopes of the Serra do Mar, with its vantage points for glimpsing part of the coast.

⋆ ⋆ Serra da Canastra

Sb 56

State: Minas Gerais (MG)

The Parque Nacional da Serra da Canastra occupies an elevated plateau south of the town of Araxá and reaches close to the border with the state of São Paulo. The nature reserve is accessed by a 75km/47-mile road.

On the first eight kilometres/nearly five miles beyond its source, the Rio São Francisco river has to negotiate three considerable drops, forming, at the third, its highest waterfall, the **Casca d'Anta**, plunging down over 180m/590ft. The river banks near the waterfall attract many daytrippers, at weekends in particular. Near the river courses, the cerrado vegetation becomes denser; however, in the steppe landscape of the nature reserve, visitors are likely to encounter numerous species of animal: anteaters, armadillos, pampa deer, pampa ostriches, maned wolves, ocelots, various species of monkey, as well as countless species of birds and butterflies.

Rio São Francisco

The reserve is framed to the south and north by mountain ranges, rising between 1,300m/4,265ft and 1,500m/4,921ft, and high plateaus. To the north, it borders the Zagaia high plateau, whilst to the south stretch the Serra do Cemitério and the Serra da Guarita, as well as the Babilônia high plateau, delimiting the valley of the Rio Grande. Near the park, the waters of the Rio Grande form the Peixoto reservoir and, a little further southeast, the large reservoir of Furnas. The park offers simple accommodation for natural scientists and small groups, as well as campsites and vending kiosques. The best season for a visit is from April to October, as rainfall is lower in that period.

Orientation

The distance to the national park from Araxá is 98km/61 miles, from Belo Horizonte 364km/226 miles. The small village of São Roque de Minas (pop 1,100) is the starting point for the 8km/5-mile dirt track to the most popular park entrance of **Portaria Casca d'Anta**, near the waterfall of the same name. From Araxá, drivers can take the road heading east to Campos Altos, turn off south halfway and carry on to São João Batista and the northern entrance of the park. There are two more entrances: the Portaria Sacramento in the west and the Portaria São Roque in the east. More information (in Portuguese) may be obtained from the IBAMA environmental protection agency, tel. (037) 34 33-11 95.

Getting there

 ARAXÁ

INFORMATION

Comtur
Praça Cel Adolfo 10
Araxá, tel. (034) 36 61-61 65
www.araxa.mg.gov.br

Araxá

The thermal spa resort of Araxá (pop 79,000), just under 100km/62 miles north of the Parque Nacional da Serra da Canastra, is situated in the central part of Minas Gerais, near the Triângulo Mineiro, the small strip of land stretching west of Minas Gerais that is bordered to the south by São Paulo, to the west by Mato Grosso do Sul and to the north by Goiás. Originally reclaimed during the gold rush by the bandeirantes, the armed pioneers who explored the Brazilian hinterland, the area around Araxá became a refuge for escaped slaves. Organizing themselves in quilombos (fortified settlements), they menaced the routes between São Paulo and the bandeirantes settlements in Goiás state. At a later stage, the town became known for the love story between Dona Beja, the **»witch of Araxá«**, and the Justice of the Peace from the town of Paracatu further northwest. In the early 19th century, Dona Beja, considered one of the most important female characters in the history of Minas Gerais, had a leading position in the local elite.

Museu Dona Beja
The museum bearing her name on the Praça Coronel Adolfo displays a collection of 18th-century furniture, household items and clothing. Erected in the early 19th century, the two-storey building with verandas is modelled on the Palácio da Ouvidoria of Paracatu, the setting for the romance between the seductive Dona Beja and her lover. Opening times: Wed – Mon 10am – 5pm.

✱ Termas de Araxá
An 8km/5-mile drive beyond the centre of Araxá brings visitors to Estância do Barreiro and the springs of Dona Beja and Andrade Júnior. These mineral springs have turned Barreiro into a spa town also offering mud baths used in the treatment of rheumatism and arthritis. The swimming centre, equipped with sauna and a warm water pool, benefits from an attractive setting with forest, waterfall and lake.

Serra do Caparaó

Sd/Se 56

States: Espírito Santo (ES) and Minas Gerais (MG)

Established in 1961, Caparaó National Park stretches across the Serra de Caparaó on both sides of the border between Espírito Santo and Minas Gerais. The park is home to the mightiest peaks of southeastern Brazil: the Pico da Bandeira, at 2,890m/9,482ft the third-highest mountain in the country, the Pico do Cruzeiro (2,860m/9,383ft), the Pico do Calçado (2,840m/9,317ft), as well as the Pico do Cristal (2,798m/9,180ft).

One of the earliest visitors to this mountainous region encompassing today's reserve was Emperor Dom Pedro II. At that time, the Pico da Neblina (3014m/9888ft), on the border with Venezuela, was still unknown, and it was assumed that the Serra de Caparaó had the highest mountain peaks in Brazil. It was the emperor who, in 1859, gave the order to raise the flag of the Empire on the highest peak. This is how the Pico da Bandeira (Peak of the Flag) got its name.

From Cachoeira de Itapemirim, the ES-185 country road leads to the national park, passing through the town of Ibitirama, situated next to the park. Starting from Belo Horizonte or Vitória, the better BR-262 federal road is recommended; at the town of **Manhuçu**, there is a turning south towards the towns of Manhumirim, Alto Jequitibá, and finally Alto Caparaó. From there, it is only a 4km/2.5-mile drive to the entrance of the nature reserve. The park has a small visitor centre (situated 6km/3.7 miles from the entrance), as well as some campsites. The drivable road ends at a viewpoint at 1,970m/6,463ft altitude; there is parking for cars, but motorbikes are not allowed. Alongside jeep tours, excursions on horseback are on offer too. Simple hotels and guesthouses (pousadas) can be found in the villages of Alto Caparaó and Alto Jequitabá.

Access and tourist infrastructure

> ! **Baedeker TIP**
>
> ### Refreshing dip
>
> The Serra do Caparaó boasts magnificent waterfalls, with the most famous being the Cachoeira do Vale Verde, do Vale Encantado and the 80m/262-ft falls of the Cachoeira Bonita. A trail leads to a viewpoint above the latter waterfall, at the foot of which hollows of up to 4m/13ft in depth promise a refreshing dip.

Thanks to the enormous variations in altitude, the vegetation of the Serra do Caparaó National Park is very diverse. In the summit areas, the rocks are only barely covered by low-growth scrubs, grasses and herbs. However, up to 1,800m/5,905ft, remains of dense Mata Atlântica (Atlantic coastal rainforest) thrive, supporting a rich animal life: ocelots, silk monkeys, pakas, pampa deer, forest foxes and a few jaguars, as well as many types of bird and insect.

Flora and fauna

Horse trails lead most of the way to the summit of the Pico da Bandeira, but the last 4.5km/2.8 miles (at least a 4-hr round trip) have to be completed on foot. Halfway, at 2,370m/7,775ft altitude, a campsite offers longer rest. After a night ascent to the summit with the help of local guides, climbers can enjoy panoramic views across the serras of Espírito Santo in the spectacular colours of sunrise. June to August is the time when there is least rain in the park, whilst in the months between November and January, the peak region is usually cloaked in mist. At night it can get fairly chilly all year round.

★ Pico da Bandeira

Teresina

Sd 48

State: Piauí (PI)
Altitude: 72m/236ft

Population: 716,000

Teresina has been the capital of Piauí since 1852. The city, with its chessboard layout, is considered the hottest in Brazil, situated in a region that due to its dry climate is one of the poorest in the country.

Temperatures above 40 °C/104 F are not unknown here. Not only Teresina, but the whole state of Piauí suffers from long periods of drought that parch the soil and make people's life a hardship. No wonder then that Piauí ranks among the least-densely populated states in Brazil and sees few tourists, even though Teresina and its extended surroundings do offer some sights worth seeing.

What to see in Teresina

Museu do Piauí

The Museum of Piauí on Praça Marechal Deodoro shows a varied collection on the history of Piauí, its archaeology, geology and folk art, but also the state's fauna and flora. Of particular interest are the fossils, as well as bone finds and prehistoric objects used by the Indians who once lived here.

Teatro Quatro de Setembro

Further east lies the Praça Dom Pedro II. Don't miss the façade of the Quatro de Setembro Theatre, built in 1894, with its doors and windows framed by neo-Gothic pointed arches.

São Benedito, Palácio do Karnak

On Praça da Liberdade rises the church of São Benedito dating from 1896, with its wood-carved doors a part of Teresina's listed heritage. Not far from here, on Avenida Antonio Freire, look for the Palácio do Karnak, built in the late 19th century in the Greco-Roman style and currently the seat of the state government. The surrounding park was designed by the famous landscape architect **Roberto Burle Marx** (1909 – 1994). It is possible to visit by booking ahead: tel. (086) 32 21-39 03.

✴ Sete Cidades (Seven Cities)

Established in 1961, the Sete Cidades National Park in the north of Piauí state lies some 210km/130 miles northeast of Teresina; access is via the BR-343 federal road to Piripiri and then another 12 km/7.5 miles on the BR-222, up to the turn for the park. The village of Piripiri, at the entrance of the national park, offers a fazenda hotel; within the reserve itself, there is a small information centre, several campsites and a hostel suitable for small groups. The best time to visit is in the driest season between June and December.

▶ VISITING TERESINA

INFORMATION

Piemtur
Centro de Convenções
Rua Acre (no number)
Tel. (086) 32 21-71 00

Informações Turísticas
Parque Encontro dos Rios
Avenida Boa Esperança
Tel. (086) 32 17-50 20 u. 32 17-95 14
www.teresina.pi.gov.br

GETTING THERE

Airport
Aeroporto de Teresina
Tel. (086) 32 25-29 47

Bus station
On the BR-343
trunk road Tel. (086) 32 18-15 14

MARKETS

The markets of Teresina sell clothing and other leatherware hardly differing from those of colonial times. Another commodity with a similarly long tradition is carvings made from cedar, umburana and piqui wood, often representing biblical figures or saints. The most important trading places for these are the Mercado Central on Praça Marechal Deodoro and the Central de Artesanato on Praça Dom Pedro II. With a bit of luck, visitors can see repentistas (travelling »improvization singers«) and violeiros (guitar players) performing on the markets.

WHERE TO EAT

▶ Expensive
Dona Irene
Rua Tenente Luís Meireles 1800 Bom Retiro district
Tel. (086) 27 42-29 01
Dishes from the era of Tsarist Russia.

Two Saturdays a month concerts from 8pm.

▶ Moderate
Tutu-Terê
Rua R Viana 257, Ingá district
Tel. (086) 26 42-50 20
Nutritious Minas Gerais dishes from the charcoal-fired oven. All credit cards accepted.

▶ Inexpensive
Don Vito
Rua Primeiro de Agosto 432
Tijuca district
Tel. (086) 27 42-15 52
Simple Italian restaurant

WHERE TO STAY

▶ Mid-range
Metropolitan Hotel
Avenida Frei Serafim 1696
Tel. (086) 32 16-80 00
www.metropolitanhotel.com.br
The leading hotel in Teresina. Business centre and internet access. Under Argentinian management.

▶ Budget
Pousada Chamonix
Rua Gonçalo de Castro 735
Alto district
Tel. (086) 26 42-32 30
www.pousadachamonix.com.br
The pousada has 21 rooms and nine chalets.

Hotel Serra da Capivara
Rodovia PI 140, Santa Luzia
São Raimundo Nonato
Tel. (089) 35 82-13 89
Only 2km/1.2 miles from the Serra da Capivara National Park, with a pool and the best restaurant in town.

Fauna and flora

The uneven terrain of the park lies at an altitude of between 100 and 300m/330 and 985ft and is characterized by a vegetation that is half **caatinga** (low dry thorn forest) and half **cerrado** (bush steppe and savannah). In the gallery forests that flourish along the watercourses, visitors can spot Amazonian plants such as the buriti palm, but also plants typical of the northeast, such as the carnauba palm. Over 600 different bird species live here. The rest of the fauna is rich in biodiversity too; expect to see pakas, marsh deer, pampas foxes, serval cats, raccoons and jaguars.

Cachoeira do Riachão

The Cachoeira do Riachão, a waterfall over 20m/65ft high, attracts many visitors. The pool that forms at its foot becomes completely empty during the dry season from June to November. However, two basins fed by natural springs, the Olho d'Água dos Milagres and the Olho d'Água do Bacuri, have water all year round.

✳ Sete Cidades and cave paintings

The main attractions, however, are the cave paintings and natural monuments of Sete Cidades, eroded sandstone formations that – with a bit of imagination – are reminiscent of cities or medieval castles. The shape of other rock formations resemble people, animals or objects, expressed in names such as Cabeça de Cachorro (Dog's Head), Urso subindo na Pedra (Bear Climbing the Rock) or Três Reis Magos (Three Wise Men). Another, extremely bizarre rock (Mapa do Brasil), has a crack in the shape of the border of Brazil. Here, the rock and cave walls feature around 70 groups of paintings, estimated to be at least 3,000 years old, although some experts reckon them to be as old as 7,000 to 14,000 years. Many of these cave paintings can be viewed, and the visitor centre can put those who are interested in touch with local guides: phone tel. (086) 33 43-13 42.

✳ ✳ Parque Nacional da Serra da Capivara

Serra da Capivara National Park, established in 1979, is situated northeast of São Raimundo Nonato and 650km/404 miles south of Teresina. The park, of great scenic beauty, is a habitat for wild cats, monkeys and over 200 species of bird. Of particular interest are the approx. 30,000 **petroglyphs**, which were probably created around 6,000 years ago, although some scientists believe them to be up to 12,000 years old. The park is home to some of the most important archaeological areas in the whole of Brazil; international teams of experts visit regularly, and in 1991 they were included in UNESCO's list of World Heritage Sites to be protected. Unfortunately, major exertions are required to access them, and getting there – on foot or by donkey – takes a lot of time; this should not be attempted without an experienced guide, drinking water and enough food. By far the easier option is to learn about the prehistoric finds in the **Museu do Homem Americano**, in the village of São Raimundo Nonato, which can be reached by bus from Teresina (approx. 10hr drive).

Fruit seller in Teresina

Torres

State: Rio Grande do Sul (RS)   **Population:** 31,000
Altitude: 16m/53ft

Torres, the most famous beach and holiday resort in Rio Grande do Sul, owes its name to the four big rock towers that push out into the sea, thus dividing up the beach into various sections: Torre do Farol, Torre do Meio, Torre da Guarita and Torre do Sul are ancient basalt formations with caves that have been washed out by the sea over thousands of years, and rock walls between 27 and 66m/88 and 216ft high.

What to see in Torres

Torre do Meio, Torre da Guarita and Torre do Sul are the rocks on Praia Guarita, where beach visitors should always be wary of the stormy seas. The beach belongs to Guarita State Park, which spreads over a large basalt elevation and offers views of one of the most beautiful stretches of coast in the south of Brazil. At Torre do Meio, steps lead to the caves formed by erosion.

★
Parque Estadual da Guarita

⏵ VISITING TORRES

INFORMATION
Casa da Turista
Avenida Barão do Rio Branco 315
Tel. (051) 36 26-55 59
www.clictorres.com.br

GETTING THERE
Bus station
Avenida José Bonifacio 524
Tel. (051) 36 64-17 87

! Baedeker TIP

Splashes of heavenly colour
The three-day Festival de Balonismo takes place in the Easter week in Torres. The annual meeting of balloonists means that numerous balloons rise up then around the southern Brazilian coastal city.

WHERE TO EAT
► Moderate
Anzol
Rua Cristovão Colombo 265
Molhes district
Tel. (051) 36 64-24 27
Very good restaurant for fish, lobster, crabs and other sea food

WHERE TO STAY
► Mid-range
Solar da Barra
Rua Plínio Kroeff 465
Mampituba district
Tel. (051) 36 64-18 11

www.solardabarra.com.br
Best hotel in Torres, boasting 169 air-conditioned apartments with TV, bar, restaurant, several very attractive swimming pools, a fitness suite with sauna and a play area for children.

► Budget
Costa Dalpiaz
Avenida Barão do Rio Branco 815
Tel (051) 36 64-32 24
Simple hotel with 22 rooms, internet access, telephone and TV

Beaches South of Torres extend 30km/18-mile long, very broad beaches, giving onto the open sea and limited by mighty fixed dunes, partly covered by vegetation. Swimmers need to watch out for the occasional strong current however.

Treze Tílias

Rk 59

State: Santa Catarina (SC)   **Population:** 4,900
Altitude: 796m/2,611ft

Treze Tílias (Thirteen Lime Trees) was founded in 1933 by Andreas Thaler (1883–1939), who was Austrian agriculture minister in the 1920s, and after leaving office led impoverished Tyrolean mountain farmers to southern Brazil, helping them set up a new life there.

The small town built in the alpine style lies in a landscape heavily reminiscent of the Central European uplands. Its inhabitants have preserved their European heritage to this day, from their Vorarlberg dialect to dirndls and lederhosen or hearty alpine dishes – the fame of the traditional hotel »Tirol«'s Austrian cuisine reaches far beyond the borders of Santa Catarina. Alongside agriculture, local tourism has become the main source of income for the little town.

There is a long tradition of woodcarving in Treze Tílias.

What to see in Treze Tílias

Wood carvers The local wood carvers are known all over Brazil: the most famous work of Godofredo Thaler, a grandson of the founder of the town, is the large figure of Christ for the Dom Bosco Cathedral in Brasília; his workshop at 260 Rua Leoberto Leal may be visited. Other artists whose workshops are open to visitors are Conrado Moser, at 392 Rua Leoberto Leal, and Werner Thaler, at 562 Rua Leoberto Leal.

Lago Schauplener On the road to Água Doce, some 6km/3.7 miles outside Treze Tílias, a leisure park extends around Lake Schauplener, which is full of local daytrippers, on weekends in particular. In Treze Tílias, visitors can book a trip to Lago Schauplener by jeep for up to four people. Amongst the sights are the Frozzer Waterfall and the Gruta de Bamberg cave. For more information and bookings, call tel. (049) 35 37-01 32.

✱ Ubajara

Se 47

State: Ceará (CE)

The Parque Nacional de Ubajara in the northwest of Ceará is the smallest Brazilian national park and seems an oasis of greenery amidst the semi-desert of the caatinga. But the nature reserve's most important attraction can be found underground: the Gruta de Ubajara, rich in stalactites and stalagmites.

The name of Ubajara comes from the Tupí-Guaraní Indian language and in translation means »Lord of the Canoe«. It goes back to a legend of the Tabajara Indians, according to which a chief is said to have lived for many years in the cave. In 1959 the area surrounding the Gruta de Ubajara was declared a national park.

✱ Landscape The nature park lies in the transitional area between the caatinga steppe of the Brazilian northeast and the permanently humid Amazonian forests. It occupies a narrow strip of the **Chapada de Ibiapaba**, which forms the northern border area between the states of Ceará and Piauí. The rugged mountains towering above the tree tops are rich in limestone formations, with caves and steep rock walls. The scenic appeal of the park is further enhanced by gurgling brooks, a small lake and waterfalls. The best time to visit the reserve is around June and July, as rainfall is lowest in this period.

Plants and animals Vegetation consists mainly of carnaúba palms, juazeiros (trees with edible fruit) and cacti. Amongst the animals, look out for wild foxes, macacos-prego (capuchin monkeys belonging to the Cebus Erxleben

▶ VISITING UBAJARA

INFORMATION

IBAMA
At the park's visitor centre
Tel. (085) 36 34-13 88

Secretaria de Turismo
Ubajara (town)
Tel. (085) 36 34-22 88

WHERE TO STAY
Next to the information centre at the entrance to the park, small groups can

find simple accommodation. This is also the starting point for walks with local guides. In the immediate vicinity of the national park, as well as in the nearby small town of Ubajara, several well-appointed pousadas offer a good night's sleep; some of them even have a swimming pool and children's play areas.

species), marsupials, hedgehogs and species of bird such as sparrow-hawks and king vultures. The nature reserve is also home to a few dozen species of snake, amongst them the jibóia (boa constrictor), as well as the coral snake.

The nature reserve's biggest tourist attraction is the Ubajara Cave, over 1,000m/1,094yd in length, which can be reached either on a 3.5km/2.2-mile long footpath or using a small cable car. The cave displays magnificent **sinter formations** (mineral deposits) and rooms named after the various rock shapes they contain: The Rose, The Horse, The Oratorium, The Curtain, The Brook, The Miracles and many more – all artificially illuminated. At the entrance to the cave, look for the Bell Stone – touch it and it will yield a bell-like sound.

✱
Gruta de
Ubajara

Ubatuba

Sc 57

State: São Paulo (SP)
Altitude: 3m/10ft

Population: 67,000

Ubatuba, a tourist spa resort on the northern stretch of coast of São Paulo state, boasts 70 beaches and numerous good hotels, and its many small bays and islands offer good conditions for diving and other watersports.

In the 18th century and the first decades of the 19th, Ubatuba was one of the exit ports for gold from the Minas and coffee from the Paraíba valley. Using entire caravans of pack animals, the precious cargo was transported here across the mountain slopes. With the decrease in local coffee production and the opening of the railway line to the port of Santos, the town's position fortunes waned, too. Ubatuba had to wait until the second half of the 20th century to rise again, this time as a beach and holiday resort.

What to see in Ubatuba

City beaches
Off the centre of Ubatuba lie Prainha do Matarazzo and, near the harbour, Praia Iperoig (also called Praia do Cruzeiro) and Praia Itaguá. These beaches are not really suitable for swimming and are lined by numerous restaurants and nightclubs. Also, Prainha do Matarazzo hosts an information post (at 273 Rua Antonio Athanásio), run by the **Tamar environmental protection project**, where various species of marine turtle are kept. In the **Aquário de Ubatuba** on Praia Iperoig, visitors can admire a range of sea creatures. The entrance is at 859 Rua Guarani. Opening times: Thu – Tue 10am – 8pm.

Around Ubatuba

Horto Florestal, waterfalls
On the country road leading to Taubaté, some 7km/4.3 miles northwest of Ubatuba, lies the Horto Florestal (Forest Park), and just one kilometre further along, the same road reaches the Ipiranguinha Waterfall. On the road leading to Paratí, look for two more waterfalls: the Cachoeira da Prumirim after 23km/14.5 miles, and the Cachoeira da Escada near Picinguaba, a listed fishing village, after 45km/28 miles.

✳
Beaches north of Ubatuba
This is just a selection of the beaches along the coastal strip between Ubatuba and Parati: Perequê Açu (2km/1.2 miles from the centre of Ubatuba), Vermelha do Norte (9km/5.6 miles), Itamambuca (12km/7.5 miles), Promirim, Puruba (25km/15.5 miles, difficult to get to), Ubatumirim (33km/20.5 miles), Fazenda (42km/26 miles), Picinguaba, Brava and Camburi (48km/30 miles). On Praia da Fazenda, look for the Casa da Farinha (Flour House) from 1935, with water wheel and mill. Ilha Comprida and Ilha das Couves (Cabbage Island) lie off Picinguaba beach.

Ponta Grossa Park
Only 2km/1.2 miles south of the centre of Ubatuba stretch the beaches Vermelha and de Tenório, on the way to Ponta Grossa Park, which has a lighthouse and the Andorinhas Cave. The next beaches along (Grande, das Toninhas, Taipá and Fora); all are suitable for

surfing. The SP-055 country road leads to the less attractive bays of Enseada (9km/5.6 miles from Ubatuba), Santa Rita, Perequê Mirim, Saco da Ribeira (12km/7.5 miles), Flamengo and Flamenguinho. **Praia das Sete Fontes**, on the hard-to-access southern side of the Ponta do Flamengo peninsula, is the first in a long series of excellent swimming beaches: da Sununga (26km/16 miles), do Lázaro, Domingos Dias, Brava do Sul, Vermelha do Sul, Costa, Fortaleza, Cedro, Bonete and finally Maranduba (30km/18.5 miles). Praia da Enseada and Praia do Saco da Ribeira, a

UBATUBA

INFORMATION
Avenida Iperoig 331
on Praia do Cruzeiro
Tel. (012) 38 33-73 00
www.ubatuba.com.br

GETTING THERE
Bus station
Rua Professor Tomás Galhardo 513
Tel. (012) 38 32-36 22

popular yachting spot accommodating around 1,000 boats, are the departure points for the schooners that take tourists to the less accessible beaches and out to Anchieta Island with its penitentiary, built in 1908 and closed in 1957. The Praia do Lázaro with its myriad cafés and hotels is on the way to the magnificent beaches of Sununga and Domingas Dias, framed by hills. At Praia da Lagoinha stand the ruins of the country's first glass factory. From here, a fishing boat can take visitors to **Praia do Bonete**, with its fine sand and weak surf, which only supports a few scattered fishing villages, a school and a small church. The tropical wealth of plants of the Mata Atlântica clings to the hills that surround the beach; a narrow trail leads through the coastal rainforest, connecting Praia do Bonete with Praia da Fortaleza on the northeastern side of the Ponta da Fortaleza peninsula. This route takes between 30 and 60 minutes to walk.

Off Ubatuba lie the Ilha das Cabras (Goats' Island), the Ilha do Mar Virado (Island of the Turbulent Sea), the Ilha das Palmas (Palm Island), the Ilha Anchieta and the Ilhota do Sul. All are perfect for snorkelling and diving.   **Offshore islands**

Valença

Sd 57

State: Rio de Janeiro (RJ)
Altitude: 560m/1,837ft

Population: 66,500

The university town of Valença – not to be confused with Valença near Salvador – was founded in 1857, at the peak of the Brazilian coffee boom.

Until 1888, this provincial town was the place within Rio de Janeiro state which arguably had the most slaves forced to work on the plantations. As the coffee monoculture declined in the first half of the 20th century, several textile industry companies settled in Valença, making a key contribution to urban growth here.

What to see in and around Valença

Matriz de NS da Glória

The parish church of Nossa Senhora da Glória, built as early as 1820 at 365 Praça Pedro Gomes Leal, houses, among other things, an image of the patron saint imported from Portugal in 1817. The locals call this church, with its two bell towers, Catedral for short. The church also houses a **museum of sacred art**, which is small but worth a look.

Praça Quinze de Novembro

Visually, Valença's centre is dominated by the old trees on Praça Quinze de Novembro. Originally laid out by French landscape gardener Auguste Glaziou, the park, reminiscent of a botanical garden, was later updated by no less a figure than **Roberto Burle Marx**.

Pico da Torre

The best view of Valença and its surroundings can be enjoyed from the 1,100m/3,609-ft summit of the Pico da Torre. The viewpoint, approx. 4km/2.5 miles from the town centre, is accessible via Rua Domingos Cosati.

✳ Balneário Ronco d'Água

A drive of around 7km/4.3 miles on the untarmacked road connecting Valença with Conservatória leads to the Ronco d'Água waterfall. The natural swimming pool at the foot of the small cascade, complete with bar and snack food stalls, is one of the most popular day trip destinations for the locals.

Vassouras

Vassouras (35km/21.5 miles from Valença, pop 31,500) was born, like Valença, out of the coffee boom and was originally the administrative centre of the region. Around Praça Campo Belo, some buildings from that time are still standing and worth a look, amongst them the former residence of the Baron of Ribeirão from 1860, which today serves as a municipal forum. The former railway station on Praça Martinho Nobrega, dating from 1875, today houses a school centre. The **Cachoeira Grande** coffee farm was also established in the 19th century. This feudal estate has been partly restored and lies on the RJ-127 country road, just under 7km/4.3 miles out of Vassouras. Guided tours take place for groups of ten or more visitors, but must be arranged in advance by phoning tel. (024) 24 71-12 64.

✳ Conservatória

The centre of Conservatória, 27km/16.5 miles from Valença, has remained practically unchanged since colonial times. In Brazil, the town of 4,000 inhabitants is known as the **Cidade das Serestas** (City

⏵ VISITING VALENÇA

INFORMATION
Avenida S Borges Graciosa 2
Tel. (024) 24 53-60 54
www.valenca.rj.gov.br

GETTING THERE
Bus station
Praça Paulo de Frontin 137
Tel. (024) 24 53-45 55

EVENTS
The Glória church and Praça Quinze form the backdrop to the popular festival of Folia de Reis, which starts every year on 20 December and keeps the town on its toes up to 6 January. During this time, dozens of marching bands strut their stuff.

WHERE TO EAT
▶ **Moderate**
Arara
RJ-145, exit Barra do Piraí
Canteiro, tel. (024) 24 53-52 28
Brazilian dishes

WHERE TO STAY
▶ **Budget**
Palmeira Imperial
Rua Nossa Senhora da Aparecida 1111
Tel. (024) 24 53-19 95
www.palmeiraimperial.com.br
Simple city hotel; 18 acceptable air-conditioned rooms with minibar, telephone and TV. It has internet access, a pool and bar, but no restaurant.

of the Serenades); this musical custom is observed by the locals every Saturday in the streets of the town. Musicians and singers hold their big get-together every year on the last Saturday in August; otherwise, visitors can find out about this tradition in the Museu das Serestas, at 99 Rua Osvaldo Fonseca.

⋆ Vitória

State: Espírito Santo (ES)
Altitude: 3m/10ft

Population: 293,000

Vitória, the capital of Espírito Santo state, was founded in 1551 on the Ilha de Vitória (Victory Island) in the bay of the same name. The colonization of this stretch of coast began on 23 May 1535, a Whitsun Sunday (Espírito Santo, translated into English, means Holy Spirit), with the foundation of Vila do Espírito Santo.

However, under constant threat from the local Tamoio Indians, the settlement was transferred in 1551 to a safe place, namely on to the Ilha de Vitória, and was renamed Vila Nova de Espírito Santo, while the old historic core has since then been called Vila Velha (Old Town).

▶ VISITING VITÓRIA

INFORMATION
Informações Turísticas
At the airport
Tel. (027) 32 35-63 00
www.vitoria.es.gov.br

GETTING THERE
Airport
Aeroporto de Vitória (E. Sales)
Av F. Ferrari
Tel. (027) 32 35-63 00

Bus station
Ilha do Príncipe
Tel. (027) 32 22-33 66

EVENTS
Vital
Carnival out of season –
in November

WHERE TO EAT
▶ **Moderate**
Pirão
Rua J Lírio 753, Praia do Canto
Tel. (027) 32 27-11 65
Imaginatively prepared fish dishes,
with all kinds of typically Brazilian
ingredients. This place has for years
ranked among the top restaurants in
Vitória.

WHERE TO STAY
▶ **Mid-range**
Senac Ilha do Boi
Rua Bráulio Macedo 417
(on Ilha do Boi island)
Tel. (027) 33 45-01 11
www.hotelilhadoboi.com.br
95 rooms, most of them with splendid
views of Vitória and the Atlantic

The swirling colours of carnival in Vitória

What to see in Vitória

Squeezed in between »inselbergs« (isolated hills) and the sea, Vitória – much like Salvador – consists of an upper and a lower town. The Upper Town (Cidade Alta), with its narrow lanes, colonial houses and churches comprises the historic centre. Several flights of steps – the most famous the **Escadaria Maria Ortiz** – connect it with the Lower Town (Cidade Baixa), the centre of the town's economic and financial activities.

Townscape

The listed chapel of Santa Luzia was built in 1551 on Rua José Marcelino and is the oldest building in town. Today it is used as an art gallery and research centre for the university of Espírito Santo. Rua José Marcelino leads to Praça D Luís Scortegagna, with the town's cathedral, erected in 1918.

Santa Luzia, cathedral

Inaugurated in 1927, the Carlos Gomes Theatre on Praça Costa Pereira is the oldest theatre in Espírito Santo. The Scala opera house in Milan served as architectural model for this magnificent building, which often houses music festivals. Visits by appointment only: tel. (027) 31 31-83 96.

✶
Teatro Carlos Gomes

On the Colina de São Francisco, on Rua Uruguai, lie the ruins of the friary of São Francisco, which was begun in 1591 under the monk Antônio dos Mártires. This was the first Franciscan building outside northeastern Brazil.

Convento de São Francisco

The Palácio Anchieta on Praça João Clímaco, today the seat of the Espírito Santo state government, was once a Jesuit college. Inside, the palace houses the tomb of the Jesuit priest **José de Anchieta** (1534–1597), who made history as the founder of São Paulo togehter wirh Manuel da Nóbrega.

Palácio Anchieta

The parliament of Espirito Santo state convenes in the Palácio Domingos Martins, built in 1606 on the site of the Nossa Senhora da Misericórdia church. The palace is named after Espírito Santo-born Domingos José Martins, one of the leaders of the 1817 rebellion in Pernambuco.

Palácio Domingos Martins

This museum in the Jucutuquara district is housed in an 18th-century country house; its collection includes furniture, a house altar and a varied collection of china. The mansion is considered one of the finest examples of Brazilian rural architecture.

✶
Museu Solar Monjardim

Also known as Pico do Frei Leonardi, the 136m/446-ft Pedra dos Dois Olhos (Two Eyed-Stone) rises up 6km/3.5 miles out of town, between the Jucutuquara and Maruípe districts. The rock takes its name from two depressions formed by erosion.

Pedra dos Dois Olhos

Morro da Fonte Grande
Situated 5km/3 miles outside the city centre, between the districts of Jucutuquara and Santo Antônio, the 312m/1,023-ft Morro da Fonte Grande (Hill of the Great Spring) forms the highest elevation within the city limits. The summit, offering a splendid panoramic view of Vitória and its bay, is crowned by several radio and TV towers.

✳ **Praia do Canto**
With its many bars and the **Parque dos Namorados** (Lovers' Park), Praia do Canto (also known as Praia do Aterro) is one of the liveliest places in town. On Saturdays, the park hosts a very popular craft market (Feira de Artesanato).

Praia de Camburi, Praia do Suá
Further north, Avenida Dante Michellini leads to Camburi Beach, 6km/3.5-mile long and one of the hotspots for local nightlife. The beach finishes at the Tubarão promontory, where the big iron ore port of the same name was established. Lying not far from the **Ilha do Boi**, Praia do Suá is the departure point for the boats that take part in the annual marine procession on 29 June, honouring St Peter.

Vitória cathedral

Baía de Vitória

Wide Vitória Bay, strewn with many small islands, is dominated by two landmarks of the town: Penedo Rock and the Ponte Castelo de Mendonça. Penedo Rock, protruding 136m/446ft out of the ocean, seems to watch over the entrance to the bay like a stone sentinel. The Darcy Castelo de Mendonça bridge, also called **Terceira Ponte**, connects the two sides of the bay.

Another bridge ensures the connection between Ilha de Vitória and **Ilha do Frade**, 8km/5 miles from Vitória. The beaches of this island, lined by rocks and reefs, mainly attract divers.

On the **Ilha do Boi** (Ox Island), 7km/4.5 miles outside the town centre, herds of cattle were once

Beach in Vitória Bay

held in quarantine before being taken to individual settlements on the mainland. Today the island is much changed, housing the most luxurious villas in town.

✳ Vila Velha

With a population of 346,000, the town of Vila Velha lies 15km/9.5 miles south of Vitória, beyond the Baía de Vitória. The Upper Town has preserved several fine colonial buildings, while the Lower Town's main attraction is its magnificent beaches.

Visible from afar, the convent of Nossa Senhora da Penha was built in 1558 on a 154m/505-ft rock. It houses many figures of Portuguese saints and paintings by the Brazilian artist **Benedito Calixto**. Also of interest is the Sala dos Milagres (Hall of Miracles), containing the votive offerings of those believers helped by the patron saint. Eight days after Easter Sunday, the Festa da Penha is celebrated here; in a night-time procession, pilgrims come in droves from Vitória, 15km/9.5 miles away, up to the convent. There are two entrances to the convent: cars enter via Rua Luísa Grinalda, pedestrians use the entrance on Praça Pedro Palácios. Opening times: Mon – Sat 5.30am – 4.45pm, Sun 4.30am – 4.45pm.

✳✳
Convento NS da Penha

🕐

Praia da Costa, one of the finest beaches in Espírito Santo state, is situated just 3km/1.8 miles from the centre of Vila Velhas. Rising up at the end of the beach, the **Santa Luzia lighthouse** was inaugurated on 7 September 1871. Close by, the 167m/548-ft Morro do Moreno attracts paragliders.

✳
Praia da Costa

Guarapari

✳ **Beaches**
Guarapari, the largest resort in southern Espírito Santo, 50km/31 miles south of Vitória, is famous for the (radioactive) **monazite sand** of its beaches, which is used to treat arthritis and other diseases. The beaches near the town centre are Areia Preta (with monazite sand), Meio, Namorados, Virtudes and Castanheiras. To the north, the beaches of Morro (4.5km/2.8 miles outide Guarapari), Três Praias (6km/3.7 miles), Setiba (12.5km/7.7miles) and Setiba Pina (13.5km/8.3 miles) are worth mentioning; all offer good surfing conditions. South of the town lie the beaches of Enseada Azul (7km/4.3 miles), Guaibura, Bacutia, Padre and Meaípe (9km/5.6 miles).

Crafts
On the beach of **Meaípe**, situated 10km/6.2 miles south of Guarapari, bone lacework made by the wives of fishermen is for sale. On Praça Jerônimo Monteiro and in other parts of town, stalls sell pottery and leather goods, lacework, items made of hemp and shells, as well as Panelas do Barro, clay pots typical of the crafts of Espírito Santo. The town's cultural institute has also set up a crafts exhibition.

Anchieta

The Jesuit priest José de Anchieta, one of the founding fathers of São Paulo, died in 1597 in the village of Reritiba, which today carries his name. The little town (pop 19,000), situated just under 30km/18.5 miles south of Guarapari, has fine beaches that attract many visitors. On 9 June, the Festa de Anchieta is celebrated here.

NS da Assunção
Of the original listed Jesuit church of Nossa Senhora da Assunção (1587), the sacristy and the two-storey Cela de Anchieta are preserved. Next to the church, look for the **Padre Anchieta** museum.

✳ **Beaches**
Just outside the town, the sandy beaches of Anchieta, Coqueiro, Balanço and Mar Vila await; these are followed, in the direction of Guarapari, by the swimming beaches of Castelhanos (4km/2.5 miles from Anchieta), Guanabara (5km/3 miles), Ubu (8km/5 miles), Praia do Além, popular with surfers, and Praia Maimbá (14km/8.5 miles). South of Anchieta, level with the small village of Iriri, the beautiful beaches of Praia dos Namorados (Lovers' Beach), Praia Santa Helena and Costa Azul are there to be enjoyed.

Marataízes

Situated 41km/25.5 miles southeast of Anchieta in the estuary of Rio Itapemirim, Marataízes (pop 26,000) is one of the biggest sea resorts in Espírito Santo. It is connected to Vitória, 116km/72 miles away, by the ES-060, the Rodovia do Sol, which, as it runs parallel to the Atlantic coast, leads to many of the beaches the state has to offer.

In the town centre, the beaches of Marataízes and Areias Pretas come ✱
recommended. South of Marataízes lie the beaches of Praia dos Cas- **Beaches**
cões (18km/11 miles), Marobá (24km/15 miles) and dos Neves
(45km/28 miles), the latter getting close to the border with Rio de Janeiro state. North of Marataízes, the line-up of swimming beaches is
no less attractive, with Barra (2km/1.2 miles), Pontal, Itacoa and Itaipava (18km/11 miles) all awaiting.

Coast north of Vitória

In Nova Almeida, a settlement 48km/30 miles from Vitória, don't **Nova Almeida**
miss the listed Igreja dos Reis Magos (Church of the Three Wise
Kings) of 1558, which used to be part of a Jesuit mission. The beach
of Barreiras is considered dirty, whereas Praia Grande and the 5km/
3-mile Praia Capuba are suitable for swimming.

Getting from Vitória to the small town of Domingos Martins (pop ✱
31,000) involves a 46km/29-mile drive west on the BR-262 federal **Domingos**
road. It was here that **Colônia Santa Isabel** was founded in 1847, the **Martins**
first German settlement in the Bra-
zilian state of Espírito Santo. The
communities of Paraju, Biriricas,
São Miguel, Melgaço, Marechal
Floriano and Santa Maria still re-
tain timber-framed houses from
the German colonial era, as well as
some events, such as the **Festa da
Imigração Alemã** (Festival of German Immigration, also simply
called summer festival) at the end
of January, and the **Festa do Chu-
crute** (Sauerkraut Festival) in Feb-

> ! ***Baedeker* TIP**
>
> **Liqueurs, wine and sweets**
> Fancy trying the local cookies, tarts or home-
> made marmalades, or sampling liqueurs and
> wines prepared to German recipes in Domingos
> Martins? The centrally located Casa do Artesa-
> nato (House of Crafts) offers an abundant
> selection for your delectation.

ruary, to keep the memory of the settlements' origins alive. The
listed **Igreja Luterana** on Praça Doutor Arthur Gerhardt dates back
to 1866, which makes it the oldest Protestant church in the whole of
Brazil.

The 1,822m/5,977-ft Pedra Azul (Blue Rock), a kind of large version ✱
of Sugarloaf, is a prominent landmark in the Espírito Santo moun- **Estadual da**
tains and can be seen from afar. It rises in the community of Aracê, **Pedra Azul**
with its strong Italian heritage, situated west of Domingos Martins in
a state-owned forest reserve administrated by the Instituto de Terras,
Cartografias e Florestas, which organizes mountain tours with experienced guides. One of the highlights, alongside the ascent of the
summit, is a visit to the huge **Gruta da Pedra Azul** or a refreshing
bath in one of the numerous natural swimming pools. For more information, contact the Estadual da Pedra Azul visitor centre on tel.
(027) 32 48-11 56.

Glossary of Brazilian geography, religion and culture

Açai palm Type of palm tree with berry-like fruit, typical for the Amazon Delta; the juice is appreciated by the locals as a thirst-quenching drink

Afoxé Followers of Afro-Brazilian religions, who during carnival take their drums to the streets

Aldeia Jesuit missionary settlement

Alvenaria Walls built using bricks or quarry stone

Arraial Small historic settlement

Atabaques Drums

Azulejos Painted wall tiles, introduced to the Iberian peninsula by the Moors and spreading from there to the Latin American colonies

Baiana Female inhabitant of Bahia state, often clad in traditional costume

Bandeirantes Adventurers who explored the Brazilian interior carrying a banner (bandeira)

Batida Sugar cane spirit diluted with fruit juices

Bossa nova Musical style born in Brazil; derived from samba, but also containing elements of jazz

Boto Amazon freshwater dolphin

Bumba Meu Boi Dance and song festival performed in different variations, where the action centres on a bull (boi)

Burití Type of palm with yellow fruit made into a liqueur-like drink; the palm fibre is used to make braidwork

Caatinga Dry steppe in the northeast of Brazil, covered with low shrubs and cacti

Cabo Cape, foothills

Caboclo Mixed-race Brazilian, with one white and one Indian parent; also used for inhabitants of the country's interior

Cachaça Sugar cane spirit

Cachoeira Waterfall

Cafuzo Mixed-race Brazilian, with one Indian and one black parent

Caiçara Coastal dweller

Caipirinha Cocktail made from sugar cane spirit, lime, sugar and crushed ice

Cajueiro Tree from the Anacardiaceae family, with edible fruit (cashew apple) and seed (cashew nut).

Câmara e Cadeia Municipal administration and jail in colonial and imperial times

Candomblé Afro-Brazilian religion

Cangaçeiro Bandit in northeastern Brazil

Capitania Brazilian fiefdom, given to Portuguese noblemen by the imperial dynasty

Capixaba Inhabitants of Espírito Santo state

Capoeira War dance developed by African slaves for self-defence, as they were not allowed to carry arms

Carioca Inhabitants of Rio de Janeiro city

Carne seca Salted, air-dried beef or goat meat

Cavalhadas Equestrian tournaments from the Iberian peninsula symbolizing the medieval battles between Moors and Christians

Caverna Cave

Cerrado Savannah landscape in the Brazilian interior

Chácara Small rural estate

Chafariz Public well

Chapada Plateau, plateau landscape

Charque Dried meat

Cinema Novo Brazilian film movement of the 1960s, presenting a critical analysis of society

Congadas Dances of African origin, culminating in the coronation of the Rei do Congo

Correios Post office

Dendê oil Palm oil frequently used in Afro-Brazilian cooking

Emboabas Name given to new settlers (arriving after those from São Paulo), who flocked to Minas Gerais during the 18th-century gold-rush

Engenho Plantation with sugar cane factory and distillery, from colonial times in particular

Favela Slum in large Brazilian cities

Fazenda Large estate, with agriculture or livestock farming

Fazendeiro Big landowner

Filho de Santo Follower of an Afro-Brazilian religion

Fonte Source

França Antárctica Colony founded by the French in Guanabara Bay in the 16th century

Garimpeiro Gold and diamond prospectors

Gaúcho Inhabitant of the state of Rio Grande do Sul

Gruta Cave

Igapó Permanently flooded, swampy forest bordering the Amazon

Igarapé Natural canal or narrow watercourse between two islands or between the mainland and an island in the Amazon region

Igreja Church

Igreja Matriz Main or original church of a settlement or town

Inconfidência Mineira Conspiracy of citizens of Ouro Preto led by Tiradentes, with the aim of achieving independence for Brazil from Portugal, which was violently quashed in 1789

Intendência Control board for gold or diamond finds, set up by the Portuguese crown

Jacarandá Rosewood tree or timber

Jagunço Bandit

Jangada Sailing boat used by the fishermen of northeast Brazil

Jardim Garden, public park

Jataí, jatobá Tree belonging to the legume family found in the Amazon and in northeast Brazil

Lagoa Lagoon, lake

Largo Square, esplanade

Literatura de Cordel »String literature«; pulp novel, taking its name from the string that was used to hang up these small booklets for sale

Macumba Strongly syncretistic Afro-Brazilian religion

Mãe de Santo Priestess of an Afro-Brazilian religion

Marajoara Highly evolved ceramics of the Pre-Columbian era from the Brazilian island of Marajó and their modern imitations

Mata Atlântica Brazilian coastal forest

Mestre Master, name given to fine artists

Minas Baroque Brazilian baroque style, best represented in Minas Gerais; its main exponent is considered to be Aleijadinho.

Monazite sand Sand formed from magmatic rock, with a high level of thorium

Morro Hill

Mulato Mulatto, mixed-race Brazilian, with one black and one white parent

Nordestino Inhabitant of northeast Brazil

Orixá Afro-Brazilian saint or deity

Pantanal Vast marsh area in Mato Grosso and Mato Grosso do Sul in western Brazil

Pardo Mulatto

Pau Brasil Brazil wood, a type of dye-wood which gave the country of Brazil its name

Paulista / Paulistano Inhabitant of São Paulo

Pedra Rock, mountain

Pedra de Lioz Marble-like stone from Portugal, which often came to Brazil as ballast on ships, and was used in the building of churches

Pedra Sabão Soapstone, a soft magnesium silicate with a greasy feel, used by sculptors

Pelourinho Pillory used for the punishment of slaves

Pico Summit

Pinga Sugar cane spirit

Pirarucu Largest freshwater fish in Brazil, lives in the Amazon Basin

Planalto High plateau

Pororoca High, torrential tidal wave rising around the mouth of the Amazon when freshwater and seawater meet

Praça Square

Praia Beach

Quilombo Fortified village, established by escaped slaves

Redução Fortified village where the Indians lived, controlled by the Jesuits

Revolução Farroupilha War of Tatters uprising; independence movement of the rebellious gaúchos, who in 1839 proclaimed the República Juliana in Santa Catarina

Rio River

Rodoviária Bus station / stop

Samba Dance based on Afro-Brazilian rhythms

Sambaqui Shell midden (deposit of shells, bone fragments and remains of cooking utensils) belonging to the shell midden cultures, proven to have lived on the coast of the Brazilian state of Santa Catarina in particular

Sé Cathedral

Senzala Slave hut

Seringueiro Rubber collector in the Amazon region

Serra Mountains, mountain range, uplands

Sertanejo Inhabitants of the Sertão

Sertão Sparsely populated, semi-desert hinterland of northeast Brazil

Sítio Farm, small estate

Sobrado House with two or more storeys

Solar Palatial house of wealthy Brazilians

Taipa Clay mixed with plant fibres, used for building

Talha Gilded carving, which in 18th-century Portuguese and Brazilian churches served as decoration for walls and ceilings

Tambaqui Freshwater fish of the Amazon region – a valuable food source

Terra firme Dry land in the Amazon Basin, higher up, thus safe from flooding

Terreiro Place of worship used for the Candomblé

Tropeiro Cattle herder or trader

Tucunaré Fish of the Amazon region, used for food

Umbanda Afro-Brazilian religion introduced by the Bantu

Vaqueiro Cattle herder

Várzea Alluvial plain

Victoria Amazônica Large water lily with floating leaves that can attain a diameter of 2m/78 inches; formerly known as »Victoria Regia«

Vila Larger settlement that was given its town charter by the Portuguese government

INDEX

PHOTO CREDITS

LIST OF MAPS AND ILLUSTRATIONS

PUBLISHER'S INFORMATION

Illustrations etc: 186 illustrations, 39 maps and diagrams, one large map
Text: Ottaviano und Elizabeth De Fiore, Robin Daniel Frommer, Odin Hug, Luciano Martinengo, Werner Voran
Translation & Editing: Kathleen Becker
Cartography: Franz Kaiser, Sindelfingen; Christoph Gallus, Hohberg; MAIRDUMONT/Falk Verlag, Ostfildern (map)
3D illustrations: jangled nerves, Stuttgart
Design: independent Medien-Design, Munich; Kathrin Schemel

Editor-in-chief: Rainer Eisenschmid, Baedeker Ostfildern

1st edition 2009
Based on Baedeker Allianz Reiseführer
»Brasilien« 6. Auflage 2008

DEAR READER,

We would like to thank you for choosing this Baedeker travel guide. It will be a reliable companion on your travels and will not disappoint you.
This book describes the major sights, of course, but it also recommends interesting events, as well as hotels in the luxury and budget categories, and includes tips about where to eat or go shopping and much more, helping to make your trip an enjoyable experience. Our authors ensure the quality of this information by making regular journeys to Brazil and putting all their know-how into this book.

Nevertheless, experience shows us that it is impossible to rule out errors and changes made after the book goes to press, for which Baedeker accepts no liability. Please send us your criticisms, corrections and suggestions for improvement: we appreciate your contribution. Contact us by post or e-mail, or phone us:

► **Verlag Karl Baedeker GmbH**
Editorial department
Postfach 3162
73751 Ostfildern
Germany
Tel. 49-711-4502-262, fax -343
www.baedeker.com
www.baedeker.co.uk
E-Mail: baedeker@mairdumont.com

Baedeker Travel Guides in English at a glance:

► Andalusia
► Bali
► Barcelona
► Berlin
► Brazil
► Budapest
► Dubai · Emirates
► Egypt
► Florida
► Ireland
► Italy
► London

► Mexico
► New York
► Paris
► Portugal
► Prague
► Rome
► South Africa
► Spain
► Thailand
► Tuscany
► Venice
► Vienna